The activities of the Council's Committee on Social and Affective
Development During Childhood have been supported primarily by
the Foundation for Child Development, a private foundation that
makes grants to educational and charitable institutions. Its main
interests are in research, social and economic indicators of children's lives, advocacy and public information projects, and service
experiments that help translate theoretical knowledge about children into policies and practices that affect their daily lives.

Social cognition and social development

A sociocultural perspective

*Based on seminars sponsored by the
Committee on Social and Affective Development During Childhood
of the Social Science Research Council*

Edited by

E. TORY HIGGINS
DIANE N. RUBLE
WILLARD W. HARTUP

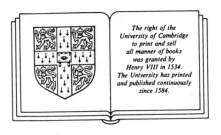

*The right of the
University of Cambridge
to print and sell
all manner of books
was granted by
Henry VIII in 1534.
The University has printed
and published continuously
since 1584.*

CAMBRIDGE UNIVERSITY PRESS

Cambridge
London   New York   New Rochelle
Melbourne   Sydney

Published by the Press Syndicate of the University of Cambridge
The Pitt Building, Trumpington Street, Cambridge CB2 1RP
32 East 57th Street, New York, NY 10022, USA
10 Stamford Road, Oakleigh, Melbourne 3166, Australia

First published 1983
First paperback edition 1985

Printed in the United States of America

Library of Congress Cataloging in Publication Data
Main entry under title:
Social cognition and social development.
(Cambridge studies in social and emotional development)
Includes bibliographies and index.
1. Socialization – Addresses, essays, lectures.
2. Child development – Addresses, essays,
lectures. 3. Social perception – Addresses,
essays, lectures. 4. Cognition – Addresses,
essays, lectures. I. Higgins, E. Tory
(Edward Tory), 1946-   . II. Ruble, Diane N.
III. Hartup, Willard W. IV. Series.
HQ783.S563   1983   303.3'2   82-12897
ISBN 0 521 24587 7 hard covers
ISBN 0 521 31370 8 paperback

Contents

List of contributors   *page* vii
Preface   ix

Part I. Introduction

1   What's social about social-cognitive development? *Diane N.*
    Ruble, E. Tory Higgins, and Willard W. Hartup   3

Part II. Social understanding and interpersonal relations

2   Social cognition and the social life of the child: stages as
    subcultures *E. Tory Higgins and Jacquelynne Eccles Parsons*   15

3   Beyond the information processed: socialization in the
    development of attributional processes *Philip R. Costanzo
    and Theodore H. Dix*   63

4   Social cognition and social interaction in childhood *Willard
    W. Hartup, Judith E. Brady, and Andrew F. Newcomb*   82

5   Social antecedents, cognitive processing, and comprehension
    of social portrayals on television *W. Andrew Collins*   110

6   The development of social-comparison processes and their
    role in achievement-related self-socialization *Diane N. Ruble*   134

7   Social cognition, social behavior, and children's friendships
    Thomas J. Berndt   158

Part III. Value internalization and moral development

8   Culture as a cognitive system: differentiated rule understand-
    ings in children and other savages *Deborah L. Pool, Richard
    A. Shweder, and Nancy C. Much*   193

v

9   Development of interpersonal values *Walter Emmerich and
    Karla Shepard Goldman*   214

10 Affective and cognitive processes in moral internalization
    Martin L. Hoffman   236

11 The internalization of altruistic dispositions: a cognitive
    analysis *Joan E. Grusec*   275

12 Social-control processes and the internalization of social
    values: an attributional perspective *Mark R. Lepper*   294

Part IV. Commentary and overview

13 Interaction and development in social cognition *Elliot Turiel* 333

14 Let's not overattribute to the attribution process: comments
    on social cognition and behavior *Eleanor E. Maccoby*   356

15 Five questions for research in social-cognitive development
    William Damon   371

16 What would my mother say? Reactions to gleanings from
    developmental studies on social cognition *Tom Trabasso*   394

    Index   405

Contributors

Thomas J. Berndt
Department of Psychology
Yale University

Judith E. Brady
Institute of Child Development
University of Minnesota

W. Andrew Collins
Institute of Child Development
University of Minnesota

Philip R. Costanzo
Department of Psychology
Duke University

William Damon
Department of Psychology
Clark University

Theodore H. Dix
Department of Psychology
New York University

Walter Emmerich
Educational Testing Service
Princeton, New Jersey

Karla Shepard Goldman
Department of Psychology
University of Colorado

Joan E. Grusec
Department of Psychology
University of Toronto

Willard W. Hartup
Institute of Child Development
University of Minnesota

E. Tory Higgins
Department of Psychology
New York University

Martin L. Hoffman
Department of Psychology
University of Michigan

Mark R. Lepper
Department of Psychology
Stanford University

Eleanor E. Maccoby
Department of Psychology
Stanford University

Nancy C. Much
Committee on Human
   Development
University of Chicago

Andrew F. Newcomb
Department of Psychology
Michigan State University

Jacquelynne Eccles Parsons
Department of Psychology
University of Michigan

Deborah L. Pool
Committee on Human
  Development
University of Chicago

Richard A. Shweder
Committee on Human
  Development
University of Chicago

Diane N. Ruble
Department of Psychology
New York University

Tom Trabasso
Department of Education
University of Chicago

Elliot Turiel
Department of Psychology
University of California,
  Berkeley

Preface

The contributions in this volume are revised versions of research presented at a conference titled "Social Cognition and Social Behavior: Developmental Perspectives," which was sponsored by the Social Science Research Council's Committee on Social and Affective Development During Childhood and held at the University of Western Ontario from November 9 to 11, 1979. The purpose of the conference was to focus on the "social" aspect of social-cognitive development, in particular, socialization or social-situational forces on the antecedent side and social behavior on the response side. Although social cognition is currently one of the most active areas in both social and development psychology, the field has been dominated by the "cognitive" aspect of social cognition, with the "social" aspect receiving relatively little attention. By focusing the conference on the "social" aspect of social-cognitive development, we hoped to reformulate some of the theoretical foundations of research in this area. Each participant was asked to address at least one of the following questions: (1) What kinds of sociocultural factors explain observed developmental changes in social cognition? (2) How do age-related changes in social cognition affect social behavior?

The conference brought together researchers who have been concerned with social developmental processes for many years and researchers who have just begun to address these questions. We believed that interaction among such participants at this stage of progress in the field would facilitate a coherent attack on some of the fundamental unresolved questions in a social-cognition approach to social development. (See Ruble, Higgins, & Hartup, Chapter 1, for further discussion of this question.) We were fortunate in bringing together an exciting group of psychologists who were actively engaged in exploring aspects of social-cognitive development from a variety of theoretical perspectives and whose enthusiasm about both their own and others' viewpoints was infectious. In addition to the chapter authors, John Coie, Carol Dweck, and Carolyn Shantz also participated in the meetings. Their contributions greatly added to the intellectual stimulation and success of the conference. The success of any conference depends on timing and on the particular "mix" of participants. Unfortunately, it is not possible to capture in print the excitement and sense of common purpose that was shared throughout these meetings, but Tom Trabasso (Chapter 16) comes very close. The contributions have benefited substantially from the interchange and discussion at the conference, as well as from the comments that the participants provided one another on early drafts. As editors, we wish to thank the authors for their editorial contribution to this volume.

The sixteen chapters are grouped into four major sections. Chapter 1 introduces the volume, describes the purpose of the conference, and raises some issues for future consideration. Chapters 2 through 7 focus on the interaction of sociocultural and cognitive factors in the development of social judgment and the utilization of social input. Chapters 8 through 12 present various perspectives on value internalization and moral development. Chapters 13 through 16 present critical overviews and commentaries on the preceding chapters, as well as on the field of social-cognitive development as a whole. We are especially grateful for the balanced perspective on social-cognitive development that these commentaries provide. Together, the chapters in this volume contain major reviews of key areas of social-cognitive development and summarize the current research programs and perspectives of many distinguished psychologists in this area.

After this book went into production, two authors changed their names too late for the changes to be incorporated. Jacquelynne Eccles Parsons is now Jacquelynne Eccles (Parsons) and Karla Shepard Goldman is now Karla Shepard.

We would like to express our sincere gratitude to the University of Western Ontario, and especially to P. T. Johnson, general manager, and the staff at Spencer Hall for contributing to the success of the conference by providing us with excellent facilities and friendly, courteous assistance. We owe a particular debt to Peter B. Read, who, as council staff to the Committee on Social and Affective Development, enthusiastically supported this project in myriad ways. We also wish to thank Susan Milmoe and her colleagues at Cambridge University Press for their editorial assistance in preparing the volume for publication. Most of all, we wish to thank the contributors, whose thoughtful and eager participation in this project made this volume possible.

Part I

Introduction

1 What's social about social-cognitive development?

Diane N. Ruble, E. Tory Higgins, and Willard W. Hartup

Empirical and theoretical interest in the area of social-cognitive development has burgeoned in recent years. Research manuals regularly include essays on this topic (e.g., Chandler & Borjes, 1982; Shantz, 1975 and in press), and edited volumes devoted to it have proliferated (e.g., Butterworth & Light, 1981; Collins, 1981; Flavell & Ross, 1981; Howe & Keasey, 1978). To a considerable extent, this effort has been closely tied to the study of cognitive development, with methods and issues being defined in terms of the traditions of that field. That is, the emphasis has been on intellectual development as a determinant of age-related changes in social understanding; the more "social" aspects have been relatively neglected. As an example of this emphasis, "Social Cognition," an essay by Shantz appearing in the forthcoming revision of *Carmichael's Manual of Child Psychology* (Mussen, in press), is included in the volume on cognitive development rather than in the volume on social development.

The way in which social cognition is conceptualized is of considerable theoretical importance. In terms of classic S-O-R models of behavior, social cognitions mediate between the social situation and the social behavior of the individual:

Social Situation → Social Cognition → Social Behavior

Chronological age may be associated with changes in each component in this scheme – in the social situations to which children are exposed, in cognitive structures and information-processing capacities, and in the response repertoire available for social interaction. Contemporary research has been heavily focused on the cognitive components of this model, most

Preparation of this chapter was facilitated, in part, by Grant No. 37215 from the National Institute of Mental Health and, in part, by New York University. We are grateful to Theodore Dix for helpful comments on an earlier draft.

particularly the development of socially relevant cognitions (e.g., descriptions of persons) and the interelations among cognitive variables (e.g., decentration, memory, and attention) and social perception (e.g., moral judgments). The direct links to the more social aspects of the model – socialization or social-situational forces on the antecedent side and social behavior on the response side – have received relatively little attention.

The primary goal of the present volume, therefore, is to help expedite a convergence of social and developmental approaches to the study of social cognition. To do this, the efforts of both social psychologists (including perspectives from anthropology and sociology) and developmental psychologists are needed and are represented by the contributors to the volume.

Existing relations across disciplines

To effect an integration of social psychology and developmental psychology in the area of social cognition would seem to be a straightforward task. Most investigators in both disciplines are constructivists, espousing views of the individual as an "active" information processor and a "lay scientist." Common substantive concerns mark the two disciplines – for example, impression formation and attribution of responsibility. Curiously, however, the two fields have remained distant from one another. Social psychologists have emphasized *process* and *structure,* focusing on the information-processing factors and cognitive structures involved in person memory and social judgment (Hastie et al., 1980; Higgins, Herman, & Zanna, 1981). In contrast, developmental psychologists have tended to emphasize *content* – that is, age- or stage-related changes in an individual's representations of others (Shantz, 1975) or conceptions of social phenomena (Damon, 1979). In the area of person perception, for example, social psychologists have focused either on cognitive mediators of social judgments, including salience, construct accessibility, cognitive heuristics, and schemas, or on the impact of prior judgments, including self-fulfilling prophecies and errors in memory. Developmental psychologists, on the other hand, have been more concerned with content issues, including age-related changes in how children describe others (Feldman & Ruble, 1981).

There are many reasons for the lack of convergence between these two disciplines. Historical and theoretical antecedents differ, as do contemporary methods and goals. Social psychology is typically deductive, marked by a preference for experimental methods that incorporate subtle manipulations for testing hypotheses about human social behavior. Developmental psychology remains heavily inductive and descriptive. Social psychologists tend to be more concerned with the internal validity of the laboratory situation, whereas developmentalists emphasize external or ecological validity.

But interest in social cognition is as strong among social psychologists as among developmental psychologists. This level of interest is reflected in journals (*Journal of Personality and Social Psychology: Attitudes and Social Cognition; Social Cognition*), in the forthcoming edition of Lindzey and Aronson's *Handbook of Social Psychology*, and in the wave of new books (Cantor & Kihlstrom, 1981; Clark & Fiske, 1982; Harvey, 1981; Hastie et al. 1980; Hastorf & Isen, 1981; Higgins, Herman, & Zanna, 1981; Kahneman, Slovic, & Tversky, 1982; Nisbett & Ross, 1980; Wyer & Carlston, 1979).

Although recent advances in cognitive science have impacted on the study of social-cognitive development, advances in adult *social* cognition have impacted little on studies of child development. By and large, social-cognitive developmentalists have not been influenced by either the issues or the phenomena described in the literature on adult social cognition. And yet, there are obvious age-related changes to be examined in the use of heuristics and social decision making (cf., Kahneman, Slovic, & Tversky, 1982; Nisbett & Ross, 1980), the role of affect in social judgment, memory, and social behavior (cf., Clark & Fiske, 1982; Hastorf & Isen, 1981), the effect of goals on social information processing (cf., Higgins, Herman, & Zanna, 1981), and the organization of social information in long-term memory (cf. Hastie et al., 1980; Wyer & Carlson, 1979). One literature that should be of special interest to developmental psychologists is concerned with the extent to which people's social judgments are "theory-driven" or "data-driven" (cf., Cantor & Kihlstrom, 1981; Higgins, Herman, & Zanna, 1981), as this problem is intimately related to the classic developmental issue of the relative importance of assimilation and accommodation in adaptation to the environment.

It is also important to link the socialization literature with the literature on social cognition. Although cognitive considerations are central to many aspects of social and personality development (e.g., interpersonal perception, conceptions of authority, moral judgments), the topic is largely missing in recent texts (e.g., Lamb, 1978; Maccoby, 1980). There are several possible reasons why little integration has occurred. Studies in social and personality development have been concerned with the manner in which external agents socialize children, the behavioral results of these socialization experiences, and individual differences in outcomes. Thus, a prevailing theme in social-development research has been the identification of the nature of external stimulus control over specific units, or types, of behavior (Kuhn, 1978). The nature of the external stimulus has been defined at various levels of analysis (e.g., subcultures, parents, schools, short-term isolation, and specific reinforcement contingencies), and a wide range of behavioral consequences has been examined (e.g., attachment, popularity, achievement, sex roles). But the basic strategy has been to connect antecedent stimulus and behavioral outcome; the role of the child has been viewed, for the most part, as relatively passive or incidental.

Research in social-cognitive development, however, has been based on the assumption that children take an active role in their own development, especially in the formation of constructs about their environment – both physical and social. Most empirical studies have focused on structural/qualitative changes occurring in the child, rather than on their antecedents or outcomes. This does not mean, of course, that these considerations are ignored in the literature on social-cognitive development. Indeed, a basic assumption in Piagetian theory is that cognitive structures emerge from the individual's commerce with the environment. But most studies in developmental social cognition have dealt with the cognitions themselves, their nature and the sequence of their development, rather than with antecedent or consequent conditions. In addition, most investigators have stressed developmental universals – the sequence of qualitative changes intrinsic in development – rather than individual differences.

The work represented in this volume is an indication that social and developmental psychology are beginning to converge in terms of methods and goals. We believe these convergences have several advantages. First, joint consideration of social-cognition and socialization processes enhances the significance of our developmental studies; for example, focusing explicitly on social antecedents can potentially enrich our understanding of when and how social concepts change. Second, the integration of social/cognition and social/personality research may provide a more complete understanding of the relation between external stimulus events (contexts) and social behavior. For example, a major contribution of social-cognitive studies to the understanding of social and personality development could be a clearer focus on the children themselves: what kinds of social information they seek and use, how they integrate social information, and how this integration affects their social judgments and behaviors. We assume that childhood socialization cannot be understood independently of the cognitions and evaluations made by children concerning social actions and that attempting to do so may lead to erroneous conclusions and inconsistent results. Thus, the scarcity of positive results relating parent behaviors to, for example, children's sex-role acquisition

(Maccoby & Jacklin, 1974) may be attributed, in part, to the ease with which children acquire sex-role rules from numerous external sources (neighbors, television, etc.). Any rules that are learned may affect the kinds of behaviors that children are attentive to, how the behaviors are interpreted or evaluated, and thus how children themselves behave. Furthermore, because cognitions are viewed as important mediators of the socialization process, the effects of specific socialization experiences cannot be evaluated independently from the cognitive-developmental level of the child.

Overall, the present volume represents an attempt to consider the *social* aspects of social-cognitive development by linking up with work from social-science disciplines (social psychology, sociology, and anthropology) as well as with traditional studies in social and personality development. Both the antecedents and consequences of social-cognitive development are considered. To accomplish this aim, each contributor was asked to address one or both of the following questions:

1. What kinds of social-situational factors may explain observed developmental changes in social perception – changes that are often assumed to be caused by cognitive factors? Empirically, this kind of question would involve a shift from examining developmental changes in social processes that are dependent variables to those that may be independent variables, such as age-related changes in predominant sources of information (e.g., adult vs. peer).

2. How do age-related changes in social cognitions affect social *behaviors,* such as performance or motivational variables, self-control, and reciprocation of friendly or aggressive acts?

Sociocultural antecedents

Almost all the chapters incorporate analyses relevant to the first question. However, the issue is addressed most explicitly by Higgins and Parsons in Chapter 2. As a point of contrast to structural accounts of developmental change, they argue that age-related changes in social environment create, in essence, developmental "subcultures" that may determine, in part, the course of social-cognitive development. Their chapter focuses, then, on a description of the nature of these subcultures (such as a shift from family to school environment) and how they may represent alternative explanations for well-known age-related changes in social cogniton.

Chapters 3 and 8, which apply a sociocultural analysis to the study of developmental changes in children's understanding and use of social rules, demonstrate the importance of a sociocultural perspective in a different sense. They question traditional conclusions regarding social-cognitive development in terms not only of how it is interpreted (social vs. cognitive) but also to the extent that age-related changes have been appropriately described. Specifically, they argue that age changes may be more a function of changing social factors than of changing intellectual ability, especially as age reversals in judgments can occur by changing the social context of the judgment. Costanzo and Dix (Chapter 3) present a social-psychological perspective. They argue that even preschool children judge events on the basis of intention, volition, and so on under some conditions. That is, they suggest that children will engage in systematic causal analyses when rules of constraint are absent–for example, when no salient external cause exists for another person's behavior. Pool, Shweder, and Much (Chapter 8) present an anthropological perspective. They argue that questions framed appropriately to the culture of childhood will elicit from young children distinctions between rule infractions (e.g., moral vs. prudential) that are very similar to those expressed by adults.

Four chapters deal with the influence of sociocultural factors on the impact of socializing agents on social cognitions and social behavior. Collins (Chapter 5) discusses developmental changes in children's comprehension of televised narratives and the social-situational factors that influence children's interpretations of what they see. One such antecedent factor concerns the knowledge and expectations that children bring with them when watching television. For example, Collins demonstrated that socioeconomic status in conjunction with developmental level affected children's comprehension of events and their inferences about the actors. For the younger children only, comprehension was better when they viewed programs representing settings similar to their own backgrounds.

The remaining three chapters in this category are concerned primarily with parental disciplinary techniques. All three focus on factors in socialization experiences that influence social-cognitive mediators of behavior. Hoffman (Chapter 10) discusses motivational/affective factors, such as parental emotion, that influence moral understanding and empathic responsiveness. He argues, for example, that the emotional arousal generated during a disciplinary encounter, depending on the level, may motivate, or interfere with, the processing of the disciplinary message. Grusec (Chapter 11) also discusses the importance of arousal in disciplinary strategies but emphasizes, rather, how such strategies affect attributional mediators of social behavior. That is, her data suggest that socialization strategies that lead children to make a stable, internal attribution for an act (e.g., I am a nice person) are more likely to foster subsequent prosocial behavior than are other types of strategies. Similarly, Lepper (Chapter 12) focuses on how social-situational factors influence children's causal attributions for socialization events. Applying well-known social-psychological phenomena (forced compliance and overjustification) to an analysis of socialization processes, he argues that social inducements that are just barely sufficient to effect compliance are most likely to lead to internalization. That is, socialization experiences that lead children to believe they acted out of personal volition are most likely to produce subsequent similar actions in the absence of external inducement.

Interestingly, there is little specific discussion in these three chapters on age-related processes per se. To the extent that developmental level influences children's processing of social information, however, these attributional/motivational accounts of disciplinary events provide a useful basis for subsequent developmental analyses. Indeed, this kind of developmental implication is evident in one of the studies reported by Grusec. Socialization strategies invoking internal, stable attributions enhanced internalization for 8-year-olds but not for younger children, presumably because younger children tend neither to view themselves in stable terms nor to make generalizations on the basis of dispositional labels (Shantz, 1975).

Finally, two chapters discuss antecedent social factors of a different sort: developmental change in social processes that are typically considered as independent variables. That is, as opposed to examining the effect of sociocultural antecedents on social concepts and behaviors, as the previously discussed chapters do, the focus of these chapters is on the development of the antecedent processes themselves. Ruble (Chapter 6) focuses on the source of information used in self-assessment. She reports a developmental shift in the self-evaluation of competence from absolute standards (e.g., completing a set number of problems) to social-comparison standards (e.g., performing better than peers). Emmerich and Goldman (Chapter 9) focus on the development of interpersonal values. Although it is commonly acknowledged that such values are important independent variables in the study of social cognition and social behavior, in that they affect the kind of information sought and how it is used, little attempt has been made to describe the developmental course of value systems. Emmerich and Goldman describe developmental shifts in social-acceptance versus individual-autonomy value orientations, which contribute to increasing value conflicts during adolescence.

Social-behavioral consequences

A few chapters attempt to examine the impact of the development of social cognition on actual social behavior. Although the need to make these links has been a concern for several years (e.g., Shantz, 1975), progress toward this goal has been slow – perhaps, in part, because operationalizing cognitions and behaviors and examining their interrelation is difficult and because the inference of cause and effect is equally difficult. This goal remains a worthy one, however; and, as demonstrated by a few chapters in this volume, an attempt to address it continues.

Two chapters that examine social behavior are by investigators associated with the social-learning tradition (Grusec and Hartup) and thus represent the addition of developmental social-cognition factors to a continuing focus on social behavior. Grusec, as described earlier (Chapter 11), has extended her previous work on the socialization of prosocial behavior to emphasize the crucial role of social-cognitive mediators that are developmentally related. Similarly, Chapter 4 by Hartup, Brady, and Newcomb represents a social-cognition perspective on a topic of long-standing interest to Hartup (e.g., Hartup, 1970): children's peer interactions. The authors first review previous attempts to relate social cognition to social interaction and discuss the methodological and interpretational difficulties inherent in many such studies, particularly those of a correlational nature. They then describe two studies demonstrating a relationship between certain kinds of social understanding (e.g., nature of reward contingencies) and children's cooperative and competitive behavior in the context of an ongoing social exchange. Their demonstration is strengthened by additional data showing that manipulations affecting social understanding had predicted effects on the children's subsequent behavior.

Three other chapters concerned with social-behavioral consequences represent a more recent blend of social-psychological and social-developmental approaches. Berndt (Chapter 7) examines the relation between intentions and behavior in children's friendships. He shows that distinctions children make in intentions to help and share with friends versus acquaintances are reflected in actual behavioral distinctions when observed unobtrusively but only when the measure of intentions and behaviors relates to similar situations. Ruble (Chapter 6) shows that developmental changes in the bases of inferences about competence are reflected in subsequent task behavior. Finally, Lepper (Chapter 12), as discussed earlier, applies well-known social-psychological principles to the problem of internalization, as reflected in behavior in the absence of external constraints.

Organization of the volume

The book is divided into four parts. Parts II and III represent a content-based distinction between the presentations. Part II concerns developmental changes in interpersonal relations and social understanding. The chapters in Part III take a new look at what traditionally has been the most fundamental concern of social/personality development: socialization of values and internalization of standards of conduct. Finally, Part IV presents commentaries by four distinguished developmental psychologists representing divergent points of view. Maccoby (Chapter 14), representing the social/personality tradition, critically evaluates the volume in terms of its contribution to our understanding of basic socialization processes. Trabasso (Chapter 16), representing the information-processing tradition, raises basic questions about the goals of the research being presented. Both Turiel (Chapter 13) and Damon (Chapter 15) are known for pioneering research programs in the study of social-cognitive development. Turiel discusses the orientation of the volume in terms of the traditional distinction between the social-learning and the cognitive-developmental approaches. Damon evaluates the contribution of each chapter by applying what he considers the five fundamental questions underlying research in social-cognitive development.

Coherence in this volume derives from two main sources: (1) the efforts of the authors to anchor children's social cognitions in the events that shape them or in social activity and (2) the small number of behavior domains in which the authors work: morality, achievement, prosocial behavior, and interpersonal relations. Even so, the contents of the volume are extremely diverse, especially with respect to measurement and method, partly because the processes connecting social experience and social cognition are not easy to observe. In fact, one might argue that methodological pluralism in this area should be encouraged rather than eschewed. Clearly, it will be with varied strategies that future investigators seek to describe the complex interconnections that characterize the development of social cognition and its social implications.

References

Butterworth, G., & Light, P. *Social cognition.* Chicago: University of Chicago Press, 1981.
Cantor, N., & Kihlstrom, J. (Eds.) *Personality, cognition, and social interaction.* Hillsdale, N.J.: Erlbaum, 1981.
Chandler, M. J., & Borjes, M. A. Social-cognitive development. In B. Wolman (Ed.), *Handbook of developmental psychology.* Englewood Cliffs, N.J.: Prentice-Hall, 1982.
Clark, M. S., & Fiske, S. T. (Eds.). *Affect and cognition.* Hillsdale, N.J.: Erlbaum, 1982.
Collins, W. A. (Ed.). *Minnesota Symposium on Child Psychology* (Vol. 14). Hillsdale, N.J.: Erlbaum, 1981.
Damon, W. Why study social-cognitive development? *Human Development,* 1979, *22,* 206–211.
Feldman, N. S., & Ruble, D. N. The development of person perception: Cognitive and

social factors. In S. S. Brehm, S. M. Kassin, & F. X. Gibbons (Eds.), *Developmental social psychology*. New York: Oxford University Press, 1981.

Flavell, J. H., & Ross, L. *Social cognitive development*. New York: Cambridge University Press, 1981.

Hartup, W. W. Peer interaction and social organization. In P. H. Mussen (Ed.), *Carmichael's manual of child psychology* (3rd ed., Vol. 2). New York: Wiley, 1970.

Harvey, J. H. *Cognition, social behavior, and the environment*. Hillsdale, N.J.: Erlbaum, 1981.

Hastie, R., Ostrom, T. M., Ebbesen, E. B., Wyer, R. S., Jr., Hamilton, D. L., & Carlston, D. E. (Eds.). *Person memory: The cognitive basis of social perception*. Hillsdale, N.J.: Erlbaum, 1980.

Hastorf, A. H., & Isen, A. M. (Eds.). *Cognitive social psychology*. New York: Elsevier North Holland, 1981.

Higgins, E. T., Herman, C. P., & Zanna, M. P. (Eds.). *Social cognition: The Ontario Symposium* (Vol. 1). Hillsdale, N.J.: Erlbaum, 1981.

Howe, H. E., Jr., & Keasey, C. B. (Eds.). *Nebraska Symposium on Motivation*. Lincoln: University of Nebraska Press, 1978.

Kahneman, D., Slovic, P., & Tversky, A. (Eds.). *Judgment under uncertainty: Heuristics and biases*. New York: Cambridge Unversity Press, 1982.

Kuhn, D. Mechanisms of cognitive and social development: One psychology or two? *Human Development*, 1978, *21*, 92–118.

Lamb, M. E. *Social and personality development*. New York: Holt, Rinehart and Winston, 1978.

Lindzey, G., & Aronson, E. (Eds.). *Handbook of social psychology* (3rd ed.). Reading, Mass.: Addison-Wesley, in press.

Maccoby, E. E. *Social development: Psychological growth and the parent–child relationship*. New York: Harcourt Brace Jovanovich, 1980.

Maccoby, E. E., & Jacklin, C. N. *The psychology of sex differences*. Stanford, Calif. Stanford University Press, 1974.

Mussen, P. H. (Ed.). *Carmichael's manual of child psychology* (4th ed.). New York: Wiley, in press.

Nisbett, R. E., & Ross, L. D. *Human inference: Strategies and shortcomings of informal judgment*. Englewood Cliffs, N.J.: Prentice-Hall, 1980.

Shantz, C. U. The development of social cognition. In E. M. Hetherington (Ed.), *Review of child development research*. Chicago: University of Chicago Press, 1975.

Shantz, C. U. Social cognition. In J. H. Flavell and E. M. Markman (Eds.), *Cognitive development*, volume in P. H. Mussen (General ed.), *Carmichael's manual of child psychology* (4th ed.). New York: Wiley, in press.

Wyer, R. S., & Carlston, D. E. *Social cognition, inference, and attribution*. Hillsdale, N.J.: Erlbaum, 1979.

Part II

Social understanding and interpersonal relations

2 Social cognition and the social life of the child: stages as subcultures

E. Tory Higgins and Jacquelynne Eccles Parsons

Age-grades are recognized divisions of the life of an individual as he passes from infancy to old age. Thus each person passes successively into one grade after another, and, if he lives long enough, through the whole series – infant, boy, youth, young married man, elder, or whatever it may be.

Radcliffe-Brown (1929)

All cultures must deal in one way or another with the cycle of growth from infancy to adulthood. . . . Discontinuity in the life cycle is a fact of nature and is inescapable. . . . Age-graded cultures characteristically demand different behavior of the individual at different times of his life and persons of a like age-grade are grouped into a society whose activities are all oriented toward the behavior desired at that age.

Ruth Benedict (1938)

Interest in age-related changes in social judgment and social concepts has increased dramatically in recent years (cf. Damon, 1977 a,b; Flavell & Ross, 1981; Howe & Keasey, 1978; Shantz, 1975). In interpreting these age-related changes, one approach has dominated. In fact, Damon (1977a) justifiably refers to this approach, inspired by the Piaget–Kohlberg perspective on social development, as a kind of "new look" in social development. Essentially, this "new look" interprets age-related changes in social cognition in terms of developmental changes in the cognitive operations and/or structures that underlie or mediate children's social judgments and concepts, changes with respect to such processes as role taking, classification, and compensation (or reversibility). This approach has contributed greatly to our understanding of the nature of social development and has increased our appreciation of the qualitative or stagelike character of this development. Unfortunately, like all powerful perspec-

The research reported by E. Tory Higgins was supported by Grant RO1 MH 31427 from the National Institute of Mental Health. We are grateful to Michael Pressley, Diane Ruble, and Richard Shweder for helpful comments and suggestions.

15

tives, the "cognitive ability" approach has also diverted attention from the investigation of important additional mediating factors. That the cognitive developmental approach matches a common bias in explaining variation in behavior – the bias toward "dispositional" attributions (e.g., ability, skills) rather than "situational" attributions (e.g., social constraints and demands, task characteristics; cf. Heider, 1958; Jones & Harris, 1967; Ross, 1977) – has undoubtedly contributed to its salience as the major explanation of developmental changes. The general purpose of this chapter is to consider, in a preliminary, speculative fashion, a particular set of "situational" factors that ought to be related to systematic developmental change, specifically, age-related changes in the culturally prescribed social life, or subcultures, of children.

Children in all cultures pass through a series of age-related phases during development (Denzin, 1977; Keniston, 1971), although the amount of discontinuity across the life cycle varies cross-culturally (see Benedict, 1938). Each phase involves characteristic social concerns, activities, social situations and settings, expectations and rules for behavior, socially approved institutions, and so on. Moreover, the behavior of adults toward, and in the presence of, children varies in different phases. For example, the responses of adults to children who violate their personal space in a queue varies dramatically as a function of the child's age, ranging from smiles for 5-year-olds to frowns for 10-year-olds (Fry & Willis, 1971). Given that these periods are fairly systematic within any given culture, one can conceptualize each phase (e.g., infancy, preschoolers, juveniles, preadolescents, adolescents) as a subculture within the more general, adult-dominated culture. The cultural character of these phases is suggested by their historical emergence: "The world that we think proper to children – fairy stories, games, toys, special books for learning, even the idea of childhood itself – is a European invention of the past four hundred years" (Plumb, 1973, p. 153). That is, the modern phase of childhood is, at least in part, a cultural product (Aries, 1962; Kessen, 1979; Plumb, 1973). Moreover, as technological and scientific advances both increased the amount of education required to carry out many social roles and permitted a large segment of society to be unproductive by vastly increasing the productivity of those who did work, additional phases of development were introduced into industrialized societies, such as adolescence.

Certainly, the general influence of subcultural factors on social judgments and behavior has been well recognized, both in the social-learning approach (e.g., Bandura & Walters, 1963) and in the "new look" approach (e.g., Kohlberg, 1969; Piaget, 1965). The influence of subcultural factors, however, has typically been considered with respect to demographic variation within a particular age phase of development, such as social class or ethnic differences in norms, values, and beliefs. Although the importance of social experience for social cognition is acknowledged, it is mainly with respect to speeding up or slowing down mental growth within a particular phase of development, providing opportunities for cognitive development, or affecting superficial content aspects of social cognition.

We are suggesting, instead, that variation in the characteristics of social life phases could be an important factor underlying the age-related changes in social cognition reported in studies using middle-class North American subjects. A similar point was made recently by Kessen (1979), who went so far as to speculate whether our current descriptions of age-related changes in children's behavioral patterns might not be a cultural artifact. Anthropologists, especially, have emphasized the importance of considering social environmental factors when interpreting differences in cognitions, rather than focusing on cognitive processing skills or intellectual level (e.g., Mead, 1932; Shweder & Bourne, in press). What they have suggested for cross-cultural comparisons, we are suggesting for comparisons across age phases.

Unfortunately, because the cognitive growth approach in developmental psychology has been dominant in recent years and because the preceding behavioristic era was largely adevelopmental in its focus, there has been little concern with the social life of the child and consequently it is currently impossible to estimate its possible effects. Moreover, there has been so little empirical research and theoretical analysis that a clear articulation of the range of social variables that might be important or of the possible mechanisms underlying their influence does not exist at present. For example, even such a dramatic shift in the social life of the child as going to school has received little descriptive or theoretical attention, even though major developmental changes in social cognition are reported as occurring approximately concurrently with this shift.

To prevent misunderstanding, it is important to clarify our strategy in this chapter. We are not advocating the position that qualitative change in the social life of children, by itself, underlies age-related changes in social cognition and social behavior. To deny the role of cognitive change in social development would, in fact, contradict our own previous descriptions of cognitive factors underlying social development (e.g., Higgins, 1981; Higgins, Fondacaro, & McCann, 1981; Parsons, 1974, in press, Parsons & Ruble, 1977). It is a useful exercise, however, to consider the extent to which the qualitative shifts in social development can be accounted for simply in terms of qualitative shifts in social life phases.[1] Certain aspects of social development that are puzzling and appear to contradict the "cognitive ability" approach to social cognition may be due to social life factors. Consideration of age-related changes in social life could eliminate the need to account for all social-cognitive changes in terms of underlying cognitive changes, which could increase the predictive validity of the "cognitive ability" approach. In addition, by reducing the subcultural background noise, the search for those changes in cognitive operations and structures that do influence social development could be facilitated.

Our general purpose, then, is to consider the role of social factors in the development of social cognition. We will, however, also consider the interrelation between social and cognitive factors in this development. It is certainly not novel to suggest that social development arises from an interaction of social and cognitive factors. There are a variety of different "social × cognitive interaction" positions that one could hold, however. Neither the traditional social learning nor the "cognitive ability" approach has given much attention to the stagelike changes in social input that may contribute to the social × cognitive interaction. Moreover, those approaches that have focused on social-age phases, most notably the psychoanalytic approach, have typically not considered the relation between age phases and intellectual growth, and, in addition, have paid attention to only a restricted range of social variables (e.g., toilet training, modes of discipline, life crises).

Our chapter has four basic aims. Our first aim is to describe a set of social or cultural dimensions along which there is systematic variation as a function of children's age, such as changes in socialization agents (e.g., parents and siblings vs. teachers and peers) and changes in social position and roles (ascribed status and subordinate position vs. achieved status and equal position). Our second aim is to illustrate the usefulness of the "social life phases" perspective both for interpreting age-related changes in social cognition that are not easily explained by other approaches and for reinterpreting previously identified developmental shifts in social cognition. Our third aim is to consider cross-cultural and demographic variability in socialization in light of this perspective. Our final aim is to use this perspective to reconsider the nature of the "social × cognitive" interaction underlying social-cognitive development.

The social life of children at different age phases

It has been recognized for a long time that the social life of children changes at different phases in their development (cf. Benedict, 1938;

Brim, 1966; Erikson, 1963; Inkeles, 1969; Parsons, 1964; Radcliffe-Brown, 1929; Sullivan, 1953). In addition, the importance of considering children's social world has been emphasized in the literature (cf. Bandura & Walters, 1963; Barker, 1968; Kessen, 1979; Parke, 1974; Vygotsky, 1962). Lewin (1935), for example, describes the impact of the social world on the "boundary zones" and regions of a child's life space. Vygotsky (1962) discusses how socializing agents provide children with structure and regulatory systems. Bandura and Walters (1963) point out the critical role of social models on children's social development. There have also been suggestions that particular age-related changes in social behavior may be due, in part, to some age-related change in social input (e.g., Keniston, 1971; Kessen, 1979; Piaget, 1965). For example, age-related shifts in the prescribed moral code and in socializing agents' disciplinary tactics concerning children's behavior have been mentioned as possible causes of developmental shifts in children's moral behavior (e.g., Bandura, 1969; Bijou, 1976; Parke, 1974). Staats (1975) has suggested that children are especially open to learning speech when they are young because their dependency upon their parents increases the strength and variety of reinforcers the parents can use in training them. Hartup (1970) has suggested that age-related changes in peer interaction probably derive, in part, from changes in reinforcement for, and models of, particular behaviors. However, to our knowledge, there has been no systematic attempt to describe and contrast the general social life of children at different age phases or to relate the qualitative changes in the social life of children to the qualitative changes in children's social cognition.

Our major interest was to explore the latter issue. We were, thus, rather disappointed to find little discussion in the literature of how the social life of children changes from the preschool years through the early adolescent years. In fact, it was even difficult to find extensive, organized accounts of the social life of children during most of the age phases. It has been necessary, therefore, to construct our account of the social life of children at different age phases from information scattered across various sources, with the empirical basis, and even accuracy, of the descriptions often being unclear. Most features of each age phase, however, have been mentioned by more than one source. Nevertheless, to have to rely on this social life data base for drawing inferences about social-cognitive development is an unhappy state of affairs, however necessary. At this stage of our knowledge, our examination of this issue is clearly speculative and is meant mainly to be suggestive of variables to be given more serious consideration in the future.

It has been argued that to discover the nature of thinking and its development it is necessary to analyze the settings and activities associated with the thinking, as well as the goals of the thinker and the environmental features relevant to each goal (cf. Brunswick, 1943; Cole, Hood, & McDermott, in press). If such environmental variables are important for cognition, they should be important for social cognition. Our purpose, then, is to consider some of the social environmental variables that may differentiate the social life of children at different age phases. Because our aim is to relate children's social life phases to the stagelike changes in their social-cognitive development, we will restrict our attention to those features of each social life phase that are relatively distinct and that emerge from, or undergo, rapid growth during a particular age phase. Of course, social life features common to different age phases could be important determinants of social cognition. For our purposes, however, it is the relatively distinctive and emergent features that are critical. Taking a sociological approach (Inkeles, 1969), we will also restrict our attention to those social life features in each age phase that are regular, recurrent, and socially structured aspects of the prototypic child's individual experience. Our description of each age phase will necessarily be sketchy, because little direct, systematic attention has been paid to this issue, but selective, because the potential sources of relevant information are overwhelming. The description will most closely resemble the phases for white, middle-class, urban/suburban children. This is appropriate, however, because this is the same demographic sample that studies of developmental social cognition have typically examined.

The description of each life phase is organized in terms of the following set of factors: socializing agents, activities and tasks, social position and roles, social contact and relationships, social restrictions and privileges, social motives and concerns. Although these factors reflect different aspects of the social life of children, they are clearly not independent because together they constitute an interconnected and integrated whole, with the different aspects interpenetrating and reinforcing each other. The major, general sources for our descriptions of the social life phases are Brim (1966), Campbell (1969), Clausen (1968), Jersild (1963), Parsons (1964), Parsons, Olds, Zelditch, and Slater (1955), Sullivan (1953), and our own personal observations.

Preschool to juvenile (from 3–5 to 6–9 years of age)

Socialization agents. With entry into elementary school, the juvenile comes under the influence of two new sets of socialization agents: specifically, the classroom teacher and related school personnel, and peers.

Classes are generally organized with a single teacher, typically female, in charge of 20 to 30 same-aged students. The role of the teacher necessitates less personal attention and nurturance than was received by the juvenile from parents and more peer socialization than was true at home. In addition to these school-related shifts in socializers, the juvenile may also be exposed to other adult socialization agents, including recreational directors, Sunday-school teachers, and a large array of peers, some of whom are of equivalent age and status and some of whom are older and more powerful.

Activities and tasks. The tasks that juveniles are exposed to in school differ from the typical preschool task in that they involve increased focus on intellectual skills where success and failure on the task is, at times, not obvious without outside evaluation. There is also an increase in the requirements to master tasks imposed on one by an authority figure in a specified time period. Age segregation makes regimentation of tasks across individuals possible and consequently increases the likelihood of comparative judgments of the speed of mastery. Children also are faced with abstracting and learning the new social-behavioral code associated with the "student" role. Recent data (Blumenfeld et al., 1979) suggest that the "curriculum" in the first years of school is more concerned with a child's acquisition of the "student" role than academic skills.

Social position and roles. When juveniles enter elementary school they have the collective status of new recruits compared to their individual status at home. Whereas previously they had one major role – the ascribed role of son or daughter in the informal organization of their home – they now have both ascribed and achieved roles as students within two major social structures, namely, a formal social structure associated with the school system and an informal social structure associated with the peer culture. Because status in both these social structures is determined in part by social skills and achievement rather than primarily by ascribed status, entry into school introduces children to achieved roles. The role of student is a task-oriented role in which performance is systematically evaluated with regard to pre-set performance standards of excellence, normative progress, and acceptable style. As such, children will vary in their status within that role depending on their performance. Further, segregating the children into grades based primarily on age, as is done in most North American schools, focuses the attention of both the teacher and the students on these status variations, making competition and social comparison probable events.

Age segregation also influences the child's position in the peer culture.

In contrast to the hierarchical status characteristic of the home and the school environment, age-segregated peer groups are often characterized by a homogeneous status structure. Most children in age-segregated groups have equivalent status. Piaget has argued that it is only within this age-segregated peer culture that consensus-based moral codes can develop. Because age segregation also narrows the power differential, the status hierarchies that do emerge within these peer groups are influenced by personal characteristics as well as ascribed characteristics. A wider range of roles and their associated status is available to the child than is true within the family. Children can select a role for themselves from among this range. In addition, juveniles within their peer groups first encounter superiority–inferiority relationships that are based on achieved characteristics. Children who interact on a regular basis will recognize that they have different statuses, that their play groups are hierarchically arranged, and that their status may vary across different groups. All these characteristics of the peer culture can serve to focus children's attention on individual differences in personality, in social skill, and in personal liabilities and strengths.

In addition to age segregation, juveniles are subject to increased sex segregation and additional pressure to assume sex roles. Separate washrooms and separate athletic events reinforce the segregation of the sexes started during the preschool period. Along with these institutionally segregated structures, the children themselves increasingly segregate their play groups by sex and put increased social pressure on children who may deviate in their playmate choices.

Social contact and relationships. Social exposure increases dramatically when juveniles enter elementary school. There is increased exposure to representatives of various statuses (e.g., sex, religion, ethnicity), as well as to a variety of adult social roles and peer personality types. Juveniles have much greater contact with peers who have a variety of personal styles to which they must accommodate. They also have the opportunity to observe how authority figures judge the behaviors and personalities of their peers, focusing attention on issues of equity. By interacting with various teachers over the early elementary school years, juveniles learn to relate to different people occupying the same role, whereas in the family the same people occupy the role of mother and father over time. In addition, children are exposed to a wider range of expectations regarding their behavior from the increased numbers of both adults and peers. Juveniles begin to participate in wider social circles that are not organized in terms of kinship. Peer relationships, unlike family relationships, are not preordained, permanent, or institutionally ascribed. Members of peer groups are responsible for maintaining control and providing nurturance within the relationship. Because peer groups are often organized according to sex, exposure to, and active interaction with, both sexes may decrease. Finally, the salience of group memberships either through uniforms or through social labeling may lead juveniles to identify with their social groups (e.g., a "bluebird," a "member of Tom's team") and to begin limiting their social network to members of their own social groups.

The ratio of children to adults changes dramatically when juveniles enter school. In addition, because of the greater chance of peers staying together from year to year than of students being with the same teacher from year to year, cohesion within the peer group is promoted. Finally, contact with peers allows juveniles to observe how other peers respond to a variety of different authority figures and different personality types.

Social restrictions and privileges. Entry into school increases both the juveniles' individual freedom and the demands for greater control of their behavior. On the one hand, juveniles are given greater freedom over their mobility, as reflected in their riding bicycles to school and taking buses alone to and from school. They are also provided with their own personal desk and chair. In addition, the interactions among peers are, to a much greater extent than earlier, outside the orbit of parental control. On the other hand, children must sit quietly for long periods of time and are expected to show restraint within the classroom and to learn a whole set of procedural rules associated with their various roles. They become subject to universalistic, common standards of dress and deportment as well as new expectations for personal conduct. These rules, however, need no longer be followed by virtue of their ascribed status, as in the family, but involve common subjection to general rules. Children are also exposed to an increase in the variety of privileges given to different students. They may become aware for the first time that the same adult gives different privileges to different children of the same age.

Social motives and concerns. Because the child has to acquire the new role of student, there is a great pressure on juveniles by both parents and teachers to be a "good boy" or "good girl" at school; the child is expected to learn respect for the teacher, consideration and cooperativeness in relating to fellow pupils, and good "work habits" (Blumenfeld et al., 1979). At the same time, peer acceptance is a major concern of the child. As a consequence of these two sets of demands, juveniles must learn to accommodate to different individuals in a variety of situations in and out of the classroom and must learn to handle conflicting goals, such as the potential conflict between the task goals that are the teacher's primary concern and the social goals of the peer group. Children also are exposed to a distinction between the obligation to be "nice" to everyone and loyal to members of one's own group (e.g., family, friends, classmates) and to the notion that one should be proud of one's own goals.

Juvenile to preadolescent (from 6–9 to 10–12 years of age)

Socialization agents. During the preadolescent period children are exposed to yet another increase in the types of socialization agents: coaches of Little League sports, instructors of dance or ballet, music teachers, camp counselors, leaders of Cubs and Brownies, directors of various classes at youth organizations such as the YMCA, YWCA, and so on.

Activities and tasks. The range of activities available to children greatly increases from the juvenile to the preadolescent period, as reflected in the increase in socialization agents. Children spend more time in activities outside the home and school in various kinds of organized activities at town centers and youth organizations, such as the YMCA and YWCA, cubs, brownies, church activities, and summer camps. In addition, there is an increase in activities for children to learn particular skills, such as learning to play a musical instrument, learning artistic skills, crafts, and dancing. There is also a sharp increase in the exposure to competitive sports for boys, providing additional social-comparison information on individual differences in skills in a wider variety of activities and situations.

Social position and roles. Whereas juveniles are the youngest age group in the elementary school, the preadolescents are the older age group in the elementary school. Thus, in the age hierarchy of the school, preadolescents have higher status. In addition, preadolescents have a greater awareness that the power of the teacher is more circumscribed than the power of their parents. During the preadolescent period, structures of prestige and power emerge within the classroom and the informal peer groups.

Social contact and relationships. The increased activities allow an increase of association with same-sex peers. Preadolescents can now drift into and out of "voluntary associations" that have relatively fluid boundaries. The strength of the peer bond relative to the teacher bond increases in this period, in part because by the later elementary school years the students have spent many years together, whereas only one year is spent with any particular teacher. Their experience with different teachers over the years also provides preadolescents with an opportunity to compare teachers and thus discover their relative merits and demerits and to discover the arbitrariness of classroom rules. The children will also have had increasing opportunities for exposure to information that can disconfirm the various stereotypes they may have formed. The peer groups during this period form into something like corporate groups that inculcate a strong sense of solidarity. The peer groups themselves develop a differentiation of roles, particularly with respect to leadership. Preadolescents develop strong relationships with the same-sex peers, and children begin to form "chum" or "bosom" relationships.

Social restrictions and privileges. During the preadolescent period the range of independent behavior increases. Generally, there is a decrease in detailed adult supervision, and, in particular, less and less of children's physical and social environment is under the direct surveillance and control of their parents. Children may also be asked to assume greater responsibilities around the school, their home, and in the organizations of which they are members. They may also acquire a job and consequently an independent source of income.

Social motives and concerns. Preadolescents seek to contribute to their chums' happiness, and they become sensitive to what matters to other people. There is a beginning of a "we" feeling that is more than just cooperation and involves collaboration in the sense of adjustment to others' needs in pursuit of mutual interests. During this period, parents, teachers, and a variety of coaches or group leaders emphasize comparison in intellectual achievement as well as in social and athletic activities. The motive to excell relative to others increases (Veroff, 1969), especially in boys.

Preadolescent to early adolescent (from 10–12 to 13–16 years of age)

Socialization agents. In contrast to elementary school students, junior and senior high school students generally have different teachers for various subjects each year and teachers of both sexes. This greatly increases the opportunities for adult influence. In addition, the significant others and reference persons for adolescents are more likely to include adults whom they have never actually met, such as glamorous or famous media figures.

Peers increase in importance as social activities and clubs take on a more formal nature. Opposite-sex peers take on a new power as socializing agents. Also, because junior and senior high schools are usually bigger than elementary schools, adolescents meet and must accommodate to a wider, more diverse set of peers.

Activities and tasks. In general, many more formal, structured activities occur in junior high school than in elementary school: athletic activities, such as wrestling, field hockey, archery, and volleyball; specialized clubs, involving such activities as photography, debating, international affairs, choral singing, and the student newspaper. Typically, adolescents are granted greater autonomy in directing school clubs and organizations. The early adolescent also has an opportunity to engage in a broader range of activities outside the school, such as joining organized clubs and formal groups in the YMCA and YWCA. As a consequence of this increase in social options, the early adolescent is faced with the need to make choices among the various alternatives. Adolescents spend more time simply having conversations with one another. There is a sudden increase in dating, "going steady," and "falling in love." Thus, the adolescent must learn new skills for interacting with the opposite sex. The adolescent is much more absorbed in the world outside the home and pursues various hobbies and personal interests that can differ from those of their parents. There is also an increased likelihood that they will have a paying part-time job outside their home. School work requires an increased amount of time, with homework assignments penetrating to a greater extent into their home life.

Social position and roles. Early adolescents are in the process of becoming an adult. Their status is marginal and varies, depending upon whether they compare themselves to younger children or older adults (see Lewin, 1939). They are not permitted to maintain childish behavior, but at the same time they are isolated from the workings of adult society. Although their role as student is increasing in importance, its transiency is also becoming more obvious; school takes on the quality of a training center for their future adult role. Although they can have part-time jobs, they are prevented from having full-time employment.

The informal peer associations during this period involve much sharper prestige stratification. Because there are more activities and a wider array of peers, status hierarchies based on activities as well as status hierarchies within groups emerge and become salient. Cliques emerge that confront adolescents with pressures to choose which way they will develop. Adolescents begin to recognize that their position or status in society does not depend simply upon their family's judgment. As the range of the early adolescents' associations widens, not only does both their capacity for getting along with different kinds of people and their repertoire of roles increase, but their awareness of group and individual differences and similarities also increases.

Most early adolescents have various positions and statuses in the different formal groups to which they belong. Consequently, they are forced to engage in a diversity of social roles. On the one hand, this diversity prepares the adolescent for future adult roles and the demands of such roles. The very diversity of roles that the adolescent must occupy, on the other hand, increases the probability of experiencing conflict among the demands of the different roles and thus forces the adolescent to develop strategies for managing role conflict.

Social contact and relationships. Early adolescence is a period of dramatic increase in the amount of contact with the opposite sex: More positive cross-sex relationships emerge both within and outside the classroom. Having a good time becomes important, and a strong hedonistic quality in social activities involves both sexes. To compete effectively in this new social domain, adolescents must learn new skills and test them in a new social arena.

Because junior and senior high schools are larger than elementary schools and draw from a wider geographical area, adolescents are exposed to individuals from a much wider range of demographic statuses and from backgrounds not encountered in their own neighborhood. Opportunities to meet and form friendships with a greater number of peers also increases. Adolescents spend much more time with their peers. In fact, the junior and senior high schools provide a population mass that is sufficiently dense to make possible the development and maintenance of an autonomous adolescent social system. The high school, especially, is the adolescent's world to a large extent, and high school activities and events have great personal significance for them. Peer associations during this period become collective organizations to satisfy and channel mutual interests. Many adolescents join clubs and gangs and become members of "crowds" and "cliques." Within these associations, adolescents have the opportunity to compare different social standards and rules, as well as share experiences that question their parents' or teachers' pronouncements. This, in part, arises from the great diversity of the members' backgrounds in peer associations and in the variety of courses they take in school.

Social restrictions and privileges. Junior and senior high school students generally have many more privileges than elementary school students. They have more control over their social life and can influence the moral climate, dress, lingo, rules of etiquette, and so on of their social life. Adolescents have greater freedom to select their friends and activities and consequently play more important roles in defining their rights and privileges. Parents are much more reluctant to constrain the social activities of their adolescent children and may even ask them what rules seem most appropriate given what the parents of other adolescents are permitting, such as how late they can stay up, how much allowance they should get, and when and how often they should date. Such responsiveness by the parents greatly increases the freedom of adolescents to control their social life. Their freedom is also increased by earning their own money, further reducing their parents' control over them. In school, they are asked to select the courses they will study and are asked by counselors, teachers, and parents to begin planning for a vocation or career and to think seriously about what their adult roles will be.

In general, then, adolescence is a period marked by inconsistencies. On the one hand, the adolescent is allowed greater freedom from adult surveillance. As a consequence, adolescents have an opportunity to practice responsibility in human relations without supervision and to learn to accept the consequences of their behavior. On the other hand, early adolescents are not permitted to participate in a variety of adult activities and decision making. Typically, they are not allowed to be self-supporting or to vote, cannot go into bars or buy hard liquor, and are not permitted to marry without adult consent. Parents themselves have conflict between the desire to give the adolescent freedom and the desire to reassert control. Finally, most adolescents recognize that a great deal of power is still vested in adults, especially in teachers, principals, counselors, and juvenile officers; thus they are reminded that their ultimate responsibility is still to an external authority.

Social motives and concerns. In early adolescence there is a high value placed upon autonomy, initiative, identity formation, and idealism, with explicit, overt acceptance or approval of adult-sponsored interests and discipline being negatively valued. There is a strong norm not to be under the control of parents and to abandon familial dependency.[2] Adolescents are motivated to gain some financial independence and to attempt to achieve self-direction and emancipation. Although, on the one hand, some aspects of adolescent culture emphasize fun and adventure, other aspects of adolescent culture emphasize career preparation and serious work toward long-range goals. There is a greater flirtation with boundary areas between propriety and immorality, with various offenses, such as staying out late, drinking, and sexual behavior, often being encouraged by the peer group.

Adolescents are concerned with the world's view of both themselves and their family and devote a great deal of energy to trying to assess what others think of them. They have a need for personal security, intimacy, and meaningful collaboration with peers. Adolescents care more about social and personal issues, political events, and religious issues. A major goal of adolescents is to make decisions about, and prepare for, future adult tasks, roles, and occupations. Preparation for one's future career is a critical aspect of this period; this, in turn, increases competition among peers for the symbols of adult status, such as positions of responsibility within student government, scholarships, or outstanding athletic performance. Adolescents are also expected to acquire and practice the social skills of adults, to experiment with what they are in relation to others, and to "try on" new behaviors and experiences. In other words, they are expected to begin the process of attaining a somewhat coherent, permanent answer to the questions "Who am I?" and "What will I become?"

Social-life phases and social-cognitive development

The purpose of this section is to provide some examples of the possible relation between changes in the social life of children and changes in their social concepts, social information processing biases, and social predictions. Our discussion of this relation is meant only to be suggestive, as our knowledge of the social life of children during different periods, as mentioned earlier, is incomplete, selective, somewhat anecdotal, and of unknown accuracy.

Some aspects of the social life of children could affect the development of their social concepts. For example, when juveniles enter elementary school they adopt the new role of "pupil" in the formal organization of the school. This role demands that certain common standards of dress, deportment, and personal conduct be followed; both parents and teachers emphasize the importance of being a "good boy" or "good girl" at school. During the preadolescent period, children are supervised by a number of different authority figures and must learn to follow the rules of various formal organizations in which they participate but over which they have little power or control. These aspects of the social life of juveniles and preadolescents should impact on their moral judgments and

beliefs. With respect to Kohlberg's (1964, 1969) stages of moral development, in particular, one would expect that during the juvenile period
there would be a sharp increase in Stage 3 moral judgments (i.e., the
interpersonal concordance or "good boy–nice girl" orientation) and that
during the preadolescent period there would be a sharp increase in Stage
4 moral judgments (i.e., orientation toward authority, fixed rules, and the
maintenance of the social order). In fact, there is evidence (Kohlberg,
1964, 1969) of a sharp increase in Stage 3 moral judgments between 7 and
10 years of age (the juvenile period) and a sharp increase in Stage 4 moral
judgments between 10 and 13 years of age (the preadolescent period). Of
course, we are not arguing that social life changes are sufficient for shifts
in moral judgments; cognitive factors also play an independent and interactive role (as discussed later). Thus, we would only predict a sharp
increase in the proportion of children at a higher stage after a shift to a
later life phase, *not* that a majority of children in the later phase would
necessarily reach the higher stage.

Changes in their relationships with those in power could also lead to a
change in the children's conceptions of authority during the juvenile and
preadolescent periods. Preschoolers are mainly under the authority of
their parents; in contrast, juveniles are under the control of a wide variety
of authority figures. These individuals provide each child with much less
personal attention and nurturance than parents, and their authority re-
sides in either institutional roles or their acknowledged expertise. If preschoolers associate authority with their parents and juveniles associate
authority with a range of adults, one might expect preschoolers to associate authority with the particular characteristics of their parents, with
attachment, and with fulfillment of their personal needs; in contrast,
juveniles would be expected to associate authority with social power,
formal status, and expertise. Damon (1977a) has found a shift from the
preschool to the juvenile period in the tendency to give Level 0 authority
knowledge responses (i.e., authority is legitimized by the personal link
between the authority figure and the self or by physical attributes of the
authority figure that the child considers to be descriptive of persons in
command) versus Level 1 authority knowledge responses (i.e., authority
is legitimized by attributes that enable authority figures to enforce their
commands).

Preadolescents interact with the same peers in a variety of situations
that provide them with the opportunity to notice that variation in the
power and performance of their peers is a function of the situation. In
addition, the selection of leaders within their informal peer groups is
based upon the achieved, rather than the ascribed, status of the members;

leaders are selected on the basis of their ability to lead the group effectively. Thus, one might expect a shift during adolescence to Level 2 authority knowledge responses (i.e., authority is legitimized by the authority figure's ability to lead and command better than subordinates, and this ability is believed to vary across different situations), which has, indeed, been found by Damon (1977a).

In his study of preschoolers' and juveniles' authority knowledge responses, Damon (1977a) also found an age-related difference in whether a peer story-dilemma versus an adult story-dilemma yielded higher level responses. The peer story-dilemma focused on a child–child authority relation (i.e., the authority relation between the captain and other players on a team) and the adult story-dilemma focused on a child–adult authority relation (i.e., the authority relation between a mother and her son or daughter). Damon (1977a) found that the preschoolers gave higher level authority knowledge responses on the adult story-dilemma, whereas juveniles gave higher level authority knowledge responses on the peer story-dilemma. As Damon (1977a) suggests, this developmental difference is probably due to differences in the social life of preschoolers and juveniles. Preschoolers do not participate regularly in formal, organized games or social activities with peers in which there is a hierarchy of power and prestige; they do, however, have frequent exposure to parental authority. Juveniles, on the other hand, have regular contact with peers in hierarchially organized activities, especially in games in which the captain is distinguished from other team members.

Changes in the social life of juveniles, preadolescents, and early adolescents should also affect their conceptions of friendship. First, juveniles' friendships should be based more on their subjective evaluations of others' personal characteristics than are preschoolers' friendships because, as described later, their social life promotes an increase in dispositional, personal judgments of others. There is, in fact, considerable evidence that between 7 and 10 years of age the establishment of friendships shifts from being based on situational factors (e.g., common activities, proximity, frequent encounters) to admiration of another person's dispositions or traits (e.g., Berndt, 1981; Damon, 1977a). Preadolescents have greater freedom to move into and out of "voluntary associations"; they interact in more activities and organizations with large numbers of different peers; and they have more control over their social relationships. Social interaction within large groups of peers, most of whom are strangers or acquaintances, should increase the need and desire for loyal support from some peer (or peers) who can be regarded as a friend. Many studies have found that the nature of friendship does shift in these directions during the late juvenile and preadolescent periods (cf. Damon, 1977a). During preadolescence, trust and loyal support become defining attributes of friendship (cf. Berndt, 1981; Selman, 1976a), and notions of "kind" acts in interpersonal relations increasingly include helping and aiding others (cf. Youniss, 1975).

The marginal status of early adolescents and the conflicting demands placed upon them create tension in their life. The pressure to achieve, to prepare for, and decide upon, future adult roles, to discover who they are, and to get along with a wide variety of different types of people create additional problems. One might expect early adolescents to experience a need to find people with whom they can share their fears, aspirations, and beliefs, and to whom they can turn when they feel overwhelmed by their tensions and problems. There is, consequently, an increase during this period in the tendency to consider as friends people who share their innermost thoughts and feelings and who assist one another with their psychological problems (cf. Damon, 1977a). Early adolescents have much greater control over their selection of friends and over the activities in which they and their friends participate. In addition, they are very aware of the eventuality of marrying an opposite-sex peer. As one might expect, early adolescents are more likely to consider friendships as relatively long-term relationships (cf. Damon, 1977a).

Other changes in the social life of children could underlie the observed developmental changes in social information processing biases. For example, certain aspects of the social life of juveniles should promote changes in the nature of their person perceptions. Social exposure increases dramatically when juveniles leave elementary school. Juveniles interact with various adults other than their parents (e.g., teachers, recreational directors) and have much greater contact with peers of different demographic status (e.g., sex, religion, ethnicity) and different personalities. They can observe how authority figures judge the behavior and personalities of their peers. Such social exposure should increase the early adolescent's tendency to describe others in terms of personal traits. Sullivan (1953) suggested that the very speed with which juveniles are exposed to people of different types would make it difficult for juveniles not to create classification systems for people. Age-segregated classrooms should further enhance this tendency, as age is removed as one of the possible and highly salient classification categories, thus shifting attention to other classifications. There is, in fact, a sharp increase between 6 and 9 years of age (i.e., the juvenile period) in the tendency for children to describe others in terms of their personal traits rather than their superficial appearance or possessions and to explain others' behaviors in terms of their underlying dispositions rather than situational factors (cf. Chandler, 1977; Livesley & Bromley, 1973; Peevers & Secord, 1973; Shantz, 1975).

Juveniles are also more under the influence and control of adult and, especially, parental sanctions and norms than pre- and early adolescents. Thus, it would not be surprising if adult sanctions and norms had a greater impact on juveniles' judgments when they are relevant to the judgmental task. Indeed, Costanzo and his colleagues found in a series of studies that developmental changes in various kinds of social judgments are better interpreted in terms of age-phase changes in sensitivity to the particular norms prevalent in the child's social context rather than in terms of cognitive deficits. In fact, when adult prohibitions or norms were irrelevant to the judgmental task, juveniles gave more "mature" social judgments, such as the use of information about intentions (see Costanzo et al., 1973; Costanzo, Grumet, & Brehm, 1974; Farnill, 1974; see also Costanzo & Dix, this volume).

Other evidence suggests that the general developmental shifts in children's weighting of intent versus outcome information when making judgments of others reflect shifts in children's social life. Using the familiar Piagetian intent/outcome moral-judgment paradigm (Piaget, 1932), Parsons (1974) provided children with a description of an event sequence and asked them to reward or punish the actor. Like the classic Piagetian studies, the sequences varied along two basic dimensions: the actor's intent and the outcome. In addition, the situational context varied with respect to the competitiveness of the situation. The competitive stories depicted situations in which an individual either performs a solo task on which few either succeed at the peak level or win while the majority either perform only adequately or fail (e.g., taking an exam, swimming in a race) or in which persons compete as team members on similar types of competitive tasks (e.g., a baseball game, a team spelling bee). The noncompetitive stories depicted situations in which an individual either completes a solo noncompetitive task (e.g., building a model plane, putting together one's scrapbook) or helps another person complete a noncompetitive task (e.g., helping a friend build a kite, watering the lawn for one's mother). Figure 1 illustrates the developmental patterns associated with the use of outcome (left graph) and intention (right graph) as evaluative cues to determine the competitiveness of the situation.

The first finding worth noting is the differential developmental patterns in the use of outcome and intent associated with the different situational contexts. If the development of evaluative judgments was primarily a function of intellectual development – that is, an age-related substitution

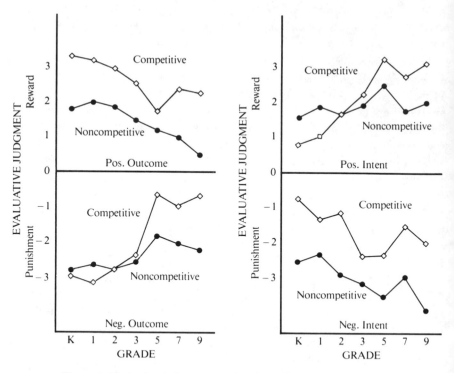

Figure 1. Evaluative judgment as a function of intent, outcome, and competitiveness of situation.

of evaluations based on internal, inferred intentions for more simplistic judgments based on concrete, observable outcomes – the curves would be more similar, differing, perhaps, in a pattern reflecting décalage, or developmental lag. That this is not the case is evidenced by the weighting of outcome, for example, which clearly varies across situations, ages, and outcomes. Why, for instance, do negative outcomes in noncompetitive situations continue to be punished, whereas negative outcomes in competitive situations lose their evaluative significance? The recent investigations of both Blumenfeld and her colleagues (1979) and Parsons (in press) suggest that classroom dynamics may be responsible for this pattern. Teachers punish consistently for misbehavior and failure to follow prescribed norms. In contrast, they rarely punish a child directly for poor academic performance. In interviewing fifth-grade children, Blumenfeld and her colleagues found that children's assessments of the relative importance of failure in these domains reflect their teachers' reinforcement patterns. The children said that it was much worse to violate a behavioral rule or to misbehave than to do poorly on an exam. Clearly, the children's evaluative judgments are being influenced markedly by the cultural norms around them.

Other studies using the Piagetian intent/outcome moral judgment paradigm have also found that the situational context has a major impact on developmental patterns. In an earlier study, Weiner and Peter (1973) found results similar to the Parsons (1974) findings in a comparison of achievement and moral contexts, and in a cross-cultural follow-up study, Salili, Maehr, and Gillmore (1976) also documented the impact of situational context on the development of evaluative judgments. Interestingly, the situational effects Salili and his colleagues found in Iran differed from the effects found by Weiner and Peter (1973) and Parsons (1974) in American samples.

The second relevant finding is the developmental shift in the use of both outcome and intent occurring at the seventh-grade level. In competitive situations at the seventh-grade level, the importance of outcome increases (i.e., positive outcomes are rewarded more and negative outcomes are punished more), whereas the importance of intention decreases (i.e., positive intent is rewarded less and negative intent is punished less). The percent of variance accounted for by each variable demonstrates this shift even more dramatically; the percent of variance accounted for by outcome jumps from 13% to 23%, whereas the percent of variance accounted for by intention drops from 29% to 17%. Interestingly, Weiner and Peter (1973) found a similar shift at the seventh-grade level in the weighting of outcome and intent (i.e., effort) for their achievement story.

What accounts for this shift? Although neither study can provide the answer directly, it may be due to the situational environment of the seventh-graders They had just begun junior high school, and the transition from elementary school to junior high school is a critical social event marked by significant changes in the expectations and social situations confronting the child. Whereas elementary school teachers may have been willing to reward achievement efforts to support strong achievement motivation, junior high school teachers may be less willing to let grades reflect effort. Junior high school is the time, after all, to get down to business in school, the time to take one's education seriously. This shift in attitude will undoubtedly be reflected in the attention paid to outcome versus effort. For example, in several school districts with which we are familiar, letter grades are first given in the seventh grade. Prior to that time, children's performance is evaluated in terms of their progress and not in terms of their relative performance. In junior high school the focus shifts. Parents may also be placing more emphasis on outcome as entry into college and other occupational training grounds is now at stake.[3] Additional evidence for our hypothesis is provided by the Salili, Maehr, and Gillmore (1976) Iranian study. They did not find the shift in importance of outcome at adolescence and explained this discrepancy in terms of the stress placed on effort over outcome in the Iranian ethics of achievement; that is, whereas adolescents are judged by their products in North America, they are judged by their effort in Iran.

A study by Simmons and her colleagues provides additional support of the impact of the junior high school environment on children's social cognitions (Simmons, Rosenberg, & Rosenberg, 1973). These investigators compared the self-concepts and person perceptions of two groups of 12-year-olds: one group in elementary school and one group in junior high school. They found a marked difference between these two groups that could not be explained by biological changes, maturational rates, cognitive levels, or relative physical size. They concluded that the difference was primarily a consequence of differences in the social environments associated with elementary and junior high schools. In other words, changes in the children's social environments had a greater effect on the social cognitions measured than did the developmental changes associated with maturation.

Changes in the social life of children may also underlie some of the developmental changes that occur in the attributional biases of children. In a recent study by Ruble, Feldman, Higgins, and Karlovac (1979), 4- and 5-year-olds, 8- and 9-year-olds, and college students watched a target actor select a preferred item from an array of either animals, colors, cartoon characters, or cars and four other actors either agree or disagree with the target actor's choice. Subjects were asked why the target actor selected the chosen object: Was it because of the actor's own personal tastes (a person attribution) or was it because the object was really good (an entity attribution)? This basic procedure was then replicated in another study with 5- and 6-year-olds, 7- and 8-year-olds, 9- and 10-year-olds, and high school students, except that subjects chose their own favorite item in each array and answered the person/entity attribution question for themselves. These studies found that 4-, 5-, and 6-year-olds were more likely to make entity than person attributions for both a target actor's choices and their own choices, whereas by the age of 9 children were more likely to make person than entity attributions. This developmental shift in attribution bias was again found in a recent study by Higgins and Bryant (in press).

From a cognitive-development perspective, one might interpret this developmental shift in attribution bias as reflecting young children's tendency to focus on concrete, observable features of the environment (i.e., the chosen object's physical properties) rather than on more abstract, covert features of the environment (i.e., the target actor's dispositions or personal tastes). Although there may indeed be a developmental shift in the attention paid or weight given to entity-based versus dispositional-based determinants of choice behavior (cf. Ruble et al., 1979), it is *not* the case that the youngest children were incapable of making dispositional attributions. Even the 4- and 5-year-olds made significantly more person attributions for the target actor's choice when the other actors unanimously disagreed with the choice (i.e., low consensus) than when they unanimously agreed with the choice (i.e., high consensus). Thus, the developmental shift was not due to a change from concrete to abstract thinking (see Piaget, 1962a; Werner, 1957).

Another explanation for the entity/person attribution shift is that children's beliefs about the causes of actions and events may initially involve little sense of personal responsibility or control over outcomes and that children's sense of personal causation increases with age. As Ruble and her colleagues (1979) point out, this explanation is consistent with evidence of both an age-related increase during this period in internal locus of control (e.g., Lifshitz, 1973) and a shift during this period in mastery orientation in achievement situations (e.g., Veroff, 1969). This change in children's sense of personal causation may, in turn, reflect a change in children's actual control over their personal lives during this period. There is, after all, a dramatic increase from the preschool to the juvenile period in children's mobility, freedom to select activities and playmates, and opportunity to function without constant adult supervision and direction.

The role of social exposure, more generally, in increasing person attributions is also suggested by the results of our most recent study (Higgins & Bryant, in press). Consistent with our previous studies, 8- and 9-year-olds and college students had a general person attribution bias when making judgments of a peer target actor. There was no person attribution bias, however, when the target was a nonpeer (e.g., a college student target for the 8- and 9-year-old subjects). Thus, 8- and 9-year-olds and college students displayed a person attribution bias only when the target was a member of a familiar age group. Presumably, frequent contact with members of one's peer group, such as in age-segregated activities, would increase one's knowledge of the variability in responses among peer group members, which, in turn, would increase one's recognition of the role of personal factors (e.g., personal taste) in behavior. Consistent with this reasoning, as one might expect, preschoolers make entity attributions even when making judgments of self and peers because their relatively limited peer contact makes them less aware of the variability in peer responses (Higgins & Bryant, in press; Ruble et al., 1979).

Finally, there are some shifts in the social life of children that could affect their predictions of others' responses and behavior. For example, in two recent studies (Higgins, Feldman, & Ruble, 1980) illustrations of separate arrays of snacks, meals, and activities were presented to 4- and 5-year-olds and 8- and 9-year-olds. They were asked to select their personal preference, the preference of their peers, and the preference of nonpeers (i.e., "grown-ups"). The 8- and 9-year-olds (juveniles) were more accurate than the 4- and 5-year-olds (preschoolers) in predicting the preferences of grown-ups; the 4- and 5-year-olds were more accurate in predicting the preferences of peers than the preferences of nonpeers.

From a traditional cognitive-development perspective, this developmental pattern would most likely be interpreted as the transition from "egocentric" to "nonegocentric" judgment (e.g., Piaget, 1965). That is, the 4- and 5-year-olds, being egocentric, would tend to select their personal preference when judging the preferences of others, which would lead to accurate judgments for similar others (peers) but inaccurate judgments for dissimilar others (grown-ups). In contrast, the 8- and 9-year-olds, being nonegocentric, would not tend to assume similarity when making judgments of others. The results of the studies, however, cannot be explained in terms of this cognitive-developmental shift. First, most of the 4- and 5-year-olds did not select their own preferences when predicting the preferences of either peers or grown-ups. Moreover, neither the 4- and 5-year-olds' accuracy in predicting peers' preferences nor their inaccuracy in predicting grown-ups' preferences could be accounted for by those subjects who did select their own preferences when making predictions. For example, only 22% of the 4- and 5-year-olds who made inaccurate predictions of grown-ups' preferences selected their own personal preference when predicting for grown-ups.

Higgins, Feldman, and Ruble (1980) describe a number of developmental differences in social experience that could underlie the developmental difference in accuracy. In terms of the present "social life phases" framework, a possible cause of the developmental change is the sharp increase in exposure to various adults (i.e., "grown-ups") that occurs when juveniles enter elementary school and begin to participate in community activities outside the home. As exposure to adults increases, the accuracy of children's knowledge about adults naturally increases.

Social experiences could also provide an alternative explanation for the shift in children's use of past achievement-related outcomes in predicting subsequent performance. Parsons and Ruble (1977) found that 3- and 5-year-old children do not make use of failure information in predicting future performance, whereas children 7 years of age and older do. Using a cognitive-development framework, they attributed this developmental change to a specific shift in the children's cognitive capacity, namely, to an increase in the child's capacity to integrate a series of past outcomes in the formation of a stable concept of one's abilities. Basing one's predictions for future performance on past performance, however, also requires that one consider the past performance as relevant and heuristically valuable. Thus, the developmental change reported by Parsons and Ruble could reflect a shift in the perceived relevance of one's past outcomes rather than a shift in the children's cognitive capacity. Preschoolers, because they are acquiring so many physical skills so rapidly, have frequent experience with failure followed by subsequent, and often dramatic, improvement. Consequently, their own past experiences provide them with little reason to conclude that past failures are predictive of future failures. Other aspects of the social environment of preschool children would support their belief in the instability of both outcomes and ability. First, because parents of preschoolers are aware of the rapid changes in the physical capacity of their children, they encourage their children to continue to try despite failures. Second, because the home environment is not age stratified, children have the opportunity to compare their performances with both older and younger people and thus observe the striking shifts in abilities that occur as one gets older. These social environmental factors should lead preschool children to perceive abilities as rather unstable and more like skills to be learned than like entities that are stable characteristics of individuals.

Recent results (Eccles-Parsons, 1982) obtained in Parsons's laboratory provide support for this interpretation. On a modified version of the procedures used by Parsons and Ruble (1977), preschoolers were just as likely as older children to attribute their outcomes to ability, but when asked to predict future performance, the younger children's attributions were unrelated to their predictions, whereas the older children's predictions were. In addition, when asked why they made their prediction, older children were more likely to cite past performance or stable ability, whereas young children were more likely to cite learning how to do the task as the causal explanation for their predictions.

In conclusion, then, there may be little in the social life of preschoolers that would lead them to conclude that performance reflects stable, underlying abilities. Entrance into elementary school alters several of these dynamics. First, classes are age stratified. Consequently, juveniles are exposed to a dramatic increase in information regarding individual differences and individual consistency across time. Second, their own maturation level will have slowed considerably. And third, as discussed earlier, it is very probable that parents' attitudes regarding the stability of performance undergo a shift at about this time. Each of these shifts should increase the perceived relevance of past performance for predictions of future performance.

Cultural and demographic variation in social-life phases

Our earlier account of social-life phases was intended to represent the sequence of life phases for a typical middle-class child in North America as it was to be related to the social-cognitive development of the typical North American middle-class child. The sequence and features of children's social life, however, undoubtedly vary greatly as a function of social class, ethnicity, sex, region, and culture. Such variation could permit a test of the hypothesis that social-life phases contribute to social-cognitive development and provide an answer to the "chicken and egg" question; that is, could the shifts in social-life phases simply reflect socialization agents' recognition of the qualitative changes in children's cognitive capacity? Certainly some changes in children's social life arise from such recognition. For example, it has been suggested that parents' use of verbal rationales, or induction, to train their children in moral behavior depends upon the parents' judgments that their child has reached a sufficient level of verbal understanding (Parke, 1974; Rosenthal & Zimmerman, 1978). Nevertheless, lower-class mothers tend not to use verbal rationales even when their children are capable of understanding them (Hess & Shipman, 1968), and lower-class children continue to use reward/punishment rationales for school performance well after middleclass children have started using "higher" level rationales (Blumenfeld et al., 1979).

It is also quite likely that some changes in children's social life are due to physical maturation. For example, the sudden changes during puberty in physical size, strength, speed, and coordination, as well as sexual strivings, obviously influence adolescents' activities, social relationships, privileges, and so on. There may even be a maturational influence on basic emotional needs and life-phase "crises" (cf. Erikson, 1963). It has been argued, however, that the nature of adolescence is due to the influence of adult values and role expectations for youth rather than physiological maturation (e.g., De Vos & Hippler, 1969; Mead, 1961; Simmons, Rosenberg, & Rosenberg, 1973) and that the role of psychological maturation has been overemphasized (see Bandura, 1964).

It is clearly important to determine whether social-life phases influence social-cognitive development independent of such intellectual and maturational factors, and cultural-demographic comparisons are one possible way to examine this issue (see Mead, 1932; Shweder & Bourne, in press). Assuming that requisite maturational level and cognitive skills could be controlled for or matched, one could examine the relationship of temporal entry into a particular life phase or of the specific features of a particular life phase and social-cognitive development. For example, although children generally move from a non-productive (i.e., not expected to contribute to the goods and services of the society) to a productive role phase, cultures differ as to when and how abruptly this shift occurs, which could influence an individual's sense of social responsibility, social position, and relationship to others.

There is, of course, a substantial literature on culture and personality concerned with the relation between parental practices and personality development (cf. Hess, 1970; Hsu, 1961; LeVine, 1970; Zigler & Child, 1973). This literature, however, has typically related general differences in child training to general differences in personal dispositions (e.g., achievement motivation, dependency) or cultural beliefs and customs (e.g., beliefs concerning illness, mourning customs). Possible cultural differences in the sequence and features of successive life phases in childhood have not been examined nor have such differences been related to differences in the social relationships and social judgments of children. There is even some question as to whether a solid body of evidence concerning cross-cultural variations in child development has been collected yet (LeVine, 1970). But there is a growing awareness of the need for just such data in evaluating the validity of our descriptions of, and causal explanation for, developmental change (cf. Super & Harkness, 1980). Harkness (1980) has argued recently that our reliance on a monocultural data base has blinded us to the impact of social variation in development and has led to our heavy reliance on maturational theories in developmental psychology.

Ideally, one could wish to obtain evidence that variations along particular social life dimensions are associated with variation in social cognition. At present, the information available simply does not permit such an analysis. Thus, this section will be restricted to providing examples of cultural and demographic variation in life phases that appear to be, or could be, related to differences in social cognition.

It is well recognized that ecological, technological, economic, and political factors can all influence socialization practices through their impact on social relationships within and outside the family and on the aims of the socialization agents (cf. Aberle, 1961; Clausen, 1968; Inkeles & Levinson, 1969; Super & Harkness, 1980). The nature of the tasks imposed by a society's technology, for instance, affects the age at which societal members first engage in serious economic activity, with such activity occurring later if the tasks are dangerous, highly complex, or performed far from home (Aberle, 1961). Among the Samburu (Kenya), for example, the abrupt initiation from boyhood into the adult phase of Moranhood occurs when males are between 13 and 20 years of age. During the Moranhood phase of life, males live as bachelor warriors in the bush away from the settlement. When they are 30 years of age or older, they enter the next adult phase of elderhood in which they live in the settlement, marry, and become decision makers (Spencer, 1970). In contrast, in the village of Kau Sai (Hong Kong), children have a production role from a very early age, with adult skills and functions being acquired gradually at home. Although the marriage ceremony formally confers adult status, adult roles are assumed gradually (Ward, 1970).

The adolescent period in North American society is quite different from either of these cases, even though the biological transition at puberty is likely to be quite similar. Compared to the Samburu, entry into and exit from the adolescent phase is much more age-related in North American society (i.e., 12 to 14 for entry, 18 to 21 for exit). The broad range of ages for entry into and exit from Moranhood among the Samburu suggests that factors other than cognitive or maturational level determine when the shift occurs in that culture. In Kau Sai there is no distinct adolescent period in which children must abruptly shift from childhood to adult roles. In fact, Kau Sai pubescents have no life choices to make because they are offered no alternatives (Ward, 1970), and Kau Sai pubescence appears to generate less conflict than does North American adolescence (Ward, 1970). It is interesting in this regard that Chinese-American adolescents who take on adult functions sooner and with less choice than Anglo-American adolescents and learn more of these functions at home react less to authority than Anglo-Americans during this period (Gardner, 1978). Similarly, Hsu (1961) and his colleagues in a study comparing youth growing up in Chicago with Chinese-American youth growing up in Hawaii attributed the low rate of rebellion among the Chinese-American youth to the clear expectations and social roles set out for children within the Chinese-American cultures. Mead (1961) has argued that forcing our adolescents to choose from a wide-ranging, ill-defined set of options is responsible for the conflicts and difficulties associated with adolescence in this culture. One can only speculate on the impact of this forced choice on the shifts in a variety of social-cognitive domains, such as moral reasoning, person perception, and identity formation.

The link between social experiences and cognitive-development patterns is also evident in the domain of competition and sensitivity to social comparison information. Ethnic groups vary in the value they place on competition. For example, whereas the Sioux Indians emphasize independence and competitiveness, the very idea of competition contradicts the Hopi Indians' sense of what they are or most want to be. Similarly, Mexican-American parents are less likely to socialize competitive behavior in their children than are Anglo-American parents. One might expect, therefore, that the developmental increase in achievement-related social comparison and competitiveness that generally characterizes development among Anglo-American children would be less evident for Hopi Indians and Mexican-Americans. Indeed, McClintock (1974) has found that competitiveness does not develop in Mexican-American and Anglo-American children at the same pace.

The goals parents have for their children and parental beliefs regarding the stability of various child behaviors offer additional examples of the cultural variations that impact on social development. In a new line of research, J. Goodnow (personal communication, 1980) asked parents in Australian-Australian and Lebanese-Australian families when they think various behavioral patterns become stable. Australian-Australian (largely of English descent) parents think that most behavioral patterns, including academic performance, are fairly stable across the years from 6 to 12. Lebanese-Australian parents, on the other hand, think that most behavioral patterns are not stable across time. It is very probable that middle-class North American parents hold beliefs similar to those of Australian-Australian parents. North American parents start asking the school for social comparison information on their children's intellectual abilities soon after they enter school. Interestingly, North American youths develop a stable concept of ability (Nicholls, 1975) by 8 and 9 years of age, and there is a dramatic shift in North American children's use of past outcomes to predict future performance between the ages of 5 and 8 (Parsons & Ruble, 1977). Are North American children's beliefs regarding the stability of intellectual abilities a consequence of their parents' attitudes? And, if so, will Lebanese-Australian children view ability as unstable for a longer development period? If our argument has merit, one would have to predict so. One would also have to predict that the developmental patterns for Australian-Australian and North American children would be similar. Goodnow's research will provide us with some very important answers.

Another important feature of modern, industrialized society that is not found in every culture is formal schooling. Great cross-cultural variation is found in adult functions learned in formal school situations with non-kindred teachers and peers and those learned at home with parents and siblings (Gardner, 1978). The formal schooling common to Western modernized societies instills in students an individual modernity, that is, a complex set of interrelated attitudes and values, including a desire for autonomy, a decreasing concern with traditional authority figures, an increased sense of personal control over one's life, and an openness to new people, experiences, and ways of doing things (cf. Inkeles, 1974; Suzman, 1974). Acquisition of such aspects of individual modernity should influence, in turn, children's social cognitions. Developmental models that chart social-cognitive growth toward a set of values based on autonomy and universal justice, such as Kohlberg's, may reflect the orientation of children toward the Western value system rather than toward some universal, culture-free sequence. If this is true, one would expect differences in sequencing and in the final end state of the social-cognitive development of children from modernized and nonmodernized societies, as well as differences among children from the same society who vary in their degree of exposure to formal Western schooling.

Socialization practices can also vary within the same society as a function of social class, gender, and so on. With respect to social class, for example, there is evidence that lower-class children, especially, participate less than middle-class children in formal organizations and extracurricular activities within the school and community (Hess, 1970). Thus, lower-class children are exposed to a smaller range of socialization agents and experience less opportunity for performing different kinds of social roles (e.g., holding office in a club) and for working cooperatively with adults. This restriction in social experience could account, in part, for the tendency of moral judgments of lower-class children to differ from those of middle-class children. There is, in fact, evidence that children who participate in social clubs and organizations tend to give more advanced moral judgments than those who do not, regardless of social class (Hess, 1970; Keasey, 1971).

The social life of lower-class children also differs with respect to the mode of social control exercised by their parents (position-oriented vs. person-oriented) and the goals that are emphasized in interpersonal communication (Bernstein, 1970). Lower-class parents are more likely than middle-class parents to respond to their child on the basis of the child's ascribed status or position (e.g., age, gender) than on the basis of the child's personal characteristics (e.g., needs, motives, skills). Lower-class parents are also more likely to emphasize social solidarity in interpersonal relationships, and, thus, compared with middle-class parents, the communication goal of reinforcing social bonds is given more weight than the communication goal of accurate transmission of the speaker's personal beliefs, attitudes, and so on (Bernstein, 1970). Although these social-class differences do not appear to affect communication style to the extent claimed by Bernstein (cf. Higgins, 1976), they could contribute to social-class differences in referential accuracy by reducing both the mental resources the lower-class children allocate to accurate information transmission versus interpersonal maintenance (cf. Higgins, Fondacaro, & McCann, 1981) and the attention they allocate to the individuating characteristics of their listener. However, as with participation in formal organizations, it is the social life of children rather than social class per se that is critical (cf. Higgins, 1976). Thus, Bearison and Cassel (1975) report that middle-class children whose parents use a person-oriented mode of social control communicate more effectively than children whose parents use a position-oriented mode of social control.

Gender differences provide yet another opportunity to explore the possible impact of social life variation on social cognitions. Two specific examples seem especially relevant: one related to achievement behaviors and one related to moral reasoning.

Henrig and Jardin (1977) argue that women are not as good as men at the role of "team player" and that, consequently, their ability to survive and prosper in the business community is thus compromised. Although we basically disapprove of theories that blame the victim, their point has some interesting implications for our position. They attribute this difference to the effect on social perceptions of one critical sex difference in preadolescent and adolescent social experiences, namely, participation in competitive athletics. They argue that participation in competitive team sports teaches cooperative, team-oriented behavior and the acceptance of collective responsibility for outcomes; these skills, they argue, are essential for survival in the corporate structure. Although no direct test has been made of their hypothesis, it is the case that many successful corporate executives have had a long history of active participation in competitive sports. Sex-differentiated participation in competitive sports could also account for sex difference in inferences concerning academic successes and failures. Girls are more likely than boys both to attribute their academic failures to lack of ability and to lower their expectancies following failure (cf. Parsons, in press; Frieze et al., 1978). High rates of failure and experiences with improvement may reduce the significance of failure for one's sense of one's abilities. Given the low probability of success each time one is up at bat in baseball or runs for a touchdown in football, and given the rapid improvements children experience in their athletic skills over the juvenile and preadolescent periods, boys may have more experiences that teach them to see failures as less a function of inability than of bad luck or inexperience than do girls. Because girls, until recently, have been denied such experiences, they are less likely to develop an unstable, experience-dependent view of ability.

Moral reasoning is a second domain in which sex differences in social life could influence the development of social cognition. High school girls score an average of one stage (Stage 3) lower than high school boys on Kohlbergian scales (Gilligan et al., 1971; Holstein, 1976; Turiel, 1973). The female sex role may be responsible for this difference. Because Stage 3 reasoning relies on interpersonal concordance and because interpersonal orientation is the hallmark of the female sex role, one should not be surprised to find the majority of women "stuck" at Stage 3. Gilligan (1977) recently has proposed another social life explanation; specifically, she argues that the sequence proposed by Kohlberg is based on a male orientation toward development in which optimal growth is directed toward autonomy, independence, and universal justice. Gilligan argues that female development follows a different course and turns on different developmental issues. Consequently, a new model for the development of moral reasoning that is more appropriate to the realities of female social life changes is necessary. Gilligan has proposed such a model, which, like the first explanation, points to the importance of differences between the social lives of boys and girls as the critical mediating factor.

"Social × cognitive" interaction

At present little direct evidence is available concerning the role of social-life phases in social-cognitive development, and even less evidence is available concerning the interaction of social-life phases and cognitive skills in shaping social-cognitive development. The scarcity of empirical evidence on these issues is, in part, a reflection of the current domination of social development by the Piaget–Kohlberg "cognitive" perspective. The "cognitive-developmental" approach, of course, does not suggest that social-cognitive development is influenced by cognitive factors alone. The interaction between the cognitive structures of the child and input from the social environment is stressed (cf. Kohlberg, 1969; Piaget, 1965). But the impact of the child's level of cognitive development on the child's response to the social environment is emphasized; social inputs are seen primarily as providing opportunities for cognitive growth (e.g., role-taking opportunities) or as important influences on the rate of cognitive development (see Kohlberg, 1969; Selman, 1971). For example, the development of role taking has been linked to the adjustments that occur during peer group conflict (e.g., Feffer, 1970; Maitland & Goldman, 1974; Piaget, 1926b; Selman, 1971).

Nevertheless, as Maccoby (1968) points out, the cognitive-developmental approach has generally led researchers to look for the determinants of cognitive growth in social development, such as correlations between level of social development and measures of cognitive ability. Indeed, positive correlations between level of social development and IQ have been taken as support for the cognitive-developmental approach (e.g., Emmerich, Goldman, & Shore, 1971; Kohlberg, 1969). Similarly, Keasey (1971) interpreted the positive relation between social participation and moral development in terms of the cognitive mediating variable of role-taking ability.

The social-life phases approach suggests a different interpretation of the role of cognitive factors in social development. For example, the positive correlation between level of social development and IQ could be due to the influence of IQ on the speed of socialization into one's current social-life phase. Similarly, the positive relation between social participation and moral development could be a consequence of the impact of social participation on moral development. After all, if a child has entered a new subculture (social-life phase) that emphasizes a higher moral level, the greater the child's participation in this new subculture, the greater will be the child's exposure to the new moral knowledge.

In this section, we will discuss various ways that social-life phases might interact with intellectual development to produce stagelike changes in social cognition. In so doing, we will consider some general issues concerning the role of cognitive factors in social-cognitive development.

One general issue concerns the interpretation of the co-occurrence of change in cognition and social cognition. From the "cognitive" perspective, the change in social cognition would be interpreted as a result of cognitive change. There are a number of problems with this position, however. First, there is no a priori reason to assume that co-occurrence involves any causal relation at all. The intellectual and social-life changes could be due to independent factors that are active concurrently, with only the social-life changes influencing social cognition. Alternatively, some social-cognition changes could be due to cognitive changes, whereas others could be due to social-life changes. In fact, the independent influence of social-life changes could explain, at least in part, why the myriad of social-cognitive changes occurring during the shift from the preschool to the juvenile phase (i.e., the preoperational/concrete operational shift) cannot be adequately accounted for by the emergence of particular cognitive skills (e.g., role taking). Second, even if a cognitive change influences social-cognitive change, it need not be the cognitive change that is co-occurring with the social-cognitive change; that is, a cognitive prerequisite for a social-cognitive change may develop in an earlier period, with its subsequent application requiring an impetus from the social world (e.g., new social relationships and activities). Damon (1977b), in fact, has described cases in which the cognitive capacity necessary for a particular level of social cognition is present for a period before its utilization. In such cases, the social-cognitive change depends on the presence of both the prerequisite cognitive acquisition and the appropriate social input. Furthermore, in these cases it is the change in the child's social life that is the immediate cause of the change in the child's social-cognitive system.

This brings us to the related issue regarding the social × cognitive interaction, namely, the kinds of intellectual changes that must occur to allow children to move from one social-cognition phase to the next. What exactly are the cognitive prerequisites at each phase? Although a detailed discussion of this issue would carry us beyond the scope of this chapter, an understanding of the role of social-life phases in social-cognitive development requires that some attention be given to this issue.

The types of intellectual change underlying social-cognitive development most often mentioned in the literature involve qualitative changes in reasoning, conceptual integration and organization, and cognitive operations (e.g., reciprocity, role taking). However, most intellectual changes during childhood are basically quantitative in nature. Social-cognitive development, to a considerable extent, may reflect these quantitative changes; in particular, the increasing social knowledge and routinization of operations that comes from experience and practice with social events. Children's knowledge of the social world is likely to increase with exposure to the social world and direct instruction about the social world (from parents, peers, teachers, the media, etc.), just as their knowledge about the nonsocial world increases with experience (e.g., their knowledge about different types of cars, flowers, and animals). Such increased knowledge could, by itself, result in developmental differences in social cognition. Higgins, Feldman, and Ruble (1980), for example, argue that the developmental increase in children's accuracy in predicting nonpeers' preferences can be explained by the increase in children's exposure to nonpeers, an exposure that would inevitably increase the children's knowledge base.

Comparable developmental increases in knowledge undoubtedly occur in a variety of social content areas. For example, the developmental increase in the weighting of intentions relative to consequences (Austin, Ruble, & Trabasso, 1977; Parsons, 1974; Piaget, 1965) and the developmental increase in the tendency to judge others' in terms of dispositions (cf. Shantz, 1975) could reflect a developmental increase in knowledge about different kinds of intentions and dispositions and how they relate to behavior. After all, the superior accuracy of a clinician as compared to a physicist in judging a mentally ill patient is more likely to reflect differences in knowledge of possible symptoms and dispositions than differences in reasoning ability. Younger children may simply know less about the possible intentions and dispositions of others, just as they know less about music, sports, or any other content area.

Exposure to more situations should lead to an increased understanding of situational norms and social scripts. Grusec (this volume), for example, suggests that children learn situation-behavior scripts from teachers in school. The developmental increase in appropriate social behavior could arise from this gradual increase in knowledge of different types of situations and the behaviors associated with each. Similarly, increased knowledge about the relation between particular facial features and particular emotions and about the emotions appropriate to particular situations could also underlie the developmental increase in the ability to identify emotions accurately from facial expressions and situational cues (cf. Deutsch, 1975; Feshbach & Roe, 1968; Izard, 1971). In fact, learning correct "definitions of the situation" and situation-appropriate behaviors could be one of the most critical aspects of social-cognitive development.

In general, there may be a lot less going on than meets the eye in both children's and adult's social judgments and behavior. In fact, it may be that the Piagetian perspective is less guilty of underestimating young children's social-cognitive skills than of overestimating adult's social-cognitive skills. In fact, current interpretations of adults' social cognition do not reflect the rational, deductive, complex thinking that Piaget has ascribed to adults.

Another relatively quantitative intellectual change that could contribute to social-cognitive development is the routinization of cognitive operations that results from practice. Shatz (1978) and Case (1978) have suggested that one factor underlying developmental increases in task performance is older children's greater experience with aspects of the task. Increased practice with an operation is assumed by these theorists to lead to increased routinization, thus reducing the mental effort required for its execution. This savings in mental effort, in turn, allows a greater proportion of a child's limited mental resources to be directed toward other aspects of the task. Such routinization has been suggested as an important factor underlying developmental improvement in interpersonal communication (Higgins, Fondacaro, & McCann, 1981; Shatz, 1978). It may underlie developmental differences in other areas of social cognition as well. With respect to moral judgment (Piaget, 1965), for example, children learn first about the consequences of their behavior because parents are concerned about their safety (not to mention the safety of plants, pets, dishes, etc.). Thus, processing information about consequences is well practiced, becoming routinized and relatively automatic. It is not surprising, therefore, that young children process consequence information more quickly and remember it better when later asked to make judgments.

Because both routinization and social knowledge increase steadily with experience, these factors alone cannot account for the qualitative, "stagelike" nature of social-cognitive development. The interaction between these cognitive factors and social-life phases, however, could account for at least some "stagelike" changes in social-cognitive development. Children who enter a new social-life phase are likely to be exposed to new, and often quite different, information about their social world, information that either was not available in their earlier social environments or was purposefully hidden from them. Information about different types of peers, for example, is generally more available to juveniles than to preschoolers, and information about heterosexual relations is generally more available to early adolescents than to juveniles or preadolescents. Thus, one would expect qualitative "stagelike" leaps in social knowledge when children enter elementary school or junior and senior high school, analogous to the leaps in knowledge about mathematics, history, and chemistry that occur when children are first exposed to these academic fields.

Entry into a new social-life phase (or subculture) may also provide the first opportunity for extensive practice in processing certain kinds of social information and using specific kinds of operations, leading to the routinization of these operations. When children enter elementary school, for example, there is a dramatic increase in the number of occasions in which they must communicate to someone with whom they share little background information. These children, therefore, must provide additional information to their listener more often than was necessary in their previous, family-based subculture. As a consequence, the probability is increased that the operations necessary for such message modification will become routinized and implemented with increasing ease and automaticity.

The opportunity to interact with and judge a variety of peers who differ in their intentions should also have an effect on the character of children's social and moral judgments. Several studies have found that preschoolers use intention information when making moral judgments of themselves even when they do not do so in making judgments of others (e.g., Costanzo, 1970; Keasy, 1977; Piaget, 1965; Rotenberg, 1979). During the preschool years the experiences children have with social judgments revolve primarily around their parents' judging them in situations in which they are associated with some negative event. The children also experience variations in their own intention and the fact that negative outcome can occur independent of, or despite, one's intentions. Finally, the preschooler learns that parents are less likely to punish accidental than intentional negative outcomes. All these experiences, especially the social significance associated with the distinction between one's own accidental versus intentional wrongdoings, should increase the likelihood that the preschool child will use intention information in making self-judgments. Children as young as 3 use this knowledge, protesting that they didn't "mean to do it" when their parents threaten punishment for a negative outcome. Similar social meaning is not attached to the intentions of others. Rarely is the preschool child called upon to judge someone else's intentions. Thus there is less need to distinguish between the intentions and outcomes of others. And because preschoolers use a limited cognitive processing space to deal with a wide array of information and problem-solving tasks, it seems reasonable that they will use a more primitive judgment algorithm in judging others, especially if there is no social significance pressuring for a more sophisticated evaluation. As children enter elementary school, they become more actively involved in judging their peers. Furthermore, distinguishing between the accidental and intentional acts of others takes on an increasingly important social significance in that peers vary more both in their intentions and in the probability of accidental negative outcomes than do parents and the other supportive adults that dominate children's preschool subculture.

It must be emphasized that we are not proposing that the "qualitative-social × quantitative-cognitive" interaction is sufficient to account for social-cognitive development. First, there are developmental changes that appear to reflect qualitative changes in cognitive operations. For example, the development of moral judgments from judgments derived from only the consequences of a stimulus person's behavior to judgments derived from both intentions and consequences probably reflects in part a development of the general ability to consider more than one factor simultaneously (see Higgins, 1981).

Second, there are social developmental changes that probably involve an interaction between qualitative changes in both social and cognitive factors. For example, the ability to control the self when making judgments of others appears to increase in a stagelike manner, with each stage requiring increasingly complex operations (cf. Higgins, 1981). This cognitive growth in the ability to control self-intrusion, however, probably interacts with social-life phases as each phase places new demands on children to control self-intrusion. For example, when preschoolers enter elementary school they meet many more people whose beliefs, attitudes, knowledge, and so on are different from their own, and control of self-intrusion thus becomes increasingly important for accurate judgments and social acceptance. Then, as elementary school children move from the early to the later grades and social comparison becomes increasingly important, children must learn the more difficult task of controlling self-intrusion even though the self is part of the comparative judgment.

In sum, most previous explanations of the stagelike nature of social-cognitive development have emphasized stagelike changes in cognitive development. Recently, however, there has been an increasing concern with the general role of stagelike changes in social input (cf. Blyth, in press; Bronfenbrenner, 1977; Cole, Hood, & McDermott, in press; Serafica, in press), as well as with the interactions between intellectual and social change (cf. Damon, 1977a; Shantz, in press) that could underlie social-cognitive development. Our analysis suggests that stagelike changes in social-cognitive development could be due to qualitative changes in social input (i.e., social-life phases), qualitative changes in cognitive operations (e.g., the number of factors that can be simultaneously coordinated), as well as a number of possible social × cognitive interactions, including a possible qualitative-social × quantitative-cognitive interaction.

Conclusions

No one seriously questions that social experience is a major factor underlying social development. There is less consensus, however, concerning the exact role of social experience in social development. In the traditional social-learning approach to social development, social experience in the form of social observation and social reinforcement is the central factor in social development. In contrast, the cognitive-developmental approach posits cognitive growth as the central factor, with social experience being regarded as providing opportunities and impetus for cognitive growth. Interestingly, there is a commonality between these approaches in that qualitative shifts in social experience during different social-life phases are only rarely given serious attention. Traditional notions of socialization also portray children as slowly acquiring the ways, skills, and customs of their society through basically uniform and continuous adult intervention and training (cf. Zigler & Child, 1973). Although this perspective on the role of social experience has predominated, an alternative perspective has received some attention in the literature, particularly from sociologists and anthropoligists. This perspective emphasizes the qualitative stagelike changes that occur in the social life of children. The purpose of this chapter has been to develop this "social-life-phases," or age subculture, perspective and to consider its implications for developmental changes in social cognition.

For a social-life-phases perspective to be reasonable or useful, there must be at least some preliminary evidence that children's social lives do change at different age phases. Although there is a definite need for more systematic, detailed research in this area, the literature does describe rather dramatic changes in the social life of children as they move from the preschool period through the juvenile, preadolescent, and early adolescent periods. In fact, at each life-phase juncture, there are qualitative shifts along a number of different dimensions of social experience. For example, entry into elementary school greatly increases children's exposure to different peers and different socialization agents, as well as their individual freedom and their responsibilities.

The changes in children's social lives during different age phases appear to be related to concomitant changes in various aspects of their social cognition. For example, increased exposure to a wide variety of peers and adults with varying personalities and statuses could contribute to the increased tendency of juveniles during this period to describe others in terms of their personal traits and to base friendships on admiration of another person's traits. Furthermore, some social-cognitive changes that occur within particular periods are more easily interpreted in terms of social-life changes than in terms of intellectual or maturational change. For example, the increased weight given to outcome versus intent information in the achievement-related judgments of seventh-graders as compared with sixth-graders probably arises from the different emphasis given to grades in junior high school as compared to that in elementary school.

Finally, to the extent that cross-cultural and demographic differences in the social-life phases of children are related to differences in social-cognitive development, a social-life-phases perspective would seem to be particularly useful and necessary. Unfortunately, little research has been concerned with cross-cultural or demographic differences in the social-life phases of children, and even less research has related such differences to differences in social-cognitive development. Nevertheless, the little evidence available does suggest that variability in social experience can account for differences in social-cognitive development. For example, social-class differences in participation in social clubs and formal organizations and in the mode of social control exercised by parents are reflected in social-class differences in moral judgments and communicative performance, respectively.

We are not suggesting, of course, that social-cognitive development is determined solely by social-life variables. Cognitive and maturational variables are clearly important, both as independent factors and in interaction with social-life variables. Greater attention, however, must be directed toward social-life variables that could influence social-cognitive development. At present, social-life phases have received, at best, benign neglect by developmental psychologists, probably in part because developmental psychologists rarely receive training in those research methodologies most relevant for obtaining such information, such as field observational methods. If the social-life-phases perspective is to be useful, however, some preliminary fact-finding or descriptive stage is necessary, including cross-cultural and demographic comparisons. It would be interesting, for example, to compare the social-cognitive responses of seventh-grade students, where grade seven is the last grade of elementary school and where grade seven is the first grade of high school. In fact, Blyth and his associates (1979) report that the relation between early maturation and self-esteem for seventh-grade boys and girls varies depending upon whether they are still in elementary school or have begun junior high school. Experimental research should also examine the effects of varying social exposure, social practice, and social demands on children's social cognition. For example, the effect of social exposure on social cognitions could be tested by giving preschoolers the opportunity to participate in aspects of juvenile (or even preadolescent) social life.

A detailed comparison of the social life of children in different age phases, in fact, might suggest the presence of developmental differences in aspects of social cognition that have not even been considered. For example, adolescents have much greater opportunity than younger children to enact various kinds of social roles, both within formal peer organizations and in part-time or summer employment, and, in addition, must seriously consider and prepare for future adult roles. Adolescents also have greater freedom to select those roles they wish to embrace and have more experience with different individuals fulfilling the same role. These social-role experiences should increase both adolescents' conception of the general nature of social roles and their knowledge of various kinds of, and techniques for resolving (e.g., role distance), role conflict (e.g., self-role and interrole conflict).

Our discussion of social-life phases was restricted to the preschool, juvenile, preadolescent, and early adolescent periods because most research on social-cognitive development has been concerned with this age range. The social-life perspective, however, is clearly relevant throughout the life-span. This perspective, in fact, has been applied to both preschool and postadolescent periods. Bronfenbrenner (1977) and Cole, Hood, and McDermott (in press), for example, have discussed the implications of the physical and social environment for infant and toddler development. The social-life-phases perspective has also been applied to socialization in adulthood, most notably by Brim (1966) and Levinson (1978).

Our account of social-life phases has also been restricted to fairly general features of each age phase. There are many other features of the social life of children that probably influence their social-cognitive development, such as family structure (e.g., family size, sex composition and age distribution of siblings, number and sex of caretakers) and interaction style (e.g., directive vs. nondirective, formal vs. informal). Moreover, some features can change during the course of development (e.g., family size, sex composition and age distribution of siblings). There is probably greater variability across children for such features than those features we have considered. Nevertheless, identification of the typical, or at least modal, family structure and interaction style at different age phases could further contribute to our understanding of the role of social-life phases in social-cognitive development.

Finally, it should be noted that the social-life-phases perspective is concerned with why rather than how children's social cognitions change. That is, this perspective is concerned with the social-life changes that contribute to social-cognitive change, but not specifically with the mechanisms involved in acquiring or modifying social-cognitive responses. Other models, in contrast, are concerned with these issues. In particular, behavioral-learning (e.g., Bijou & Baer, 1961; Staats 1975), social-learning (e.g., Bandura, 1969), and cognitive-developmental (e.g., Kohlberg, 1969; Piaget, 1965) processes have all been proposed to explain the acquisition and modification of social-cognitive responses.

In sum, the social-life-phases perspective of social-cognitive development is restricted in scope and highly speculative as many pieces in the puzzle are missing. This chapter has been conceived to provide a rough framework to guide the search for the missing pieces. Admittedly, once the numerous gaps are filled, we may find a different picture from that imagined. It is clear, however, that the current picture of social-cognitive development only partially represents, and occasionally misrepresents, the nature of children's changing social reality.

Notes

1 We are not suggesting, of course, that the effects of social factors are independent of cognition. Clearly, as Turiel (this volume) points out in his commentary, cognition is involved both in processing social input and in the mental representation of those changes induced by social input. Social factors can have no effects on social judgments and behaviors unless they result in some cognitive change (e.g., increased social knowledge). However, rather than being stimulated by some general shift in intellectual skills or reasoning ability, it is possible that the shift in social cognition could be stimulated by the social environment.

2 This is not to say that early adolescents totally reject their parents' values or standards or that independence from parents has not begun prior to early adolescence. Parental influence remains strong during this period, especially with respect to career-related decisions, and dependence upon adults gradually decreases throughout development (see Bandura, 1964). There is a shift between the juvenile and early adolescent periods, however, in the relative orientation toward peers versus adults, in part reflecting a shift in children's perception of the source of their need satisfaction (see Floyd & South, 1972).

3 It may also be that junior high school teachers cannot monitor their students' efforts as effectively as elementary school teachers because of the greater number of students under their supervision.

References

Aberle, D. F. Culture and socialization. In F. L. K. Hsu (Ed.), *Psychological anthropology.* Homewood, Ill. Dorsey Press, 1961.

Aries, P. *Centuries of childhood.* New York: Knopf, 1962.

Austin, V. D., Ruble, D. N., & Trabasso, T. Recall and order effects as factors in children's moral judgments. *Child Development,* 1977, *48,* 470–474.

Bandura, A. The stormy decade: Fact or fiction? *Psychology in the Schools,* 1964, *1,* 224–231.

Bandura, A. *Principles of behavior modification.* New York: Holt, Rinehart and Winston, 1969.

Bandura, A., & Walters, R. H. *Social learning and personality development.* New York: Holt, Rinehart and Winston, 1963.

Barker, R. G. *Ecological psychology.* Stanford, Calif.: Stanford university Press, 1968.

Bearison, D. J., & Cassel, T. Cognitive decentration and social codes: Communicative effectiveness in young children from differing family contexts. *Developmental Psychology,* 1975, *11,* 29–36.

Benedict, R. Continuities and discontinuities in cultural conditioning. *Psychiatry,* 1938, *1,* 161–167.

Berndt, T. J. Relations between social cognition, nonsocial cognition, and social behavior:

The case of friendship. In J. H. Flavell & L. Ross (Eds.), *Social-cognitive development: Frontiers and possible futures.* Cambridge University Press, 1981.

Bernstein, B. A sociolinguistic approach to socialization: with some reference to educability. In F. Williams (Ed.), *Language and poverty: Perspectives on a theme.* Chicago: Markham, 1970.

Bijou, S. W. *Child development: The basic stage of early childhood.* Englewood Cliffs, N.J.: Prentice-Hall, 1976.

Bijou, S. W., & Baer, D. M. *Child development: A systematic and empirical theory.* New York: Appleton-Century-Crofts, 1961.

Blumenfeld, P., Bossert, S., Hamilton, U. L., Wesselo, C., & Meece, J. *Teacher talk and student thought: Socialization into the student role.* Paper presented at the Conference on Teacher and Student Perceptions of Success and Failure, Pittsburgh, Pa., 1979.

Blyth, D. A. Mapping the social world of an adolescent: Issues, techniques, and problems. In F. C. Serafica (Ed.), *Social cognitive development in context.* New York: Guilford Press, in press.

Blyth, D. A., Simmons, R. G., Bulcroft, R., & VanCleave, E. *Pubertal development in different school settings; A longitudinal analysis of early maturers.* Paper presentated at meetings of the Society for Research in Child Development, San Francisco, 1979.

Boehm, L. The development of independence: A comparitive study. *Child Development,* 1957, *28,* 85–92.

Brim, O. G. Socialization through the life cycle. In O. G. Brim & S. Wheeler (Eds.), *Socialization after childhood: Two essays.* New York: Wiley, 1966.

Bronfenbrenner, U. Soviet methods of character education: Some implications for research. *American Psychologist,* 1962, *17,* 550–564.

Bronfenbrenner, U. *Two worlds of childhood.* New York: Russell Sage Foundation, 1970.

Bronfenbrenner, U. Toward an experimental ecology of human development. *American Psychologist,* 1977, *32,* 513–531.

Brunswick, E. Organismic achievement and environmental probability. *Psychological Review,* 1943, *50,* 255–272.

Campbell, E. Q. Adolescent socialization. In D. A. Goslin (Ed.), *Handbook of socialization theory and research.* Chicago: Rand McNally, 1969.

Case, R. Intellectual development from birth to adulthood: A neo-Piagetian interpretation. In R. S. Siegler (Ed.), *Children's thinking: What develops?* Hillsdale, N.J.: Erlbaum, 1978.

Chandler, M. J. Social cognition: A selective review of current research. In W. F. Overton and J. J. Gallagher (eds.), *Knowledge and development.* New York: Plenum, 1977.

Clausen, J. A. Perspectives on childhood socialization. In J. A. Clausen (Ed.), *Socialization and society.* Boston: Little, Brown, 1968.

Cole, M., Hood, L., & McDermott, R. *Ecological invalidity as an axiom of experimental cognitive psychology.* Cambridge, Mass.: Harvard University Press, in press.

Costanzo, P. R. Conformity development as a function of self-blame. *Journal of Personality and Social Psychology,* 1970, *14,* 366–374.

Costanzo, P. R., Coie, J. D., Grumet, J. F. & Farnill, D. A re-examination of the effects of intent and consequence on children's moral judgment. *Child Development,* 1973, *44,* 154–161.

Costanzo, P., Grumet, J., & Brehm, S. The effects of choice and source of constraint on children's attributions of preference. *Journal of Experimental Social Psychology,* 1974, *10,* 352–364.

Damon, W. *The social world of the child.* San Francisco: Jossey-Bass, 1977. (a)

Damon, W. The nature of social-cognitive change in the developing child. In W. F. Overton and J. J. Gallagher (Eds.), *Knowledge and development.* New York: Plenum, 1977. (b)

Denzin, N. K. *Childhood socialization*. San Francisco: Jossey-Bass, 1977.

Deutsch, F. Effects of sex of subject and story character on preschoolers' perceptions of affective responses and intrapersonal behavior in story sequences. *Developmental Psychology*, 1975, *11*, 112–115.

Devereux, E. C. The role of peer group experience in moral development. In J. P. Hill (Ed.), *Minnesota Symposium on Child Psychology* (Vol. 4). Minneapolis: University of Minnesota Press, 1970.

De Vos, G. A., & Hippler, A. E. Cultural psychology: Comparative studies of human behavior. In G. Lindzey & E. Aronson (Eds.), *The handbook of social psychology* (2nd ed. Vol. 4). Reading, Mass.: Addison-Wesley, 1969.

Eccles-Parsons, J. *The development of attributions, expectancies and task persistence*. Unpublished manuscript, University of Michigan, 1982.

Emmerich, W. Developmental trends in evaluations of single traits. *Child Development*, 1974, *45*, 172–183.

Emmerich, W., Goldman, K. S., & Shore, R. E. Differentiation and development of social norms. *Journal of Personality and Social Psychology*, 1971, *18*, 323–353.

Erikson, E. H. *Childhood and society* (2nd ed). New York: Norton, 1963.

Farnill, D. The effects of social judgment set on children's use of intent information. *Journal of Personality*. 1974, *42*, 276–289.

Feffer, M. Developmental analysis of interpersonal behavior. *Psychological Review*, 1970, *77*, 197–214.

Feshbach, N. D., & Roe, K. Empathy in six and seven year olds. *Child Development*, 1968, *39*, 133–145.

Flavell, J. H., & Ross, L. (Eds.). *Social cognitive development: Frontiers and possible futures*. Cambridge: Cambridge University Press, 1981.

Floyd, H. H., & South, D. R. Dilemma of youth: The choice of parents or peers as a frame of reference for behavior. *Journal of Marriage and the Family*, 1972, *34*, 627–634.

Frieze, I., Parsons, J., Johnson, P., Ruble, D., & Zellman, G. *Women and sex roles*. New York: Norton, 1978.

Fry, A. M., Willis, F. N. Invasion of personal space as a function of the age of the invader. *Psychological Record*, 1971, *21*, 385–389.

Gardner, H. *Developmental psychology: An introduction*. Boston: Little, Brown, 1978.

Garvey, C., & Hogan, R. Social speech and social interaction: Egocentrism revisited. *Child Development*, 1973, *44*, 562–569.

Gilligan, C. In a different voice: Women's conceptions of self and of morality. *Harvard Educational Review*, 1977, *47*, 481–517.

Gilligan, C., Kohlberg, L., Lerner, J., & Belenkep, M. Moral reasoning about sexual dilemmas: The development of an interview and scoring system. *Technical Report of the President's Commission on Obscenity and Pornography*. Washington, D.C.: U.S. Government Printing Office, 1971.

Gottman, J. M., & Parkhurst, J. T. A developmental theory of friendship and acquaintanceship processes. In W. A. Collins (Ed.), *Minnesota Symposia on Child Psychology* (Vol. 13). Hillsdale, N.J.: 1980.

Harkness, S. The cultural context of child development. In C. M. Super & S. Harkness (Eds.), *Anthropological perspectives on child development: New directions for child development* (Vol. 8). San Francisco: Jossey-Bass, 1980.

Harr, R. The conditions for a social psychology of chidhood. In M. P. M. Richards (Ed.), *The integration of a child into a social world*. Cambridge University Press, 1974.

Hartup, W. W. Peer interaction and social organization. In P. H. Mussen (Ed.), *Carmichael's manual of child psychology* (3rd ed. Vol. 2). New York: Wiley, 1970.

Heider, F. *The psychology of interpersonal relations*. New York: Wiley, 1958.

Henrig, M., & Jardin, A. *The managerial woman.* New York: Anchor/Doubleday, 1977.

Hess, R. D., Social class and ethnic influences on socialization. In P. H. Mussen (Ed.), *Carmichael's manual of child psychology* (3rd ed. Vol. 2). New York: Wiley, 1970.

Hess, R. D., & Shipman, V. C. Maternal attitudes toward the school and the role of the pupil: Some social class comparisons. In A. H. Passow (Ed.), *Developing programs for the educationally disadvantaged.* New York: Teachers College, Columbia University Press, 1968.

Higgins, E. T. Social class differences in verbal communicative accuracy: A question of "Which question?" *Psychological Bulletin,* 1976, *83,* 695–714.

Higgins, E. T. Role-taking and social judgment: Alternative developmental perspectives and processes. In J. H. Flavell & L. Ross (Eds.), *Social cognitive development: Frontiers and possible futures.* Cambridge: Cambridge University Press, 1981.

Higgins, E. T., & Bryant, S. Consensus information and the "fundamental attribution error": The role of development and in-group versus out-group knowledge. *Journal of Personality and Social Psychology,* in press.

Higgins, E. T., Feldman, N. S., & Ruble, D. N. Accuracy and differentiation in social prediction: A developmental perspective. *Journal of personality,* 1980, *48,* 520–540.

Higgins, E. T., Fondacaro, R., & McCann, D. Rules and roles: The "communication game" and speaker-listener processes. In W. P. Dickson (Ed.), *Children's oral communication skills.* New York: Academic Press, 1981.

Higgins, E. T., Herman, C. P., & Zanna, M. P. (Eds.). *Social cognition: The Ontario Symposium* (vol. 1). Hillsdale, N.J.: Erlbaum, 1981.

Holstein, Development of moral judgments: A longitudinal study of males and females. *Child Development,* 1976, *47,* 51–61.

Howe, H. E., Jr., & Keasey, C. B. (Eds.). *Nebraska Symposium on Motivation.* Lincoln: University of Nebraska Press, 1978.

Hsu, F. L. K. (Ed.). *Psychological anthropology.* Homewood, Ill.: Dorsey Press, 1961.

Imamoglu, E. O. Children's awareness and usage of intention cues. *Child Development,* 1975, *46,* 39–45.

Inkeles, A. Society, social structure, and child socialization. In J. A. Clausen (Ed.), *Socialization and society.* Boston: Little, Brown, 1968.

Inkeles, A. Social structure and socialization. In D. A. Goslin (Ed.), *Handbook of socialization theory and research.* Chicago: Rand McNally, 1969.

Inkeles, A. The school as a context for modernization. In A. Inkeles & D. B. Holsinger (Eds.), *Education and individual modernity in developing countries.* Leiden: Brill, 1974.

Inkeles, A., & Levinson, D. J. National character: The study of modal personality and sociocultural systems. In G. Lindzey & E. Aronson (Eds.), *The Handbook of social psychology* (2nd ed. Vol. 4). Reading, Mass.: Addison-Wesley, 1969.

Izard, C. E. *The face of emotion.* New York: Appleton-Century-Crofts, 1971.

Jersild, A. T. *The psychology of adolescence* (2nd ed.). New York: Macmillan, 1963.

Jones, E. E., & Harris, V. A. The attribution of attitudes. *Journal of Experimental Social Psychology,* 1967, *3,* 1–24.

Keasey, C. B. Social participation as a factor in the moral development of preadolescents. *Developmental Psychology,* 1971, *5,* 216–220.

Keasey, C. B. Young children's attribution of intentionality to themselves and others. *Child Development,* 1977, *48,* 261–264.

Keniston, K. Psychological development and historical change. *Journal of Interdisciplinary History,* 1971, *11,* 329–345.

Kessen, W. The American child and other cultural inventions. *American Psychologist,* 1979, *34,* 815–820.

Kohlberg, L. Development of moral character and moral ideology. In L. W. Hoffman & M.

L. Hoffman (Eds.), *Review of child developmental research* (Vol. 1). New York: Russell Sage Foundation, 1964.

Kohlberg, L. Stage and sequence: The cognitive-developmental approach to socialization. In D. A. Goslin (Ed.), *Handbook of socialization theory and research*. Chicago: Rand McNally, 1969.

LeVine, R. A. Cross-cultural study in child psychology. In P. H. Mussen (Ed.), *Carmichael's manual of child psychology* (3rd ed. Vol. 2). New York: Wiley, 1970.

Levinson, D. J. *The seasons of a man's life*. New York: Knopf, 1978.

Lewin, K. Psycho-sociological problems of a minority group. *Character and Personality*, 1935, *3*, 175–187.

Lewin, K. The field theory approach to adolescence. *Americal Journal of Sociology*, 1939, *44*, 868–897.

Lifshitz, M. Internal-external locus-of-control dimension as a function of age and the socialization mileu. *Child Development*, 1973, *44*, 538–546.

Livesley, M. J. & Bromley, D. B. *Person perception in childhood and adolescence*. London: Wiley, 1973.

Maccoby, E. E. The development of moral values and behavior in childhood. In J. A. Clausen (Ed.), *Socialization and society*. Boston: Little, Brown, 1968.

Maitland, K. A., & Goldman, J. R. Moral judgment as a function of peer group interaction. *Journal of Personality and Social Psychology*, 1974, *30*, 699–704.

McCandless, B. R. Childhood socialization. In D. A. Goslin (Ed.), *Handbook of socialization theory and research*. Chicago: Rand McNally, 1969.

McClintock, C. G. Development of social motives in Anglo-American and Mexican-American children. *Journal of Personality and Social Psychology*, 1974, *29*, 348–354.

Mead, M. An investigation of the thought of primitive children, with special reference to animism. *Journal of the Royal Anthropological Institute*, 1932. *62*, 173–190.

Mead, M. *Coming of age in Samoa*. New York: Morrow, 1961.

Miller, D. R. Psychoanalytic theory of development: A re-evaluation. In D. A. Goslin (Ed.), *handbook of socialization theory and research*. Chicago: Rand McNally, 1969.

Nicholls, J. G. Causal attributions and other achievement-related cognitions: Effects of task outcome, attainment value and sex. *Journal of Personality and Social Psychology*, 1975, *31*, 379–389.

Nisbett, R., & Ross, L. *Human inference: Strategies and shortcomings of social judgment.* Englewood Cliffs, N.J.: Prentice-Hall, 1980.

Parke, R. D. Rules, roles, and resistance to deviation: Recent advances in punishment, discipline, and self-control. In A. Pick (Ed.), *Minnesota Symposia on Child Psychology* (Vol. 8). Minneapolis: University of Minnesota Press, 1974.

Parsons, J. E. *Causal attributions and the role of situational cues in the development of children's evaluative judgments*. Unpublished dissertation, University of California at Los Angeles, 1974.

Parsons, J. E. Expectancies, values and academic choice: Origins and change. In J. Spence (Ed.), *Assessing achievement*. San Francisco: Freeman, in press.

Parsons, J. E., & Ruble, D. N. The development of achievement-related expectancies. *Child Development*, 1977, *48*, 1075–1079.

Parsons, T. *Social structure and personality*. London: Free Press, 1964.

Parsons, T., Bales, R. F., Olds, J., Zelditch, M., & Slater, P. E. *Family, socialization and interaction process*. New York: Free Press, 1955.

Peevers, B. H., & Secord, P. F. Developmental changes in attribution of descriptive concepts to persons. *Journal of Personality and Social Psychology*, 1973, *27*, 120–128.

Piaget, J. *Judgment and reasoning in the child*. New York: Harcourt, Brace, 1926. (a)

Piaget, J. *The language and thought of the child*. New York: Harcourt, Brace, 1926. (b)

Piaget, J. *Play, dreams and imitation in childhood.* New York: Norton, 1951.

Piaget, J. *The moral judgment of the child.* New York: Free Press, 1965. (Original trans. published, 1932.)

Plumb, J. H. The great change in children. *Annual editions: Readings in human development, 1973–1974.* Guilford, Conn.: Dushkin, 1973.

Radcliffe-Brown, A. R. Age organization-terminology. *Man,* 1929, *29*(13), 21.

Rocissano, L. Object play and its relation to language in early childhood. *Dissertation Abstracts International,* 1980, *40*, 5041B. (University Microfilms No. 8009537)

Rosenthal, R. L., & Zimmerman, B. J. *Social learning and cognition.* New York: Academic Press, 1978.

Ross, L. The intuitive psychologist and his shortcomings: Distortions in the attribution process. In L. Berkowitz (Ed.), *Advances in experimental social psychology* (Vol. 10). New York: Academic Press, 1977.

Rotenberg, K. J. *The development of moral judgment of self and other in children.* Unpublished doctoral dissertation, University of Western Ontario, 1979.

Ruble, D. N., Boggiano, A. K., Feldman, N. S., & Loebl, J. H. A developmental analysis of the role of social comparison in self-evaluation. *Developmental Psychology,* 1980, *16*, 105–115.

Ruble, D. N., Feldman, N. S., Higgins, E. T., & Karlovac, M. Locus of causality and use of information in the development of causal attributions. *Journal of Personality* 1979, *47*, 595–614.

Salili, F., Maehr, M. L., & Gillmore, G. Achievement and morality: A cross-cultural analysis of causal attribution and evaluation. *Journal of Personality and Social Psychology,* 1976, *33*, 327–337.

Selman, R. L. Taking another's perspective: Role-taking development in early childhood. *Child Development,* 1971, *42*, 1721–1734.

Selman, R. L. The development of interpersonal reasoning. In A. Pick (Ed.), *Minnesota Symposia on Child Psychology* (Vol. 10). Minneapolis: University of Minnesota Press, 1976. (a)

Selman, R. L. Social-cognitive understanding. In T. Lickona (Ed.), *Moral development and behavior.* New York: Holt, Rinehart and Winston, 1976. (b)

Selman, R. L., Lavin, D. R., & Brion-Meisels, S. Developing the capacity for self-reflection: A look at troubled children's conceptions-in-theory and conceptions-in-use. In F. C. Serafica (Ed.), *Social cognitive development in context.* New York: Guilford Press, in press.

Serafica, F. C. The development of friendship: An ethological-organismic perspective. In F. C. Serafica (Ed.), *Social cognitive development in context.* New York: Guilford Press, in press.

Shantz, C. U. The development of social cognition. In E. M. Hetherington (Ed.), *Review of child development research* (Vol. 5). Chicago: University of Chicago Press, 1975.

Shantz, C. U. Children's understanding of social rules and the social context. In F. C. Serafica (Ed.), *Social cognition and social relations in context.* New York: Guilford Press, in press.

Shatz, M. The relationship between cognitive processes and the development of communication skills. In H. E. Howe, Jr., & C. B. Keasey (Eds.), *Nebraska Symposium on Motivation.* Lincoln: University of Nebraska Press, 1978.

Shweder, R. A., & Bourne, E. J. Does the concept of the person vary cross-culturally? In A. J. Marsella & G. White (Eds.), *Cultural conceptions of mental health and therapy.* New York: Reidel, in press.

Simmons, R. G., Rosenberg, F., & Rosenberg, M. Disturbance in the self-image at adolescence. *American Sociological Review,* 1973, *38*, 553–568.

Spencer, P. The function of ritual in the socialization of the Sambaru Moran. In P. Mayer (Ed.), *Socialization: The approach from social anthropology*. London: Tavistock, 1970.

Staats, A. W. *Social behaviorism*. Homewood, Ill. Dorsey Press, 1975.

Sullivan, H. S. *The collected works of Harvey Stack Sullivan* (Vol. 1). Edited by H. S. Perry and M. L. Gawel. New York: Norton, 1953.

Super, C. M. & Harkness, S. *Anthropological perspectives on child development: New directions for child development* (Vol. 8). San Francisco: Jossey-Bass, 1980.

Suzman, R. M. Psychological modernity. In A. Inkeles & D. B. Holsinger (Eds.), *Education and individual modernity in developing countries*. Leiden: Brill, 1974.

Turiel, E. *A comparative analysis of moral knowledge and moral judgments in males and females*. Unpublished manuscript, Harvard University, 1973.

Veroff, J. Social comparison and the development of achievement motivation. In C. P. Smith (Ed.), *Achievement-related motive in children*. New York: Russell Sage Foundation, 1969.

Vygotsky, L. S. *Thought and language*. Cambridge, Mass.: MIT Press, 1962.

Ward, B. E. Temper tantrums in Kau Sai: Some speculations upon their effects. In P. Mayer (Ed.), *Socialization: The approach from social anthropology*. London: Tavistock, 1970.

Weiner, B., & Peter, N. V. A cognitive-developmental analysis of achievement and moral judgments. *Developmental Psychology*, 1973, *9*, 290–309.

Werner, H. *Comparative psychology of mental development*. New York: International Universities Press, 1957.

Youniss, J. Another perspective on social cognition. In A. Pick (Ed.), *Minnesota Symposia on Child Psychology* (Vol. 9). Minneapolis: University of Minnesota Press, 1975.

Zigler, E., & Child, I. L. (Eds.). *Socialization and personality development*. Reading, Mass.: Addison-Wesley, 1973.

3 Beyond the information processed: socialization in the development of attributional processes

Philip R. Costanzo and Theodore H. Dix

According to the cognitive dynamics of attribution theory, our understanding and evaluation of persons and behavior are mediated by causal analysis (cf. Jones & Davis, 1965; Jones & McGillis, 1976; Kelley, 1967, 1972). This analysis is believed to be distinctly rational and guided by formal rules of inference. Its emphases are (1) on human action and social contexts as information, (2) on individuals as natural and logical information processors, and (3) on attributions, the inferences about the causes and characteristics of social life that are the result of this information analysis. Although the rules and devices of attribution theory were proposed as descriptive tools to allow an idealized portrayal of interpersonal reasoning, the current theoretical and research literature has tended to reify them. This trend is particularly evident in the burgeoning literature on the development of social cognition. In this literature the child's acquisition of structures for the apprehension of personal conduct is increasingly being viewed as coextensive with the acquisition of formal information processing heuristics. Thus, it is currently common to research the development of such formal analytic structures as the augmentation principle, the consensus principle, and the schemas of multiple sufficient and multiple necessary cause (cf. DiVitto & McArthur, 1978; Dix, Herzberger, & Erlebacher, 1978; Ruble et al. 1979; Shultz et al. 1975). Although such research is important and interesting, its centrality to current efforts to understand the development of social perception is disconcerting on two counts. First, it tends to assume that phenomena such as trait labeling and moral appraisal are contingent on secondary processes of cognitive elaboration rather than on the primary and immediate processes that accompany naive social observation. Its characterization of social perception as logic relegates to a secondary position the acquisition of beliefs and standards through socialization. Second, as a

63

result of its emphasis on cognitive skills and the mediating logical calculi of attribution processes, research in social-cognitive development has indirectly restricted the search for socialization antecedents of social perception and self-perception. Although skill at information integration undoubtedly increases with age and affects developing social behaviors, social perception emerges within a specific social context and is fundamentally influenced by the norms, beliefs, and social institutions common in the child's social life. Although we do not wish to indict the study of the development of causal-analytic structures, we would like to suggest that an accurate and balanced view of social-cognitive development will grant a central position to socialization and social experience as determinants of social inference and interpersonal reasoning.

Toward this end we propose a model that divides social perception processes into two classes:

(1) Interpretations of persons and events acquired through prior content-specific social experience and applied as rules or values believed to govern the types of conduct being observed

(2) Interpretations based on the relatively content-independent, logical-deductive processes detailed in attribution and cognitive-developmental theories

In latter sections of this chapter we will present a more detailed account of these processes and their operation during social interaction. But first, to present a cogent argument for the two-process model, it is important to share with you the research we have done at Duke University that impelled this formulation. The basic kernels of discontent with heuristically based models of the development of social perception occurred gradually as a consequence of four studies performed in the early and mid seventies. These studies focus on two prominent research areas within social-cognitive development, the development of moral judgment and the development of the discounting principle.

The Duke studies

Study 1: Costanzo, Coie, Grumet, and Farnill (1973)

The first study began as an attempt to reexamine Piaget's proposition that in the development of moral judgment the child moves from a concrete focus on the consequences of behavior to a more subjective focus on the actor's intentions for performing behavior. Numerous studies generated by Piaget's (1948) original formulation have shown that subjects younger than 7 fail to discriminate between malicious or benign intent when read a pair of stories about children engaging in misdeeds and asked to judge the seriousness of those misdeeds. Instead, these young children appear to make moral judgments on the basis of the amount of damage caused, whereas for older children the amount of objective damage is subordinate to subjective intent. The young child's failure to use intentions has been commonly viewed as a cognitive-developmental deficit in social information processing, that is, the ability to make and apply accurate inferences about the inner states of others.

What was clear at the time of the Costanzo et al. study was that Piaget's simple two-stage model of moral reasoning was compatible with emerging frameworks in the study of adult attribution. In the Jones and Davis (1965) theory of correspondent inference, for example, dispositions are attributed to actors when the actors' behavior and its outcomes are believed to *correspond with* an underlying trait. Such behavior-to-trait correspondence is believed present only when the effects of a behavior are believed to have been intended by the actor. Whether a behavior's effects were intended or unintended, in turn, is determined by observing the quality and intensity of the actor's behavior and the social conditions that surround it. Once the effects of action are recognized as intended, reliable inferences about the actor become possible. Thus, because it is believed to be unintentional, brushing against a friend in a crowded subway will not be seen to correspond with the trait aggressiveness, whereas the same act in the context of a bitter argument, because now intentional, will be seen to correspond with the trait aggressiveness.

When correspondent inference theory is coupled with Piaget's moral judgment framework, a portrayal of the *development* of trait attribution processes emerges. The combined perspective suggests that young children's reliance on consequences over intentions may reflect their belief in the *unequivocal correspondence* between behavior and dispositions. The young child infers that actors' traits directly correspond – in magnitude and kind – with their observed behavior and its consequences. With increasing cognitive sophistication, however, children come to adopt the more conditionally correspondent focus suggested by correspondent inference theory in which intentionality is a prerequisite to belief in behavior-trait correspondence and, thus, trait inference.

To explore this conceptual hybrid, we sought first to provide a more rigorous demonstration of the development of intention-based judgments than had been accomplished to date. This was necessary because the classical Piagetian paradigm had serious limitations. First, Piaget's stories always depicted acts that yielded accidental, not intended, outcomes. Second, they were restricted to acts that had negative, damage-related outcomes. Third, his stories confounded intentions with consequences: Positive intentions were always followed by large negative outcomes and negative intentions were always followed by small negative outcomes.

To eliminate these limitations, we elicited children's moral evaluations of story characters who produced either positive or negative outcomes and whose intentions were either positive or negative. Like Piaget, we observed a developmental increase in the importance of intention information when the consequences of depicted action were negative: Kindergarten children evaluated actors who produced negative consequences without consideration of the actor's intentions, whereas older children evaluated actors with positive intentions more positively than actors with negative intentions. The surprise came, however, when consequences were positive. In the positive consequence condition, children as young as 5 rated actors with good intentions more positively than actors with bad intentions. Thus, even the youngest children in this study demonstrated the ability to infer intentions and to use them for moral evaluation. To maintain, then, that cognitive-developmental deficits in these skills caused the failure to make intention-based judgments when consequences were negative becomes problematic. In place of a skill development position, we proposed that failure to use information about intentions could reflect age differences in the social norms that guide social judgment. Younger children might more often assign blame in line with beliefs about adult norms than older children because those norms are so central to their daily lives. In turn, adult norms might differ for positive and negative behavior. When outcomes are negative, adults may be upset regardless of the child's intentions, whereas when outcomes are positive, adult response may be mediated by inferences about the child's intentions. Thus, adults may reward positive outcomes when intended but are unlikely to praise happy accidents or malicious intentions gone awry. When coupled with the young child's concern with adult sanctions, such differential response to positive and negative outcomes by adults could account for age differences in the use of information about intentions. If this analysis is correct, developmental change in moral judgment would reflect not cognitive deficits and their subsequent amelioration but age changes in sensitivity to particular norms prevalent in the child's social context.

Study 2: Farnill (1974)

To assess this norm-constraint hypothesis directly, Doug Farnill, in collaboration with his mentor, John Coie, manipulated the extent to which moral strictures were relevant to particular judgments. If young children's moral evaluations are indeed governed by sensitivity to adult moral strictures, then judgments that are not of the good–bad type might be less dominated by the desirability of outcomes and more influenced by information about intentions. If cognitive deficits prevent intention-based judgments, on the other hand, use of intentions should be absent regardless of the precise nature of the judgment required. To test this line of reasoning, Farnill presented 5-, 7-, and 9-year-olds with videotapes of a boy moving flowerpots at his mother's request. The boy ends up breaking either one or four pots (consequences) and does so because of either maliciousness, ineptness, or the occurrence of an unavoidable accident. The relevance of moral rules was manipulated by asking (1) which boy is naughtier (norm relevant) or (2) which boy would be most helpful on a cooperative task involving dexterity (norm irrelevant). For moral judgments, the standard Piagetian findings were replicated. The youngest children felt that the boy who broke four pots was naughtier than the boy who broke only one pot, and this judgment was unaffected by whether damage resulted from maliciousness, ineptness, or unavoidable accident. Moral judgments sensitive to these intention dimensions did not emerge until the early school years. For judgments about who would make a skilled cooperator, however, results were different. Even the youngest children rated the well-intentioned accident victim more positively than either the malicious or the inept actor. Thus, like the Costanzo et al. (1973) study, the Farnill (1974) result suggests that deficits in the ability to infer intentions were not present among subjects who made consequence-based moral judgments. On the contrary, younger children demonstrated accurate knowledge of the intentions underlying behavior but simply assessed misconduct according to rules different from those of older children. Thus, the unconditional correspondence between outcomes and intentions that we expected would characterize the person inferences of young children seems typical only when adult sanctions or norms are relevant to the judgment task. When judgments are not moral in kind or are made about positive acts, even kindergartners recognize and use intentions in social inference.

Study 3: Costanzo, Grumet, and Brehm (1974)

In a third study we examined the development of correspondent inferences by examining children's judgments about the attitudes held by others. In several studies with adults, Jones and his colleagues found that inferences about the attitudes held by actors who advocated various political positions were heavily influenced by whether those actors had freely chosen to advocate their position or had no choice in the position they would advocate (Jones & Harris, 1967; Jones et al. 1971). These investigators predicted and found that the attitude of the actor was inferred to correspond more with the position advocated when the actor had chosen the position advocated than when the actor had had no choice. On the basis of Piaget's work it seemed likely that the young child would not adopt such a conditionally correspondent position but might instead feel that actors' attitudes were reflected directly in behavior, that is, in the position advocated. Thus, like intentions, the internal factor of preference might not mediate social judgment in the young child.

Under the rubric of Kelley's (1967) attribution theory, numerous subsequent studies have examined the development of such person inferences. In his discounting principle, Kelley (1972) argues that observers will discount the presence of possible internal causes when external causes for an observed act are present. Developmental investigations of this hypothesis show that adults and children older than about 8 do in fact show such discounting. When story characters are rewarded for, or commanded to engage in, particular behaviors, they are believed to be less intrinsically motivated to engage in those behaviors than story characters who perform the same behaviors in the absence of external incentives (Heller & Karabenick, 1978; Karniol & Ross, 1976, 1979; Shultz et al., 1975; Smith, 1975). Prior to age 7, the opposite inference, termed *adding,* seems prevalent: That is, characters rewarded for, or commanded to engage in, an activity are believed to be more intrinsically interested in that activity than characters who engage in the activity without external incentives (Karniol & Ross, 1976, 1979; cf. Kun, 1977; Leahy, 1979; Shultz & Butkowsky, 1977). As with failures to use information about intentions for moral judgment, failures to discount are commonly thought to reflect deficits in information processing, in this case the absence of formal social information processing schema. In the present context, use of information about an actor's free choice, the discounting schema position, would predict that children would increasingly discount the presence of an attitude when actors do not freely choose the position they advocate and that this developmental change reflects the emergence of formal abilities related to use of the discounting principle. Our findings on moral judgment, on the other hand, suggest that free choice might fail to mediate social judgment only when judgment relates to adult norms. When adult norms are irrelevant, even young children might infer that behavior and attitudes correspond most strongly when behavior is freely chosen.

To test these positions we designed an experiment analogous to the

Jones and Harris (1967) study but more suited to children. First-, third-, and sixth-grade children observed a videotape of a child choosing between two available toys and subsequently playing with either the chosen or the unchosen toy. When the actor played with the chosen toy, choice was either free or adult approved. When the actor was denied play with the chosen toy, play with the chosen toy was prohibited by either an adult command or environmental constraint, that is, the toy was out of reach. If the skill deficit position was correct, young children might fail to use information about choice but rely instead upon play behavior when inferring which toy the actor preferred. If the internal state preferences were seen as irrelevant only when adult rules were present, on the other hand, chosen toys would be seen as preferred in all instances except when choice was in conflict with adult sanction.

Our results showed that the adult-constraint position was more accurate. There were no age differences in attitude attribution when the source of constraint was environmental. First-graders were as likely as third-graders and sixth-graders to rate actors as liking freely chosen and played-with toys more than toys that were played with because the preferred toy was out of reach. Developmental differences emerged, however, when the source of constraint was an adult prohibition. As predicted from correspondent inference theory, older children rated actors as liking the unplayed-with toy more if it was unplayed-with because of adult prohibition than in the absence of adult prohibition. Younger children, however, rated actors as liking toys not played with because of adult prohibition less than when no adult prohibition was present. Thus, when adult norms were absent, younger children, like older ones, produced conditional inferences in which attributions of liking for toys corresponded with toys played with only when actors freely chose those toys. When implicit or explicit adult norms were present, however, these same children, unlike older children, ignored choice information and inferred that liking corresponded with those adult norms.

Study 4: Grumet (1975)

Finally, in her dissertation Judy Grumet (1975) replicated and extended the Costanzo, Grumet, and Brehm (1974) investigation. She reasoned that if the presence of adult norms restricted the use of information about internal states for young children, then older children, and even adults, might show the same restricted focus if behavior was constrained by norms they perceived as particularly valid. She adopted the complete design of the Costanzo, Grumet, and Brehm study and, in addition, included a condition in which the source of constraint for toy play emanated from a same-sexed peer rather than an adult. Because the importance of peers increases during childhood, peer norms might be seen as particularly valid by older children and, like adult norms for younger children, restrict the use of information about internal states. This prediction was upheld. Replicating the results of the original study, Grumet found that when peers determined which toy was played with, younger children (6 and 7 years) did *not* attribute liking on the basis of the actor's behavior (i.e., the toy actually played with) as they did when choice was determined by adults. In fact, peer constraint tended to enhance the impact of choice on the preference attributions of the young children. Peer constraint, on the other hand, reduced the impact of actor choice for older children, just as adult constraint did for younger children. For older children, the played-with-toy was believed preferred more when its choice was determined by peer pressure than when choice was determined by environmental constraint. In short, older children evaluate another child's attitude to be congruent with that of a peer constrainer in the same way that younger children view another child's attitude to be congruent with that of an adult constrainer. In both instances the critical feature is the conformity of the actor with an appropriate reference norm.

Implications of the Duke studies

Although they do not demonstrate, of course, that emerging inferential skills are unimportant to social perception, the Duke studies do demonstrate in two important literatures on social-cognitive development that age-related changes in social perception occur in the absence of differences in the ability to infer the internal states of others. In the area of moral judgment, Costanzo and his colleagues (1973) and Farnill (1974) show that the young child's failure to consider intentions occurs only when outcomes are negative or adult norms are salient. Because intentions influence moral judgment in these children in other circumstances, failure to use intentions does not appear to reflect deficits in the ability to infer others' internal states. For the development of the discounting principle similar effects emerged. Costanzo, Grumet, and Brehm (1974) and Grumet (1975) found that young children fail to discount intrinsic interest only when the external constraints on behavior emanate from adults. These same children discount intrinsic interest when external constraints are environmental or emanate from peers. In addition, older children, who discount when behavioral constraints come from adults, fail to discount when constraints come from peers.

It is difficult to construct a cognitive skills explanation of these findings. In line with Piaget (see Flavell, 1963) and Flavell and Wohlwill (1969), it could be argued that such differences across stimulus and response domains reflect decalages in the application of social-cognitive structures. Just as conservations of number, quantity, and weight develop at different ages, so use of intentions might develop first for positive, then for negative, behaviors, and the use of the discounting principle might develop first when external constraints on actions are environmental and only later when constraints emanate from persons. Such an explanation suggests two things about differences across stimulus or response domains. First, it suggests that such differences are developmental, that older children manifest formal structures in the same and in more domains than younger children, and, second, that age differences reflect differences across domains in the ease with which formal cognitive skills can be applied, that is, differences in such factors as the salience, abstractness, or complexity of the stimulus event or the child's familiarity with the elements that define it. But at present such an explanation is unconvincing on two counts. First, it lacks precision and is, therefore, difficult to test. It is unclear what task factors might distinguish domains studied or how familiarity might be measured so that social events could be reliably classified according to their processing difficulty. Thus, at present the concept of decalage and the distinction between formal and functional task factors tend to be more descriptive than explanatory. Second, some data from the Duke experiments argue against a decalage interpretation. In the Farnill (1974) study, for example, the stimuli were identical across conditions that elicited differential use of information about intentions in young children. Only the type of judgment, how helpful versus how naughty, changed. If these questions differed in difficulty, the one that elicited the "least mature" judgments, the moral evaluation question, would seem the more familiar to young children. Judgments about who would make a competent helper are probably less prevalent in the lives of young children than judgments about what constitutes good or bad conduct. The crossover interaction between age and source of constraint observed by Grumet (1975) is particularly problematic for a competence explanation, as the older children "fail" to discount in conditions where the younger children appear to discount.

These findings lead us to propose that the developmental changes in social inference observed in the Duke studies and other social-cognitive research may depend on developmental change in reference norms as much as on developmental change in cognitive skill. Although cognitive-developmental factors may be important, developmental change in social cognition need not reflect emerging analytic structures but can instead be due to age-related changes in subcultural norms or adopted beliefs about appropriate conduct and social life in general. Thus, whereas some judgments related to discounting and moral evaluation certainly depend on reasoning skills, some seem governed by simpler processes concerned with knowledge of social norms and their application to observed behavior.

The two-process model

We would like to propose a two-process model of the development of social attributions, which distinguishes attributions determined by formal reasoning from attributions determined by the norms and beliefs prevalent in the child's social context. The first of these processes is formal informational analysis. By formal informational analysis we mean a social inference process guided by logical structures and characterized by a systematic and logical consideration of relevant social information. Such analysis necessarily rests on the development of basic reasoning skills and is believed by current attribution theorists (Jones & Davis, 1965; Jones & McGillis, 1976; Kelley, 1967, 1972) to involve hypothesis testing through use of particular types of covariation information and schemas for inferring logical relationships among causes and effects. Because it rests on formal reasoning skills, Process 1 is distinctly rational and developmental. Thus, as stressed by cognitive-developmental and attribution researchers, many attributions must be inferred from logically relevant information surrounding observed acts and will presumably develop as the cognitive prerequisites of those inferences develop.

Laboratory research verifies that with age social inferences do increasingly reflect logical patterns of social information processing. Children increasingly infer traits and causes for behavior that are consistent with social covariation information, such as information about the stability of behavior across situation (the distinctiveness principle) and its normativeness across persons (the consensus principle) (DiVitto & McArthur, 1978; Dix, Herzberger, & Erlebacher, 1978; Herzberger & Dix, 1980; Ruble et al., 1979). In addition, research on attribution schemas, believed to guide inference when covariation information is absent, demonstrates comparable developmental change. With age, children increasingly recognize logically necessary relations among possible causes for behavior and between causes and effects. Thus, information about one possible cause increasingly affects judgments about other possible causes, and the strengths of causes and effects are increasingly balanced as the logical interrelationships depicted in attribution schemas come to be understood (Karniol &

Ross, 1976, 1979; Kun, 1977; Shultz et al., 1975; Smith, 1975). Evidence suggests, as well, that the complexity of particular inferences can determine whether children at particular ages will make them (DiVitto & McArthur, 1978; Kun, 1977; Shultz et al., 1975).

Developmental change in the formal analytic skills that define Process 1 will under certain conditions create age differences in children's construction of actual social events and, therefore, may influence social development in important ways. The emergence of social comparison, for example, may be related to acquisition of the consensus principle or comparable Process 1 structures and may alter the basis for children's inferences about their athletic, social, and mental abilities and their personal characteristics (Ruble et al., 1980). Similarly, research on prosocial behavior suggests that behavior attributed by children to internal dispositions generalizes more and occurs more in the absence of adults than behavior attributed to external socialization pressures (Grusec et al., 1978; cf. Hoffman, 1970; Lepper, 1973). Developmental advances in the application of Kelley's discounting principle, therefore, may affect whether particular kinds of social experience have general or specific effects. In addition, the emergence of general skills at information integration (cf. Bearison & Isaacs, 1975; Collins, Berndt, & Hess, 1974; Dix, 1980) will likely influence children's daily social behavior when Process 1 factors are brought into play.

The second process in the two-process model is norm application and concerns attribution that is governed not by rational information analysis but by the acquisition of more content-specific social beliefs about persons and behavior. It involves the observation of particular beliefs in one's social context and their subsequent retrieval as explanation when behavior that falls within their range of application is observed. Because it is linked with the child's specific social experiences, Process 2 is not necessarily rational nor developmental and, in general, involves cognitive processes more elementary than those that guide formal causal analysis. Consider the development of attributions based on racial stereotypes. These are likely acquired not by observing covariation between racial characteristics and stereotypic patterns of behavior but by observing in one's familial and peer interaction speech and behavior that expresses racial beliefs directly. When behavior reflecting these beliefs is subsequently observed, attributions for that behavior may result from a simple process of behavior-belief matching. Similar accounts of how social judgment is acquired have been advanced by Bandura and McDonald (1963) and Mischel and Mischel (1976). Although not essentially developmental, Process 2 attributions are likely to change with age for a number of reasons. Norms prevalent within children's lives will differ across age subcultures. Experiences needed for norm acquisition are often age-specific. Older children will have had quantitatively more social experience than younger children. Finally, cognitive development will permit increasingly differentiated and abstract systems of social cognition and more effective application of norms previously acquired.

A variety of studies with both children and adults supports this conceptualization by showing that people tend to adopt attributions they observe during social interaction. Thus, children whose sharing is attributed by an adult to altruistic dispositions subsequently share more than children whose sharing is attributed to external pressures (Grusec et al., 1978). Comparable effects have been obtained by Dienstbier and his associates (1975). Miller, Brickman, and Bolen (1975) found that labeling children neat or able tended to increase neatness and ability, an effect observed as well for cooperativeness and competitiveness by Jensen and Moore (1977). A series of studies by Dweck and her colleagues (1978) also suggest the importance for children of observing particular attributions during social interaction. Dweck has been successful at alleviating performance decrements in underachievers using an attribution retraining procedure that enabled underachievers to experience success and to offer effort rather than ability attributions for their failures (Dweck, 1975). She has also found that the tendency for girls to attribute academic failure to ability deficits and boys to effort deficits corresponds to actual differences in the attributions that teachers offer males and females when explaining failure in the classroom (Dweck et al., 1978). Even adults have been shown to adopt attributions for behavior offered as a matter of course during social encounters (Kiesler, Nisbett, & Zanna, 1969; Kraut, 1973; Paulus, Shaffer, & Downing, 1977). Because social life is complex, which of the many observed attributions will be adopted will likely depend on numerous factors related to the persons observed and the situations in which they are observed. All of this work suggests that attributions are not rational but suggestible and highly sensitive to the beliefs of others within a social context.

We wish to stress three points concerning the role of social norms and beliefs in the development of attributional processes. First, situations probably differ in the extent to which social norms and formal analytic reasoning determine attributions. As the Duke studies discussed earlier suggest, social norms may constrain or preempt formal causal analysis when observed behavior directly reflects an important social norm. The applied norm provides a sufficient, self-evident interpretation more or less automatically such that complex logical analysis is never activated.

Some situations, on the other hand, distinctly call for precise logical analysis, demanding that inferences follow implicit rules of fairness or rational judgment. Legal proceedings and psychology experiments are two such situations. Formal analysis might also occur when norms conflict or are inapplicable, and genuine uncertainty, therefore, exists. Experiments on attribution processes may inflate the extent to which social judgment appears guided by logical analysis, as Langer (1978) has noted, because they elicit concerns about the logical accuracy of responses. In fact, the two-process distinction made here parallels Langer's distinction between rational, mindful action and automatic, script-based action (Langer, 1978; Langer, Blank, & Chanowitz, 1978). She argues that social interaction proceeds without much informational analysis as long as events follow general socially prescribed patterns and that formal analytic processes are involved only when normal patterns are violated (cf. Goffman, 1974). Finally, for some situations attributions may reflect both Process 1 and Process 2. Such interrelations are discussed later.

Second, in addition to preempting formal causal analysis, social norms guide causal analysis when such analysis does occur. The complexities of social life and limitations in human information processing make an ideal, objective analysis impossible. Even when covariation information is collected or causal schemata are applied, by necessity a limited number of concepts and causes guide processing by directing attention, segmenting continuous action into discrete acts, and defining the types of situations, behaviors, and causes believed relevant. Such beliefs likely come from the individual's social world view adopted during socialization. Thus, when observing an aggressive behavior, we are unlikely to collect information about covariation between aggression and fruit juice consumption or left-handedness but quite likely to do so for covariation between aggression and alcohol consumption or sex.

This view is consistent with conceptions of social inference process emerging from studies of how prior theories and expectations influence formal analysis in adults. This research suggests that even adults, with their arsenal of formal reasoning skills, often detect actual covariation only poorly and substantially overestimate the amount of covariation present between variables that prior beliefs suggest should be related (see Nisbett & Ross, 1980). These phenomena are clearly evident in studies of illusory corrections (Chapman, 1967; Chapman & Chapman, 1967, 1969; Hamilton & Gifford, 1976; Hamilton & Rose, 1980). Chapman and Chapman, for example, found that trained psychiatrists and college students with no clinical experience or training in diagnostic testing felt that particular projective test responses would be associated with the same clinical symptoms (Chapman & Chapman, 1967). Furthermore, when mock client folders were presented to these groups, both clinicians and students tended to perceive in the mock cases relationships between particular symptoms and particular Rorschach responses that appeared plausible but which, in fact, were not present (Chapman & Chapman, 1969). Thus, it appears that commonly shared beliefs about relationships between various behaviors or conditions, rather than observation of actual relationships, determined these clinical judgments. Comparable findings emerge from a series of studies by Hamilton and Rose (1980). They also presented subjects with a series of descriptions of persons that included information about occupations and personal traits. When asked to estimate the frequency with which traits and occupations co-occurred, subjects tended to perceive relationships congruent with occupational stereotypes (e.g., salesman-talkative) even when those relationships were absent and failed to perceive relationships incongruent with occupational stereotypes (e.g., salesman-quiet) even when present. In their review of literature on prior belief and attribution, Nisbett and Ross (1980) state that one conclusion is certain: "The layperson's perceptions of social traits . . . are not simple products of data observation. The layperson's theories influence perceptions of covariation much more than do the data themselves, and the accuracy of these perceptions therefore depends less on the layperson's covariation detection capabilities than on the accuracy of the theories" (p. 108). The development of social perception, therefore, may depend less on the acquisition of covariation-detection capabilities and other cognitive skills than on the acquisition of socialized beliefs and theories of behavior.

Our third point about socialization in attribution development is that perceptions of persons and behavior, because acquired in a social context, may not be adopted solely on the basis of their logical consistency or their accuracy at characterizing observations. Like overt acts, beliefs about the meaning of behavior may be subject to social contingencies and shaped by their actual and anticipated consequences. In fact, young children are confronted with a pervasive system of parental rules, beliefs, and sanctions well before they are capable of a thoroughgoing cognitive appraisal of the adequacy and "correctness" of such strictures. These explicitly and implicitly communicated rules are adopted (i.e., internalized) by children without an attributional analysis. To sustain the notion that the development of adult social perception tendencies is a matter of the maturation of "cool" cognitive capacities, one has to logically maintain that the affect- and consequence-moderated internalized value strictures somehow disappear, or lose their meaning, or are subsumed by our ever-increasing rational capacity. To the contrary, we would speculatively offer that it is our developing rational capacities that are subsumed by our primitive, affect-laden, and largely irretrievable rule structures.

The maturation of cognitive skill and processing flexibility allows adult perceivers to manipulate incoming information to fit the precepts and central values of subtly socialized belief structures. Internalized values acquired in a social context in early childhood do not go away but come to function, instead, as the unseen and largely unacknowledged "directors" of our contemporary social perceptions and inferences.

Although the idea that attributions can reflect motivational as well as cognitive factors is not new (cf. Miller & Ross, 1975; Nisbett & Ross, 1980), we are proposing that the issue must be broadened. *Developmentally acquired motives* are pervasive and perhaps nonconscious. Such life-continuous affectively laden perspectives can be conceptually distinguished from the largely contemporaneous hedonic and self-serving motives that have been used to qualify the premises of information-guided attribution theory. The major suggestion that follows upon the above reasoning is that to understand the attributional habits of *both* children and adults the study of developing social cognition must be conjoined with the study of socialization (particularly the acquisition of internalized belief structures). Putting it another way, if a large portion of attribution is a matter of nonconscious, but rationally appearing, norm application (i.e., Process 2), it becomes quite important to examine the manner in which we acquire and internalize norms. Unfortunately, in the current study of attributional development, energy seems almost entirely focused upon the acquisition of cognitive skills and structures.

Overlap and co-action of Process 1 and Process 2

Although formal analysis and norm application can be distinguished in theory, in practice they are often intertwined. Several ways in which they can operate conjunctively have already been discussed. Thus, we have noted that social norms often guide causal analysis for lay perceivers as theory guides experimentation for research scientists. We have also noted that social contingencies may bias analysis of social information and that norms may determine when causal analytic skills will be invoked. In addition, attribution based on norm application will be affected by emerging skill at formal informational analysis. Although norm application is simpler than covariation analysis, it still requires basic cognitive skills, which will change with development. Thus, norms will differ in complexity and abstractness. At times they may have to be inferred from patterns of overt behavior rather than observed directly in speech. Their application will require discrimination of behaviors and situations to which they apply. Furthermore, norms may conflict, or vivid information that contradicts them may be confronted. In such circumstances, formal informational analysis may be invoked by children who understand the significance of relevant evidence. Thus, the two general processes that characterize our model of attribution processes are interdependent.

When a distinction is drawn between the initial formulation of an attribution and its subsequent use to interpret ongoing behavior, the interrelationships between Process 1 and Process 2 become yet more complex. It is possible, for example, for an attribution to be formulated initially as the result of formal analysis of information about covariation but to be subsequently applied as an established belief according to less complex, norm-application processes. It is also possible for an attribution that is acquired by observation during social interaction to be applied subsequently as a possible cause within Kelley's multiple sufficient cause schema. We have emphasized, however, that complex cognitive processes are often not involved during either acquisition or application.

Summary

This chapter questions the common view that the development of social perception is primarily a product of the development of formal, information-analytic structures. Such a view overemphasizes the role of logical analysis in the formation of the child's emerging understanding of behavior and tends to ignore socialization as a central force in shaping the child's world view. We argued that socialized beliefs require far less cognitive skill to acquire and apply than do formal judgment calculi and, furthermore, that those beliefs can determine whether causal analysis will occur and what type of analysis it will be if it does occur.

A two-process model of social perception and its development that attempts to delineate the roles played by systematic developmental change in reasoning skills and more arbitrary socialization experiences was proposed. Process 1, which describes the logic of social perception, involves the perceiver in a rational and informationally balanced appraisal of social events. It develops as cognitive skills develop. Process 2 involves the perceiver in evaluating persons and their behavior in relation to that perceiver's construction of appropriate behavioral norms. It develops with the observation of social rules and beliefs during social interaction. To buttress the two-process distinction, we presented a series of studies which suggest that, in two central research areas in social-cognitive development, moral judgment and schema-guided attribution, understanding social perception requires an understanding of how socialization introduces specific proclivities into social inference. As the study of attributional processes has largely ignored such socialization influences, it is our hope that the foregoing speculative analysis will provoke inquiry into the social as well as cognitive antecedents of social inference.

References

Bandura, A., & McDonald, F. J. Influence of social reinforcement and the behavior of models in shaping children's moral judgments. *Journal of Abnormal and Social Psychology*, 1963, *67*, 274–281.

Bearison, D., & Isaacs, L. Production deficiency in children's moral judgments. *Developmental Psychology*, 1975, *11*, 732–737.

Chapman, L. J. Illusory correlation in observational report. *Journal of Verbal Learning and Verbal Behavior*, 1967, *6*, 151–155.

Chapman, L. J., & Chapman, J. P. Genesis of popular but erroneous diagnostic observations. *Journal of Abnormal Psychology*, 1967, *72*, 193–204.

Chapman, L. J., & Chapman, J. P. Illusory correlation as an obstacle to the use of valid psychodiagnostic signs. *Journal of Abnormal Psychology*, 1969, *74*, 271–280.

Collins, W. A., Berndt, T., & Hess, J. Observational learning of motives and consequences for televised aggression: A developmental study. *Child Development*, 1974, *45*, 799–802.

Costanzo, P., Coie, J., Grumet, J., & Farnill, D. A reexamination of the effects of intent and consequence on children's moral judgments. *Child Development*, 1973, *44*, 154–161.

Costanzo, P., Grumet, J., & Brehm, S. The effects of choice and source of constraint on children's attributions of preference. *Journal of Experimental Social Psychology*, 1974, *10*, 352–364.

Dienstbier, R. A., Hellman, D., Lehnhoff, J., Hillman, J., & Volkenaar, M. C. An emotion-attribution approach to moral behavior: Interfacing cognitive and avoidance theories of moral development. *Psychological Review*, 1975, *82*, 299–315.

DiVitto, B., & McArthur, L. A. Developmental differences in the use of distinctiveness, consensus, and consistency information for making causal attributions. *Developmental Psychology*, 1978, *14*, 474–482.

Dix, T. H. *The development of judgments based on knowledge of social roles.* Unpublished doctoral dissertation, Northwestern University, 1980.

Dix, T. H., Herzberger, S. D., & Erlebacher, A. *Using consensus information: A developmental study of Kelley's attribution theory.* Paper presented at the 86th Annual Meeting of the American Psychological Association, Toronto, 1978.

Dweck, C. S. The role of expectations and attributions in the alleviation of learned helplessness. *Journal of Personality and Social Psychology*, 1975, *31*, 674–685.

Dweck, C. S., Davidson, W., Nelson, S., & Enna, B. Sex differences in learned helplessness (II) The contingencies of evaluative feedback in the classroom and (III) An experimental analysis. *Developmental Psychology*, 1978, *14*, 268–276.

Farnill, D. The effects of social judgment set on children's use of intent information. *Journal of Personality*, 1974, *42*, 276–289.

Flavell, J. *The developmental psychology of Jean Piaget.* New York: Van Nostrand, 1963.

Flavell, J., & Wohlwill, J. Formal and functional aspects of cognitive development. In D.

Elkind & J. Flavell (Eds.), *Studies in cognitive development: Essays in honor of Jean Piaget.* New York: Oxford University Press, 1969.

Goffman, E. *Frame analysis.* New York: Harper & Row, 1974.

Grumet, J. *Effects of adult and peer sanctions on children's attributions of preference.* Unpublished doctoral dissertation, Duke University, 1975.

Grusec, J., Kuczynski, L. Rushton, J., & Simutis, Z. Modeling, direct instruction, and attributions: Effects on altruism. *Developmental Psychology,* 1978, *14,* 51–57.

Hamilton, D., & Gifford, R. Illusory correlation in interpersonal perception: A cognitive basis of stereotypic judgments. *Journal of Experimental Social Psychology,* 1976, *12,* 392–407.

Hamilton, D., & Rose, T. Illusory correlation and the maintenance of stereotypic beliefs. *Journal of Personality and Social Psychology,* 1980, *38,* 832–845.

Heller, K., & Karabenick, J. *Children's use of the discounting principle in understanding choice behavior.* Paper presented at the 86th Annual Meeting of the American Psychological Association, Toronto, 1978.

Herzberger, S. D., & Dix, T. H. *The development of integrated impressions of others.* Unpublished manuscript, Northwestern University, 1980.

Hoffman, M. Moral development. In P. H. Mussen (Ed.), *Carmichael's manual of child psychology* (3rd ed., Vol. 2). New York: Wiley, 1970.

Jensen, R., & Moore, S. The effect of attribute statements on cooperativeness and competitiveness in school-age boys. *Child Development,* 1977, *48,* 305–307.

Jones, E. E., & Davis, K. E. From acts to dispositions: The attribution process in person perception. In L. Berkowitz (Ed.), *Advances in experimental social psychology* (Vol. 2). New York: Academic Press, 1965.

Jones, E. E., & Harris, V. A. The attribution of attitudes. *Journal of Experimental Social Psychology,* 1967, *3,* 1–24.

Jones, E. E., & McGillis, D. Correspondent inference and the attribution cube: A comparative reappraisal. In J. H. Harvey, W. J. Ickes, & R. F. Kidd (Eds.), *New directions in attribution research* (Vol. 1). Hillsdale, N.J.: Erlbaum, 1976.

Jones, E. E., Worchel, S., Goethals, G., & Grumet, J. Prior expectancy and behavioral extremity as determinants of attitude attribution. *Journal of Experimental Social Psychology,* 1971, *7,* 59–80.

Karniol, R., & Ross, M. The development of causal attributions in social perception. *Journal of Personality and Social Psychology,* 1976, *34,* 455–464.

Karniol, R., & Ross, M. Children's use of a causal attribution schema and the inference of manipulative intentions. *Child Development,* 1979, *50,* 463–468.

Kelley, H. H. Attribution theory in social psychology. In D. Levine (Ed.), *Nebraska Symposium on Motivation* (Vol. 1). Lincoln: University of Nebraska Press, 1967.

Kelley, H. H. Causal schemata and the attribution process. In E. Jones, D. Kanouse, H. Kelley, R. Nisbett, S. Valins, & B. Weiner (Eds.), *Attribution: Perceiving the causes of behavior.* Morristown, N.J.: General Learning Press, 1972.

Kiesler, C., Nisbett, R., & Zanna, M. On inferring one's belief from one's behavior. *Journal of Personality and Social Psychology,* 1969, *11,* 321–327.

Kraut, R. E. Effects of social labeling on giving to charity. *Journal of Experimental Social Psychology,* 1973, *9,* 551–562.

Kun, A. Development of magnitude-covariation and compensation schemata in ability and effort attributions of performance. *Child Development,* 1977, *48,* 862–873.

Langer, E. Rethinking the role of thought in social interaction. In J. Harvey, W. Ickes, & R. Kidd (Eds.), *New directions in attribution research* (Vol. 2). Hillsdale, N.J.: Erlbaum, 1978.

Langer, E., Blank, A., & Chanowitz, B. The mindlessness of ostensibly thoughtful action:

The role of "placebic" information in interpersonal interaction. *Journal of Personality and Social Psychology,* 1978, *36,* 635–642.

Leahy, R. Development of conceptions of prosocial behavior: Information affecting rewards given for altruium and kindness. *Developmental Psychology,* 1979, *15,* 34–37.

Lepper, M. Dissonance, self-perception, and honesty in children. *Journal of Personality and Social Psychology,* 1973, *25,* 65–74.

Miller, D. T., & Ross, M. Self-serving bias in the attribution of causality: Fact or fiction? *Psychological Bulletin,* 1975, *82,* 213–225.

Miller, R. Brickman, P., & Bolen, D. Attribution versus persuasion as a means for modifying behavior. *Journal of Personality and Social Psychology,* 1975, *31,* 430–441.

Mischel, W., & Mischel, H. A cognitive social-learning approach to morality and self-regulation. In T. Lickona (Ed.), *Moral development and behavior.* New York: Holt, Rinehart and Winston, 1976.

Nisbett, R., & Ross, L. *Human inference: Strategies and shortcomings of social judgment.* Englewood Cliffs, N.J.: Prentice-Hall, 1980.

Paulus, D., Shaffer, D., & Downing, L. Effects of making blood donor motives salient upon donor retention: A field experiment. *Personality and Social Psychology Bulletin,* 1977, *3,* 99–102.

Piaget, J. *The moral judgment of the child.* Glencoe, Ill. Free Press, 1948.

Ruble, D., Boggiano, A., Feldman, N., & Loebl, J. Developmental analysis of the role of social comparison in self-evaluation. *Developmental Psychology,* 1980, *16,* 105–115.

Ruble, D., Feldman, N., Higgins, E. T., & Karlovac, M. Locus of causality and the use of information in the development of causal attributions. *Journal of personality,* 1979, *47,* 595–614.

Shultz, T., & Butkowsky, I. Young children's use of the scheme for multiple sufficient causes in the attribution of real and hypothetical behavior. *Child Development,* 1977, *48,* 464–469.

Shultz, T., Butkowsky, I., Pearce, J. W., & Shanfield, H. Development of schemas for the attribution of multiple psychological causes. *Developmental Psychology,* 1975, *11,* 502–510.

Smith, M. C. Children's use of multiple sufficient cause schema in social perception. *Journal of Personality and Social Psychology,* 1975, *32,* 737–747.

4   Social cognition and social interaction in childhood

Willard W. Hartup, Judith E. Brady,
and Andrew F. Newcomb

The diverse essays assembled in this volume and the recent publication of other volumes in the area of social cognition and social behavior (Flavell & Ross, 1981; Glick & Clarke-Stewart, 1978) attest to the efforts of contemporary psychologists from various fields to achieve a more holistic understanding of development. The field of developmental psychology has been partitioned somewhat arbitrarily into the study of perceptual, cognitive, social, and affective development; however, we have little evidence to suggest that development in any one domain proceeds without influencing, or being influenced by, development in others. Moreover, the disjointed model of development implied by such independent lines of inquiry would seem counterintuitive. It is the eventual synthesis of related theories and substantiating evidence from different orientations that will advance understanding of the development of the whole child. The ideas presented in this volume illustrate the value to both the cognitive and the social developmentalist of integrating the approaches of both fields of study in attempting to explain the relation between social cognition and social behavior.

We argue in this chapter that if we are to continue to successfully relate our understanding of social-cognitive development and social interaction, traditional approaches to the study of each must be reexamined and new methods of study proposed. This chapter concerns the manner in which cognitive processes and the developmental constraints upon them influence the pattern and course of interaction occurring between the child and other individuals. As researchers interested in the development of social relationships and in the impact of children's social understanding on those relationships, we have limited our discussion to a consideration of conceptions of the knowledge of persons and social interaction and an

82

evaluation of their utility for explaining the linkages between social cognition and social behavior.

We first review the use of one theory about the acquisition of knowledge about the physical world, specifically that proposed by Piaget, as an analog for explaining the acquisition of knowledge about persons and events. Implicit in the assimilation of cognitive developmental theory to the study of social behavior has been the assumption that the principles governing development within the physical and social domains are isomorphic. However, there are certain properties unique to persons and social interaction suggesting that different explanations may be necessary to account for the acquisition and utilization of social knowledge. In the second section, schemas or scripts are discussed as an alternative conception of social knowledge, allowing for the probabilistic nature and the susceptibility to contextual factors that characterize social interaction.

The third section, entitled "Linkages between social cognition and social behavior," is devoted to a discussion of the contributions and limitations of each perspective in clarifying the linkages between cognition and action. The two subsequent sections emphasize the need to consider developmental change and contextual influences, respectively, when attempting to disentangle behavior and cognition. Finally, two brief empirical illustrations are presented that address specific questions about the ways in which behavioral differences observed between groups of children may be explained by differences in cognitive developmental level and/or by differences in the context of interaction. Finally, the implications for future research on social cognition and social behavior of these and other studies are discussed.

Physical knowledge as an analog for social knowledge

Most developmental research on social cognition to date consists of an extension of Piaget's developmental theory of cognition about the physical world to the social domain. Two questions have typified this line of inquiry: First, how do children conceptualize persons and events, and second, how do children draw inferences about another person's inner psychological experiences (Shantz, 1975)? Before the age of 7, children emphasize prominent, observable, and surface characteristics in evaluating persons and actions. Investigators of developmental changes in children's descriptions of others have found that young children mainly use attributes about physical appearance or actions to describe another person. Older children evidence far greater complexity and differentiation in their descriptions than younger children, relying on more abstract inferences about another's motives, dispositions, and values (Livesley & Bromley, 1973; Peevers & Secord, 1973). This initial reliance on the surface attributes of social objects and events and the subsequent shift to greater utilization of more complex spatial and temporal information parallels observations of developmental changes in cognitions within the physical domain. At least within the context of person perception, the use of the Piagetian cognitive model to describe social phenomena has proved successful.

Recently, however, several researchers have questioned the equating of social cognition and cognition about the physical world. Glick (1978) suggested that fundamental differences between social objects and physical objects preclude the direct translation of classic developmental models of cognition to explain a wide range of social-cognitive phenomena. He argued that the classic Piagetian model requires a stable and, in principle, specifiable environment for the integration of schemas and the development of cognitive structures. Whereas predictability and stability may characterize the physical world, the social world seems to be less certain and more sensitive to a variety of factors defining the context of social experience.

Although Damon (1981) disagreed that the objects of social cognition were inherently different from objects of physical cognition, he did argue that different relations *between* objects characterize each domain. Social individuals have the capacity to establish mutual intentional relations. The potential for such relations is unique to the social world, and, therefore, it is the understanding of intent and mutuality that distinguishes social cognition and cognition of the physical world. The study of social cognition is further complicated by the fact that universality of social experience cannot be assumed. Although different children may grow up in a physical world those laws are essentially static, children's conceptions of social relations are constrained by the nature and meaning of these relations within a given cultural context (Berndt, 1981).

Empirical investigations provide support for the distinctive nature of social cognition. If cognition in the social domain were indeed congruent with cognition in the physical domain, one would expect individuals to apply the same logical, deductive strategies used in understanding the physical world to the solution of social problems. Although this issue has not been addressed in developmental research, the failure of adults to use such strategies when asked to evaluate social stimuli has been documented repeatedly by social psychologists. Adults appear to use intuitive strategies whose outcomes frequently contradict those that would be derived from a logical, mathematical model for judgment (Nisbett & Ross,

1980; Schank & Abelson, 1977). Persons and events appear to be quickly labeled and categorized on the basis of preexisting beliefs or theories, whereas certain cognitive strategies seem to enable individuals to reduce complex inferential tasks to simple judgments of comparability (Nisbett & Ross, 1980). Belief systems and judgmental heuristics may be economical in reducing and organizing information; however, to the extent that they are inaccurately applied in any given situation, errors in judgment may be made. Nisbett and Ross (1980) identified five potential sources of error in judgment such that the conclusions drawn deviate from those predicted by the application of the logical principles of scientific reasoning. Errors may be made in the accurate and complete *description* of a person or an event; errors may be made in the *detection of covariation* between events; errors may be made in drawing *causal inferences;* errors may be made in the *prediction* of future behavior or events; or errors may be made in the *testing of beliefs* or theories about persons or events. Any of these errors may have particular consequences for subsequent judgment and behavior.

Nisbett and his colleagues (1976) found that brief hearsay recommendations conveyed in a face-to-face interaction were more effective in persuading college students to select given courses than more exhaustive and stable recommendations based on surveys of past students. Similarly, Kahneman and Tversky (1973) found that adult subjects ignored population base rates in predicting the group membership of particular individuals. Nisbett and Borgida (1975) observed that consensus information was frequently ignored by subjects attributing causality. Subjects appeared willing to interpret extreme behavior as modal even when they were told that very few people behaved in this way. Using a Bayesian model of analysis, Trope and Burnstein (1975) found that the impact of out-of-role behaviors (i.e., behaviors not congruent with situational demands) on individuals' attributes or evaluations was much greater than the impact of in-role or situationally congruent behaviors. Nisbett and his colleagues (1976) explain this apparent disregard of substantiating evidence in terms of the relative impact of abstract versus concrete information. Base rate information is abstract and in many experimental situations is deviant from an individual's a priori expectations (Wyer & Carlston, 1979). On the other hand, anecdotal information, face-to-face interaction, or personal observation is more immediate and may elicit strategies for interaction or modes of evaluation more quickly than less specific and more abstract information.

Results of developmental investigations also reveal differences between social and nonsocial cognition. Relationships between social cognitive abilities and other measures of intelligence vary with the sex of the child, socioeconomic status, and the measures used. Although it appears that age changes in conceptions of social relations are part of a general cognitive shift from an emphasis on external and superficial characteristics of objects to their more abstract qualities (Flavell, 1977), efforts to link the development of cognitive skills in the social and physical domains have failed to reveal a consistent correlation between the two. The most frequently reported correspondence is a moderate correlation between performance on conservation tasks and role-taking tasks, and even this result is not found consistently across studies (Shantz, 1975). In addition to the low-to-moderate reliability of measures in both domains, Berndt (1981) argued that differences in content and task domains make it unlikely that a strong correlation between measures of social and nonsocial cognition will be found.

Knowledge of social interaction

Alternative models drawn from social psychology and from the study of information processing and comprehension may provide a better account of the adult data than the logical, mathematical model heretofore proposed. D'Andrade (1972), for example, claimed that individuals have stored schematic representations of social interaction within their culture that may override or restructure any social information being presented. Thus, what constitutes an adaptive strategy in the domain of "social problem-solving" may be a shorthand or script that reduces the complexity of social stimuli and facilitates the generalization as well as the discrimination of behavior across a variety of social contexts (Glick, 1978).

The concept of a script was proposed by Schank and Abelson (1977) to describe how people organize information in order to understand discourse. The construct has since been elaborated to denote hypothesized, abstract cognitive structures that, when activated, facilitate comprehension of a variety of event-based situations including ongoing social interaction. Scripts may include expectations about the order as well as the occurrence of events (Abelson, 1981). In addition, rules for interaction, accompanying props, and obligatory as well as optional actions are all specifiable within a script (Nelson, 1981).

The concept of a script or a scriptlike abstract knowledge structure is not unique to the study of social behavior. It appears that very few objects or events are experienced as unique but, instead, are understood on the basis of an individual's preexisting cognitive structures. Theories of sensory perception, language, and cognition as well as theories of social understanding and social behavior currently posit the existence of abstract shemata into which new experiences are assimilated (Nisbett & Ross, 1980). Evidence of scripted event knowledge is accumulating from a variety of sources including studies of memory processing, social understanding, and discourse comprehension. Studies of both children and adults reveal the constructive nature of memory-processes (Bransford & Franks, 1971; Paris & Lindauer, 1977), and the ways that memory is constructed appear to be consistent with the hypothesis of scripted knowledge structures. Individuals tend to reinterpret or transform selected information in ways that make that information more useful. Superior recall of script-based stories as opposed to nonscript-based material (Bower, Black, & Turner, 1979) and the difficulty subjects experience in distinguishing actual sentences that have been presented from logical elaborations of those sentences (Paris & Lindauer, 1977) can be interpreted as additional evidence for the construction and retention of scripts of logically sequenced information or action. Bower, Black, and Turner (1979) also observed that, when asked to recall a series of events presented out of their usual sequential order, subjects reordered the events in a manner more closely approximating their anticipated sequencing than their actual presentation. In sum, these results are compatible with the hypothesis that existing cognitive structures may be imposed to facilitate retention of new information.

Nelson (1981) asked children between the ages of 3 and 8 to describe a number of events varying in familiarity and conventionality. She found that recalled events contained similar elements in a similar order at different recall times. In addition, recall of common experiences was markedly similar across children. Nelson posits that, through repeated participation in routine interactions, children construct scenarios of expected actions. She suggests that early scripts may be taught by adults who structure given situations, provide goals or instruction, and allow children to assume the requisite roles. As Garvey (1974) has demonstrated, fantasy and sociodramatic play provide rich sources of information about children's scripts. Events staged in dramatic play suggest that children also possess knowledge of social roles that they as yet have not assumed in real life.

In empirical investigations of discourse comprehension, Stein and Glenn's (1979) hypothesis that story material is retained in an episodic manner led them to predict better recall of information relating to the logical sequence of events (i.e., initiating events, actions, and direct consequences) than elaborative or less directly related information. In comparing the recall of first- and fifth-graders, these investigators concluded that, despite the superior recall of all types of information by fifth-graders, listeners at both grade levels seemed to make distinctions between different types of information, recalling more of the core elements necessary to the understanding of the story. The greater preoccupation of very young children with detail and their inability to discriminate crucial from incidental elements of a logical sequence are taken as evidence that young children have as yet constructed few scripts. The ability to construct scripts and to then make use of them depends on the ability to recognize causal relations or to draw causal inferences and thus link elements in a logical sequence. Stein and Glenn (1979) cite evidence that children as young as 6 years of age are capable of organizing and logically sequencing simple narratives. Their results are consistent with Brown's (1976) observations that the presence of causal relations facilitates the construction in recall of accurate temporal sequences by young children.

Although the abilities necessary to understand stories about social activities may differ significantly from the abilities necessary to interpret social interaction, Stein and Goldman (1981) argue that the study of story grammars has implications for the study of understanding interpersonal relations. In each domain the individual must draw causal inferences in order to link isolated events. What is more, the inferences made depend upon the interaction of already existing knowledge systems and the information presented in the new situation. In attempting to understand a story, individuals rely not only upon the story content presented but upon their own expectations about social interaction. Because social encounters involve more than one person, an understanding of social interaction implies an understanding of others' behavior as well as that of the individual. Just as the story material must be understood within the context of already existing knowledge systems, so the behavior of others is often interpreted with respect to one's own actions.

Stein and Goldman carry further this discussion of the implications of story comprehension by stating that both processes assume an actor's behavior is understood to be motivated and goal directed. Given this overlap, the study of social understanding may be furthered by an application of the analytic tools devised for models of discourse processing – models that share the underlying assumption that existing knowledge structures partially determine understanding and that, concurrently, changes are induced in existing knowledge structures as a function of interchange with the environment (Forbes, 1978). However, application of a comprehension model to the understanding of social behavior also allows for a probabilistic knowledge structure suited to the uncertainty and susceptibility to contextual influence characterizing the social domain. Given this analysis, Glick (1978) concludes that social cognition may involve the processing of different types of information by modes different from those implied by physical cognition.

Proponents of script theory do not claim that all understanding of social interaction is dependent upon the construction and activation of scripts. There may be circumstances under which alternative forms of processing may predominate (Abelson, 1976; Wyer & Carlston, 1979), and yet the use of scripts for repeatedly encountered interactions frees attention from ongoing activity to allow consideration of obstacles or deviations in the anticipated routine. To the extent that individuals encounter similar experiences, scripts provide a shared knowledge base for interaction with unfamiliar as well as familiar others. The scripts of individuals may vary as a function of prior experience, hence scripts may or may not match across new situations or across individuals. Perhaps the apparent egocentric nature of some interactions between young children may reflect their lack of shared scripts.

Linkages between social cognition and social behavior

To what extent has the translation of a classic cognitive developmental model into a model of social cognition or the adoption of a script-based theory of social knowledge advanced understanding of the relation between social cognition and social behavior? From a Piagetian perspecitve, cognitive developmental theory proposes that the acquisition of logical problem-solving operations and the changes associated with the development of social knowledge may be described in terms of organizational transformations (Damon, 1977). The underlying theoretical assumption is that the way in which children conceptualize others has more or less direct implications for the ways in which children interact with others. Attempts to relate social-cognitive skills, in particular role-taking abilities, to behavioral competence with peers follow directly from Piaget's suggestion that interpersonal conflict is necessary to foster cognitive development. Peer interaction, which focuses attention on the differences between children's respective constructions of the world, provides a context in which social cognitive skills can develop. Research in this area, however, has been limited almost exclusively to the correlation of individual differences in cognitive skills presumed to underlie social functioning and individual differences in selected behaviors observed in isolated social situations in the laboratory or in natural settings. These correlational analyses frequently yield conflicting results, depending upon the techniques used to assess social-cognitive competence and upon the behaviors targeted for observation.

Correlational investigations and training studies have revealed low to moderate concordances between role-taking skills and measures of helping and sharing behavior as well as negative correlations between role-taking and aggressive or antisocial behaviors. Comparable numbers of studies, however, have failed to reveal significant relations between role-taking and social behavior. Rubin and Schneider (1973) obtained a moderate correlation between communicative role-taking skills and measures of helping and generosity for 7-year-old children. Rothenberg (1970) found that role-taking was related to being described by peers as gregarious and friendly, and Deutsch (1974) found that good communicative role-taking skills were associated with more frequent positive interactions with peers. However, Zahn-Waxler, Radke-Yarrow, and Brady-Smith (1977) found that neither social nor perceptual role-taking competence predicted helping or comforting among children between the ages of 3 and 7. Rushton and Wiener (1975) also failed to find a relation between role-taking abilities and two measures of prosocial behavior among 7- to 11-year-olds, although they did note some generality across prosocial indices. Feshbach and Feshbach (1969) found that the relation between empathic skills and antisocial behavior varied as a function of age and sex. High empathy was positively related to aggression among 4- and 5-year-old boys, negatively related for 6- and 7-year-old boys, and unrelated for girls at both age levels. The variability of these findings may be partially explained by the multidimensional quality of perspective-taking. Kurdek and Rodgon (1975) correlated the perceptual, cognitive, and affective perspective-taking scores of kindergarten through sixth-grade children: Task interrelations were inconsistent, low, and nonsignificant, leading to the conclusion that perspective-taking is a multifaceted construct.

Although it has been difficult to demonstrate age differences in the relation between social-cognitive development, as indexed by role-taking tasks, and social behavior, some investigators have found differences in social-cognitive abilities between children according to their delinquency or aggressiveness. Selman (1976) found differences on three measures of social reasoning between a clinic population of 7- to 12-year-old boys who were experiencing difficulties in learning and in relating to peers as contrasted with a matched sample of more competent peers. By contrast, it is interesting to note that the performance of the clinic children on measures of logical problem solving in the physical domain was comparable to that of their matched peers.

Cutrona and Feshbach (1979) argued that differences in aggressive and prosocial behavior among third-, fourth-, and fifth-grade children may be associated with differences in the information attended to in social interaction. The tendencies of children to recall and to utilize dispositional as well as situational information about hypothetical actors were compared. Children who referred to feelings, motives, or personality traits in substantiating their evaluations of story characters were rated by teachers as less aggressive and more prosocial than children who evaluated story characters on the basis of external or situational circumstances. Cutrona and Feshbach posited that children who do not make use of psychological information about others may not be able to temper their own behavior in response to the behavior of others. However, children attuned to the feelings of others may have learned to recognize and respond to others' needs. They conclude that children's cognitive styles, as reflected by the social information to which attention is given in social interaction, have direct implications for children's behavior with others.

Dodge (1980) found significant differences in the responses of aggressive and nonaggressive second-, fourth-, and sixth-grade boys to negative interactions in which the intentions of other actors were ambiguous. Although it has been argued that aggressive children may fail to integrate cues of intentionality in mediating their hostile responses, it was demonstrated that aggressive as well as nonaggressive boys retaliated more often when peers intended to cause negative outcomes than when negative outcomes were clearly unintended. Aggressive and nonaggressive boys differed only in their response to situations in which a peer's intentions were unclear or ambiguous; the aggressive children responded aggressively, whereas the nonaggressive children restrained themselves from retaliation. Dodge concluded that, in this instance, social attribution and social behavior interact and that the interpretations children make of the behavior of others have significant implications for the behavior they subsequently elicit from their peers. Children who impute hostile intentions in an ambiguous situation and who behave aggressively may be more likely to experience rejection and mistrust from peers (who anticipate continued aggression from them) than do children who give their peers the benefit of the doubt.

Several investigators have studied the effects of training in role-taking skills on subsequent behavior. Chandler (1973), for example, found that delinquent adolescents who had participated in a 10-week role-taking training program committed significantly fewer delinquent acts in an 18-month follow-up period than delinquents who had not received the training. Spivak and Shure (1974) observed improvements in the social behavior of preschoolers who had been participants in a program designed to increase their sensitivity to others, their awareness of the consequences of their behavior, and their consideration of alternative behaviors. Although these findings suggest that changes in social-cognitive competence may be associated with behavioral changes, one cannot conclude that these training experiences were necessary or sufficient to modify social interaction.

A theory of script-based knowledge of social events suggests a somewhat different approach to the study of the relation between social cognition and social behavior. Rather than correlating indices of social-cognitive and behavioral competence, investigators observe ongoing behavior and infer the existence of scripts from evidence of roles being acted out. Given the value of scripts in reducing the complexity of social stimuli and streamlining the processing of information, it would seem reasonable to hypothesize that scripts might also guide behavior. In fact, scripts play a dual role in psychological theory: as comprehension, or knowledge, structures and as performance structures (Abelson, 1981). Evidence of roles being played out by adults in familiar interactions suggests that behavior may be guided by the same or similar structures that facilitate comprehension. What is more, observations of routinized interactions among preschool children (e.g., turn-taking and sociodramatic) have been interpreted as indications that children also have internalized scripts for at least some frequently encountered interactions (Garvey, 1974; Garvey & Berndt, 1975). Researchers, however, are just beginning to speculate about the conditions under which scripted knowledge will be translated into observable behavior. It remains for future research to examine those contextual factors that elicit the "playing out" of scripted knowledge during social interaction.

Although it would appear from the studies cited here that social cognition influences social behavior, it is not apparent whether this influence reflects the mediation of cognitive factors such as role-taking ability and the ability to construct and enact scripts or the importance of noncognitive factors such as social norms, prior social experience, or particular aspects of the social context. Although it may not be possible at this juncture to separate the influences of these two sets of factors, it is important to acknowledge in theory and in empirical investigation the potential operation of each.

Developmental constraints on the cognition-behavior relation

In an attempt to account for developmental changes in the relation between social cognition and social behavior, Berndt (1981) adopted a model for predicting behavioral intention from a weighted sum of attitudes and norms developed by social psychologists (Ajzen & Fishbein, 1977). Ajzen and Fishbein posit that any factor influencing an intention to act must operate through its influence on one of the following components: (a) attitudes toward performing that act (a function of the perceived consequences of that behavior and the valences of those consequences); (b) beliefs about expectations of the reference groups to which one belongs; (c) personal beliefs about what one should do; and (d) the motivation to comply with social or personal expectations. Thus, the model assumes a strong relation between social cognition and social behavior at all ages.

Berndt (1981) added a developmental dimension to this model by suggesting that changes in the attitudinal, normative, or motivational components of the equation or in the respective weights of these components could account for changes in social behavior. For example, larger weighting of anticipated consequences of behavior accompanied by minimal or zero weighting of normative components would yield predictions of moral judgment consistent with hypotheses about the behavior of young children drawn from cognitive-developmental theory. Similarly, a relatively higher valence for compliance with personal belief systems as opposed to compliance with the expectations of social groups might be predictive of postconventional levels of moral reasoning. However, whereas this model may serve as a valuable heuristic for evaluating the *intention* to act in a given situation or for assessing a person's prediction of individual behavior, it seems less likely to aid in the prediction of behavior in ongoing interaction.

The original model defined outcome as behavioral intention and assumed that intention was synonymous with action. But there may be other factors, particularly contextual ones, that make the acting out of behavioral intentions more or less likely. It may be argued that the contextual constraints that contribute to action or lack of action are reflected in the attitudinal component – the component that reflects the interaction of anticipated consequences of behavior and the relative valence of those consequences. The nature and valence of anticipated consequences are determined in part by the individual's previous social history in similar situations. For example, the parents of the empathic subjects in Cutrona and Feshbach's (1979) study may have practiced inductive forms of discipline, pointing out to their children the effects of their behavior on other persons. Information about the affective states of others has become salient for them, and they will select this type of information as a future guide for their own behavior. Evaluation of anticipated consequences is also influenced by an individual's more immediate "history" of preceding behaviors within the context of the current interactions. As it stands, the model is not falsifiable, and, therefore, its ultimate utility in generating testable hypotheses leading to refinement of the model is questionable. More definitive specification of factors influencing attitudes toward behavior may aid researchers in developing a more parsimonious model to predict social behavior from social cognition.

Alternatively, it may be posited that developmental changes in the cognitive processes presumed to underlie social interaction should be reflected, in some fashion, in social action. For example, if young children, as compared with older children, attend mainly to the observable and salient aspects of a social situation, their observations of someone else's behavior should have an impact on their actions that overrides more abstract social knowledge. If social comparisons are limited to motor skills and not to intellectual skills among younger children, then such comparisons should also impose constraints on their social interactions. Girgus and Wolf (1975) found that 5-year-old children were unable to correctly identify pairs of filmed social encounters as different when facial expressions, vocal intonations, or movements of actors varied across particular paired scenarios. Young children were as accurate as older children in judging sameness across pairs, but the authors concluded that young children tend to perceive many everyday social interactions as equivalent. It is not evident that young children simultaneously coordinate information, particularly more abstract, rulelike ideas, from a multiplicity of sources to guide their actions. Among older children, more complex effects involving the integration of a variety of information sources should be evident – even though the processes underlying this integration may be difficult to specify.

As children mature, their abilities to control and focus their attention on relevant cues improve (Markman, 1977). Discriminative and classificatory skills are refined. Older children spontaneously implement rehearsal and other constructive strategies to facilitate retention and retrieval of information. By the age of 10 to 12 years, children's social understanding has become relatively sophisticated. Comprehension (and even metacomprehension) undergoes change with advances in age. Older children are able, therefore, to handle a multiplicity of processing requirements, taking into account and reconciling numerous considerations in their efforts to cope with the demands of the specific situation.

The study of social understanding in context

The results of those studies attempting to link social cognition and social behavior underscore the need to examine how social understanding functions as a determinant of social interaction *in context.* Correlational methodologies constitute a relatively weak strategy for constructing developmental theories of socialization that combine children's social understanding and their social behavior. The lack of correspondence reported between measures of cognitive and social competence may reflect no more than differences in the amount and the nature of information in "real-life" social encounters as compared to laboratory and hypothetical situations (Damon, 1977; Shantz, 1975). Halliday (1977) and Shultz and Butkowsky (1977) provided evidence, for example, that conclusions drawn about the inferential reasoning skills of young children may be virtually inseparable from the means by which those data were collected. Halliday (1977) argued that any task involves a specific series of cognitive processes and that failure at a given task would not necessarily imply an absence of cognitive skill. Shultz and Butkowsky (1977) demonstrated that 5-year-old children who were unable to apply multiple sufficient cause schemes in their evaluation of hypothetical, verbally presented stories nevertheless evidenced competent application of those schemes in response to the presentation of behavior on videotape. Shultz and Butkowsky's results call into question that tacit, but pervasive, assumption that hypothetical behavior is not analyzed any differently from "real" behavior. Given the extensive use of this stratagem in studies of children's social attributions, we would do well to look for cross validation of results using other paradigms.

Recent adult social psychological research is replete with examples of how one's preconceptions of interpretations of a social situation may influence the aspects of an interaction attended to and recalled as well as the evaluation of the actors involved. Zadny and Gerard (1974) demonstrated that the ascription of a specific intention to an actor, prior to observing the actor's behavior, biases attention and recall in favor of intent-related actions. These investigators go on to suggest that, in the course of ongoing interaction, individuals surmise the intent of another at the outset of the interaction and that inferred intent selectively focuses attention on particular aspects of the other's subsequent behavior. A bias favoring such a strategy would presumably ease the cognitive demands of social interactions.

Nevertheless, Word, Zanna, and Cooper (1974) and Snyder and Swann (1978) have demonstrated the consequences of social perception for interpersonal interaction. Word, Zanna, and Cooper (1974) used an interracial interview situation to demonstrate that individuals with given preconceptions about another may behave in such a way as to elicit behavior confirmatory to their original conceptions. White interviewers treated black confederate job applicants in a less positive manner than white confederates. Subsequently, confederate interviewers, trained to behave as the rejecting white interviewers had, were effective in eliciting reciprocal negative behavior from naive white interviewees. Word and his colleagues argued that the negative quality of some interactions may not necessarily stem from any negative qualities inherent in the actors but from the dynamics of their interaction. Thus, Snyder and Swann (1978) led college students to erroneously attribute hostility to their opponents in a reaction-time task. Given false conceptions, these students elicited behavior from their opponents that confirmed their initial expectations. In addition, they found not only that the opponent came to behave as had been expected but that some opponents began to see themselves as hostile. It was concluded that these students had succeeded in "socializing" hostility within the laboratory.

It seems unlikely that analogous processes of selective attending and eliciting behavioral confirmation of preconceptions would not also be operative among children. Presumably, children form expectations about particular interactions and act in accordance with those expectations. To date, however, developmental research has been characterized by a lack of concurrent and independent measurement of cognition and social behavior during the course of interaction. Investigators have chosen either to assess cognition using a laboratory instrument or to draw inferences from observed behavior without measuring cognitions directly. What has been missing has been knowledge about the nature of social interaction from the child's point of view, an appreciation of the impact of development on that knowledge, and an examination of the effects of knowledge or perception on interaction.

To illustrate one way in which future investigations may explore the constraints of cognitive development upon social understanding and social behavior and, at the same time, examine the understanding of social interaction in the context of ongoing social exchange, we now describe two studies of children's simultaneous use of multiple information sources. Our experimental paradigm is an analog of social interaction. A programmed confederate assumes the role of the subject child's partner in a game-playing situation. Although the constrained quality of this interaction may limit the ability to generalize our findings, we believe that such research demonstrates the value of employing a variety of paradigms for the generation and evaluation of hypotheses regarding the extent to which cognitive development modulates social development and vice versa.

Two investigations of social understanding in context

The two studies that follow[1] concern children's utilization of two sources of information as determinants of their social behavior: (a) instructions defining reward contingencies, and (b) the actions of the person(s) with whom the individual interacts. These sources of information variance were studied by placing first-, third-, and fifth-grade children in two-person situations. Each child was told that he or she would play a board game called Spinning Wheels with another child of the same age and sex – a child ostensibly seated in an adjacent room. The role of the companion child, however, was actually played by a second experimenter.

The gameboard consisted of ten circles, sectored into colored spaces, and interconnected by bridges. By moving alternately from opposite ends of the gameboard, players could progress from one circle to the next by landing exactly on the bridges. On each trial, the subject child or the companion was confronted with a choice of moving the other player's marker two or four spaces. A cooperative response moved the other player's marker either the greater distance toward a bridge without moving it beyond or landed the marker on a bridge, thus permitting access to the next circle. A competitive response moved the other player's marker either the smaller distance or beyond a bridge, thus necessitating another trip around the circle. Throughout the game, both children's markers were advanced to allow the subject child to keep track of his or her own and the other player's progress.

Forty boys and forty girls from each of the three grade levels were randomly assigned to four experimental conditions. Experimenter's instructions established cooperative or competitive incentives. Under cooperative incentive conditions, players were told that they would share rewards equally based upon their combined progress around the gameboard, whereas under competitive incentive conditions, only the player progressing farther around the gameboard was to be rewarded. Preprogrammed responses were made by the second experimenter (i.e., the bogus companion) – either 100% cooperative or 100% competitive – to provide information about the other player's behavior. The children thus received information about their companion's behavior that was either congruent or incongruent with the "rules of the game." That is, the instructions inducing cooperation were paired with either cooperative or competitive companions, and instructions inducing competition were paired with one of the same two companion conditions.

The children's social behavior was measured in instrumental terms by the proportion of cooperative choices made by the subject for the companion child at critical points in the game and the proportion of cooperative choices made on routine trials. Critical points in the game were defined as those occasions on which the child had the opportunity to force the companion to skip over a bridge; the remaining trials were considered "routine."

Three-way analyses of variance – grade by incentive condition by companion behavior – were computed for each of these proportion scores. As expected, the impact of incentive condition and companion behavior on cooperation varied with the developmental status of the child. At all ages the subject's behavior was related to the companion's behavior on both critical and routine trials. With cooperative companions, the children were cooperative; with competitive companions, they were competitive. However, the effects of incentive conditions varied according to age. The reward contingencies had little effect on the behavior of first-graders, who were equally cooperative under both cooperative and competitive incentive conditions. On the other hand, third- and fifth-graders responded differentially to the two incentive conditions; they were more cooperative under cooperative incentive conditions and more competitive under competitive reward distribution. Among third-graders, the two information sources were additive; each information source was related to cooperation independent of the other. The behavior of the fifth-graders, however, was consistent with a multiplicative model of information integration. These children were biased toward cooperation whenever a cooperative cue was present – either in combination with another cooperative cue or in combination with a competitive one.

Predictions about the companion's behavior were sought at three points during the game – once in advance of playing the game, once before a routine trial, and once before a critical trial – as independent evidence of the children's interpretations of the game-playing situation. A significant grade by incentive interaction revealed that the anticipation of cooperation in advance of playing the game was almost entirely suppressed under "winner take all" conditions among third-graders and fifth-graders, whereas the expectation of cooperation among first-graders was at a chance level. Predictions of cooperation prior to the start of the game under shared-reward conditions continued to be suppressed among third-graders and approximated chance response among first-graders. Only the fifth-grade children anticipated cooperation under shared-reward conditions. There was also a significant grade by companion interaction for the children's expectations during the course of the game. The accuracy of prediction with competitive companions increased from a chance level at first-grade to virtual certainty by fifth grade. Both first- and fifth-graders

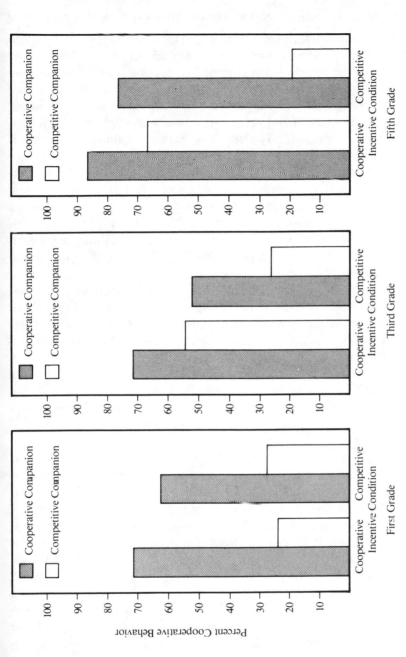

Figure 1. Mean percent cooperation scores for first-, third-, and fifth-grade children by incentive condition and companion response for critical trials (Study 1).

were significantly above chance level in accurately predicting the response of their companion when the companion was cooperative.

Taken as a whole, the results suggest that developmental differences in children's utilization of pertinent social information may determine the nature of their social interaction. The fifth-grade children integrated the two types of information and seemingly did so within a normative framework favoring cooperation. This suggests that the development of normative activity, be it cooperative or competitive, may complicate the manner in which social information is utilized. In contrast, the behavior of first-graders was predicted from the companion's behavior alone. When asked, both before and after the game, first-graders were able to restate the reward contingencies but, as they did not act in accordance with them, their understanding of the reward contingencies may have been insufficient to carry over from the instructional phase of the game to the interactive phase. The chance-level prediction of cooperation prior to the beginning of the game by first-graders under both incentive conditions supports this interpretation. However, it should also be noted that third-graders did not anticipate cooperative behavior from their partners under cooperation-inducing incentives, although they behaved differently under the two incentive conditions.

Markman (1977, 1979) argued that young children's comprehension failures result from superficial processing. Kindergarten to sixth-grade children were presented with instructions on how to perform an activity such as a magic trick and then were asked to demonstrate that activity. Crucial information necessary to the execution of the task was omitted, and age differences were observed in children's recognition of their failure to understand and in their awareness that necessary information was omitted. The youngest children did not become aware of the need for additional information until they attempted to act out the instructions. Markman posited that the youngest children were more passive listeners; they did not mentally execute the steps required to accomplish the task as they were presented. Follow-up investigations, comparing the presence and absence of demonstration accompanying the instructions, revealed that removing the necessity of mental processing facilitated the young children's ability to recognize that the experimenter's instructions were incomplete. Given these results, it might be hypothesized that if our subjects had been exposed to a set of strategies for playing the Spinning Wheels game, their understanding of reward contingencies and the subsequent translation of those contingencies into interaction would have been facilitated. Alternatively, providing the children with external cues to remind them of the reward contingencies may facilitate their continued application throughout the game.

A second study was thus designed to examine the effects of two interventions with the younger children: (a) a strategy aimed at improving understanding the basic task and (b) a strategy aimed at mainstreaming knowledge about the reward contingencies during the interaction with the companion. The experimental procedure was identical to that used in the first experiment, with the exception that each child was exposed to one of four extra treatments: (a) *rehearsal of strategies;* (b) *scorekeeping during the social interactions;* (c) *rehearsal with scorekeeping;* or (d) *no facilitation.* Children in the two rehearsal conditions practiced enhancing and hindering the progress of the companion's markers around the gameboard before information about the reward contingencies was given and before interacting with their partners. After mastering the alternative strategies, these children were then presented with the incentive instructions, that is, the reward contingencies. Children in the scorekeeping groups were provided with equipment to keep a running tally of the rewards distributed during the game itself. Children in the no facilitation group were presented with the incentive instructions only, thereby replicating the procedure used in Experiment 1. It was predicted that rehearsal and scorekeeping would both enhance the young children's use of the incentive information through improved understanding of the basic task and through heightened salience of the reward contingencies.

Equal numbers of first-grade boys and girls ($N = 160$) were randomly assigned to each of the four experimental conditions in each treatment group. Three-way analyses of variance were computed for proportion of both critical and routine choices. The companion's behavior influenced cooperation in critical situations, whereas incentive information influenced cooperation in both critical and routine situations. Although there were no interactions of treatment with either incentive or companion's behavior, subsequent analyses based on the a priori hypotheses revealed the following: First, incentive information had no significant effect on the behavior of the children in the no-facilitation group, thus replicating the results obtained in the initial study. Second, among the children receiving rehearsal alone, scorekeeping alone, or rehearsal *with* scorekeeping, the two information sources were additive – cooperation was more extensive under "shared rewards" than "winner take all."

These results indicate that first-graders use incentive information to guide their behavior when they are provided with appropriate cognitive strategies to mediate the application of abstract knowledge to task perfor-

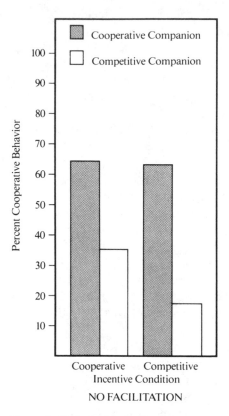

Figure 2. Critical trials replication mean percent cooperation scores for no facilitation condition by incentive condition and companion response (Study 2).

mance. Predictions about the companion's behavior were also sought before the start of the game and once each before a routine and a critical trial. Although children in all intervention conditions tended to predict that their companions would behave in keeping with the reward contingencies before the start of the game, only under the rehearsal-with-score-keeping conditions did the children discriminate significantly between incentive conditions in their predictions, anticipating cooperation under shared rewards and competition under "winner take all." Accuracy in predicting the companion's behavior did not differ across intervention conditions or reward contingencies. However, predictions tended to be least accurate when the companion's behavior was not consistent with the reward contingencies in effect, particularly when companions "behaved" competitively even though cooperation was called for.

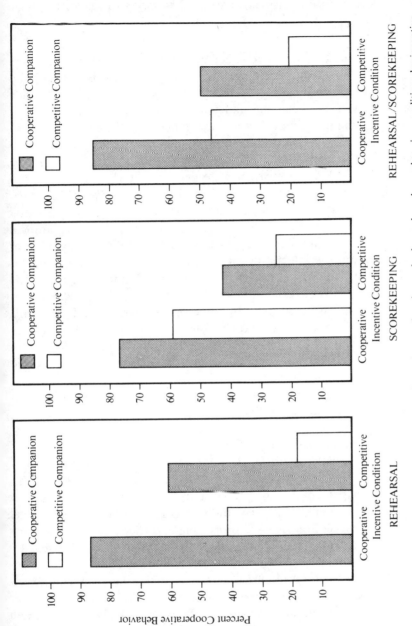

Figure 3. Mean percent cooperation scores for rehearsal, score-keeping and rehearsal, and scorekeeping conditions by incentive condition and companion response for critical trials (Study 2).

Implications

The results of these investigations demonstrate the manner in which cognitive processes and the developmental constraints upon them may influence the pattern and course of social interaction. Efforts were made simultaneously to examine the understanding of social behavior and to measure ongoing interaction in the same experimental context. Developmental differences in children's responses to the congruence between another's behavior and the rules governing reward distribution could be accounted for, at least in part, by differences in the children's ability to use the incentive information provided and by differences in the nature of the interaction that these children anticipated. We have assumed that competent or adaptive social interaction requires attention to situational features, the encoding of relevant situational information, integration of that information, the selection of a behavioral strategy, the implementation of that strategy, and, finally, the assessment of the effects of that behavior. A child must respond to the behavior of another, make appropriate attributions as determined by situational constraints and the child's own experience, and use these attributions as guides in further commerce with the other individual. In effect, adaptive behavior requires both the simultaneous and successive consideration of the other interactors and the context in which their interaction occurs.

Although the psychological complexities of social interaction are extraordinary, there is every reason to assume that these complexities can be unraveled. The construction, receipt, transformation, storage, retrieval, and interrelation of social information takes place, as Flavell (1977) has suggested, "in the same head as the processing of non-social information," and it would be surprising if there were no parallels to be found between perception, comprehension, and utilization of social and nonsocial information. Moreover, there is every reason to believe that we can refract social information processing and its use in social interaction at least as effectively as we can refract the child's processing of nonsocial information.

The success of future research on the cognitive mediators of social behavior, however, requires the reevaluation of certain assumptions about social knowledge and the interrelationship of knowledge and action. For example, age differences in children's evaluations of actors have been assumed to reflect differences in judgment criteria, but Sedlak (1979) suggests that even children as young as 8 years of age represent intentional information and use intention in their evaluations of actors' behaviors. The results of Dodge's (1980) observations corroborate this conclusion, as he noted that children responded differently to aggressive behavior as a function of the intent imputed to the aggressor. Developmental differences may be attributed, instead, to differences in understanding or processing. Using Schmidt's (1976) three-phase model for identifying another's plan, Sedlak hypothesized that differences between child and adult judgments originate in the plan schema, or the external consistency phases, of plan determination. After selecting some outcome as a goal, adults presumably elaborate this impression by filling in additional information implied by the acceptance of that particular goal. Before the hypothesized plan is accepted, the adult also compares the plan against observations of the actor's behavior. Children's evaluations, which diverge from adultlike judgments, suggest less complete elaboration of hypothesized plans or failure to adequately search for confirming or disconfirming evidence during the external consistency phase of plan determination.

Gnepp, Klayman, and Trabasso (in press) studied the sources of information children use to infer the affective states of others. They observed the same hierarchy of preferred information sources operative at three age levels: preschool, second grade, and college. They acknowledge that developmental differences may be attributable to accessibility of information, to changes in the ability to perceive or to interpret information, or to changes in the ability of children to resolve cognitive conflict. Markman (1977) argued that as individuals develop they become more active in monitoring and evaluating their own cognitive activities. The results of our research are consistent with these hypotheses about age changes in cognitive processing. We believe that the differences in the use of incentive information and feedback about a companion's behavior between first and fifth grade do not reflect differences in preferred sources of information so much as differences in the accessibility of information to children of varying ages. The findings suggest that the functional equivalence of stimuli across ages cannot be assumed but must be demonstrated.

What implications do these conclusions about cognitive processing have for the study of social interaction? Most research derived from attribution theory focuses on the manner in which individuals process information to form an impression of others. The study of the relation between perception and behavior, however, might be furthered by examining the ways in which perceivers construct the information that they process. Snyder, Tanke, and Berscheid (1977) cite evidence for the self-fulfilling nature of social impressions, proposing that impressions constrain social exchange in ways that cause others to behave so as to confirm the perceiver's initial expectations. Similar dynamics were implied in Dodge's (1980) study of children's aggressive behavior. Children's interpretations of others' behavior had direct implications for the behavior that peers subsequently elicited from each other. Such findings suggest the need to revise currently accepted models of dyadic interaction. Actors are guided by their own perceptions as well as by the impressions or expectations of others. Individuals tend to elicit behavior that confirms their prejudices, implying that social perceptions may be the cause as well as the consequence of social acts. A model that accounted for this aspect of mutual influence would reflect yet another way in which cognitions mediate social exchange.

Finally, investigators will need to measure social behavior and social cognition in the same context if we are to further our understanding of the interaction of cognition. Although children in our second study behaved differently under cooperative and competitive incentive conditions, in only one instance did they anticipate significantly different behavior from their companions as a function of the incentive condition. The fifth-grade children in the first study were the only children to reliably predict cooperative actions from their partners under cooperation-inducing incentives. These observations illustrate the danger of assuming that behavior and cognitions are synonymous, that they can be readily inferred from each other, and that they are susceptible to the same contextual constraints. Multiple and independent assessment of cognitions and actions is required if our understanding is to match the complexity of the phenomena under investigation.

Too often, the term *social cognition* signifies an effort to demonstrate either that individual differences in cognitive abilities are correlated with individual differences in social competence or that information about the social world is isomorphic with information in the physical world. The challenge facing the social developmentalist is not to formulate a theory of cognition about social objects but to describe the maintenance of coherent social interaction in context, for the individual is not only an observer of the social domain but an actor within it, and social knowledge is acquired and maintained interactively. In our view, more interesting inquiries would address the manner in which the cognitive processes, and the developmental constraints upon them, determine the pattern and course of social interaction ongoing between the child and other individuals.

Note

1 These two studies are the basis of a doctoral dissertation submitted by Judith E. Brady to the Graduate School, University of Minnesota.

References

Abelson, R. P. Script processing in attitude formation and decision-making. In J. S. Carroll & J. W. Payne (Eds.), *Cognition and social behavior*. Hillsdale, N.J.: Erlbaum, 1976.

Abelson, R. P. Psychological status of the script concept. *American Psychologist*, 1981, *36*, 715–729.

Ajzen, I., & Fishbein, M. Attitude-behavior relations: A theoretical analysis and review of empirical research. *Psychologic Bulletin*, 1977, *84*, 888–918.

Berndt, T. J. Relations between social cognition, non-social cognition, and social behavior: The case of friendship. In J. Flavell & L. Ross (Eds.), *Social cognitive development* Cambridge: Cambridge University Press, 1981.

Bower, G. H., Black, J. B., & Turner, T. J. Scripts in memory for text. *Cognitive Psychology*, 1979, *11*, 177–220.

Bransford, J. D., & Franks, J. J. The abstraction of linguistic ideas. *Cognitive Psychology*, 1971, *2*, 331–350.

Brown, A. The construction of temporal succession by preoperational children. In A. D. Pick (Ed.), *Minnesota Symposia on Child Psychology* (Vol. 10). Minneapolis: University of Minnesota Press, 1976.

Chandler, M. J. Egocentrism and antisocial behavior: The assessment and training of social perspective taking skills. *Developmental Psychology*, 1973, *9*, 326–332.

Cutrona, C. E., & Feshbach, S. Cognitive and behavioral correlates of children's differential use of social information. *Child Development*, 1979, *50*, 1036–1042.

Damon, W. *The social world of the child*. San Francisco: Jossey-Bass, 1977.

Damon, W. Exploring children's social cognition on two fronts. In J. H. Flavell & L. Ross (Eds.), *Social cognitive development*. Cambridge: Cambridge University Press, 1981.

D'Andrade, R. *Cultural belief systems*. Unpublished manuscript, University of California, at Irvine, 1972.

Deutsch, F. Observational and sociometric measures of peer popularity and their relationship to egocentric communication in female preschoolers. *Developmental Psychology*, 1974, *10*, 745–747.

Dodge, K. A. Social cognition and children's aggressive behavior. *Child Development*, 1980, *51*, 162–170.

Feshbach, N. D., & Feshbach, S. The relationship between empathy and aggression in two age groups. *Developmental Psychology*, 1969, *1*, 102–107.

Flavell, J. *Cognitive development*. Englewood Cliffs, N.J.: Prentice-Hall, 1977.

Flavell, J. H. & Ross, L. (Ed.), *Social cognitive development*. Cambridge: Cambridge University Press, 1981.

Forbes, D. Recent research on children's social cognition. In W. Damon (Ed.), *Social cognition: New directions in child development*. San Francisco: Jossey-Bass, 1978.

Garvey, C. Some properties of social play. *Merrill-Palmer Quarterly of Behavior and Development*, 1974, *20*, 163–180.

Garvey, C., & Berndt, R. *The organization of pretend play*. Unpublished manuscript, Johns Hopkins University, 1975.

Girgus, J. S., & Wolf, J. Age changes in the ability to encode social cues. *Developmental Psychology*, 1975, *11*, 118.

Glick, J. Cognition and social cognition: An introduction. In J. Glick & K. A. Clarke-Stewart (Eds.), *The development of social understanding*. New York: Gardner Press, 1978.

Glick, J., & Clark-Stewart, K. A. (Eds.) *The development of social understanding*. New York: Gardner Press, 1978.

Gnepp, J., Klayman, J., & Trabasso, T. A hierarchy of information sources for inferring emotional reactions. *Journal of Experimental Child Psychology*, in press.

Halliday, M. S. Behavioral inference in young children. *Journal of Experimental Child Psychology*, 1977, *23*, 378–390.

Kahneman, D., & Tversky, A. On the psychology of prediction. *Psychological Review*, 1973, *80*, 237–251.

Kurdek, L. A., & Rodgon, M. M. Perceptual, cognitive, and affective perspective taking in kindergarten through sixth-grade children. *Developmental Psychology*, 1975, *11*, 643–650.

Livesley, W. J., & Bromley, D. B. *Person perception in childhood and adolescence*. London: Wiley, 1973.

Markman, E. Realizing that you don't understand: A preliminary investigation. *Child Development*, 1977, *48*, 983–992.

Markman, E. Realizing that you don't understand: Elementary school children's awareness of inconsistencies. *Child Development*, 1979, *50*, 643–655.

Nelson, K. Social cognition in a script framework. In J. Flavell & L. Ross (Eds.), *Social cognitive development: Frontiers and possible futures*. Cambridge: Cambridge University Press, 1981.

Nisbett, R., & Borgida, E. Attribution and the psychology of prediction. *Journal of Personality and Social Psychology*, 1975, *32*, 932–943.

Nisbett, R., Borgida, E., Crandall, R., & Reed, H. Popular induction: Information is not necessarily informative. In J. S. Carroll & J. W. Payne (Eds.), *Cognition and social behavior*. Hillsdale, N.J.: Erlbaum, 1976.

Nisbett, R., & Ross, L. *Human inference: Strategies and shortcomings of social judgment*. Englewood Cliffs, N.J.: Prentice-Hall, 1980.

Paris, S. G., & Lindauer, B. Constructive aspects of children's comprehension and memory. In E. C. Kail & J. W. Hagen (Eds.), *Perspectives on the development of memory and cognition*. Hillsdale, N.J.: Erlbaum, 1977.

Peevers, B. H., & Secord, P. F. Developmental changes in attribution of descriptive concepts to persons. *Journal of Personality and Social Psychology*, 1973, *27*, 120–128.

Rothenberg, B. Children's social sensitivity and the relationship to interpersonal competence, intrapersonal comfort, and intellectual level. *Developmental Psychology*, 1970, *2*, 335–350.

Rubin, K. H., & Schneider, F. W. The relationship between moral judgment, egocentrism, and altruistic behavior. *Child Development*, 1973, *44*, 661–665.

Rushton, J. P., & Wiener, J. Altruism and cognitive development in children. *British Journal of Social and Clinical Psychology*, 1975, *14*, 341–349.

Schank, R. C., & Abelson, R. *Scripts, plans, goals, and understanding*. Hillsdale, N.J.: Erlbaum, 1977.

Schmidt, C. F. Understanding human action: Recognizing the plans and motives of other persons. In J. S. Carroll & J. W. Payne, (Eds.), *Cognition and social behavior*. Hillsdale, N.J.: Erlbaum, 1976.

Sedlak, A. J. Developmental differences in understanding plans and evaluating actors. *Child Development*, 1979, *50*, 536–560.

Selman, R. L. Toward a structural analysis of developing interpersonal concepts: Research with normal and disturbed preadolescent boys. In A. D. Pick (Ed.), *Minnesota Symposia on Child psychology* (Vol. 10). Minneapolis: University of Minnesota Press, 1976.

Shantz, C. U. The development of social cognition. In E. M. Hetherington (Ed.), *Review of child development research* (Vol. 5). Chicago: University of Chicago Press, 1975.

Shultz, T. R., & Butkowsky, I. Young children's use of the scheme for multiple sufficient causes in the attribution of real and hypothetical behavior. *Child Development*, 1977, *48*, 464–469.

Smith, M. C. Cognizing the behavior stream: The recognition of international action. *Child Development*, 1978, *49*, 736–743.

Snyder, M., & Swann, W. B. Behavioral confirmation in social interaction: From social perception to social reality. *Journal of Experimental Social Psychology*, 1978, *14*, 148–162.

Snyder, M., Tanke, E., & Berscheid, E. Social perception and interpersonal behavior: On the self-fulfilling nature of social stereotypes. *Journal of Personality and Social Psychology*, 1977, *35*, 656–666.

Spivak, G., & Shure, M. B. *Social adjustment of young children*. San Francisco: Jossey-Bass, 1974.

Stein, N. L., & Glenn, C. G. An analysis of story comprehension in elementary school children. In R. O. Freedle (Ed.), *New directions in discourse processing* (Vol. 2). Norwood, N.J.: Ablex, 1979.

Stein, N. L., & Goldman, S. R. Children's knowledge about social situations: From causes to consequences. In S. Asher & J. Gottman (Eds.), *The development of friendship*. Cambridge: Cambridge University, Press, 1981.

Trope, Y., & Burnstein, E. Processing the information contained in another's behavior. *Journal of Experimental Social Psychology*, 1975, *11*, 439–458.

Word, C. O., Zanna, M. P., & Cooper, J. The nonverbal mediation of self-fulfilling prophecies in interracial interaction. *Journal of Experimental Social Psychology*, 1974, *20*, 109–210.

Wyer, R. S., & Carlston, D. E. *Social cognition, inference, and attribution*. Hillsdale, N.J.: Erlbaum, 1979.

Zadny, J., & Gerard, H. B. Attributed intentions and information selectivity. *Journal of Experimental Social Psychology*, 1974, *10*, 34–52.

Zahn-Waxler, C., Radke-Yarrow, M., & Brady-Smith, J. Perspective-taking and prosocial behavior. *Developmental Psychology*, 1977, *13*, 87–88.

5 Social antecedents, cognitive processing, and comprehension of social portrayals on television

W. Andrew Collins

Television, invented and propagated to entertain, has gradually become the focus of more popular and scientific attention in the study of children than any other socialization force except family and school. As has been the case with several other topics in the study of social development (see Sears, 1975), interest in television has emerged from circumstances that are partly ecological and demographic, partly historical-political, and partly scientific. From the perspective of social effects on children, the impetus can be stated simply: Television has been thought to convey to children a unique variety and volume of social models that could socialize attitudes, behaviors, and expectations about social life. The extensive research literature on television and children (Comstock et al., 1978) largely reflects the deterministic tone of this statement; the predominant questions have been whether and in what ways children generally are affected by television viewing. Much less attention has been given to the responses of children of varying ages, abilities, and social backgrounds to social models that commonly occur on television.

In this chapter I review some recent research on developmental and individual differences in children's understanding of the social behaviors, roles, and relationships portrayed in typical programs. A major premise of these studies is that the effects of televised social models are partly determined by cognitive, social, and individual characteristics that affect children's representations of what they see. The research itself involves examining children's processing across a variety of television programs, with the goal of specifying some sources and effects of variability in comprehension. Later in the chapter I will discuss how analysis of natu-

Preparation of this chapter was facilitated by Grant No. 24197 from the National Institute of Mental Health to W. Andrew Collins and by support from the Boys Center for the Study of Youth Development, Omaha, Nebraska.

rally occurring social stimuli may be of value in the study of social cognition and social behavior.

Views on the effects of television

Relatively few of the large number of studies on the effects of television have focused on the child as a viewer (for reviews see Comstock et al., 1978; Stein & Friedrich, 1975). Rather, the field has been influenced by its sociological forebears toward a "dominant-image" view (e.g., Gerbner, 1972; Liebert, Neale, & Davidson, 1973) concerned primarily with the incidence of certain types of content, like violence. In this view the frequency of a behavior's occurrence, not the viewer's perception of its function or significance within a narrative, is socially influential; the most frequently occurring images determine the major effects of television. Viewers, whether children, youth, or adults, are commonly pictured as passive recipients of a series of salient images, from which they make no attempt to extract unique social meanings. The most influential psychological formulation in the past decade of research on television and children, Bandura's theory of observational learning (e.g., Bandura, 1965, 1969; Goranson, 1970), has often been assimilated to a dominant-image view, despite Bandura's (e.g., Bandura, 1977) recent focus on retention processes and the relevance of the context of modeled action to performance.

A more differentiated view of effects appears in other psychological perspectives on television and children (e.g., Comstock et al., 1978; Feshbach & Singer, 1971; Leifer, Gordon, & Graves, 1974; Liebert, Neale, & Davidson, 1973; Maccoby, 1964; Siegel, 1975; Stein & Friedrich, 1975). Rather than being determined primarily by salient social models (e.g., violence, prosocial behavior), postviewing behavior is also seen partly as a function of extra-presentation age and social-group correlates of postviewing behaviors. For example, postviewing aggressive behavior may be influenced by (1) the results of antecedent social learning (e.g., internalization of social and moral values, previous direct or vicarious experience with the observed behaviors) and (2) states and circumstances subsequent to viewing (e.g., opportunities for behavior and their circumstances, including provocation, existing or expected sanctions, and emotional arousal). These correlates of outcome behaviors are assumed to heighten or reduce viewers' motivations to adopt salient social behaviors from television programs; the implicit equation is one in which the separate motivational factors are weighted and combined to determine an outcome. In short, age-related and individual differences in outcomes are largely seen as the result of variation in the nature and extent of socialization of pertinent behavioral and emotional tendencies.

The role of comprehension

Emphases on the occurrence of certain types of models and motivational factors in the social outcomes of viewing have largely overshadowed issues of whether and how children process social models in typical programs. Yet television portrayals are considerably more complex and more subject to vagaries in comprehension than the laboratory analogs in most research on basic modeling processes. Younger, less cognitively skilled viewers may process these complex materials differently or less adequately than older viewers. Furthermore, besides predicting certain categories of social actions, antecedent social experiences may influence children's attention to, and retention of, portrayals of television characters and events, which in turn mediate the social influence of many television programs (Omanson, 1979).

An example illustrates this point. A commonly portrayed character in many typical entertainment programs is the "double-dealer," who superficially appears benevolent but is subtly and gradually revealed to be malevolent. Preschool and young grade school viewers may well fail to comprehend the duplicity in such a characterization (Collins & Zimmermann, 1975) and in many instances may evaluate the character's behavior more positively than the plot warrants. According to prevailing theories of behavioral effects, a duplicitous character would probably thus be more readily emulated than one for whom contextual cues were more consistently negative. Young viewers in particular would be more affected by such a model than older, more experienced viewers, who would be apt to recognize the pertinent negative cues, discount the apparently positive ones, and evaluate the character negatively.

Other factors besides developmental ones may also affect children's comprehension. Children who are especially familiar with an ambiguous character's social role and the circumstances of the portrayed behavior are in a better position to weigh apparently conflicting cues. For example, in one instance of pilot research, some young children were interviewed after seeing a plot in which the focal characters in a plot were a duplicitous white plain-clothes policeman and a Hispanic community organizer, whose laudable intentions were confounded by a contentious manner. White children viewed the Hispanic character more negatively than the policeman, and justified their evaluation by citing matters of appearance and interpersonal style. Non-white children, however, seemed to recognize the underlying goals of the Hispanic character in their explanations and judge him more positively. In other views of children's responses to social models, social factors like class or ethnic background have been considered important correlates of the viewer's tendency to engage in the modeled behaviors. Imitation of the minority character by minority children might be attributable either to a strong base-line tendency for members of the same social group to engage in a behavior or a motivation to emulate the behavior of a model with whom they could readily identify. In our view, the effects of the similarity between model and viewer in the present example probably also reflect more cognitive components, such as the attention-directing function of similarity and preference (cf. Bartlett, 1932; Krebs, 1970) and the facilitative effects of prior knowledge on the processing of the particulars of the plot in which the model is portrayed. In the remainder of the chapter, I will discuss some research findings relevant both to age-related strategies for processing information from complex programs and to the ways in which a child's prior relevant social experiences affect comprehension of social information on television.

Developmental aspects of comprehension

At this point, more extensive evidence is available about developmental differences in comprehension of typical television programs than about the differential effects of individual experience and predispositions. Most information about developmental aspects of processing comes from studies of children's understanding of dramatic programs produced for adults. These narrative programs – action-adventure programs, family dramas, situation comedies – are devised with sufficient complication to keep adult viewers interested; the particulars of the plots are often subtle, inexplicit, and interspersed with extraneous or tangentially relevant material. We have focused on the extent to which children of different ages retain two kinds of information from these complex television plots: (1) *explicit events* that occur in single scenes of the program, particularly those that are essential to the sense of the plot, and (2) *implicit information* that is not explicitly mentioned or depicted but is implied by the relations between scenes. For example, consider the following two hypothetical explicit events: Character *A* observes Character *B* steal something; later, *B* jumps *A* from behind as *A* enters a room. The causal relation between these two events (that *B* jumped *A* because *A* witnessed the theft he committed) is only implicit in the program and must be inferred by the viewer. We have been especially interested in this process of *temporal integration,* in which viewers must infer the relations among discretely presented units of information across time (Collins, 1977).

The measures used to assess comprehension are developed in several steps. The first task is an event analysis similar to that suggested by Warren, Nicholas, and Trabasso (1979) and by Omanson (1979), in which the essential elements of the plot and the relations among them are represented. Subsequently, panels of adults are asked to rate the importance of the content items and also to retell the story, including the essential elements. These panels generally show considerable agreement (across studies, between .76 and .94) about the essential items of content in programs. Next, children are asked open-ended questions about the plot to elicit words and phrases that are likely to be understandable to children when referring to the programs. Finally, multiple-choice recognition items are written to cover the essential information in the narrative, using wordings for stems and for both correct and incorrect alternatives that come from the children's responses in the pretest interviews.

One example may clarify the nature of the recognition measure. An explicit content item might concern a violent act ("When Luke was walking in the alley he . . . saw a man steal some money"). Another might concern a later act of violence ("When Luke walked into the office, another man . . . jumped on him from behind"). A subsequent question then concerns the cause of the fight ("Someone jumped on Luke . . . because Luke knew he had stolen the money"). The first two questions deal with explicit content; the third, with an inference about the implicit cause–effect relation between them. The measure thus taps children's abilities to verify the occurrence of on-screen events and the implicit relations among them. In addition, choices of incorrect alternatives, which are constructed to represent specific comprehension errors, permit both an analysis of difficulties in understanding programs and an assessment of the effects of guessing and response bias. Other nonrecognition procedures, selected according to the purpose of individual studies, are used to supplement the recognition measure.

Comprehension of explicit and implicit content

This approach has been used in several studies of children's comprehension. A brief review of one (Collins et al., 1978) illustrates the research strategy and exemplary findings. The stimulus program was an hour-long action-adventure show composed of two parallel subplots edited into four different versions. One version, the *simple* version, consisted of one of the plots. The second, or *complex,* version of the program contained the same plot, and in addition intermingled it with the second subplot, which was not necessary for comprehension of the basic story line. The third and fourth versions were *jumbled* renderings, in which scenes from the simple and complex versions were randomly ordered. This manipulation, which was designed to permit examination of effects of plot organization and complexity on processing by children of different ages, is described here to illustrate the stimulus variations over which the general comprehension patterns we found have been obtained.

In the experiment, one of these four versions was shown to second-, fifth-, and eighth-grade children ($N = 292$). After viewing, the children completed a recognition-items test about discrete scenes in the show and about the causal relationships that existed among the scenes. Second-graders remembered a significantly smaller proportion of the explicit content than did older children, adolescents, and adults. On these items, second-graders recalled an average of only 66% of the content that adults had judged as essential to the plot; fifth-graders recalled 84% of these scenes, and eighth-graders recalled 92%. These age differences occur regardless of plot length; and they parallel age trends reported in studies of situation comedies (Collins, 1970; Newcomb & Collins, 1979) and other action-adventure programs, including a period Western (Collins, in preparation).

Even when they do remember important explicit events, however, younger children often fail to grasp the interscene relations that also carry important information. Performance on the recognition measure of implicit information – the content that is not explicitly presented but is implicit in the relationships between discrete scenes – is shown in Figure 1. Second-graders had an overall mean score of fewer than half (47%) of the inference items adults had agreed upon as essential, and fifth- and eighth-graders scored 67% and 77%, respectively. However, as Figure 1 shows, children's ability to make the inferences required for understanding implicit information varied with the version of the stimulus program they watched. It is clear from both boys' and girls' data that fifth- and eighth-graders comprehended best in the two ordered conditions. This pattern is also apparent in the data for girls at the second-grade level, although their mean scores are markedly lower than those of older children. However, second-grade boys in all four conditions perform at chance level on this measure of inferences.

Second-graders' poor performance on the recognition inference items does not appear to be only an artifact of their poor knowledge of individual scenes. The conditional probabilities for correct inferences provide evidence of this, given that the children knew at the time they were tested

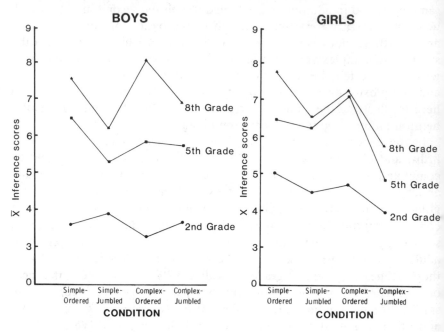

Figure 1. Boys' and girls' mean scores for inferences about the content of four versions of an action-adventure drama. (Data from Collins, Wellman, Keniston, & Westby, 1978.)

either both of the relevant premise scenes, only one of them, or neither one. It was possible to determine from questionnaire measures and supplementary interview probes whether individual children knew the two discrete scenes or the *premises* on which each of the inference items was based. The shaded bars in Figure 2 represent the probability that inference items were answered correctly, given that children knew both requisite pieces of discrete information. Clearly, the likelihood of correctly integrating important information about the plot across temporally separate discrete scenes is relatively small for second-graders; the probability is less than 50%, just greater than chance. The probabilities for fifth- and eighth-graders are considerably higher (68% and 75%, respectively). By contrast, the likelihood of correct inferences when there is evidence at testing that children know only one, or neither, of the premise scenes (shown in Figure 2 by the shaded bars) is just greater than chance at all three grade levels. Thus, given knowledge of the discrete, explicit scenes older children are more likely than younger children to infer the implied relationships among them.

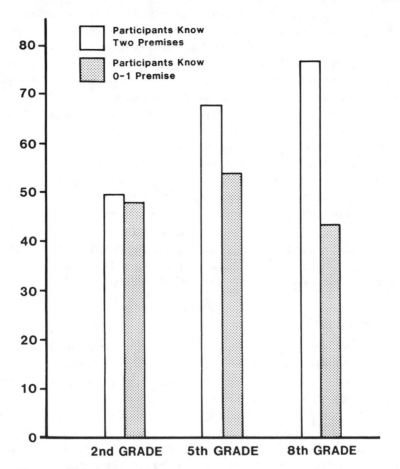

Figure 2. Conditional probabilities for correct inferences about relations between program events, given that both premises of the inference are known or that only one or neither of the premises is known. (Data from Collins, Wellman, Keniston, & Westby, 1978.)

Developmental differences of the sort described here have been replicated in studies of a number of different types of commercial dramatic television progams. As do developmental differences in comprehension of other kinds of materials, these age-related patterns appear to reflect emergence of strategies for "going beyond the information given." We have attempted in recent studies (Collins, in preparation; Purdie, Collins, & Westby, 1979) to examine whether this characterization is an apt one by tracing the course of processing during viewing. Briefly described, the procedure involves interrupting viewing at different points for different subgroups of children and then testing the children's knowledge of explicit content and inferences up to the point of interruption. Viewing is resumed after testing; and all children answer recognition items and interview questions about the remainder of the show when the program is over. One group of children sees the entire program without interruption and is then tested on the full battery of recognition items to provide a check on possible contamination of postinterruption answers in the other three conditions.

The interruption procedure revealed that children tested on content they had seen only minutes before performed no better than children who were asked the same questions at a later time. Apparently the comprehension difficulties of young grade school viewers are not attributable simply to forgetting; nor do they result from the interferences of intervening information, when children are tested without interruption at the end of a lengthy program. Rather, throughout the program the recognition of explicit content and inferences of implicit relationships was poorer for second-graders than for fifth- and eighth-graders.

Processing social cues

From this vantage point, let us now turn to some research in which we examined age-related comprehension of cues relevant to the evaluation of a televised social model, namely, motives for an antisocial act and the causal relation between motives and aggression.

In this study (Purdie, Collins, & Westby, 1979) the stimulus program was an edited version of a commercial-network action-adventure drama. The plot involved a man searching for his former wife to prevent her from presenting damaging testimony against him in a kidnapping case. He finds the house where she is hiding and shoots at her. His goal is thwarted by the arrival of law officers, and he is taken away in handcuffs. In editing the main events of the plot were retained, but some extraneous material and all commercials were deleted. We manipulated narrative sequence by creating one version in which the temporal distance between relevant premise scenes was reduced. Thus, in the *distal-motive version*, the protagonist's motives and aggression appeared in scenes that were approximately four minutes apart. In the *proximal-motive version*, motive and aggression information were presented in immediate sequence. One or the other of the two versions was then shown to 200 randomly selected second- and fifth-grade girls and boys.

As in our other research, there were pronounced grade differences on the recognition measure of comprehension. At both grade levels, however, children who saw the motive and aggression cues next to each other understood the implicit motive-aggression relationship better than children who saw the cues separated from each other. Apparently, reducing the distance between relevant cues facilitated integration of information about the protagonist's motive and aggression, especially for the second-graders. The conditional probability for correct inference items, given that children answered both discrete premises correctly, was .52 for proximal-motive viewers in the second grade, whereas distal-motive-condition second-graders made correct inferences at chance level (.29). Fifth-graders' probabilities were higher and essentially equal in both viewing conditions. Both age groups performed at chance level when only one, or neither, explicit premise was known.

These variations in children's recognition of explicit and implicit information about the motives and action of the character in the program influenced their impressions of the goodness or badness of the aggressor. Evaluations were assessed using a graduated-squares procedure (Costanzo et al., 1973), in which six size-graduated squares are labeled from "very bad" to "very good." Children point to the square that shows how good or how bad the character is. Children who answered all three motive-aggression inference questions correctly were significantly more negative in their evaluations of the aggressor than were children who understood two or fewer inferences. Whether motives and aggression were proximally or distally portrayed also affected evaluation. At both grades, distal-motive viewers evaluated the character less negatively then proximal-motive viewers, particularly following portrayal of the aggressive action. Thus, children's inferences about critical links were related to evaluative responses that potentially affect adoption of observed behaviors.

Children's representations of programs

Thus far the emphasis has been on what children fail to understand from typical portrayals. Let us now take another perspective on the problem: granted that – compared to older viewers – young grade school children comprehend less of the essential explicit and implicit content of programs, what *do* they take away from typical portrayals of characters and events? Recent analyses indicate that representations of programs are heavily affected by the knowledge about persons and sequences of events that children bring to viewing.

For example, in the study just described (Collins et al., 1978) two-thirds of the second- , fifth- , and eighth-graders were interrupted at one or the other of two points that had previously been agreed upon by adult

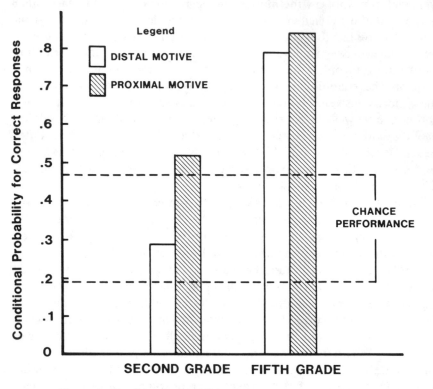

Figure 3. Conditional probabilities for correct responses by second- and fifth-grade children in the distal-motive and proximal-motive viewing conditions.

raters as suspense points, or scenes after which something noteworthy obviously was going to happen. During these interruptions, the children were asked what they thought was going to happen next and why, and their predictions were coded according to whether or not they mentioned events from the program in explaining their answers. (The predictions were not coded for accuracy.) The majority of the fifth- and eighth-graders (78% and 68%, respectively) predicted events that invoked, or followed from, the sequence of plot occurrences prior to interruption. For example, following a scene in which a murderer meets a panhandler who resembles the man he had killed, *relevant* predictions often involved the likelihood that the murderer would confuse the man with his earlier victim and provoke further mayhem ("He'll think he didn't kill the wino and will go after this guy"). Second-graders rarely (28% of the cases) predicted events that followed from the earlier events of the shows. Instead, they appeared to answer on the basis of the immediately preceding scene alone.

A typical prediction made by these children was simply that the villain would give the old panhandler some money. In many instances, of course, the common action sequences that young children cite are high-probability occurrences that can aid in understanding observed behavior. They are examples of what have been called *schemata* (e.g., Bartlett, 1932; Neisser, 1976) or *scripts* (Schank & Abelson, 1977), that is, group-ings of actions that are called into play when key parts of the action or characteristic settings are encountered. For example, in the instance of the killer and the panhandler, knowing that someone asks for money may initially suggest a sequence in which a handout is granted (even though it is inconsistent with the traits of the character in question here).

How do such expectations about social events enter into comprehension of social narratives? At this point only a speculative account can be offered. In constructing a representation, mature viewers may use increasingly more specialized action sequences. At one level comprehension may be based on various standard sequences that are evoked by details of the portrayal. For example, from seeing police in uniforms, even a young child could understand that the plot was a police story and could infer that police were chasing someone who was guilty of some transgressions and so forth. Thus, certain types of program-elicited *common knowledge* are likely to be represented in children's understanding. On the other hand, certain variations or embellishments on these simple sequences represent more *program-specific knowledge,* or more special-ized understandings, that would probably be typical only of older children. Applying these distinctions to the stimulus program studied by Collins and his associates (1978), the show probably evoked *common knowledge* about (1) policeman, (2) a murder committed by one of the characters, (3) this same person's being shot or apprehended by the police in the end, and (4) buying groceries (which the protagonist did repeat-edly in order to cash his forged checks; buying groceries is likely to be understood even by young children [Nelson, 1978]). *Program-specific knowledge* included information that (1) some nonuniformed characters were policemen, (2) the murder at the beginning occurred because the victim surprised the villain during a theft (a motive inference), and (3) the purpose behind buying groceries was cashing "fake" checks to get money.

These categories of content recently have been examined by Collins and Wellman (1980) in interview protocols from the children who partici-pated in the study by Collins and his associates (1978). The children had been asked to retell the narrative so that "someone would be able to tell what happened in the show." Wellman first had adults code content propositions from these interviews into either the program-elicited common knowledge or the program-specific knowledge categories (proportion of agreements was .98). He then noted the frequency with which children mentioned one or the other category of content in their narratives. As Table 1 shows, among second-graders the mean proportion of children who mentioned the content that fit scripts readily known by all age groups was 81%, but the mean proportion of these younger children who mentioned more specialized knowledge was only 16%. Fifth- and eighth-graders were just as likely as younger children to mention common knowledge, but many more older viewers mentioned program-specific knowledge. The relevant mean proportions in fifth and eighth grades were 55% and 98%, respectively, compared to 16% for second-graders. Thus, for viewers whose expectations coincide with what the actors do, think, and feel, both the explicit and implicit events in a television portrayal are probably relatively easy, because observations can be assimilated readily. For viewers who lack pertinent schemata or scripts, comprehension is probably more difficult.

In the study by Collins and his associates (1978), however, younger children mentioned some details just as frequently as older children but fewer program-specific details; and their comprehension of the program was generally poorer. Perhaps young viewers, even when they know many relevant scripts, apply them less flexibly than older children in comprehending new experiences. That is, once a script has been instantiated by a salient cue (e.g., the label "police" or seeing uniformed characters), younger children may behave as though the program simply follows a standard script; as a result, they may fail to notice or may ignore ways in which the program varies from the script. Consequently, central explicit and implicit details or particular narratives may be short-circuited by rigid expectations of actors and actions. More knowledgeable viewers may more readily recognize the significance of departures from scripts and process them as significant aspects of stories that override action scripts.

This view of age-related differences in comprehension difficulty is a working hypothesis for future research. The tendency to short-circuit attention to unique, essential features of dramatic plots may be consequential for social learning in cases where reliance on early instantiated, limited knowledge could result in misleading impressions of actors and their behavior. For example, in the case of the double-dealing character in the preceding sequence, behavioral and appearance cues may initially instantiate a script for benevolent behavior, although in the details of the

Table 1. *Proportions of children who mentioned common-knowledge and program-specific contents in retelling the televised narrative*

	Common-knowledge content				Program-specific content		
Grade	Police	Murder	Bad guy caught	Buying groceries	Show premise	Villain's crime	Forgery
Second	9/17	12/17	15/15	16/17	2/17	3/17	1/17
Fifth	10/19	14/19	19/19	19/19	7/19	12/19	12/19
Eighth	3/14	12/14	12/14	14/14	13/14	14/14	14/14

program the character is actually revealed, subtly and by small increments, to be malevolent instead.

Individual differences in social knowledge and comprehension

Recently, evidence has emerged in our research indicating that prior social experiences may underlie individual variations, as well as developmental differences, in children's comprehension. These individual differences may be especially pronounced within younger age groups, whose comprehension of the explicit content of programs is often poor. In a recently published study (Newcomb & Collins, 1979), individual differences were found in the understanding of typical televised social portrayals. The experiment involved equal numbers of children from both lower-socioeconomic and middle-socioeconomic samples (SES) at the second, fifth, and eighth grades. One set of children, including all these subgroups, viewed an edited version of a commercial network show featuring middle-class characters; the second set of participants saw a show with a similar plot line featuring lower-class characters. Family composition and the complexity of the programs were similar, and the two recognition measures constructed for the study were of similar degrees of difficulty.

When the children were tested for understanding of the events, the inferred causes of action, and the emotions of the characters, second-grade children performed best when the social-class milieu portrayed in the program was similar to their own. Figure 4 shows these results. Middle-SES second-graders who viewed the middle-class show inferred more about the causes of actions and the feelings and emotions of the characters than lower-SES youngsters who watched the middle-class shows; and lower-SES second-graders who watched the lower-class characters inferred more of the same kind of information from that plot than

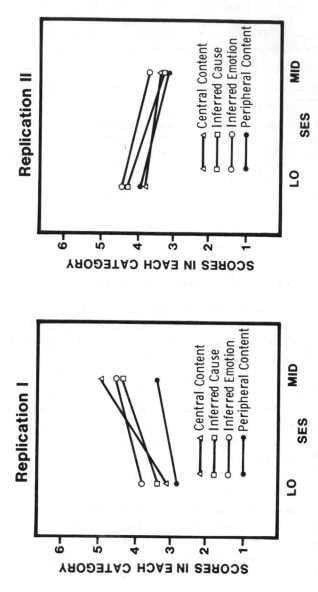

Figure 4. Mean correct answers on explicit- and implicit-content recognition items for middle- and lower-SES second-graders who watched middle-class characters (Replication I) or working-class characters (Replication II). (Data from Newcomb & Collins, 1979.)

did the middle-class children who watched the lower-class program. These effects do not appear at the fifth- and eighth-grade levels. Thus, for the younger children, with more limited cognitive skills for understanding television programs, seeing the action portrayed in settings similar to their own backgrounds helped them acquire relevant information from the program; their difficulties in comprehending shows, which have been attributed to developmental factors, were most evident when the types of roles, characters, and settings portrayed in the program were unfamiliar. Thus, if TV characters and events do not conform to social expectations, young viewers may be even less than ordinarily likely to understand actions, motives, and feelings in television programs.

Despite the salutary effects of pertinent social experiences for second-graders, however, preadolescent and adolescent viewers in the study again appeared to use selective and inferential strategies more effectively than the younger children. Even the best-performing second-graders were still significantly less accurate than fifth- and eighth-graders. Furthermore, conditional probabilities were again computed to determine whether, if the children knew the central explicit contents of the scenes, they were also likely to know the implicit content – the causes of actions and the emotional states of actors. These probabilities were significantly higher for fifth-graders than for second-graders, indicating that information implied by on-screen events was more likely to be grasped by older viewers than by younger ones.

Other evidence of individual differences in comprehension comes from a recently completed study (List, Collins, & Westby, 1981) of the effects of sex-role stereotypes on comprehension of conventional versus nonconventional sex-role portrayals in television dramas. In this research, third-graders' degree of sex-role stereotyping was assessed. Their comprehension of explicit content and inferences after viewing both a conventional and a nonconventional portrayal of a female character were then tested in a within-subjects design using recognition procedures. Understanding of the two programs was clearly affected by children's sex-role expectations. When high-stereotype children made errors of comprehension, the errors significantly reflected traditional sex-role expectations, whereas low-stereotype viewers more often made errors consonant with less-traditional expectations. These findings cannot be explained by differences in ability between the two groups nor by differential difficulty of the two programs or measures. Furthermore, a separate group of high- and low-stereotype third-graders who answered the recognition items without having seen the programs chose among the alternative answers at chance level. Sex-role expectations apparently were cued by the content of the programs and, in turn, influenced children's perceptions of plot events. Thus, social expectations as commonplace as sex-role stereotypes affect children's representations of content in television programs.

Conclusions

I have attempted to outline here some aspects of children's representations of television portrayals of social models. In the view I have proposed, the social stimuli purveyed by television are at the center of a causal configuration, in which what children select and remember about the portrayals they observe are shaped by prior social and cognitive growth, and the resulting representations in turn mediate the social effects of viewing. The evidence to date indicates that, after watching typical dramatic programs, grade-school and preadolescent children construct representations that vary considerably in how accurately and completely they reflect the content of portrayals. Furthermore, their evaluations of the portrayed characters and actions appear to vary concomitantly with comprehension.

Age-related differences in cognitive strategies for processing social content across the time span of typical dramatic narratives clearly contribute to variation in representation of acts and the contexts in which they occur. In addition, variability in social understanding depends heavily on viewers' prior knowledge of a variety of social experiences. Pre-viewing experiences, circumstances, and states have long been recognized as pertinent to the prediction of behavior after viewing; but judging from our evidence, the effects of these factors may partly reflect their influence on the way in which the social portrayals themselves are understood and remembered.

At present there is little basis for saying how social knowledge is represented and how it enters into comprehension of social portrayals. The most extensive evidence comes from theory and research on prose narratives (Bower, 1978a; Bower, Black, & Turner, 1979; Mandler & Johnson, 1977; Warren, Nicholas, & Trabasso, 1979; Schank & Abelson, 1977; Stein & Glenn, 1979), but few details are known and several contending perspectives presently guide research efforts (Omanson, 1979). The most detailed account of the role of prior knowledge in understanding stories is the scripts approach (Schank & Abelson, 1977), in which prior knowledge, in the form of stereotypes of event sequences, enables inferences about gaps in the linkages between the actions or states of the story characters. These scripts, which are abstracted from previous experiences in similiar situations, make possible hierarchical representations of plots.

One difficulty, as Bower (1978b) notes, is that scripts may often not be clearly distinguishable from a conceptually cumbersome aggregation of similar experiences elicited in different circumstances. Schank and Abelson (1977), however, emphasize the abstract, categorical quality of scripts. Like other views of the role of schemata in processing of social information (e.g., Cantor & Mischel, 1977; Hastie, in press; Judd & Kulik, in press; Taylor & Crocker, in press), the scripts formulation implies hierarchical information structures in which the highest, most abstract levels are supported by a rich store of specific experiences or bits of information at lower levels. Such structures affect both encoding (Bower, 1977: Markus, 1977; Rogers, Kuiper, & Kirker, 1977) and retrieval (Cantor & Mischel, 1977; Hastie, in press; Zadny & Gerard, 1974) of information about newly encountered persons and events. Neisser's (1976) characterization applies generally to current views of the effects of structures in social information processing:

A schema is like a *format* in a computer programming language. Formats specify that information must be of a certain sort if it is to be interpreted coherently. . . . Information can be picked up only if there is a developmental format ready to accept it. Information that does not fit such a format goes unused. Perception is inherently selective. (p. 55)

Little attention has been given to the assessment of relevant schemata in studies of social cognition. In most research, manipulations have been introduced to activate certain commonly available schemata, which have then been observed to affect memory for a stimulus (e.g., Cantor & Mischel, 1977; Taylor & Crocker, in press). Recently, however, Bower, Black, and Turner (1979) and Nelson (1978), the latter working with children, have attempted to specify knowledge of scripts in memory and language tasks, and social psychologists (e.g., Markus, 1977; Rogers, Kuiper, & Kirker, 1977) have also examined the nature of certain social schemata and their role in the processing of new stimuli. Their strategies are potentially applicable to comprehension of important aspects of social portrayals in television narratives. One focus of future research should be further specification of the nature and representation of social knowledge and its role in children's processing of social stimuli like television programs.

In addition to knowledge about social interactions and events, two other kinds of general knowledge also affect comprehension of televised narratives and thus continue to be central to our analysis of children's processing. One is knowledge of the usual form and structure of stories. In recent research on prose stories (e.g., Mandler & Johnson, 1977; Poulsen et al., 1978; Stein & Glenn, 1979), preschool and young grade school children's relatively poor recall of story details has appeared to be related to a less adequate general structure according to which story details might be parsed. More recently, Sedlak (1979) has suggested that young children fail to comprehend the actions and events in a narrative because they assume different interpretations of the various actors' intentions or plans. Sedlak's approach is congruent with recent dissertation research by Wilensky (1978), in which the importance of perceived goals and intentions to narrative comprehension is further specified. Both approaches specify inferential steps that characterize the processing of narratives by older children, but are used less reliably by younger ones.

A third kind of knowledge that affects processing of audiovisually presented narratives is familiarity with certain cinematic conventions (Tada, 1969). Baggett (1979) has recently found that an audiovisually presented narrative had identifiable structure and meaningful breakpoints that corresponded semantically to the breakpoints in a prose version of the same narratives. The way in which information was conveyed in the two media differed markedly, however. Formal features of programs, such as camera angles and the use of background music, and visual techniques for compressing time and signaling breaks in action carry considerable information for viewers whose experience permits their meaning to be recognized. At present, however, little is known about the interaction of social knowledge and knowledge of the presentation conventions common to television programs.

Potential effects of comprehension on behavior

Implications of variations in comprehension of television portrayals for behavioral effects on children and adolescents have been addressed in relatively few studies, and those in which direct measures of both comprehension and behavior have been taken (e.g., Leifer & Roberts, 1972) have yielded null findings. In this regard, the literature parallels discouraging empirical efforts in the areas of attitude–behavior relationships (e.g., Ajzen & Fishbein, 1977) and social-cognition–behavior correspondences (e.g., Shantz, 1975). Nevertheless, several researchers have found behavioral differences that are suggestive of links between children's representations of programs and subsequent behavior. Such links should be further examined. For example, Collins, Berndt, and Hess (1974) found that kindergarten and second-grade children who had watched an action-adventure program had difficulty remembering the relationship of the motive and consequence cues to the aggressive action. Although such cues appear to moderate the behavioral effects of observed aggression (Bandura, 1965; Berkowitz & Geen, 1967; Berkowitz & Rawlings, 1963), kindergartners and second-graders in the research remembered the aggressive scene but only infrequently knew its links with the motives and consequences. Collins (1973) further reported behavioral differences that ostensibly reflect cognitive processing differences such as those previously described. This research involved inserting commercials between scenes of negative motives and negative consequences for aggression and the violent scene itself. Under this condition, third-graders' postviewing tendencies to choose aggressive responses increased, in comparison to children of the same age who saw the three scenes in immediate sequence. Although no measure of comprehension was available, the task of inferring relations between aggressive action and the pertinent motive and consequence cues was probably more difficult for the first group than for the second, a result, most likely, of the temporal separation imposed by the commercials. There was no evidence of behavioral differences among the sixth- and tenth-graders who saw both types of programs.

It is impossible to estimate what part of the variance in the social impact of television is due to incomplete or distorted comprehension of what children see; comprehension is only one factor in a very complex equation for television effects. However, we have found marked variability of children's comprehension of socially pertinent content during the middle-childhood and adolescent years; and we can point to suggestive evidence of concomitant effects on behavior in the laboratory. These two empirical thrusts indicate that social-cognitive components of the viewing process should become a term in the effects equation that guides future research.

Implications for the study of social cognition

The formulation advanced here of the source and nature of difficulties in children's understanding of common social models emerged from studies of television portrayals. In our research, we have noted a number of instances in which predictions about the effects of social models are different from, or more differentiated than, those that would be made from extant social-modeling formulations. Perhaps social-cognitive analyses of other natural social stimuli could similarly supplement and inform research on children's social cognition. In several other instances, like Lepper's (this volume) studies of messages to children in classrooms, social-cognitive analyses have been enriched by in vivo investigations of the stimuli typically encountered by children. It may be profitable to diversify our analytic efforts to examine the range and nature of social-cognitive tasks involved in children's typical social experiences. Such analyses, in fine-tuned oscillation with laboratory work, would be useful both in constructing more accurate laboratory analogs and in testing the sufficiency of the analogs once they have been constructed. Perhaps, with appropriate adjustments for the nature of the phenomena under study, social-cognition researchers could experience some of the benefits that social-behavior scholars have enjoyed as a result of renewed involvement in studies of children in natural settings.

A corollary to the need for in vivo research on social cognition is the need to give explicit attention to the social antecedents of social-cognitive functioning, or – the other way around – the social-cognitive sequelae of social experiences. Thus far in our own research we have relied on differential studies, investigating comprehension of social portrayals as a function of group differences in social class, attitudes and expectations, and behavioral tendencies. We have little sense of the ways in which mundane social experiences are represented in memory and then enter into construing new social experiences. In other social-cognitive domains, more is known about the effects of specific experiences on social cognition: Lepper and Ruble (this volume) have examined social contingencies that appear to be correlated with certain attributional processes, for example. Despite several generations of research on parent–child and peer relations, however, we still know relatively little about the nature and functioning of the social-cognitive sequelae of primary social interactions with parents and with different configurations of peers. Nor do we know how, or to what extent, television portrayals affect expectations about more or less common social occurrences. Judging from the few studies to date, problems like these may be more central to the social-cognition–behavior relationship than had previously been recognized. Perhaps better understanding of the effects of social experience on social cognition will enable us to specify more adequately the ways in which social cognition affects social behavior.

References

Ajzen, I., & Fishbein, M. Attitude-behavior relations: A theoretical analysis and review of empirical research. *Psychological Bulletin, 1977, 84,* 888–918.

Austin, V., Ruble, D., & Trabasso, T. Recall and order effects as factors in children's moral judgments. *Child Development, 1977, 48*(2), 470–474.

Baggett, P. Structurally equivalent stories in movie and text and the effect of the medium on recall. *Journal of Verbal Learning and Verbal Behavior, 1979, 18*(3), 333–356.

Bandura, A. Influence of models' reinforcement contingencies on the acquisition of imitative responses. *Journal of Personality and Social Psychology, 1965, 1*(6), 589–595.

Bandura, A. A social-learning theory of identificatory processes. In D. A. Goslin (Ed.), *Handbook of socialization theory and research.* Chicago: Rand McNally, 1969.

Bandura, A. *Social learning theory.* New York: Wiley, 1977.

Bartlett, F. C. *Remembering.* Cambridge: Cambridge University Press, 1932.

Berkowitz, L., & Geen, R. The stimulus qualities of the target of aggression: A further study. *Journal of Personality and Social Psychology,* 1967, *5,* 364 368.

Berkowitz, L., & Rawlings, E. Effects of film violence on inhibitions against subsequent aggression. *Journal of Abnormal and Social Psychology,* 1963, *66*(5), 405–412.

Bower, G. H. On injecting life into deadly prose. Paper presented to the meeting of the Western Psychological Association, Seattle, 1977.

Bower, G. Experiments on story comprehension and recall. *Discourse Processes,* 1978, *1,* 211–231. (a)

Bower, G. Representing knowledge development. In R. Siegler (Ed.), *Children's thinking: What develops?* pp. 349–362. Hillsdale, N.J.: Erlbaum, 1978. (b)

Bower, G. H., Black, J. B., & Turner, T. J. Scripts in memory for text. *Cognitive Psychology,* 1979, *11,* 177–220.

Cantor, N., & Mischel, W. Traits as prototypes: Effects on recognition memory. *Journal of Personality and Social Psychology,* 1977, *35,* 38–48.

Collins, W. A. Learning of media content: A developmental study. *Child Development,* 1970, *41*(4), 1133–1142.

Collins, W. A. The effect of temporal separation between motivation, aggression and consequences: A developmental study. *Developmental Psychology,* 1973, *8*(2), 215–221.

Collins, W. A. *Temporal integration and inferences about televised social behavior.* Paper presented as part of a symposium on Cognitive Processing of Television Content: Perspectives on the Effects of Television on Children, at the biennial meeting of the Society for Research in Child Development, New Orleans, March 1977.

Collins, W. A., & Wellman, H. M. *Social scripts and developmental changes in representations of televised narratives.* Unpublished manuscript, Institute of Child Development, University of Minnesota, 1980.

Collins, W. A. *Developmental and individual differences in children's responses to television.* Manuscript in preparation.

Collins, W. A., Berndt, R., & Hess, V. Observational learning of motives and consequences for television aggression: A developmental study. *Child Development,* 1974, *45,* 799–802.

Collins, W. A., Wellman, H., Keniston, A., & Westby, S. Age-related aspects of comprehension of televised social content. *Child Development,* 1978, *49,* 389–399.

Collins, W. A., & Zimmerman, S. A. Convergent and divergent social cues: Effects of televised aggression on children. *Communication Research,* 1975, *2,* 331–347.

Comstock, G., Chaffee, S., Katzman, N., McCombs, M., & Roberts, D. *Television and human behavior.* New York: Columbia University Press, 1978.

Costanzo, P., Coie, J., Grumet, J., & Farnill, D. A reexamination of the effects of intent and consequence on children's moral judgemtns. *Child Development,* 1973, *44,* 154–161.

Feldman, N. S., Klosson, E. C., Parsons, J. E., Rholes, W. S., & Ruble, D. N. Order of information presentation and children's moral judgments. *Child Development,* 1976, *47,* 556–559.

Feshbach, S., & Singer, R. *Television and aggression: An experimental field study.* San Francisco: Jossey-Bass, 1971.

Gerbner, G. Violence in television drama: A study of trends and symbolic functions. In G. Comstock & E. Rubinstein (Eds.), *Television and social behavior* (Vol. 1). Washington, D.C.: U.S. Government Printing Office, 1972.

Goranson, R. E. Media violence and aggressive behavior: A review of experimental research. In R. Berkowitz (Ed.), *Advances in experimental social psychology,* pp. 2–31. New York: Academic Press, 1970.

Hastie, R. Schematic principles in human memory. In E. T. Higgins, C. P. Herman, and M. P. Zanna (Eds.), *The Ontario Symposium on Personality and Social Psychology: Social cognition. Hillsdale, N.J.: Erlbaum, in press.*

Judd, C. M., & Kulik, J. Schematic effects of social attitudes upon information processing and recall. *Journal of Personality and Social Psychology,* in press.

Krebs, D. L. Altruism: An examination of the concept and a review of the literature. *Psychological Bulletin,* 1970, *73,* 258–302.

Leifer, A., Gordon, N., & Graves, S. Children's television: More than mere entertainment. *Harvard Educational Review,* 1974, *44,* 213–245.

Leifer, A., & Roberts, D. Children's responses to television violence. In J. Murray, C. Rubenstein, & G. Comstock (Eds.), *Television and social behavior* (Vol. 2). Washington, D.C.: U.S. Government Printing Office, 1972.

Liebert, R., Neale, J., & Davidson, E. *The early window: Effects of television on children and youth.* Elmsford: N.Y.: Pergamon Press, 1973.

List, J., Collins, W. A., & Westby, S. *Comprehension and inferences from traditional and nontraditional sex-role portrayals.* Unpublished manuscript, University of Minnesota, 1981.

Maccoby, E. Effects of the mass media. In M. Hoffman & L. W. Hoffman (Eds.), *Review of child development research* (Vol. 1), pp. 323–348. Chicago: University of Chicago Press, 1964.

Mandler, J., & Johnson, N. Remembrance of things parsed: Story structure and recall. *Cognitive Psychology,* 1977, *9,* 111–151.

Markus, H. Self-schemata and processing information about the self. *Journal of Personality and Social Psychology,* 1977, *35,* 63–78.

Neisser, U. *Cognition and reality.* San Francisco: Freeman, 1976.

Nelson, K. How children represent knowledge of their world in and out of language: A preliminary report. In R. Siegler (Ed.), *Children's thinking: What develops?* pp. 255–274. Hillsdale, N.J.: Erlbaum, 1978.

Newcomb, A. F., & Collins, W. A. Children's comprehension of family role portrayals in televised dramas: Effects of socioeconomic status, ethnicity, and age. *Developmental Psychology,* 1979, *15*(4), 417–423.

Omanson, R. *The narrative analysis.* Unpublished doctoral dissertation, University of Minnesota, 1979.

Poulsen, D., Kintsch, E., Kintsch, W., & Premack, D. *Children's comprehension and memory for stories.* Unpublished manuscript, University of Colorado, 1978.

Purdie, S., Collins, W. A., & Westby, S. *Children's processing of motive information in a televised portrayal.* Unpublished manuscript, Institute of Child Development, University of Minnesota, 1979.

Rogers, T. B., Kuiper, R. G., & Kirker, W. S. Self-reference and the encoding of personal information. *Journal of Personality and Social Psychology,* 1977, *35,* 677–688.

Schank, R., & Abelson, R. *Scripts, plans, goals, and understanding.* Hillsdale, N.J.: Erlbaum, 1977.

Sears, R. Your ancients revisited: A history of child development. In E. M. Hetherington (Ed.), *Review of child development research* (Vol. 5), pp. 1–73. Chicago: University of Chicago Press, 1975.

Sedlak, A. J. Developmental differences in understanding plans and evaluating actors. *Child Development,* 1979, *50*(2), 536–560.

Shantz, C. U. The development of social cognition. In E. M. Hetherington (Ed.), *Review of child development research* (Vol. 5). Chicago: University of Chicago Press, 1975.

Siegel, A. Communicating with the next generation. *Journal of Communication,* 1975, *25,* 14–24.

Stein, A., & Friedrich, L. Impact of television on children and youth. In E. M. Hetherington (Ed.), *Review of child development research* (Vol. 5), pp. 183–256. Chicago: University of Chicago Press, 1975.

Stein, N., & Glenn, C. An analysis of story comprehension in elementary school children.
In R. Freedle (Ed.), *Advances in discourse processes* (Vol. 2). Hillsdale, N.J.: Erlbaum, 1979.

Tada, T. Image-cognition: A developmental approach. In *Studies of Broadcasting*, pp. 105–
173. Tokyo: Nippon Hoso Kyokai, 1969.

Taylor, S., & Crocker, J. Schematic bases of social information processing. In E. T. Higgins, C. P. Herman, and M. P. Zanna (Eds.), *The Ontario Symposium on Personality
and Social Psychology: Social cognition*. Hillsdale, N.J.: Erlbaum, in press.

Warren, W., Nicholas, D., & Trabasso, T. Event chains and inferences in understanding
narratives. In R. Freedle (Eds.), *Advances in discourse processes* (Vol. 2). Hillsdale,
N.J.: Erlbaum, 1979.

Wilensky, R. *Understanding goal-based stories.* Research Report No. 140, Yale University,
Department of Computer Sciences, 1978.

Zadny, J., & Gerard, H. B. Attributed intentions and informational selectivity. *Journal of
Experimental Social Psychology*, 1974, *10*, 34–52.

6   The development of social-comparison processes and their role in achievement-related self-socialization

Diane N. Ruble

For various historical reasons, approaches to the study of socialization have traditionally focused on what socializing agents, especially parents, *do* (e.g., types of punishment used, age of toilet training) and how their actions affect individual differences – e.g., children who are high or low in aggressiveness, dependency, or masculinity/femininity. This approach is well illustrated by the correlational studies in the 1950s and 1960s of Sears and his associates (Sears, Maccoby, & Levin, 1957; Sears, Rau, & Alpert, 1965). Although the socialization of individual differences continues to be an issue of obvious interest and importance, the results of this kind of research have often been disappointing. One problem may have been the failure to consider children as active participants in their own socialization. As part of the socialization process, children must learn the social rules by which society functions *and* begin to apply these guidelines to the self. Thus, in this sense, children may be viewed as actively seeking information about themselves and their social environment. This orientation to social development has been labeled a "self-socialization" process (e.g., Maccoby & Jacklin, 1974).

The major purpose of this chapter is to examine the developing use of social-comparison information, a type of information that is essential to the self-socialization process. Self-socialization may be viewed as being oriented toward two major goals: (1) determining how one is supposed to behave (norm acquisition goals) and (2) determining how good one is at this particular type of behavior (self-evaluation goals). In many, or most, cases, a realistic assessment of both the appropriateness and the adequacy

Preparation of this chapter was facilitated, in part, by Grant No. 16278 from the National Science Foundation, and, in part, by Grant No. 34694 from the National Institute of Mental Health. I am grateful to Nina Feldman, Karin Frey, Ellen Grosovsky, E. Tory Higgins, and Thane Pittman for helpful comments on an earlier draft and to Linda Worcel for technical assistance.

or quality of one's characteristics and behaviors depends on information received about others (Veroff, 1969). Note that this conceptualization expands somewhat the meaning of social comparison, in that this term has traditionally referred primarily to self-evaluation (Festinger, 1954). In addition to (and probably temporally prior to) comparing for self-evaluative purposes, however, socialization involves learning about social rules. That is, children must learn to define, for example, what high ability levels are, what behaviors are appropriate for males and females, and what constitutes appropriate and inappropriate interpersonal assertiveness. Although this form of knowledge involves comparisons with others, it should be distinguished from personal evaluation (e.g., Am I good at math? Am I an adequate female?). This distinction may be relevant to interpreting inconsistencies in the literature concerning when children engage in social comparison, a point that will be reiterated later in the chapter.

The focus of the present analysis is on achievement-related social comparison, as most of the relevant research has concerned assessment of performance and abilities. Here, the self-socialization goal confronting children is the determination of their own areas of competence and relative strengths and weaknesses. Such decisions, in turn, can help them delimit their current and future behavioral options. Although the following review of empirical work is limited primarily to this single area, it seems likely that developmental trends observed for achievement may be quite similar to self-socialization processes in many other areas of social development, such as sex roles or aggressiveness. That is, children can presumably learn about the appropriate range of most kinds of characteristics and behaviors by comparing their peers with each other and with themselves. Thus, although differences in socialization processes no doubt occur across domains of social behavior, it is assumed here that the study of the development of achievement-related social comparison is relevant to an understanding of social development more generally.

The origin of research interest in social comparison is typically attributed to Festinger (1954), who noted that there seems to be a strong motivation in most individuals to evaluate their opinions and abilities. When unambiguous criteria are not available, people look to others for subjective standards of ability levels. That social comparison is a pervasive process is now well documented in the social-psychological literature (e.g., Darley & Goethals, 1980; Latane, 1966; Suls & Miller, 1977) and is obvious from casual observations of human behavior. In academia, for example, the meaning of most indices relevant to self-evaluation – for example, number of publications, teacher ratings – can be determined only by comparisons with other academicians. Indeed, the frequency of social comparison has evidently seemed so high that empirical research based on Festinger's theory has typically ignored the question of whether social-comparison information is actually used and has focused instead on the kinds of social comparison in which individuals typically engage (e.g., with *whom* do people choose to compare?).

In turning to the development of social-comparison processes, however, the question of whether or not such information is used obviously takes on considerable significance. The point at which social comparison begins to have an impact on children may be considered as a kind of milestone in the self-socialization process because the nature of evaluations made about the self and others is likely to change dramatically once comparative standards become important. Children's perceptions of how well they are doing relative to their immediate peers may have a profound impact on their self-concepts, self-evaluations, and interpersonal relationships, independent of their actual performance level (Levine, in press; Levine, Mendez-Caratini, & Snyder, 1982). For example, the results of several field studies in elementary schools have suggested that shifts in the types of reference groups available for comparison can dramatically alter the level of self-esteem of poor students (Schwarzer, Jerusalem, & Lange, 1981) and academically handicapped children (Strang, Smith, & Rogers, 1978). Also, in other research, academic self-concept was shown to be much more strongly related to within-classroom (comparative) achievement than to absolute levels of achievement (Rogers, Smith, & Coleman, 1978). Thus, one might argue that the study of social comparison is of greatest interest during childhood, because this is when initial self-conceptions are being formed. Once children have defined their capacities and characteristics, subsequent information received (including social comparison) is likely to have less impact because such information is interpreted in terms of concepts already formed (Bartlett, 1932).

In a seminal theoretical chapter, Veroff (1969) suggested that young children do not automatically use social-comparison information under conditions of ambiguity, as Festinger's theory would suggest, until *after* the early years of school. Instead, according to Veroff, the basis of young children's self-evaluation is autonomous motivation, that is, judgments based on absolute performance and comparisons with the self. Subsequent conceptual analyses have generally supported these conclusions (Suls & Mullen, 1982; Suls & Sander, 1979). In some respects, this proposal is surprising because one would think that children would begin to use comparative standards soon after entering school. The amount of time children spend with peers changes dramatically as children leave home and enter school, and they have ample opportunity to make comparisons. Furthermore, in the school setting the primary focus is on achievement, which is often intensely oriented toward the comparative evaluation of abilities (Pepitone, 1972). *But,* in these settings, do young children automatically seek to compare? What kinds of things do they learn? What effect does this information have?

The development of the use of social-comparison information

In the past few years my colleagues and I have conducted several studies concerned with these kinds of questions. In our initial studies we focused on a central tenet of social comparison theory: that an individual cannot fully evaluate his or her performance except in relationship to how others have done. That is, although individuals are likely to feel more pleased about themselves and to evaluate their abilities and efforts more highly after successfully completing a task than after failing, such self-evaluations should also be influenced by how others did in the same situation. For example, they should feel less pleased about a success at a task that everyone can accomplish than at one in which most others have difficulty. This line of reasoning is consistent with the empirical findings and attributional analysis of achievement presented in Weiner (1974).

The basic design of our studies involved children at different age levels working on a task and receiving information concerning the outcome of their own performance as well as the outcomes of peers. They were then asked to evaluate themselves and the task along various dimensions. Although the basic design was similar across studies, a number of variations were included (e.g., within vs. between subjects variables, different response measures, different tasks) to provide converging evidence across studies. In each case, however, somewhat to our surprise, we found that the self-evaluations of children at different age levels showed essentially no use of social-comparison feedback by children until at least 7 years of age (Boggiano & Ruble, 1979; Ruble, Parsons, & Ross, 1976; Ruble et al., 1980). That is, the young children's ratings of, for example, ability or task difficulty were based exclusively on whether or not they had successfully completed the task (an absolute standard in Veroff's terms), and it was only for older children that such judgments were affected by the information about how well other children had done.

To illustrate, in one study we attempted to make social-comparison information particularly salient (Ruble et al., 1980, Study 2). First, the comparative feedback was made meaningful to children's future outcomes. That is, the children had to make predictions about how well they would do on a subsequent task under conditions in which they could maximize their rewards and minimize their costs by making an accurate assessment of their competence, and accuracy could be determined only in terms of social comparison. In addition, the actual outcome of the task was left ambiguous (i.e., 50% correct) so that the children would have difficulty labeling their performance as a clear success or failure without additional information.

Kindergartners and second- and fourth-graders played a ball-throwing game and were told that several other children their age had played the game. Performance was manipulated so that all children successfully hit the target area two out of four times, an ambiguous outcome. Thus, children could estimate their competence at the task only by attending to the social-comparison information about how well the other children did.

The experimenter then explained to the subjects that they would have the opportunity to play the ball-tossing game a second time in competition for prizes with two same-sex peers. The number of possible prizes was made contingent on both performance and *accurate* self-appraisal. Manipulation checks indicated that, as with the earlier studies, even the youngest children attended to, and remembered, the information given about their own and other children's scores, indicating their ability to judge relative outcomes accurately when explicitly asked to do so. Additional questioning indicated that they also understood the costs of inaccurate predictions (both for under- and over-estimating their own relative ability level).

Thus, the children could optimize their outcomes by accurate self-appraisal, which they could get only from the social-comparison information. Nevertheless, only the fourth-graders based their prediction on competence information gleaned from relative performance. The younger children failed to use the inference that they had high ability at a task to select a level of difficulty that would increase the number of rewards they could win. Indeed, for the kindergarten children, the predictions for the three information conditions were identical, as shown in Table 1. The other measures showed a similar pattern of results such that only fourth-graders expressed less certainty in beating others and lower self-perceptions of ability when they did poorly relative to others. Furthermore, consistent with these findings, analyses of the open-ended responses indicated that, relative to both kindergartners and second-graders, fourth-graders gave significantly more responses relevant to social comparison to explain their ability evaluations (e.g., "I must be pretty good because I beat all the others").

In contrast to the direct self-evaluative measures, the second-graders as

Table 1. *Mean predictions and certainty and ability ratings as a function of grade level and social-comparison condition*

Grade and dependent variable	Condition		
	Failure	Control	Success
Kindergarten			
Predictions	1.1	1.1	1.1
	(.74)	(.88)	(.88)
Certainty	2.9	2.8	3.0
	(.91)	(1.1)	(.85)
Ability	2.9	2.7	3.3
	(.88)	(.82)	(.48)
Second			
Predictions	0.5	1.0	0.7
	(.71)	(.67)	(.82)
Certainty	2.4	2.3	2.7
	(.63)	(.64)	(.50)
Ability	2.5	2.8	2.8
	(.71)	(.42)	(.63)
Fourth			
Predictions	0.4	1.1	1.7
	(.52)	(.32)	(.48)
Certainty	2.1	2.4	3.1
	(.55)	(.81)	(.37)
Ability	2.2	2.8	2.7
	(.63)	(.42)	(.48)

Note: The prediction measure ranges from 0 to 2, and the other, measures range from 1 to 4. n = 10 per cell. Standard deviations are in parentheses.
Source: Ruble et al. (1980).

well as the fourth-graders did show use of social-comparison information on one measure – a kind of strategic decision. Children at these grade levels who had experienced relative failure were more likely to choose unknown others as future competitors than were children who succeeded. In addition, in light of the consistent failure of the younger children to be influenced by information regarding relative performance, it is important to note in this study that even the youngest children reported greater certainty of beating one versus two others. Thus, the younger children did make use of some kinds of information when estimating their likely outcome, suggesting that their failure to respond to social comparison was not simply due to the use of an insensitive measure.

In summary, the main point is that converging evidence from several studies, which employed a range of design variations and response measures, suggests that the impact of social-comparison information on children's self-evaluations is negligible until surprisingly late in their development. However, perhaps the use of verbal measures in these studies underestimated the role of peer comparisons in children's evaluations of competence. It seems possible that observations of competence-related behaviors would reflect a level of inference that young children are unable to verbalize.

Evidence bearing on this point is available from another of our recent studies (Boggiano & Ruble, 1979). In this study, the impact of peer comparisons on achievement-related *behavior* was examined by using an intrinsic/extrinsic motivation (overjustification) paradigm. Studies using this paradigm have repeatedly shown that offering a reward to an individual for engaging in an enjoyable activity will undermine that individual's subsequent interest, as evidenced by a decrease in frequency of choice of that activity when the reward is discontinued (Deci, 1975; Lepper & Greene, 1978). However, reward may not always undermine subsequent interest. Based on theories suggesting that intrinsic interest results from perceptions of competence and self-determination (Deci, 1975; White, 1959), recently several investigators have postulated that rewards conveying information regarding competence should sustain, rather than undermine, interest (Arkes, 1978; Karniol & Ross, 1977; Lepper & Greene, 1978). Thus, it would be predicted that if children receive information that they are competent at a task, their interest should be maintained even if they have received an external reward for engaging in the task.

This prediction becomes quite interesting in light of the findings from the social-comparison studies reported earlier, which suggest that the nature of children's inferences of competence shift dramatically during the early school years. Specifically, older children's interest in a task should be affected by competence information conveyed in terms of peer comparisons. In contrast, for children under 7 or 8 years of age, interest should be affected by competence information conveyed only in absolute, but *not* relative, terms.

To test this hypothesis, children at two age levels (4 and 5 years and 8 to 10 years) engaged in a task of high initial interest. The children either anticipated a reward made contingent on task engagement alone or upon meeting a performance standard (i.e., competence information based on absolute performance level). In addition, the children either were or were not provided with information regarding their performance relative to

Table 2. *Transformed percent of time spent playing target task*

Contingency of reward to performance	Social comparison condition		
	Others better (indicating incompetence)	Others worse (indicating competence)	No information
Younger Children			
Performance contingent	.33 (.44)	.29 (.41)	.45 (.62)
Task contingent	.17 (.23)	.20 (.27)	.19 (.27)
Control (no reward; no standard)			.52 (.73)
Older children			
Performance contingent	.21 (.28)	.49 (.67)	.39 (.55)
Task contingent	.25 (.32)	.50 (.68)	.21 (.29)
Control (no rewards; no standards)			.49 (.68)

Note: Raw percentiles in parentheses.
Source: Boggiano and Ruble (1979).

peers (i.e., competence information conveyed in social-comparison or relative terms).

As expected, the pattern of results indicated that the preschool children were primarily affected by the performance contingency of the reward but not the social-comparison information. As shown in Table 2, the undermining effect of reward did *not* occur when attaining the reward was made contingent on meeting an absolute standard of performance (as shown by comparing the top row to the base-line control). That is, although the preschoolers' interest in the task was undermined when the reward was made contingent on task engagement alone, their interest was maintained when they met an absolute standard of competence. However, social-comparison information indicating *relative* competence or incompetence had no effect on the subsequent interest of the younger children, as shown by comparing across columns. For example, their interest was undermined by rewards both when they performed better and when they performed worse than peers. In contrast, social-comparison information superseded the effect of the absolute standard for the older children, such that their interest was maintained primarily when they viewed themselves as *relatively competent* (middle column).

These results strengthen the earlier conclusions regarding developmental changes in social-comparison processes by showing identical age shifts in terms of a behavioral measure that indirectly reflects children's inferences about their own competence. These findings also begin to suggest the importance of understanding the changing nature of children's self-evaluations. For example, a startling implication of this study is that a teacher promising a nursery school child a gold star for being the best in the class in reading may inadvertently *undermine* the child's subsequent interest in reading because of the child's failure to make an inference about competence on the basis of information conveyed in relative terms.

Steps involved in the development of social comparison

In many respects the findings from our studies were inconsistent with our intuitions about social comparison among young children. Everyday observations suggest that even preschool children are concerned with "being the biggest or the best" or with making sure they received as many candies or birthday presents as their friends or siblings. Indeed, some previous research has suggested that even nursery school children engage in some kinds of social comparison (Mosatche & Bragonier, 1981) and are influenced by it on some measures, such as self-reinforcement after being differentially reinforced relative to a peer (Masters, 1971). It was, in fact, because the findings were surprising that we conducted multiple studies using very different methodologies and response measures.

How may we reconcile these apparent discrepancies? One possibility is that, similar to recent models of the development of perspective taking (Flavell, 1977), several steps or levels in the social-comparison process develop at different times. I turn now to a descriptive analysis of the elements involved in social comparison and attempt to determine what dimensions characterize developmental changes in this process.

For the purpose of this analysis, I have broken the social-comparison process down into three levels, which are presented in Table 3. *Background factors* refer to three prerequisite elements of social comparison: (1) basic cognitive capacities necessary for making comparisons, (2) an interest or motivation to compare, and (3) understanding of strategies for making social comparisons, such as making comparisons with similar others. Each background element contributes to a subsequent *inference,* such as a self-evaluation of competence resulting from social comparison. The inference, in turn, is postulated to have some specific *behavioral effects* for the individual, such as influencing affect experienced, future options, or performance.

Table 3. *Elements in the social-comparison process*

Background factors ⟶	Inferences (e.g., self-evaluation of ability) ⟶	Change or behavioral effects
Basic capacities	Concrete to abstract	Affect
Interest or motivation	Perception or stability	Performance
Strategies	Self-reflective inferences	
	Social-experiential factors	

Background factors

Data from diverse sources are examined below, many of which were not designed to address the questions of social comparison directly. Taken together, these data suggest that many of the background capacities, motivations, and strategies are present in children much before they are able or inclined to make self-evaluation inferences based on such factors.

Basic capacities. The process of comparing oneself with another on some behavior or characteristic may be quite complex and involves several types of prerequisite information-processing capacities and sets of knowledge. For example, to engage in the process at all, children must be aware that people differ in capacities, characteristics, and opinions. The suggestion that young children (under 7 years) are egocentric in their view of the world – that is that they do not recognize differences in perspective between themselves and others (e.g., Flavell et al., 1968) – may mean that social comparison is difficult for children at this age (Veroff, 1969). However, several studies indicate quite clearly that even preschool children are cognizant of differences across individuals in such skills as verbal comprehension (Shatz & Gelman, 1973) and motor abilities (Markman, 1973). In addition, in two studies 4- and 5-year-olds, 8- and 9-year-olds, and undergraduates were shown to make different predictions of preference (for snacks, meals, and activities) for different dissimilar others (e.g., "2-year-olds" vs. "grown-ups"). Furthermore, at every age group, it was rare for subjects to select their own preference when predicting preferences for both similar and dissimilar others (Higgins, Feldman, & Ruble, 1980). Thus, these studies show that young children make distinctions among different points of view even when their own viewpoint has previously been expressed.

Another type of prerequisite information-processing capacity concerns the recognition of relative standing of outcomes. Several lines of evidence suggest that children under 7 years of age are capable of such processes. First, the work of Trabasso and his colleagues on transitive inferences suggests that young children are capable of this kind of logical operation as long as the availability of the information at the time of the judgment is ensured, as through memory training (e.g., Bryant & Trabasso, 1971; Trabasso & Riley, 1974). These findings suggest that children have the *capacity* to make quite complex forms of comparisons, assuming the cognitive operation is similar to the social operation. Presumably, then, they should be able to infer, for example, that Jill can run faster than Susan (given the appropriate intermediary propositions). Indeed, some research shows that at 5 years children are able to form reasonably accurate hierarchies of running skills (Morris & Nemcek, 1978).

A second line of evidence pertinent to children's understanding of relative outcomes concerns the manipulation checks employed in the studies described earlier. In each study, children at all ages accurately reported whether they had performed better or worse relative to others when specifically asked, once again suggesting that the *capacity* to compare is present at an early age.

Interest or motivation. A second possible explanation for findings that comparative self-evaluation is a late-developing process concerns children's level of interest in peers' behaviors and opinions. Although young children may be capable of recognizing relative standing, they may not typically be motivated to do so (Veroff, 1969). There is little information available concerning the development of children's motivation to engage in social comparison. Veroff (1969) defined social-comparison interest as a choice of a moderate-difficulty task, operationalized in terms of social norms (i.e., "a task that most, some, or few children your age can do"). According to Veroff, selecting a task that "some can do and some cannot" indicates high social-comparison motivation because it is assumed that the child is using social comparison as a basis to make a choice that has the potential for providing maximum information about children's capacities relative to others. Consistent with his hypothesis concerning the development for social-comparison motivation, Veroff (1969) found striking age differences in the choice of moderate difficulty tasks. At the kindergarten level, more than 80% of the children chose the easy task, whereas less than 10% chose the moderate task. In contrast, by fourth grade more than 50% of the children chose the challenging task.

Although these findings are consistent with the results of other related studies (cf. Ruble & Boggiano, 1980) and with Veroff's predictions, they do not provide unequivocal information concerning children's changing interest in social comparison. Age-related shifts in task-difficulty choices may reflect a number of possible processes, and there is no independent evidence from this type of study that the children have any awareness about the implication of their choices for social-comparison knowledge. As Veroff notes, one alternative explanation concerns increasing awareness of the social desirability of choosing challenging tasks. Other explanations have been suggested by Nicholls (1978) and Harter (1975, 1978).

Thus, to examine the question of social-comparison motivation more directly, we developed a discrete behavioral measure of interest. By pushing a button on a videotape monitor the children were able to see a peer's progress on a speed task and compare it to their own (Ruble, Feldman, & Boggiano, 1976). Kindergartners and first- and second-graders performed the task in a situation in which they were free to compare or not to compare their own performance with that of a peer. In addition, so that extraneous factors would not influence their expression of interest in comparison, both the actual interaction and the nature of the information received were controlled.

As would be expected from Veroff's (1969) hypothesis, the mean number of times the children pushed the button to observe their partner's score increased significantly with age. However, it is important to note that even the youngest children exhibited more than a minimal interest in social comparison. They pushed the button nearly four times on the average and the total *amount* of time they spent viewing their partner's progress did *not* differ from that of the older children.[1] In addition, when asked "why" they had looked at their partner's scoreboard, the majority of the children at all age levels gave a reason relevant to social comparison, indicating that they wanted to know how well the peer was doing. Thus, although these results suggest that interest in social comparison may increase during the early years of school, they also suggest that both interest and understanding of social comparison are present in kindergarten-age children. On the basis of this latter finding, it seems reasonable to conclude that interest level per se probably is not sufficient to account for the young children's failure to utilize social-comparison information in the earlier studies.

Strategies. A third possible explanation for the apparent developmental changes in the impact of social-comparison information concerns the strategies employed during the comparison process. Different approaches to the social-comparison process (e.g., preference for similar others vs. standard setters) could result in vastly different outcomes and conclusions from the process at different ages (Suls & Mullen, 1982). However, the most striking finding from studies in this area is the *similarity* across age levels in comparison-seeking strategies, at least among school-age subjects.

For example, Feldman (1978) examined developmental changes in the characteristics of others presumed to be salient to individuals involved in ability assessment. Theoretical and empirical support has emerged both for the similarity base (whether the chosen person is like the subject in some way) and for a standard-setter base (whether the chosen person is known to excel at the task) (e.g., Feldman & Ruble, 1981; Festinger, 1954; Samuel, 1973; Suls & Sanders, 1979; Zanna, Goethals, & Hill, 1975). In the study, both types of characteristics were varied.

Subjects received one story about an actor working on a task described as one at which males, females, or both sexes excelled. They were told that the actor wanted to find out his or her own level of ability on that kind of task. The option of comparing work with six others who varied in sex and ability level (high, average, low) was given to the actor. The subject was asked to rank order the six others and then rate degree of interest. The presumed amount of the actor's interest in comparing with each target other was the major dependent measure, indicated on a scale ranging from 1 to 6 ("not at all" to "a lot").

The results showed that all age groups used both sex (similarity) and ability (standard setting) bases of comparison in making their predictions, with same-sex and one-step upward comparisons being the dominant choice. In addition, virtually all the subjects showed a clear strategy during the first two choices; both were either sex-related (e.g., same-sex average and high ability choices) or ability-related (e.g., same- and opposite-sex high ability choices). The only age-related difference was that fourth-graders showed the strongest interest in comparing with a high ability choice and the least interest in viewing a low ability other, a finding possibly related to developmental changes in reasons presumed to motivate social comparison, described later. Similarity across age levels in the nature of preferences for comparison others has also been shown in a study using a behavioral measure (Dinner, 1976). In sum, social-comparison strategies concerning choices of comparison others are evident in young children and show little qualitative change with increasing age.

Summary. Three types of background factors assumed to be prerequisite to engaging in social comparison have been reviewed. None of these show striking developmental changes in young children that seem sufficient to account for the large shifts observed in the use of social comparison occurring between 7 and 9 years of age. Basic capacities, interest, and mature strategies relevant to social comparison are all present by 6 years of age. Nevertheless, possibly important age-related changes have also been indicated, such as an increase in interest with age and a heightened preference for standard-setting choices at the fourth-grade level. Further research is needed to assess the role of these factors in emerging social-comparison processes and the cognitive and environmental changes that promote their development.

Inference factors

The preceding review leads to the hypothesis that the best explanation for these developmental changes involves different ways of processing and weighting social-comparison information at the time that inferences are drawn as opposed to changes in children's capacities to evaluate them-selves or to compare others' performances with their own. Although there is little directly relevant research available, an analysis of the task of making social comparisons suggests that four factors seem most likely to affect the use of social comparison during the inferential process: (1) changes from *concrete to abstract judgments,* (2) changes in recognizing the *stability* of personality characteristics and abilities, (3) changes in tendencies to make *self-reflective* inferences – a kind of actor/observer dif-ference, and (4) social-environmental changes in pressure to engage in social comparison.

Concrete to abstract. One way to characterize developmental changes is in terms of a shift from overt/concrete to covert/abstract application of social-comparison information. For example, as mentioned earlier, very young children are aware of relative outcome differences between them-selves and others and even appear to use such information for concrete and external measures, such as equalizing the number of rewards re-ceived (e.g., Masters, 1971). However, findings from other research (Mosatche & Bragonier, 1981) suggest that preschool children are more likely to make comparisons involving concrete categories (i.e., posses-sions and activities) than more abstract categories (i.e., abilities, atti-tudes, and status). Also, the information gained from this comparison process may not be translated into a realization of their implications for more internal or abstract measures, such as judgments of competence (e.g., Ruble et al., 1980) or behaviors based on judgments of competence (Boggiano & Ruble, 1979; Spear & Armstrong, 1978). That is, it appears that children's initial comparisons are at an overt, physical level, not involving inferences that are at least one step removed from concrete differences; and only later do such comparisons have any deeper meaning for self-concept.

This characterization of a shift in the inferential process may be related to distinctions made concerning cognitions about nonsocial phenomena (Flavell, 1977), such as focusing on observable characteristics rather than unobservable transformations. Similar shifts have also been reported concerning other areas of *social* cognition. For example, when asked to give impressions of an adult or another child, children younger than 7 or 8 years of age tend to refer primarily to overt, physical characteristics or behaviors (e.g., hair, clothing), whereas older children are more likely to mention abstract internal qualities of the other (e.g., likes or dislikes, degree of friendliness) (cf. Feldman & Ruble, 1981; Livesley & Bromley, 1973; Shantz, 1975). Parallel developmental trends have also been shown in recent research on children's causal attributions concerning their own or another's preferences among an array of items (Ruble et al., 1979). With increasing age, there was a shift away from viewing the choice as being due to the concrete properties of the entity (e.g., color) toward viewing the choice as something internal to the person (e.g., personal taste). Thus, there is evidence from a variety of sources that shifts from concrete to abstract judgments may represent an important developmental change coincident with, and possibly central to, changes in the social-comparison process.

Perceptions of stability. A related way to characterize age changes in the use of social-comparison information concerns whether or not the inference involves the perception of stability, such as personal dispositions or traits. Normally people are motivated to infer the dispositional or stable determinants of a performance (Darley & Goethals, 1980). Young children may not perceive the world, themselves, or other people in terms of stable characteristics that allow for predictability across time. Indeed, in reality many skills do actually change quite rapidly for young children. Thus, during an achievement activity, their concern may be primarily with how to improve current, visible skills (e.g., to get more correct answers), not with evaluating more stable concepts such as ability. With the increased recognition that characteristics may be stable, the 7- to 9-year-old child in effect discovers that there is a wealth of heretofore ignored information about people. A new tendency to look for stable attributes may well lead to greater interest in comparative evaluation of both self and others.

Recently, we began a series of studies to examine developmental changes in children's tendencies to infer stable causal structures in people, as defined by the ability to generalize and note consistencies in behavior. In one study (Rholes & Ruble, in press), 5- and 6-year-olds and 9- and 10-year-olds were shown behaviors of other children on videotape that pretesting had shown would elicit uniform trait and ability attributions. The children were asked to predict how the actor would behave in related situations. As expected, the older children based their predictions on the traits or abilities revealed in the actor's behavior. In contrast, younger children failed to make logical predictions even when they were asked to attach a label to the behavior (e.g., generous) in advance of making predictions. Thus, there is some support for the idea that young children tend not to perceive consistencies in behavior[2] and may therefore not socially compare when inferences require the perception of stability over time. The results of a recent investigation by Barenboim (1981) are consistent with this hypothesis in that use of psychological constructs was found to precede chronologically and to predict psychological *comparisons*.

Self-reflective inferences. Another way to characterize developmental changes in the social-comparison process concerns the ability to translate information received in the environment back to its implications for the self. As children recognize that individuals have important, enduring characteristics, the ability to self-reflect may also lead children to recognize the possibility of enduring characteristics in themselves.

Indeed, several lines of indirect evidence suggest that the initial focus of social comparison may be external (outside of the self) and only later do children realize that the same kinds of relationships in others or in the outside world may apply to the self. First, this kind of phenomenon was suggested in a previous study (Ruble, Feldman, & Boggiano, 1976). An apparent lag was observed between knowledge and behavior in terms of young children's failure to translate the information they received from social comparison under competitive conditions back to the implications for their own performance. Second, preschool children have been shown to use social norm information to make logical inferences of task difficulty information involving hypothetical *other* children (Shaklee, 1976). Finally, a third set of more directly relevant studies has shown that preschool children were able to evaluate differentially the characteristics of *another* individual, presented on videotape, on the basis of social-comparison or consensus information (Feldman & Ruble, 1980; Ruble et al., 1979; Shultz & Butkowsky, 1977). Such findings emphasize once again that developmental changes in the use of social-comparison information for self-evaluation do not seem attributable to young children's deficits in prerequisite cognitive capacities, as they do make logical comparisons for other children.

This apparent self/other difference is quite intriguing, in part because it is opposite to hypotheses concerning other areas of social judgments (Ruble & Rholes, 1981). For example, with regard to moral judgments, it has been suggested that younger children will have an earlier understanding of intentionality when making judgments about their own acts as opposed to those of another child (Keasey, 1977). Why, then, might it be that children show an earlier awareness of social comparison for others than for themselves? One possible explanation involves a kind of attributional egoism (cf. Snyder, Stephan, & Rosenfield, 1978) – a self-centered view in which perceptions of positive and negative outcomes act to protect or enhance one's self-esteem. Thus, young children's tendency to ignore social-comparison information relevant to their own outcomes, particularly when it indicates failure, may represent a basic assumption that "what I want [i.e., success] is what I got." In Piaget's (1972) terms, this kind of thinking represents the young child's logical realism – an inability to distinguish desires from what is real. Some support for this explanation is found in a study of preschool children (Morris & Nemcek, 1982). When asked to rank children in their group on the basis of running speed, children erred primarily by nominating themselves and their friends as faster than they were. Because numerous studies have suggested that this kind of egocentric thought decreases with age (cf. Higgins, 1981), it seems possible to explain a self/other difference in the use of social-comparison information in terms of an egocentric or egoistic bias, which should decrease with age.

A second possible explanation concerns information-processing factors such as focus of attention (Taylor & Fiske, 1978), rather than motivational ones. For example, children may have different perceptions of the relative importance of personal versus situational contributions to the outcome when they are in the situation themselves than when they are judging others, similar to the actor/observer distinction in attribution research (Jones & Nisbett, 1971). That is, when performing a task, children's primary focus of attention is most likely directed externally toward the specific features of the task that they (as actors) are engaged in and away from reflections about themselves and their abilities. Thus, it should, in some sense, be "easier" to evaluate the performance of another, who is directly and concretely observable, than to evaluate oneself.[3] Because salience effects are especially pronounced in young children (e.g., Pryor et al., 1981), assessment of performance based on direct experience with the task may dominate especially the youngest children's evaluations. Research is currently under way to examine these hypotheses regarding an actor/observer difference underlying developmental changes in social comparison.

Social-experiential factors. A final, very general, type of explanatory factor concerns social-environmental changes with age in the emphasis placed on social comparisons, such as an increasing use of relative criteria for grades or praise. Intuitively, it does seem that children are exposed to an ever-increasing array of contests and competitive games (Higgins & Parsons, this volume). At present, however, very little research has addressed this issue. One possible prediction is that children between 6 and 8 years of age, who are in a time of transition, will have greater knowledge of relative standings and exhibit more comparative behavior if their parents or the classroom environment stresses relative standards of behavior.

The nature of social comparison among young children

Let me now turn to a different kind of issue, one that is of particular interest to us in our current research. Despite the apparent failure of children under 7 to 9 years to make *inferences* about their own competence on the basis of social-comparison information, some of the research discussed earlier suggests that social comparison *is* evidenced in many aspects of young children's behavior – for example, interest in comparing possessions or performance progress or maintaining equity of rewards. What does social-comparison behavior mean for the young child? In addition to viewing social comparison as a multistep process, with different aspects of the process developing at different ages (as discussed with reference to Table 3), I would like to propose that the same *behavior* (i.e., making an overt comparison) may also serve different *functions* for children at different ages.[4] Thus, discrepant conclusions about *when* social comparison develops (e.g., Masters, 1971; Mosatche & Bragonier, 1981; Ruble et al., 1980; Suls & Sanders, 1979; Tesser, 1981) and whether social comparison precedes or follows self-evaluation (Ausubel, Montemayor, & Svajian, 1977; Eisert & Kahle, 1982) may be due, in part, to varying definitions or functions represented across studies.

The use of the term *social comparison* in the present chapter has so far implied a hierarchical distinction (e.g., *A* is better than *B*) consistent with one of the goals of making comparisons: self-evaluation. As mentioned earlier, however, there may be other goals involved, such as the acquisition of norms. Two types of phenomena illustrate this point.

First, social comparison may be directed at uncovering *similarities*, partly to define norms and ensure the appropriateness of behavior. Similarity comparison may also occur both as part of an acquaintanceship/ friendship process (Gottman & Parkhurst, 1980) and as a part of a "reflection" process (Tesser, 1981) – that is, to "bask in the reflected glory" of a close associate's accomplishments (Cialdini et al., 1976). These reasons for similarity comparisons may be relevant to a developmental analysis. For example, social comparison may be more likely to represent reflection goals than self-evaluation goals when the relevance of the behavior to one's self-definition is low (Tesser & Campbell, 1980). Therefore, as the self-relevance of abilities is likely to be low until after the early years of school, reflective or similarity-based comparisons are likely to dominate among young children (Tesser, 1981). There is some evidence that young children are particularly interested in establishing similarities between themselves and their peers (Mosatche & Bragonier, 1981). Consensus-producing questions (e.g., "Who likes ice cream?" and "Who has a blue paintbrush?") followed by enthusiastic hand-raising is a common occurrence among preschoolers. In their observational study of friendships, Gottman and Parkhurst (1980) suggest that solidarity comparisons (e.g., "I'm doing mine green/Me too") are especially important in the acquaintanceship process of 3- to 5-year-olds. Among 6-year-olds, there is greater interest in comparisons that emphasize individualism or contrast ("I'm doing mine green/I'm doing mine blue"). Karin Frey and I have recently completed observational studies of the frequency of consensus questions, solidarity comparisons, and contrast comparison among peers in kindergarten to fourth-grade classrooms (Ruble & Frey, 1982).

Second, there is some indication that young children may be less interested in performance *assessment* and more interested in the other child's specific *technique* than older children. Indeed, in one of our earlier studies responses to open-ended questions about an actor's reason for wanting to compare revealed a significant age-related increase in responses relevant to comparative evaluation (e.g., wanting to see who was doing better). The primary difference was that the youngest children were more concerned with comparing to get answers than the other age group (Feldman & Ruble, 1977).

Summary and conclusions

I have argued that social comparison is a basic process during early social-ization. With regard to the area of achievement, it seems obvious that to set realistic aspirations for themselves children must develop a sense of *relative* capacities. Although there is often a heavy emphasis placed upon comparative evaluation from the moment children enter school, a review of evidence leads to the surprising conclusion that social-comparison information has little impact on children's self-evaluation or on behaviors based on self-evaluations until at least 7 or 8 years of age. Furthermore, this is true even though most of the prerequisite cognitive skills, motivations, and strategies are evident during the preschool years. I have tried to highlight two main questions about the development of social comparison that we are currently working on:

1. *Why* this shift occurs: What social and cognitive factors may lead to different ways of processing and using social comparison for self-assessment in the 7 to 9 age range?
2. What *functions* do social comparison processes serve at different ages? There was some suggestion that early functions are related more to norm acquisition goals or concerns with appropriateness of behavior than to self-evaluation.

Let me conclude by suggesting that an analysis of the emergence of social comparison of achievement may serve as a basis for a more general understanding of early self-socialization. To gain a fuller knowledge of their own characteristics and values and to regulate their own behaviors within a range of acceptability, children must be able to compare themselves with others on a wide range of characteristics.

We have begun to explore these more general implications of the social-comparison process in terms of the acquisition of sex roles. The basic idea is that in the same way that children reach a point where social-comparison processes become highly important in evaluating areas of *competence* there is probably a similar point where children also begin to compare themselves in terms of appropriate masculine or feminine behaviors. Indeed, in a study just completed, we showed that children become highly responsive behaviorally to sex-related comparison information only after they have stably categorized themselves as males or females. That is, a single viewing of a commercial portraying a gender-neutral toy in a context that made it seem appropriate for only one sex had a dramatic effect on children's subsequent behavior with, and attitudes about, that toy – but only for children who had attained the stage of gender constancy (Ruble, Balaban, & Cooper, 1981). These results suggest that attaining a stable gender identity may represent a stage in development in which children actively seek information from peers about what is appropriate for their own sex and act in accordance with it. This study thus illustrates the potential generality and importance of social-comparison processes for early self-socialization.

Notes

1 The inconsistencies between the two measures most likely reflect an increased proficiency with age in making comparisons. That is, the younger children probably needed longer intervals each time they pushed the button to acquire the information they were seeking.
2 Conflicting data were recently reported by Heller and Berndt (1981), who concluded that 5- and 6-year-olds do expect behavior to be consistent over time and across situations. Although a number of methodological and interpretational issues may be relevant to explaining this discrepancy (Barenboim, in press; Rholes & Ruble, in press), it is clear that many questions remain about the specific conditions in which young children expect cross-situational stability.
3 It is interesting to note, in this context, that one recent study made self-evaluation particularly salient by portraying own outcomes externally on a video monitor along with outcomes of others. Consistent with the focus-of-attention hypothesis, even first- and second-graders showed clear effects of social-comparison information in their self-evaluations (Levine, Mendez-Caratini, & Snyder, 1982).
4 The contribution of Karin Frey in the development of these ideas is gratefully acknowledged.

References

Arkes, H. R. Competence and the maintenance of behavior. *Motivation and Emotion,* 1978, *2*(3), 201–211.

Ausubel, D. P., Montemayor, E., & Svajian, P. N. *Theory and problems of adolescent development.* New York: Grune & Stratton, 1977.

Barenboim, C. The development of person perception in childhood and adolescence: From behavioral comparisons to psychological constructs to psychological comparisons. *Child Development,* 1981, *52*, 129–144.

Barenboim, C. A response to "Predictions of future behavior, trait ratings, and responses to open-ended questions as measures of children's personality attributions," by T. J Berndt and K. A. Heller. In S. R. Yussen (Ed.), *The development of reflection.* New York: Academic Press, in press.

Bartlett, F. C. *Remembering.* Cambridge: Cambridge University Press, 1932.

Boggiano, A. K., & Ruble, D. N. Competence and the over-justification effect: A developmental study. *Journal of Personality and Social Psychology,* 1979, *37*, 1462–1468.

Bryant, P. E., & Trabasso, T. Transitive inferences and memory in young children. *Nature* 1971, *232*, 456–458.

Cialdini, R. B., Borden, R. J., Thorne, A., Walker, M. R., Freeman, S., & Sloan, L. R Basking in the reflected glory: Three (football) field studies. *Journal of Personality and Social Psychology,* 1976, *34*, 366–375.

Darley, J. M., & Goethals, G. R. People's analyses of the causes of ability linked performances. In L. Berkowitz (Ed.), *Advances in experimental social psychology,* (Vol. 13) New York: Academic Press, 1980.

Deci, E. L. *Intrinsic motivation.* New York: Plenum, 1975.

Dinner, S. H. *Social comparison and self-evaluation in children.* Unpublished doctoral dissertation, Princeton University, 1976.

Eisert, D. C., & Kahle, L. R. Self-evaluation and social comparison of physical and role change during adolescence: A longitudinal analysis. *Child Development,* 1982, *53,* 98–104.

Feldman, N. S. *Developmental changes in social comparison interest.* Paper presented at American Psychology Association, San Francisco, September, 1978.

Feldman, N. S., & Ruble, D. N. *A developmental study of actor/observer differences in the use of social comparison information.* Paper presented at the Eastern Psychological Association Meetings, Hartford, Conn., April 1980.

Feldman, N. S., & Ruble, D. N. Awareness of social comparison interest and motivations: A developmental study. *Journal of Educational Psychology,* 1977, *69,* 579–585.

Feldman, N. S., & Ruble, D. N. The development of person perception: Cognitive versus social factors. In S. S. Brehm, S. M. Kassin, & F. X. Gibbons (Eds.), *Developmental social psychology: Theory and research.* New York: Oxford University Press, 1981.

Feldman, N. S., & Ruble, D. N. Social comparison strategies: Dimensions offered and options taken. *Personality and Social Psychology Bulletin,* 1981, *7,* 11–16.

Festinger, L. A theory of social comparison. *Human Relations,* 1954, *7,* 117–140.

Flavell, J. H., Botkin, P. T., Fry, C. L., et al. *The development of role taking and communications skills in children.* New York: Wiley, 1968.

Flavell, J. H. *Cognitive development.* Englewood Cliffs, N.J.: Prentice-Hall, 1977.

Gottman, J., & Parkhurst, J. A Developmental theory of friendship and acquaintanceship processes. In W. A. Collins (Ed.), *Minnesota Symposium on Child Psychology* (Vol 13). Hillsdale, N.J.: Erlbaum, 1980.

Harter, S. Developmental differences in the manifestation of mastery motivation on problem-solving tasks. *Child Development,* 1975, *46,* 370–378.

Harter, S. Effectance motivation reconsidered. Toward a developmental model. *Human Development,* 1978, *21,* 34–64.

Heckhausen, H. *The anatomy of achievement motivation.* New York: Academic Press, 1967.

Heller, K. A., & Brendt, T. J. Developmental changes in the formation and organization of personality attributions. *Child Development,* 1981, *52,* 683–691.

Higgins, E. T. Role taking and social judgment: Alternative developmental perspectives and processes. In J. H. Flavell and L. Ross (Eds.), *Social cognitive development: frontiers and futures.* Cambridge: Cambridge University Press, 1981.

Higgins, E. T., Feldman, N. S., & Ruble, D. N. Accuracy and differentiations in social prediction: A developmental study. *Journal of Personality,* 1980, *48,* 520–540.

Jones, E. E., & Nisbett, R. E. *The actor and the observer: Divergent perceptions of the causes of behavior.* Morristown, N.J.: General Learning Press, 1971.

Karniol, R., & Ross, M. The effect of performance-relevant and performance-irrelevant rewards on children's intrinsic motivation. *Child Development,* 1977, *48,* 482–487.

Keasey, C. B. Young children's attribution of intentionality to themselves and others. *Child Development,* 1977, *48,* 261–264.

Latane, B. Studies in social comparison. Introduction and overview. *Journal of Experimental Social Psychology,* 1966, *2,* (Supplement 1), 1–5.

Lepper, M. R., & Greene, D. *The hidden costs of rewards.* Hillsdale, N.J.: Erlbaum, 1978.

Livesley, W. J., & Bromley, D. B. *Person perception in childhood and adolescence.* New York: Wiley, 1973.

Levine, J. M. Social comparison and education. In J. M. Levine and M. C. Wang (Eds.), *Teacher and student perceptions: Implications for learning.* Hillsdale, N.J.: Erlbaum, in press.

Levine, J. M., Mendez-Caratini, G., & Snyder, H. N. Task performance and interpersonal attraction in children. *Child Development,* 1982, *53,* 359–371.

Maccoby, E. E., & Jacklin, C. N. *The psychology of sex differences.* Stanford, Calif.: Stanford University Press, 1974.

Markman, E. M. *Factors affecting the young child's ability to monitor his memory.* Unpublished doctoral dissertation, University of Pennsylvania, 1973.

Masters, J. C. Effects of social comparison upon subsequent self-reinforcement behavior in children. *Journal of Personality and Social Psychology,* 1968, *10*(4), 391–401.

Masters, J. C. Social comparison by young children. *Young Children,* 1971, *27,* 37–60.

Morris, W. N., & Nemcek, D. The development of social comparison motivation among preschoolers: Evidence of a step-wise progression. *Merrill-Palmer Quarterly,* 1982, *28,* 413–425.

Mostatche, H. S., & Bragonier, P. An observational study of social comparison in preschoolers. *Child Development,* 1981, *52,* 376–378.

Nicholls, J. G. The development of the concepts of effort and ability, perception of academic attainment, and the understanding that difficult tasks require more ability. *Child Development,* 1978, *49,* 800–814.

Pepitone, E. A. Comparison behavior in elementary school children. *American Educational Research Journal,* 1972, *9,* 45–63.

Piaget, J. *The child's conception of the world.* Totosa, N.J.: Littlefield, Adams, 1972.

Pryor, J. B., Rholes, W. S., Ruble, D. N., & Kriss, M. *A developmental analysis of salience and discounting in social attribution.* Manuscript submitted for publication, 1981.

Rholes, W. S., & Ruble, D. N. *Children's understanding of dispositional characteristics of others. Child Development,* in press.

Rogers, C. M., Smith, M. A., & Coleman, J. M. Social comparison in the classroom: The relationship between academic achievement and self-concept. *Journal of Educational Psychology,* 1978, *70,* 50–57.

Ruble, D. N., Balaban, T. D., & Cooper, J. Gender constancy and the effects of sex-typed television toy commercials. *Child Development,* 1981, *52,* 667–673.

Ruble, D. N., & Boggiano, A. K. Optimizing motivation in an achievement context. In B. Keogh (Ed.), *Advances in special education* (Vol. 1). Greenwich, Conn.: JAI Press, 1980.

Ruble, D. N., Boggiano, A. K., Feldman, N. S., & Loebl, J. H. A developmental analysis of the role of social comparison in self-evaluation. *Developmental Psychology,* 1980, *16,* 105–115.

Ruble, D. N., Feldman, N. S., & Boggiano, A. K. Social comparison between young children in achievement situations. *Developmental Psychology,* 1976, *12,* 192–197.

Ruble, D. N., Feldman, N. S., Higgins, E. T., & Karlovac, M. Locus of causality and the use of information in the development of causal attributions. *Journal of Personality,* 1979, *47,* 595–614.

Ruble, D. N., & Frey, K. S. *Social comparison and self-evaluation in the classroom: A naturalistic study of peer interaction.* Paper presented in a symposium on Social Comparison: Implications for Education, American Educational Research Association, New York, March 1982.

Ruble, D. N., Parsons, J. E., & Ross, J. Self-evaluative responses of children in achievement setting. *Child Development,* 1976, *47,* 990–997.

Ruble, D. N., & Rholes, W. S. The development of children's perceptions and attributions about their social world. In J. H. Harvey, W. Ickes, & R. F. Kidd (Eds.), *New directions in attribution research* (Vol 3). Hillsdale, N.J.: Erlbaum, 1981.

Samuel, W. On clarifying some interpretations of social comparison theory. *Journal of Experimental Social Psychology,* 1973, *9,* 450–465.

Schwarzer, R., Jerusalem, M., & Lange, B. *The development of academic self-concept with respect to reference groups in school.* Paper presented at the International Society for Behavioral Development meetings, Toronto, August 1981.

Sears, R. R., Maccoby, E. E., & Levin, H. *Patterns of child rearing*. Evanston, Ill.: Row, Paterson, 1957.

Sears, R. R., Rau, L., & Alpert, R. *Identification and child rearing*. Stanford, Calif.: Stanford University Press, 1965.

Shaklee, H. Development in inferences of ability and task difficulty. *Child Development*, 1976, *47*, 1051–1057.

Shatz, M., & Gelman, R. The development of communication skills: Modifications in the speech of young children as a function of listener. *Monographs of the Society for Research in Child Development*, 1973, *38* (5), 1–38.

Shultz, T. R., & Butkowsky, I. Young children's use of the scheme for multiple sufficient causes in the attribution of real and hypothetical behavior. *Child Development*, 1977, *48*, 464–469.

Shantz, C. The development of social cognition. In E. M. Hetherington (Ed.), *Review of child development research* (Vol. 5). Chicago: University of Chicago Press, 1975.

Snyder, M. L., Stephan, W. G., & Rosenfield, D. Attributional egotism. In J. H. Harvey, W. Ickes, & R. F. Kidd (Eds.), *New direction in attribution research*, (Vol. 2). Hillsdale, N.J.: Erlbaum, 1978.

Spear, P. S., & Armstrong, S. Effects of performance expectancies created by peer comparison as related to social reinforcement, task difficulty, and age of child. *Journal of Experimental Social Psychology*, 1978, *25*, 254–266.

Strang, L., Smith, M. D., & Rogers, C. M. Social comparison, multiple reference groups, and self-concepts of academically handicapped children before and after mainstreaming. *Journal of Educational Psychology*, 1978, *70*, 487–497.

Suls, J. M., & Miller, R. C. (Eds.). *Social comparison processes: Theoretical and empirical perspectives*. Washington, D.C.: Hemisphere/Halsted, 1977.

Suls, J. M., & Mullen, B. From the cradle to the grave: Comparison and self-evaluation across the life-span. In J. M. Suls (Ed.), *Social psychological perspectives on the self*. Hillsdale, N.J.: Erlbaum, 1982.

Suls, J. M., & Sanders, G. S. Social comparison processes in the young child. *Journal of Research and Development in Education*, 1979, *13*, 79–89.

Taylor, S. E., & Fiske, S. T. Salience attention, and attribution: Top of the head phenomena. In L. Berkowitz (Ed.), *Advances in experimental social psychology* (Vol. 1). New York: Academic Press, 1978.

Tesser, A. *Self-evaluation maintenance processes: Implications for relationships and development*. Paper presented at the Nashville Conference on Boundary Areas in Psychology: Developmental and Social, June 1981.

Tesser, A., & Campbell, J. Self-definition: The impact of the relative performance and similarity of others. *Social Psychology Quarterly*, 1980, *43*, 341–347.

Trabasso, T., & Riley, C. A. On the construction and use of representations involving linear order. In R. L. Solso (Ed.), *Contemporary issues in cognitive psychology*. Hillsdale, N.J.: Erlbaum, 1974.

Veroff, J. Social comparison and the development of achievement motivation. In C. P. Smith (Ed.), *Achievement related motives in children*. New York: Russell Sage, 1969.

Weiner, B. (Ed.). *Achievement motivation and attribution theory*. Morristown, N.J.: General Learning Press, 1974.

White, R. W. Motivation reconsidered: The concept of competence. *Psychological Review*, 1959, *66*, 297–333.

Zanna, M. P., Goethals, G. R., & Hill, J. F. Evaluating a sex-related ability: Social comparison with similar others and standard setters. *Journal of Experimental Social Psychology*, 1975, *11*, 86–93.

7 Social cognition, social behavior, and children's friendships

Thomas J. Berndt

The pleasures that children derive from their friendships are obvious to all observers. Children show their happiness when with their friends, they drop other activities to spend time with friends, and they frequently rely on friends for advice and support. Psychological research on children's friendships has increased rapidly in recent years, as researchers have attempted to determine the most important features of friendship and the changes in these features with age (Asher & Gottman, 1981; Foot, Chapman, & Smith, 1980; Rubin, 1980). In most studies, children have been asked to respond to general questions such as "How do you know that someone is a best friend?" The responses have been viewed as direct evidence of children's conceptions of friendship. In addition, they often have been interpreted as indirect evidence of the characteristics of children's actual friendships.

In this chapter a different approach to the investigation of children's friendships is described. The new approach involves the coordinated exploration of social cognitions related to friendship and the social behavior of friends. The primary reason for linking measures of social cognition and social behavior was not to validate the findings of social-cognitive research against a behavioral criterion. Instead, the primary goal was to obtain a more complete understanding of friendship than that provided by either type of measure when used alone. Previous social-cognitive research revealed several important aspects of friendships and their development, but a single method can hardly be expected to provide a full picture of a phenomenon as complex as friendship. The joint investigation of cognition and behavior was selected as a means for the discovery of aspects of friendship that had been neglected or overlooked in past research.

Findings from a recent series of studies suggest that the new approach can lead to an increase in the precision and scope of knowledge about children's friendships. To anticipate briefly, the recent research has indi-

158

cated that features of friendship vary with sex as well as with age. Under certain conditions, girls distinguish more sharply between close friends and other peers than do boys. In addition, the new studies have suggested that certain types of conflicts are intrinsic to friendship. On the one hand, friends perceive themselves as equals, and they help or share with each other when these behaviors promote equality in their outcomes. On the other hand, children compete rather than share with a friend if sharing could lead to their "losing" or appearing inferior to the friend. Similarly, children try to respond sensitively to their friends' needs and desires, but they do not believe that they should always do what their friends want. Instead, they strike a balance between responsiveness and independence. Finally, not all features of friendship change with age. Some important features appear to remain fairly constant across a large age range.

Theories of the development of friendship are not extensively discussed in this chapter because few theories exist and they are not very detailed. Youniss (1980) drew from the writings of Piaget (1932/1965) and Sullivan (1953) the general hypothesis that age changes in friendship reflect transformations in the meaning of reciprocity. Youniss reported data on children's conception of friendship that are consistent with his hypothesis, but he gave little attention to several issues that must be considered in a complete theory. For example, he did not present specific hypotheses about the antecedents of developmental changes in friendship or the consequences of individual differences in friendship. These comments are not meant as a criticism of Youniss's work. He has identified an element of friendship that can serve as an integrative principle in the description of developmental changes. Moreover, his description and that of Sullivan (1953) were considered in the generation of specific hypotheses for the studies reported later in this chapter. Nevertheless, these writings and the rest of the literature do not contain a formal theory of friendship that could be tested in a program of research. Before such a theory can be constructed, more detailed information about children's friendships is needed.

The chapter is divided into three major sections. In the first section, the previous social-cognitive research is briefly reviewed and discussed. In the second section, the studies that included the simultaneous examination of social cognition and social behavior are described. In the final section, conclusions about current knowledge regarding the development of friendship are followed by a discussion of the questions that may be most productive in future research.

Children's conceptions of friendship: a general view

Several reviews of the social-cognitive literature on friendship have been published recently (Berndt, 1981d; Bigelow & LaGaipa, 1980; Selman, 1981). Consequently, a full review will not be given in this chapter. Instead, the major similarities and differences between studies will be emphasized.

All studies have used the same basic procedure. Children have been asked one question or a series of general and open-ended questions about friendship, for example, "What is a friend?" (Youniss, 1980), "Why is it nice to have friends?" (Reisman & Shorr, 1978), and "How can you tell that someone is a best friend?" (Berndt, 1981d). Occasionally, children have been asked about their own friends (Damon, 1977). Occasionally, children have been told a story or have been shown a filmstrip about friendship before they were asked any questions (Selman, 1981). The amount of probing done after children's initial responses has varied across studies. In some cases interviewers were free to change questions so that they could determine what children meant by specific statements and how the children dealt with counterexamples (Damon, 1977). In other cases no probing was possible because children were tested in large groups and answers were written (Bigelow, 1977). These differences seem to be relatively unimportant, because all researchers appear to have obtained similar sets of responses. In other words, children made similar statements about friends and friendship regardless of the specific question they were asked or the amount of probing done.

Coding of friendship conceptions: specific categories versus stages

Great differences between studies are found in the manner that researchers coded and summarized the children's data. Several researchers chose the option of coding the responses into specific categories devised after inspection of the data (Berndt, 1981d; Gamer, 1977). Other researchers used previous writings on friendship as a guide to the selection of specific categories (Bigelow, 1977; Riesman & Shorr, 1978). Previous writings were not used to generate hypotheses about the categories that are most important in children's friendship conceptions or age changes in these categories. Rather, they simply suggested ways of classifying the data collected.

Empirically derived specific categories have been used in research with subjects ranging from preschool age to later adulthood (Berndt, 1981d; Bigelow & LaGaipa, 1980; Hayes, 1978; Riesman & Shorr, 1978). In their major conclusions, the results of different studies are consistent with one another, so the typical findings can be illustrated with two studies by Berndt (1981d). Children from kindergarten to sixth grade most frequently said that a friend was someone who played with them or did other activities with them. These responses did not change with age. References to play alone decreased with age in other studies, whereas references to common activities increased (Bigelow, 1977; Riesman & Shorr, 1978). Apparently, children at all ages agree that friends spend time interacting with each other; young children seem more likely to describe these interactions as play.

Children from kindergarten to sixth grade frequently said that friends behave prosocially toward each other and do not fight with each other. These responses were more commonly mentioned by older children. On the other hand, Bigelow (1977) did not find any regular age trends for references to prosocial behavior.

References to the intimacy of conversation between friends increased dramatically between third and sixth grade. Kindergarten and third-grade children rarely said that they talk about problems with friends or even that they share secrets with them. References to friends' loyalty also increased between third and sixth grade. Young children rarely said that their friends did (or did not) stick up for them when they were in trouble with adults or other peers; they rarely said that their friends talked (or did not talk) about them behind their backs. All studies have found an increase in concerns with intimacy and loyalty as children approach adolescence. Intimacy seems to be the only major category that shows sex differences. Girls tend to stress intimacy more than do boys.

Finally, young children often said that a friend was someone whom they knew and liked or someone who called them a friend. These responses were less common in older children, probably because older children assumed that these characteristics were essential to friendship and so felt no need to mention them. Two other categories were mentioned less often. Especially in the higher grades, children said a friend was faithful, a person who would not leave them for someone else. Children also mentioned attributes of a person that make it pleasant to be friends with them (e.g., "She's a nice girl"). These responses did not vary regularly with age. References to faithfulness and to the attributes of a friend seem to have been obtained by other researchers. However, they have been classified differently. For example, faithfulness is sometimes treated as a component of loyalty, and references to the attributes of a friend are sometimes coded into several different categories (cf. Bigelow, 1977).

As an alternative to the use of the specific categories, several researchers have attempted to score children's friendship conceptions for the level or stage of reasoning that they represent. Selman's (1981) model is probably the best known (but see also Damon, 1977). Selman argued that there are stages in the development of friendship conceptions that closely correspond to levels of social perspective-taking ability. Children at the lowest level of perspective taking cannot distinguish their own perspective from that of other people. They also confuse the subjective, or psychological, and the objective, or physical, aspects of the social world. At the corresponding stage of friendship conceptions, Stage 0, children regard everyone they play with as a friend, but they assume the friendship lasts only as long as they are playing together.

At Level 1 of perspective taking, children understand that other people may think or feel differently than they do, but they cannot take two perspectives into account simultaneously or understand themselves from another person's perspective. At Stage 1 of friendship conceptions, children view a friend primarily as someone who helps them or does things for them. Because they cannot understand another's view of them, they do not recognize their responsibility to help in return.

At Level 2 of perspective taking, children can understand another's view of them and consider reciprocal perspective. Friendship at Stage 2 means cooperation: Each child tries to take account of the other child's preferences. At this stage, however, there is no sense of an enduring relationship between friends. Any instance of noncooperation or conflict is regarded as terminating the friendship.

At Level 3 of perspective taking, children can take the view of a third party with respect to an interaction between two people. This achievement leads to a new appreciation of mutuality in Stage 3 friendships. Friendships are defined by mutual support and mutual understanding. Friendship is regarded as an intimate relationship that is maintained during minor conflicts. Often, the stress of intimacy leads to a possessive relationship. One friend may insist that the other be available and responsive under all circumstances.

Level 4 of perspective taking is typically found only in adolescence and adulthood. Individuals can recognize a general perspective on events, one common to the society at large. They also realize that there are various levels at which people's perspective may be similar or different. For example, people may agree about superficial information but disagree about its interpretation. Stage 4 of friendship conceptions reflects a new balance of friendship and individuality. People understand that friends are dependent on each other; for example, they rely on each other for support. Nevertheless, friends retain a measure of independence, particularly with regard to other interpersonal relationships. Friends are free to see other people and spend time with them. The new appreciation of a friend's need for independence breaks down the possessiveness of Stage 3 friendship conceptions.

Selman's (1981) model of the development of friendship conceptions is more complex and differentiated than the preceding description implies. He also has identified six issues that apply to friendship: friendship formation, closeness and intimacy, trust, jealousy, conflicts and their resolution, and friendship termination. Children's responses during an interview about friendship are coded first for the issue to which they refer and then for the stage of reasoning that they represent. Examples illustrating responses at each stage for each issue are contained in a detailed scoring manual (Selman & Jaquette, 1977).

A third group of researchers stand midway between those who code responses into specific categories and those who derive overall stage scores. Youniss (1980) described his data on age changes in friendship conceptions as generally illustrating a transformation in the meaning of reciprocity. Nevertheless, he also classified children's responses under the headings of playing and sharing, helping, mutual understanding, and so on. Bigelow (1977) proposed that specific categories for friendship conceptions can be combined into three general stages. At the lowest stage, children emphasize the rewards and costs of friendship. At the next stage, children are concerned with a friend's character as judged against conventional standards. At the highest stage, children are concerned with the psychological elements of friendship, particularly intimacy and empathy.

Measures of friendship conceptions: a brief critique

Despite the large number of studies and reviews of research on children's friendship conceptions, few writers have explicitly compared the alternative techniques for coding and analyzing the data obtained. In a brief discussion, Selman (1981) suggested two possible advantages to the use of a stage model rather than specific categories. First, he suggested that researchers using specific categories may misinterpret the meaning of children's responses because they do not probe the responses fully. However, this criticism concerns a detail of interviewing procedure rather than the choice of how to code and summarize the data once it is collected. In addition, if misinterpretations of children's responses frequently occurred, they would reduce the reliability of the data and lead to inconsistencies in findings across studies. An Selman pointed out, the findings of studies that have employed different coding systems are largely consistent with one another. For example, all researchers report that a concern with the intimacy of friendships, which Selman placed at Stage 3, first appears during adolescence. Consequently, it is doubtful that insufficient probing or the use of specific categories have led to any substantial misinterpretation of children's responses.

Second, Selman suggested that the derivation of categories on an empirical or intuitive basis is less desirable than the use of an explicit theory when exploring a new domain of reasoning. Selman's own coding system is only partly based on theory, however. It is structured partly by levels of perspective taking and partly by the six specific issues that were not generated from any theory. Nonetheless, Selman's model is based on theory in a way that the alternative technique for coding and analysis is not. One major purpose of his research was to determine if developments in children's conceptions of friendship could be subsumed by a general model of cognitive development, in particular, the structural model of Piaget (1970) and Kohlberg (1969). Therefore, the metric by which he has scored children's responses is their maturity, that is, their position in a stage sequence formulated on the basis of previous theory and research on cognitive development. In contrast, researchers who have coded children's responses into specific categories have been interested, first, in the features of friendship that are important to children and, second, in age changes in the importance of these features. The metric for judging importance is the frequency with which responses reflecting each feature are expressed. The similarity in the methods and the major findings of research using the two approaches may obscure this fundamental difference in purpose and measurement.

One problem with all the previous research is that it does not provide very specific information about any single aspect of friendship. For example, all researchers agree that children expect friends to help and share with each other, although there is some dispute regarding how these expectations change with age. Berndt (1981d) reported an increase with age in children's comments about prosocial behavior between friends, but Bigelow (1977) did not. Selman (1981) suggested that prosocial behavior is not considered at Stage 0 of friendship conceptions. In his model, it is not until Stage 2 that children recognize their own need to help, and share with, a friend. Other researchers have suggested that children believe they should share with a friend before they believe they need to help him or her (Damon, 1977; Youniss, 1980). Conducting additional interviews with open-ended questions about friendship is probably not the best way to resolve the dispute. It may be better to ask a more precise question or set of questions about the role of prosocial behavior in friendship.

Several important and unanswered questions can be generated easily. For example, how much do children expect friends to help, and share with, each other? Does the amount of sharing and helping expected from friends vary with age? Is more sharing and helping expected from close friends than from children who are not close friends? These questions can be answered if children make judgments about friends' prosocial behavior on a structured Likert-type response scale. Use of a structured response scale also eliminates a potential artifact in research with open-ended questions, the confounding effect of verbal fluency or ability.

Another set of questions would transform the study of social cognitions about friendship from the general or ideal realm to the realm of children's actual friendships. For example, how much do children say they would help, and share with, one of their own friends? Does what children say they would do correspond to what they actually do? Answers to these questions would begin to link friendship conceptions to friends' behavior. They would clarify not just how children's ideas about friendship change with age but how friendships themselves change.

Prosocial behavior between friends: studies of social cognition and behavior

A progression from the general exploration of friendship conceptions to a specific focus on prosocial behavior seems appropriate for several reasons. In the popular and theoretical literature on friendship, the degree to which friends help and share with each other has always been emphasized (e.g., Sullivan, 1953). Nevertheless, empirical research on the significance of prosocial behavior in friendships is scarce and inconsistent. As just mentioned, the findings from previous social-cognitive research do not clearly indicate whether or not there are age changes in children's expectations for prosocial behavior between friends. Older children may or may not expect friends to share with, or help, each other more than younger children. Children at any given age may or may not say that they would share with, or help, one of their own friends more than other classmates.

Evidence on the actual behavior of friends also presents a confusing picture. In two studies (Fincham, 1978; Wright, 1942), children shared more with a stranger than with a best friend, apparently because they believed the stranger was in greater need. Children shared more with a child whom they regarded as a close friend than with another classmate in one study (Staub & Sherk, 1970), but no difference between friends and other classmates was found in another study (Floyd, 1964). In research on children's bargaining, close friends either made bargains similar to those of children who felt neutral toward each other or they decided on a less equal distribution of rewards than other children (Benton, 1971; Morgan & Sawyer, 1967). In the most recent studies, friends more frequently interacted with each other and had more harmonious interactions than did other classmates when the children were watching a movie or working together on a task (Foot, Chapman, & Smith, 1977; Newcomb & Brady, 1982; Newcomb, Brady, & Hartup, 1979). These studies show more positively toned interactions between friends than nonfriends, but sharing and helping were not measured directly.

The previous research provides surprisingly little support for the commonsense hypothesis that friends will act more prosocially toward each other than will nonfriends. Reasons for the inconsistencies in results are difficult to discern. Comparisons between studies are hard to make because different methods and measures were used. The group of nonfriends also varied. Sometimes the nonfriend group included strangers; sometimes they were children who disliked each other; and sometimes they were classmates who had only moderate liking for each other. In addition, the research contains little information about age changes in friends' prosocial behavior, because most studies included children at one age or from a narrow age range. In view of these problems, a new research program on prosocial behavior in children's friendships seemed necessary.

At this point, three studies in the research program have been completed. All studies included observations of helping or sharing between friends. All studies included measures of children's prosocial intentions toward a friend, that is, the amount that they said they would help and share with a friend (cf. Fishbein & Ajzen, 1975). Additional questions were used to investigate various factors that might affect prosocial intentions. The measure of intentions and its associated questions were designed as an extension of previous social-cognitive research on friendship. Because of the similarity in measures across studies, later ones partly clarify the results and interpretation of earlier ones. Nevertheless, there are important differences between the studies. They included children at different ages and employed different research designs. Instead of focusing on a single question, they were planned as a broad exploration of sharing and helping in children's friendships.

Study 1: sharing between friends in middle childhood

The primary purpose of the first study (Berndt, 1981b) was to determine whether or not prosocial intentions and behavior are greater for pairs of close friends than for pairs of classmates who are not close friends. Age changes in prosocial intentions and behavior during middle childhood also were examined.

Method. The study included 116 children from kindergarten, second, and fourth grades. The children were asked first to name their best friends and then to rate their liking for each of their same-sex classmates on a 5-point scale consisting of 5 circles of increasing size. The smallest circle was labeled "don't like"; the largest was labeled "like very much, as much as a best friend." Children's nominations and ratings were used in combination to pair each child with a specific friend or another classmate. Children were considered close friends if at least one of them had nominated the other as a best friend and their ratings for each other averaged 4.0 or more. Children were considered simply as classmates if neither child had nominated the other as a best friend and they had not indicated a high degree of liking for each other. Children were never paired with a child who had indicated that he or she disliked them.

After the pairings were made, each child was interviewed individually. To assess children's prosocial intentions, they were asked how much they would help, or share with, their partner in the study, the friend or other classmate paired with them, in four specific situations. For example, they were asked if they would let their partner ride a new bicycle that they had just received. If they said they would, they were asked how long they would let the partner ride it. Children responded on a 5-point scale consisting of 5 squares of increasing size. The smallest was labeled "not at all"; the largest was labeled "as long as he (she) wants." Use of the 5-point scale increased the comparability of responses across subjects and reduced the impact of differences in children's verbal skills. The final measure of prosocial intentions was derived by summing the scores for all four situations.

After indicating what they would do in each situation, children were asked three questions designed to measure possible determinants of their intentions (see Berndt, 1981d; Fishbein & Ajzen, 1975). They were asked how much they thought they should help or share with their partner, how much their partner would expect them to help or share, and how much they wanted to help or share.[1] The order of the three questions was randomized; they were answered with the 5-point scale used for prosocial intentions.

In another session randomly scheduled before or after the interviews, the pairs of friends or other classmates were observed as they worked on a task that provided them with opportunities to share with each other.[2] Each child was given a design to color, but the two children were told that they would need to share a single set of crayons. For the first half of the trials, one child was given the crayons first. The amount of time that child let the other child use the crayons served as the measure of sharing. For the remainder of the trials, the other child had the crayons first and could choose how much to share with his or her partner.

Children were told that they would receive a prize for how much they completed on their own design. The experimenter indicated how well they were doing by giving them nickels after each trial. The child who colored more on each trial received two nickels; the child who colored less received one nickel. The rewards ensured that sharing the crayons had some cost for the children. Children who shared for a longer time were likely to receive fewer rewards than their partners. The reward structure could promote competition if children regarded themselves as losing on a trial when they received fewer nickels then their partners. In other words, rather than thinking mainly about how much of their own design they could complete, they may have considered whether they completed more and got more nickels than their partner.

Boys' and girls' prosocial intentions toward friends. The results for prosocial intentions were clear but unexpected. Boys and girls agreed on how much they would help and share with classmates, but girls said they would help and share with friends more than with other classmates and boys said they would act similarly toward friends and other classmates. For both boys and girls, intentions did not vary between kindergarten and fourth grade. Intentions to help and share were strongly correlated with children's reports of how much they thought they should, and how much they wanted to, share and help. Intentions were uncorrelated with children's reports of how much their friend or classmate expected them to share and help.

The sex differences in intentions may be related to findings in previous research that suggest girls have smaller and more exclusive friendship groups than do boys. Girls tend to have fewer close friends than boys, and girls tend to make fewer new friends during the course of a school year than boys do (Eder & Hallinan, 1978). In addition, girls who have many friends at the beginning of a school year tend to make fewer friends during the year than do other girls; the opposite is true for boys (Berndt & Hoyle, 1981). These data suggest that girls are more likely than boys to limit the size of their friendship groups. Children's reports on their interactions with peers indicate that girls spend most of their time with a single other girl; boys most often play with a group of other boys (Savin-Williams, 1980; Waldrop & Halverson, 1975). During adolescence, girls express more concern with the intimacy of friendships than boys do (Berndt, 1981d; Douvan & Adelson, 1966). The girls' emphasis on intimacy is probably related to their preference for dyadic interactions with friends, because intimate conversations are more likely in dyads than in larger groups. Finally, when another classmate joins a pair of friends who are already engaged in an interaction, boys more rapidly acknowledge and include the classmate in their interaction than do girls (Feshbach, 1969; Feshbach & Sones, 1971). For girls, the boundary between friends and nonfriends seems to be sharper than for boys.

A sex difference in the exclusiveness of friendships can explain the effects for prosocial intentions. By responding in an extremely positive way toward a close friend, girls help maintain the friendship. By responding less positively to other classmates, girls discourage future interactions and maintain the boundary between friends and nonfriends. In so doing, they may preserve the intimacy of their small friendship group. In contrast, boys who have many friends cannot afford to treat any particular friend in an especially positive way, because all their other friends will demand the same treatment. Boys apparently treat classmates who are not yet close friends as potential friends. By helping and sharing with them, boys invite further interaction and may ultimately increase the size of their friendship network. These speculations would be more convincing, however, if it was clear that the pattern of sex differences in intentions was not an accidental result. Later studies provided evidence on this point.

Prosocial behavior between friends: sharing or competition. Children's behavior toward friends also varied with sex, but the pattern was different from that for prosocial intentions. Children never shared significantly more with friends than with other classmates. Girls shared the crayons fairly equally with their partners, regardless of whether the partner was a close friend or another classmate. Second-grade boys who had control of the crayons for the first half of the trials and fourth-grade boys who had control of the crayons for the last half of the trials shared significantly *less* with friends than with other classmates. In addition, when their partner asked for the crayon, boys at all ages tended to comply with friends' requests less often than with classmates' requests. Girls usually complied with the requests of both friends and other classmates. Finally, a measure of equality in outcomes, the discrepancy between the amounts colored by the two children in a pair, showed larger discrepancies for boys paired with friends than for boys paired with other classmates. Discrepancies were low for girls in both conditions.

The entire pattern of results can be explained by assuming that girls adopted the polite solution of sharing equally with any partner; boys shared the crayons fairly equally with classmates who were not close friends, but when their partner was a friend, they tried to get more done on the task and get more nickels than their friend by sharing the crayons less. In other words, boys who were friends apparently viewed the task as a competitive one. They tried to win the competition or at least to avoid losing by keeping the crayons for themselves most of the time.

Other research indicates that the boys' competition with friends is not an isolated result. Staub & Noerenberg (1981) also found that third- and fourth-grade boys shared less with a friend than with another classmate under certain conditions, and they suggested competition between friends as a possible explanation. When playing games on which competitive responses were measured directly, male high school students and male students attending a large, business-oriented college competed more with friends than with strangers (Oskamp & Perlman, 1966; Swingle & Gillis, 1968). Moreover, in a recent study of attitudes toward competition, boys expressed more agreement than girls with statements such as "I try to do better work than my friends" and "My friends want to do better work than me" (Ahlgren & Johnson, 1979).

In explaining the results of the current study, two questions must be answered. First, why did girls aim for equality with close friends and other classmates? Previous research often has shown that girls and women prefer equality over competition to a greater degree than do boys and men (e.g., Kahn, Nelson, & Gaeddert, 1980; Skarin & Moely, 1976). When two girls are engaged in an interaction, they apparently are more concerned with achieving interpersonal harmony by trying for equality than they are with achieving superiority over another. The reason that girls' preference for exclusive friendships does not directly affect their sharing with friends and classmates is not entirely clear. Exclusiveness may affect girls' prosocial behavior only if sharing and helping might be used to initiate an interaction with another child, or if girls have a choice between interacting with two other girls when one of them is a close friend and the other is not (e.g., Feshbach & Sones, 1971). When girls are already engaged in an interaction with another girl, they seem to regard fair and equal sharing as most satisfying, unless the other girl is someone they really dislike (Benton, 1971).

Second, why do boys compete more with friends than with other class-mates? On the one hand, friends may feel less constrained to act politely toward each other. All boys may have been ready to compete with each other on the task, but they may have felt free to do so only when paired with a close friend. This view is compatible with the assumption that boys competed with friends because it made the task enjoyable: It was a friendly competition. On the other hand, boys may not enjoy competing with a friend, but they may feel compelled to do so when the only alternative is losing a game to a friend. Because friends are similar to each other, they often compare themselves to each other and they assume that they are equal in most important respects (Rubin, 1980; Tesser, 1981; Youniss, 1980). However, if one friend loses a game to the other, it is clear that the friends are not equal. Because this conclusion violates a basic principle of the friendship, it can be quite disturbing. In this view, the competiton between boys who were friends was a serious and unpleasant matter for both of them.

The two contrasting interpretations of the friends' competition cannot be tested with the data from the first study. They could be tested if children's reactions to the task and to their partner's behavior were assessed. Alternatively, they could be tested indirectly by varying the reward structure for the task and determing the effects on children's behavior. Previous research has demonstrated that friends do not compete with each other in all situations. Often friends cooperate more than do other classmates (Newcomb & Brady, in press; Newcomb, Brady, & Hartup, 1979). Competition seems most likely when friends cannot easily achieve the outcome of equality. In this first study, children could try for equality across a series of trials, as girls seemed to do. They could not attain an equal number of rewards on each trial, however. If equality was possible on each trial, boys and girls might try for equality more often and share more often with close friends than with nonfriends. Furthermore, if this result was obtained, it would suggest that friends do not enjoy competing with each other because they avoid any real competition when they can.

Relations between social cognition and social behavior. The correlations between the measures of prosocial intentions and actual sharing were low and mostly nonsignificant, although they were slightly higher for friends than for other classmates (average rs = .24 and −.05, respectively). The low correlations are not surprising because the two types of measures showed different effects for the most important independent variables, sex and friendship. In most previous research, low correlations between measures of social cognition and social behavior have been regarded as casting doubt on the reliability or the validity of the social-cognitive measures, the behavioral measures, or both (see, e.g., Enright & Sutterfield, 1980; Shantz, 1975). Problems of reliability and validity do not seem to be a plausible explanation for the correlations in Study 1, because the findings for both intentions and behavior were consistent with data from previous research. Instead, the problem seems to be the lack of correspondence between the situations to which each measure referred (Ajzen & Fishbein, 1977). Children were asked about their intentions to help and share with their partner in situations that were drawn from everyday life. None of the situations was implicitly or explicitly competitive. Children had opportunities to share with their partner in a game that could have been viewed and apparently was viewed as competitive. Previous research suggests that strong correlations between the measures of intentions and behavior would not be expected in this case and would be expected only if both measures referred to similar types of situations.

Study 2: changes in friendships and their effects on prosocial intentions and behavior

The major purpose of the second study (Berndt, 1981a) was to determine if changes in children's friendships that naturally occur during the course of a school year are associated with changes in children's prosocial intentions toward friends and their actual behavior. Pairs of friends were formed in the fall of a school year. At that time, data on the friends' prosocial intentions and behavior were collected. In the spring of the same school year, the same pairs of childen were interviewed and observed again. By that time, some of the pairs were expected to be no longer close friends. A relation between the decrease in the strength of these friendships and decreases in the children's prosocial intentions and behavior was expected.

The primary measures in the study were altered in two important ways from those used in Study 1. First, the measure of prosocial intentions included two situations that were comparable to the task situations in which prosocial behavior was observed. By increasing the correspondence between the measures of intentions and behavior, this change was expected to increase the correlations between them. On the other hand, the change precluded an attempt to replicate the sex difference in friends' prosocial intentions that seemed to be related to the exclusiveness of girls' friendships. Because the sex difference in Study 1 held for situations that were noncompetitive, it was less likely to appear when implicitly competitive situations (like the task situations) were included in the measure of intentions.

Second, the reward structure for the tasks used to measure friends' prosocial behavior was altered so that the two children could receive an equal number of rewards on each trial. This change was expected to reduce friends' competition with each other and increase their prosocial behavior, because neither friend would lose if they tried for equality. Several writers have proposed that the preference for equality between friends increases with age (see Youniss, 1980). This hypothesis was tested by including children from the first and fourth grades in the study.

Finally, a new measure was added in Study 2. As was mentioned briefly, the prosocial intentions of children in the first study were unrelated to their judgments about how much their partner expected them to share and help. Because no relations were found either for friends or for classmates, the results imply that children ignored their friend's expectations when deciding how much to share and help. On the basis of theory, common sense, and past research (e.g., Newcomb, Brady, & Hartup, 1979), this conclusion appears implausible. In Study 2, children again were asked about the friend's expectations, but they also were asked how they would respond to a specific request by the friend. The new question more directly examines children's sensitivity to a friend's desires.

Method. The study included 86 children from the first and fourth grades. On the basis of best-friend nominations and ratings of liking, each child was paired with a close friend in October of the school year. Children then were asked about their intentions to help, and share with, the friend in one session; in another session they were observed as they did two tasks with the friend. The interviews and observations were repeated in March of the school year with the same pairs of children, whether or not they were still close friends. Only one pair of children failed to complete both the fall and the spring assessments, because one child moved during the school year.

As already mentioned, two of the situations in the measure of prosocial intentions were modeled on the tasks for prosocial behavior. For example, children were asked if they would share some crayons that they brought from home with their friend when they and the friend were drawing pictures that might win prizes at the school art show. After children had responded to all four situations, they were asked the new question about what they would say if the friend asked them to share or help in one of the previous situations for the maximum possible time. For example, they were asked if they would share the crayons for the entire time that they had to draw if their partner asked them to. (A situation was chosen for which children had not said originally that they would share or help as much as was possible.) In addition, the original question about the friend's expectations was changed to "How much would (name of friend) think you should share (or help)?" One reason for changing the wording of the question was that "expect" has two distinct meanings: what a person is likely to do and what a person should do. The latter meaning is more appropriate when judging children's consideration of a friend's wishes. A second reason for changing the question was to ensure that the previous results were not an artifact of a particular phrasing.

Children's prosocial behavior toward their partner was observed on the task of sharing crayons used in the first study and an additional task for helping. One child in each pair was given an activity to do individually. The other child had the option of helping the first one or working on a separate activity. To increase the cost of helping, children received fewer rewards (nickels) on each trial if they spent more time working with their partner than on their own. On both tasks, however, equality in rewards was an option on each trial. Both children in a pair received the same number of rewards if they colored the same amount with the crayons. Both children received the same number of rewards on the other task if the child with the opportunity to help spent some time helping and some time working on his or her own activity.

Changes in prosocial intentions and behavior with age and time. With the revised measure of prosocial intentions, the effects of age and time on children's responses were significant and the effects of sex were not. Fourth-graders said they would help, and share with, their partner more than did first-graders. The difference between first- and fourth-graders' intentions increased between the fall and the spring, primarily because first-graders reduced the amount that they said they would help, and share with, their partners. First-graders also reduced the amount that they said they should and would really like to share and help.

Children's actual behavior also varied with age and with time. In both the fall and the spring, fourth-graders helped their partners for a longer time and less often refused to share with them than did first-graders. How long children shared the crayons and how often they refused to help their partner did not differ for first- and fourth-graders in the fall, but they did differ in the spring. First-graders shared less with their partners and more often refused to help their partners in the spring than in the fall; fourth-graders' responses did not change over time. Two interactions with sex were found, but they were weak and not easily interpretable.

These findings provide support for two major conclusions. First, under conditions in which children can easily achieve equality in rewards, prosocial intentions and prosocial behavior between friends increase with age. The changes between first and fourth grade in children's intentions and behavior are consistent with the hypothesis that the development of friendship is marked by a growing preference for equality (Youniss, 1980). When viewed in the context of the Study 1 results, the findings also are consistent with the more specific hypothesis that children shift with increasing age from competing with friends to responding sensitively to their friends' needs and desires (Sullivan, 1953). These hypotheses would be better supported, however, if they were confirmed by children's reports on their own goals or motives when doing the experimental tasks.

Second, a decrease in the strength of a friendship leads to decreases in the friends' prosocial intentions and behavior. The changes in first-graders' intentions and behavior between the fall and the spring can be explained in this way. Decreases in the strength of the friendships between the original pairs of children seem more likely for first-graders than for fourth-graders, because the stability of friendships increases with age (Hartup, 1970). On the other hand, age changes in the stability of friendships were not immediately obvious in Study 2. Most children at both first and fourth grade continued to name their partner as a best friend and continued to give a high rating of liking for their partners. The children's responses may have been affected by a particular kind of experimental artifact, however. After being interviewed about their partner and working on tasks with him or her in the fall, children may have been primed to mention the partner as a close friend when the study resumed in the spring.

Other evidence suggested that friendships were less stable in first-graders than in fourth-graders. When all the close friends that children had in their grade were considered, the percentage that lasted from the fall to the spring was significantly higher for fourth-graders than for first-graders (78% and 57%, respectively). In addition, in the spring fourth-graders appeared to be closer friends with their partners than were first-graders, More fourth-graders than first-graders named their partner as their very best friend or one of their two or three closest friends (55% and 26%, respectively). It seems fair to conclude that a number of the first-graders' friendships did grow weaker during the course of the school year. The weakening of these friendships led, in turn, to a reduction in first-graders' prosocial intentions and their actual behavior.

Relations between intentions and behavior. The similarity in the pattern of effects for prosocial intentions and actual behavior is prima facie evidence for a correlation between them. Across both time periods, the average correction between scores for prosocial intentions and for actual sharing and helping was .50. The correlations ranged from .34 to .61 and all of them were statistically significant. The correlations illustrate that children frequently do what they say they will do, if their words and deeds are examined for comparable situations (Ajzen & Fishbein, 1977). On the other hand, the correlations are not high enough to consider the two types of measures as equivalent or to use a measure of intentions as a replacement for behavioral measures.

Responsiveness to a friend and personal freedom. The results presented thus far clearly imply that good friends are responsive to each other's needs and requests. The only apparent exceptions to this conclusion were obtained in the individual interviews. As in Study 1, children's prosocial intentions were unrelated to their attributions about how much their partners thought they should help and share with them. The lack of a relation suggests that children ignored their partners' expectations when deciding what to do in each situation. Responses to the specific question about how they would react if a friend asked them to share or help for the maximum possible time differed in the fall and in the spring. In the spring, children acceded to the request and decided to share or help more than they had originally planned. In the fall, children did not increase the amount they planned to share or help. First-grade girls actually said they would share or help less if the friend asked them to do so for the maximum possible time.

Such a complicated pattern of results for two specific questions should be interpreted cautiously. Nevertheless, the findings can be explained by assuming that children are concerned with their own independence even when they are responding to another's requests. They maintain a sense of personal control over their actions by saying that their decisions about what to do were influenced primarily by what they think they should and want to do, not by a friend's opinions about what they should do (cf. Jones & Nisbett, 1971). Moreover, if they believe a friend's request for assistance is unreasonable and infringes on their rights to decide for themselves, they may ignore or reject the request (see Brehm & Cole, 1966). These examples illustrate that responsiveness to a friend may not only conflict with children's self-interest; it may also conflict with what children perceive as a legitimate need for personal freedom.

Study 3: continuity and change in childhood and adolescent friendships

Several writers have assumed that the most dramatic changes in friendship occur between middle childhood and adolescence (see Maas, 1968). For example, Sullivan (1953) argued that the development of particularly close and intimate friendships in the years shortly before adolescence leads to a sharp contrast between the interactions of friends and nonfriends. According to Sullivan, young children typically show the same insensitivity and competition with friends and nonfriends alike. As they approach adolescence, children begin to respond sensitively to the needs and desires of the particular person who becomes a close friend. Sullivan assumed that interactions with a close friend have a long-term impact on children's personality and their social behavior toward all other children (see Mannarino, 1976, 1979), but he most strongly stressed the distinctive character of interactions between friends. The major purpose of the third study (Berndt, 1981c) was to test Sullivan's hypothesis by examining age changes in generous and helpful behavior toward friends or other classmates between fourth and eighth grade.

Two additional purposes of the study were to clarify the interpretation of previous findings on friends' prosocial intentions and behavior. First, sex differences in intentions toward friends and other classmates were assessed. When intentions to share and help in noncompetitive situations were investigated (Study 1), girls showed more prosocial intentions toward friends than toward other classmates and boys did not differentiate between friends and other classmates. When the intentions measure included situations that corresponded to the experimental tasks and thus potentially involved competition (Study 2), there were no sex differences in responses. In the third study, the measure of intentions included situations that were neither implicitly nor explicitly competitive. Because the situations were similar to those in the first study, a comparable pattern of effects was expected. Of course, the same effects might not be obtained if sex differences in friendships also change with age.

Second, children were asked to report their goals or motives when they did tasks that allowed them to behave generously or helpfully toward a friend or other classmate. The children's reports could provide support for the hypotheses that close friends prefer equality to competition and that the preference for equality over competition increases with age (Sullivan, 1953; Youniss, 1980).

Method. The study included 118 children from fourth, sixth, and eighth grade. They first named their best friends and rated their liking for all their same-sex classmates. Then they were paired either with a close friend or with another classmate, using the same procedure as in the first study. In a later session, they indicated their prosocial intentions toward their partner for four specific situations. The situations were like those in Study 1, but they were altered so that they were more appropriate for older children and adolescents (e.g., helping the partner complete a project for a class show after you have completed your own project).

In another session, the pairs of friends or classmates were observed as they performed two tasks. The first task was similar to the Kagan and Madsen (1972) measure of generous behavior. Children were shown two alternative ways of distributing rewards (pennies) to themselves and to their partner. The alternatives varied on different trials, but one alternative was always more generous to the partner than the other. In addition, one alternative usually provided an equal number of rewards for the child and the partner. Children made their choices at the same time but had no knowledge of their partners' choices.

For the second task, the two children worked together to make a flag out of small paper triangles. One child was assigned to do a section of the flag that was twice as large as the other child's section. The experimenter pointed out the imbalance to the children and said that the child with the smaller section could help the partner if he or she wanted to help. The experimenter made it clear, however, that each child would be rewarded only for the work completed on his or her own section of the flag.

After completing both tasks, children were asked to report their motives when doing each one. They were presented with four alternatives: (1) equality ("try to get the same number of pennies as my partner"); (2) competition ("try to get more pennies than my partner"); (3) own gain ("try to get as many pennies as I could"); and (4) altruism ("try to get a lot of pennies for my partner"). Children indicated their most important motive when doing each task. They also made attributions about their partner's most important motives.

Sex differences in prosocial intentions. The findings for the measure of prosocial intentions exactly matched those in Study 1. Girls said they would help and share more with friends than with other classmates; boys said they would treat friends and classmates alike, in roughly the same way that girls treated classmates. No effects of age were found. Prosocial intentions were strongly correlated with children's reports of what they should do and really liked to do but uncorrelated with their reports of what their partner thought they should do. The results confirm that in noncompetitive, everyday situations girls distinguish more sharply between close friends and other classmates than do boys. In the earlier discussion, the sex differences in intentions were related to the greater exclusiveness of girls' friendships than boys' friendships. The current findings imply that the sex differences in exclusiveness remain fairly constant between kindergarten and eighth grade.

Age changes in friends' and classmates' prosocial behavior. The frequency of generous and helpful behavior between friends was similar to that between other classmates at fourth and sixth grade. At eighth grade, friends were more generous and helpful to each other than were other classmates. In view of Sullivan's (1953) hypothesis that children develop close friendships in the years shortly before adolescence, the absence of friend-classmate differences in prosocial behavior before eighth grade is surprising. On the other hand, the hypothesis that the differentiation between friends and classmates increases with age seems more important for the theory than the exact age at which differences emerge for specific tasks.

Children's reports on their own and their partners' motives indicate that the age changes in friends' behavior were influenced by a shift in the balance of motives for equality and competition. Most children said that they tried to get either the same number of rewards as their partner (equality) or more rewards than their partner (competition). The relative emphasis on these two motives did not vary for friends and classmates at fourth or sixth grade. At eighth grade, children paired with friends said their partners tried more often for equality than competition. Children paired with classmates said their partner more often competed with them than tried for equality. Comparable effects were not found for children's reports on their own motives, probably because children were unwilling to say they were competing even when they believed a classmate was competing with them. These findings indicate that the growing difference between friends' and classmates' behavior was a function of a growing preference for equality over competition among friends.

Conclusions

The three studies that have been described in detail were focused on friends' prosocial behavior and related social cognitions. The findings from the research demonstrate conclusively that the role of prosocial behavior in friendships can be understood only with reference to specific types of situations or contexts. The situational context affects how friends interpret each other's behavior, what goals prosocial behavior can serve, and what factors limit or constrain how prosocially friends behave toward each other. Consequently, in different contexts prosocial behavior is an indicator of different aspects of friendship. Three aspects are particularly relevant to the recent studies: the exclusiveness of friendships, the balance of equality and competition in friendship, and the balance between responsiveness to a friend's desires and one's own independence.

Sharing and helping in exclusive friendships

By helping or sharing with a close friend, children can confirm that they and the friend have a special relationship; they are part of a special group. Conversely, by refusing to help or share with a classmate who is not a close friend, children can discourage further interaction and signify that the classmate does not have a favored relationship with them. In these ways, sharing and helping preserve the boundary between friends and nonfriends, between the ingroup and the outgroup. If friends help and share with each other more than with nonfriends, they are likely to have an exclusive friendship group, a group that does not easily expand to include new persons.

Results from several types of research suggest that girls have more exclusive friendship groups than do boys. In the studies presented earlier, girls said they would help and share with a friend more than with another classmate in everyday, noncompetitive situations. Boys said that they would help and share with friends less than did girls; boys said they would treat a close friend in the same way that they treated another classmate whom they liked to a moderate degree. The children's responses could not be directly related to their behavior with friends and nonfriends because their behavior was not observed in a similar situational context.

In other research, however, girls did show greater differentiation in their behavior toward friends and nonfriends than did boys (Feshbach, 1969; Feshbach & Sones, 1971). In addition, girls tended to have fewer close friends, to make new friends less rapidly, and to prefer interactions with a single other child more than did boys (Berndt & Hoyle, 1981; Eder & Hallinan, 1978; Savin-Williams, 1980; Waldrop & Halverson, 1975). Taken together, the research suggests that girls are more likely than boys to limit the size of their friendship group. Apparently, girls use differences in their prosocial behavior toward friends and nonfriends as one means of setting a limit on the number of friends they have.

The sex difference in the exclusiveness of friendships may be related to a greater emphasis on the intimacy of friendships among girls than among boys (Berndt, 1981d; Douvan & Adelson, 1966). It is possible, however, that girls have exclusive friendships before they have intimate ones. In previous studies of friendship conceptions, neither boys nor girls expressed much concern with the intimacy of friendships before adolescence. The data on prosocial intentions, on friendship networks, and on play preferences suggest that girls have more exclusive friendships than do boys from kindergarten on. Moreover, the sex difference in exclusiveness does not seem to change markedly with age. On the other hand, girls' friendships might appear to be more intimate than boys' friendships during middle childhood as well if a different measure of intimacy were used.

The importance of sex differences in friendship was not obvious from previous social-cognitive research. Many researchers stressed age changes in friendship conceptions and ignored other possible sources of variation. Information about sex differences in children's responses often is not reported. In many cases, it seems that the possibility of significant differences in boys' and girls' friendship conceptions was not even examined. Comments about the exclusiveness of friendships have been obtained in previous social-cognitive research, but they have been classified with comments about faithfulness (Berndt, 1981d) or linked to the issues of jealousy and possessiveness (Selman, 1981). Sex differences in the frequency of these comments seldom have been reported, but the apparent absence of sex differences may reflect the insensitivity of previous measures. The sex differences in prosocial intentions were obvious only when children were asked about their behavior toward one of their own friends, when intended behavior toward friends was compared with intended behavoir toward another classmate, and when children indicated how much they planned to share or help rather than whether or not they would share or help at all. Such specific comparisons are rare in other social-cognitive research.

Speculations about the origins of the sex differences in friendship have been offered by previous writers (e.g., Lever, 1978; Waldrop & Halverson, 1975). For example, boys usually are assumed to play team sports that require large numbers of participants more often than do girls. Boys may want a large group of friends to ensure sufficient numbers for playing games. Conversely, girls may have more experience in dyadic interactions with their mothers than do boys. Girls may develop a preference for dyadic interactions that they transfer to their peer relationships. These speculations have not been carefully tested, but they illustrate the potential influence of experiences with parents and with peers on patterns of friendship. The impact of social experience on children's friendships has not been emphasized in past research. Instead, the importance of cognitive development has been stressed. A more balanced exploration of the effects of cognitive development and social experience on children's friendships would be desirable.

Finally, it is necessary to stress that both boys' and girls' friendships are exclusive to a degree. All children must distinguish to some extent between close friends and other classmates. Even though girls seem to regard this distinction as more significant than do boys, there is substantial similarity between the friendships of boys and girls. It also is important to note that the negative connotation of exclusiveness may not be deserved. Peer groups that readily expand to include newcomers frequently are regarded as more desirable than exclusive groups. On the other hand, maintaining an exclusive group may be the only way to preserve the intimacy of the friendships within it. In general, greater knowledge of the correlates of exclusiveness in friendship groups is required before a final judgment is made about their desirability.

Equality versus competition between friends

When two friends are doing an activity together, they may help or share with each other so that their final performance on the activity is similar. For example, if they are working on their homework together, one may help the other with some of the problems so that they can both get a good grade. In such cases, helping and sharing are used to maintain or restore the equality between the friends (Youniss, 1980). Friends need not try for equality, however. They could compete with each other and try to show that their performance is superior to that of the friend. Rather than wanting to help each other with their homework, they may want to see how well each of them can do without any help from the other. In short, the amount of prosocial behavior that friends show toward each other can be adjusted to achieve the goals of equality or competition.

Sullivan (1953) suggested that young children are likely to compete with their friends; older children and adolescents are likely to try for equality. Our data provide substantial support for this hypothesis. When the alternative was losing to a partner, boys between kindergarten and fourth grade competed more and shared less with a friend than with another classmate. In contrast, sharing and helping increased between first and fourth grade when these behaviors could lead to equality in the rewards received by a child and a close friend. Between fourth and eighth grade, children's generous and helpful behavior increased more for close friends than for other classmates. Children's attributions about the friends' and classmates' motives confirmed that the age changes in the friends' behavior were due to a growing preference for equality over competition.

Although the major findings are consistent with Sullivan's hypothesis, additional results suggest two important qualifications. First, young children do not always compete with their friends. In Study 2, first-graders shared more with their partners in the fall than in the spring of the school year. The decrease in sharing over time seemed to reflect a decrease in the strength of their friendships with the partner during the course of the school year. In other words, when the first-graders were close friends with their partner, they shared more equally and, apparently, competed less often than when they were no longer such close friends. These data are consistent with other research demonstrating that first- and third-graders who are close friends have more cooperative and harmonious interactions than do other classmates, even under conditions that encourage competition (Newcomb, Brady, & Hartup, 1979).

Second, in certain situations friends seem strongly motivated to compete with each other at all ages. In Study 1, the boys' competition with friends seemed to be particularly intense because children could not achieve equality in rewards on each trial. They could only win or lose by getting more or fewer rewards than their partners. In research with male college students (Tesser & Smith, 1980), friends were less helpful to each other than were strangers if their help could have allowed a friend to attain a higher score than themselves on a task highly relevant for their self-evaluations (e.g., a measure of their academic ability). These findings suggest that competition between friends is especially likely when they are forced to compare their relative performance on tasks measuring an important ability or skill. The outcome of competition in such situations indicates that one friend is inferior to the other. Because friends regard themselves as equals, such an outcome may be unpleasant for the winner and the loser. The conflicts that can follow competitive interactions may explain why close friends avoid them when they can, even at first grade, by trying for equality. The empirical research suggests that boys may have more problems with competition in friendships than do girls. On the other hand, situations in which girls are likely to compete with friends may have been not yet identified.

Responsiveness and independence in friendships

Children expect their friends to accede to their requests for sharing and helping. They use a friend's responsiveness to indicate the closeness of the friendship (cf. Kelley, 1979). Nevertheless, when a friend asks them to share or help, children may refuse to comply. Of course, children simply may be unwilling to go out of their way to do what the friend asks. They may be unwilling to accept the costs of prosocial behavior. In other cases, children may refuse to honor the request because they regard it as infringing on their own independence. If the friend makes an extreme request or does not seem to be truly in need, children may feel entitled to disregard the request. It is as if they said: "The obligations of friendship go only so far; I also have my own rights."

The recent studies contained relatively little data on the potential conflict between responsiveness and independence in friendships. In all three studies, children preferred to attribute their own sharing and helping to a personal choice rather than to compliance with the friend's demands. Their prosocial intentions were influenced by how much they thought they should and wanted to share or help, not by their judgments of the friend's expectations. Moreover, when faced with an extreme request by a friend, children sometimes reacted negatively, saying they would share and help less than they had originally planned.

Selman (1981) described the conflict between responsiveness to a friend and one's own independence as the central issue at the highest stage for friendship conceptions, found in late adolescence and adulthood. It seems likely, however, that younger children appreciate this conflict even if they do not discuss it as explicitly as do adolescents and adults. In a simple form, conflicts of this type are found in early and middle childhood. For example, preschool children want friends who are reliable playmates, friends who are usually willing to play with them when they ask (Corsaro, 1981). When children say that they have other things to do and, therefore, will not play with a friend, they are asserting the primacy of independence over responsiveness. Once children agree to play together, they must decide what to play. Conflicts about what and how to play frequently arise in children's interactions (Gottman & Parkhurst, 1980; Lubin, 1981). In resolving these conflicts, children must decide how much they should give in to a friend and how much they should insist on their own preferences. Again, responsiveness and independence are in opposition.

The degree to which these conflicts affect children's friendships is difficult to judge. Friends may most often limit their requests to what they believe the other child will consider legitimate. Conflicts in play may be settled by a set of standard procedures or primitive rules of fairness, for example, "first we'll do what you want and then we'll do what I want." Nevertheless, the balance between responsiveness and independence should be further investigated. In adults' close relationships, individuals' agreement on this balance seems to affect both satisfaction with a relationship and its stability (Braiker & Kelley, 1979; Harvey, Wells, & Alvarez, 1978).

What more is there to discover?

At the beginning of this chapter, the discovery of aspects of friendship that had been overlooked in previous research was proposed as the major goal for a new research program. The joint investigation of social cognition and social behavior was suggested as one means for reaching this goal. As the preceding section illustrates, the research program summarized in this chapter was successful in exposing or clarifying aspects of friendship that had received little emphasis in the past. Of course, there is more to discover. Little detailed information about features of friendship besides prosocial behavior is available. For example, no behavioral research on the expression of intimacy and loyalty in children's friendships has been done. With rare exceptions (e.g., Diaz & Berndt, in press), these features of friendship have been investigated only with responses to open-ended questions. The significance of play or mutual interaction has been examined in recent studies using naturalistic observations (Gottman & Parkhurst, 1980; Lubin, 1981), but it has almost never been studied in completely natural settings. As a result, there are few reports on when and where friends usually interact with each other or what they do when they are together.

New discoveries will also come from the exploration of new questions. Detailed investigations of interactions between friends would be particularly valuable in clarifying how friends develop a common understanding of their own relationship. For example, in certain interactions friends face judgments about how exclusive they want their relationship to be. If one child invites a best friend over to play, is he or she free to invite other friends as well? If two best friends are talking together, would they expect each other to discourage other classmates who want to join their conversation? These questions imply that friends must negotiate with each other about the importance of the boundary between their own friendship and the larger peer group.

Competitively structured interactions, such as athletic events, may also evoke a process of negotiation between friends. Should the friends compete with each other or should they refuse to play unless they can be on the same team? If they must play against each other, as in singles' tennis, should they always play to win or try to make each one's wins and losses roughly equal? If one child does win consistently, can friends agree that the inequality between them is unimportant because "it's just a game"? These questions reflect a series of judgments that friends must make when they interact in competitive situations.

Issues of responsiveness versus personal freedom potentially apply to the greatest range of situations. How do children decide when a friend's request is legitimate and when it is extreme? How do they decide whether to play with a friend or continue with an individual activity? Friends may try to make such decisions together, coming to agreement through discussion. In contrast, the decisions could be made by one child's unilateral action, or they could provoke an extended conflict.

The process by which friends resolve conflicts concerning exclusiveness, competition, and responsiveness versus independence is likely to affect their friendships in the long term as well. Changes in the exclusiveness of a relationship may change its intimacy. Changes in friends' interpretation of the outcomes of competition between them may affect their judgments about their overall similarity and equality. Finally, changes in the agreements friends reach about their obligations to respond to each other rather than go their own ways may affect the frequency with which they interact.

Because all the questions about processes ask what actually happens when friends interact and how they interpret these events, they call for the coordinated investigation of social cognition and social behavior. In addition, investigations of the process of interaction between friends suggest a new metric for judging the importance of different aspects of friendship. In the short term, processes that are important for the friendship should have a major influence on children's reports of the satisfaction they derive from it. In the long term, processes important for the friendship should significantly affect whether it grows or decays with time. Few friendships are satisfactory in all respects, but the ones that provide the most important sources of gratification are likely to be the closest and most stable of children's friendships.

Notes

1 In the earlier paper (Berndt, 1981d), a general hypothesis about development changes in the relative importance of the three possible determinants of prosocial intentions was presented and discussed. The findings in the research program do not provide much support for the hypothesis, because age changes in the correlations between responses to the three additional questions and prosocial intentions were rare. Other research suggests that the questions used to measure the three determinants may not adequately distinguish between them (Miniard & Cohen, 1981). Consequently, the general hypothesis might be better tested with one of the other techniques outlined in Berndt (1981d).
2 Children's behavior also was observed on a second task that provided opportunities for children to help their partners. Responses on this task did not vary with age, sex, or friendship, probably because little helping occured.

References

Ahlgren, A., & Johnson, D. W. Differences in cooperative and competitive attitudes from the 2nd through the 12th grades. *Developmental Psychology*, 1979, *15*, 45–49.

Ajzen, I., & Fishbein, M. Attitude-behavior relations: A theoretical analysis and review of empirical research. *Psychological Bulletin,* 1977, *84,* 888–918.

Asher, S. R., & Gottman, J. M. (Eds.). *The development of children's friendships.* Cambridge: Cambridge University Press, 1981.

Benton, A. A. Productivity, distributive justice, and bargaining among children. *Journal of Personality and Social Psychology,* 1971, *18,* 68–78.

Berndt, T. J. Age changes and changes over time in prosocial intentions and behavior between friends. *Developmental Psychology,* 1981, *17,* 408–416. (a)

Berndt, T. J. The effects of friendship on prosocial intentions and behavior. *Child Development,* 1981, *52,* 636–643. (b)

Berndt, T. J. *Generosity and helpfulness between friends in early adolescence.* Manuscript submitted for publication, 1981. (c)

Berndt, T. J. Relations between social cognition, nonsocial cognition, and social behavior: The case of friendship. In J. H. Flavell & L. D. Ross (Eds.), *Social cognitive development: Frontiers and possible futures.* Cambridge: Cambridge University Press, 1981. (d)

Berndt, T. J., & Hoyle, S. G. *Sociometric measures of friendship: Age changes, sex differences, and temporal stability.* Manuscript submitted for publication, 1981.

Bigelow, B. J. Children's friendship expectations: A cognitive-developmental study. *Child Development,* 1977, *48,* 246–253.

Bigelow, B. J., & LaGaipa, J. J. The development of friendship values and choice. In H. C. Foot, A. J. Chapman, & J. R. Smith (Eds.), *Friendship and social relations in children.* New York: Wiley, 1980.

Braiker, H. B., & Kelley, H. H. Conflict in the development of close relationships. In R. L. Burgess & T. L. Huston (Eds.), *Social exchange in developing relationships.* New York: Academic Press, 1979.

Brehm, J. W., & Cole, A. H. Effect of a favor which reduces freedom. *Journal of Personality and Social Psychology,* 1966, *3,* 420–426.

Corsaro, W. A. Friendship in the nursery school: Social organization in a peer environment. In S. R. Asher & J. M. Gottman (Eds.), *The development of children's friendships.* Cambridge: Cambridge University Press, 1981.

Damon, W. *The social world of the child.* San Francisco: Jossey-Bass, 1977.

Diaz, R. M., & Berndt, T. J. Children's knowledge of a best friend: Fact or fancy? *Developmental Psychology,* in press.

Douvan, E., & Adelson, J. *The adolescent experience.* New York: Wiley, 1966.

Eder, D., & Hallinan, M. T. Sex differences in children's friendships. *American Sociological Review,* 1978, *43,* 237–250.

Enright, R. D., & Sutterfield, S. J. An ecological validation of social cognitive development. *Child Development,* 1980, *51,* 156–161.

Feshbach, N. Sex differences in children's modes of aggressive response toward outsiders. *Merrill-Palmer Quarterly of Behavior and Development,* 1969, *15,* 249–258.

Feshbach, N., & Sones, G. Sex differences in adolescent reactions toward newcomers. *Developmental Psychology,* 1971, *4,* 381–386.

Fincham, F. Recipient characteristics and sharing behavior in the learning disabled. *Journal of Genetic Psychology,* 1978, *133,* 143–144.

Fishbein, J., & Ajzen, I. *Beliefs, attitudes, intentions, and behavior: An introduction to theory and research.* Reading, Mass: Addison-Wesley, 1975.

Floyd, J. M. K. Effects of amount of reward and friendship status of the other on the frequency of sharing in children (Doctoral dissertation, University of Minnesota, 1964). *Dissertation Abstracts,* 1965, *9,* 5396–5397. (University Microfilms No. 65-00120)

Foot, H. D., Chapman, A. J., & Smith, J. R. Friendship and social responsiveness in boys and girls. *Journal of Personality and Social Psychology,* 1977, *35,* 401–411.

Foot, H. D., Chapman, A. J., & Smith, J. R. *Friendship and social relations in children.* New York: Wiley, 1980.

Gamer, E. *Children's reports of friendship criteria.* Paper presented at the meeting of the Massachusetts Psychological Association, Boston, May 1977.

Gottman, J. M., & Parkhurst, J. T. A developmental theory of friendship and acquaintanceship processes. In W. A. Collins (Ed.), *Minnesota Symposium on Child Psychology* (Vol. 13). Hillsdale, N.J.: Erlbaum, 1980.

Hartup, W. W. Peer interaction and social organization. In P. H. Mussen (Ed.), *Carmichael's manual of child psychology* (3rd ed., Vol. 2). New York: Wiley, 1970.

Harvey, J. H., Wells, G. L., & Alvarez, M.D. Attribution in the context of conflict and separation in close relationships. In J. H. Harvey, W. Ickes, & R. F. Kidd (Eds.), *New directions in attribution research* (Vol. 2). Hillsdale, N.J.: Erlbaum, 1978.

Hayes, D. S. Cognitive bases for liking and disliking among preschool children. *Child Development,* 1978, *49,* 906–909.

Jones, E. E., & Nisbett, R. E. The actor & the observer: Divergent perceptions of the causes of behavior. In E. E. Jones, D. E. Kanouse, H. H. Kelley, R. E. Nisbett, S. Valins, & B. Weiner (Eds.), *Attribution: Perceiving the causes of behavior.* Morristown, N.J.: General Learning Press, 1971.

Kagan, S., & Madsen, M. C. Rivalry in Anglo-American and Mexican-American children of two ages. *Journal of Personality and Social Psychology,* 1972, *24,* 214–220.

Kahn, A., Nelson, R. E., & Gaeddert, W. P. Sex of subject and sex composition of the group as determinants of reward allocations. *Journal of Personality and Social Psychology,* 1980, *38,* 737–750.

Kelley, H. H. *Personal relationships: Their structures and processes.* New York: Halsted Press, 1979.

Kohlberg, L. Stage and sequence: The cognitive-developmental approach to socialization. In D. A. Goslin (Ed.), *Handbook of socialization theory and research.* New York: Rand-McNally, 1969.

Lever, J. Sex differences in the complexity of children's play and games. *American Sociological Review,* 1978, *43,* 471–483.

Lubin, D. *Children's social behavior and understanding of social processes.* Paper presented at the Vanderbilt University conference on Boundary Areas in Psychology: Developmental and Social, Nashville, Tenn. June 1981.

Maas, H. S. Preadolescent peer relations and adult intimacy. *Psychiatry,* 1968, *31,* 161–172.

Maccoby, E. E., & Jacklin, C. N. *The psychology of sex differences.* Stanford, Calif.: Stanford University Press, 1974.

Mannarino, A. P. Friendship patterns and altruistic behavior in preadolescent males. *Developmental Psychology,* 1976, *12,* 555–556.

Mannarino, A. P. The relationship between friendship and altruism in preadolescent girls. *Psychiatry,* 1979, *42,* 280–284.

Miniard, P. W., & Cohen, J. B. An examination of the Fishbein-Ajzen behavioral-intentions model's concepts and measures. *Journal of Experimental Social Psychology,* 1981, *17,* 309–339.

Morgan, W. R., & Sawyer, J. Bargaining, expectations, and the preference for equality over equity. *Journal of Personality and Social Psychology,* 1967, *6,* 139–149.

Newcomb, A. F., & Brady, J. E. Mutuality in boys' friendship relations. *Child Development,* 1982, *53,* 392–395.

Newcomb, A. F., Brady, J. E., & Hartup, W. W. Friendship and incentive condition as determinants of children's task-oriented social behavior. *Child Development,* 1979, *50,* 878–881.

Oskamp, S., & Perlman, D. Effects of friendship and dislinking on cooperation in a mixed motive game. *Journal of Conflict Resolution*, 1966, *10*, 221–226.

Piaget, J. *The moral judgment of the child*. New York: Free Press, 1965. (Originally published, 1932.)

Piaget, J. Piaget's theory. In P. H. Mussen (Ed.), *Carmichael's manual of child psychology* (3rd ed., Vol. 1). New York: Wiley, 1970.

Reisman, J. M., & Shorr, S. I. Friendship claims and expectations among children and adults. *Child Development*, 1978, *49*, 913–916.

Rubin, Z. *Children's friendships*. Cambridge, Mass.: Harvard University Press, 1980.

Savin-Williams, R. C. Social interactions of adolescent females in natural groups. In H. C. Foot, A. J. Chapman, & J. R. Smith (Eds.), *Friendship and social relations in children*. New York: Wiley, 1980.

Selman, R. L. The child as a friendship philosopher: A case study in the growth of interpersonal understanding. In S. R. Asher & J. M. Gottman (Eds.), *The development of children's friendships*. Cambridge: Cambridge University Press, 1981.

Selman, R. L., & Jaquette, D. The development of interpersonal awareness (a working draft): A manual constructed by the Harvard–Judge Baker Social Reasoning Project, January 1, 1977.

Shantz, C. U. The development of social cognition. In E. M. Hetherington (Ed.), *Review of child development research* (Vol. 5). Chicago: University of Chicago Press, 1975.

Skarin, K., & Moely, B. E. Altruistic behavior: Analysis of age and sex differences. *Child Development*, 1976, *47*, 1159–1165.

Staub, E., & Noerenberg, H. Property rights, deservingness, reciprocity, friendship: The transactional character of children's sharing behavior. *Journal of Personality and Social Psychology*, 1981, *40*, 271–289.

Staub, E., & Sherk, L. Need for approval, children's sharing behavior, and reciprocity in sharing. *Child Development*, 1970, *41*, 243–252.

Sullivan, H. S. *The interpersonal theory of psychiatry*. New York: Norton, 1953.

Swingle, P. G., & Gillis, J. S. Effects of the emotional relationship between protagonists in the Prisoner's Dilemma. *Journal of Personality and Social Psychology*, 1968, *8*, 160–165.

Tesser, A. *Self-evaluation maintenance processes and interpersonal relationships*. Paper presented at the Vanderbilt University conference on Boundary Areas in Psychology: Developmental and Social, Nashville, Tenn., June 1981.

Tesser, A., & Smith, J. Some effects of task relevance and friendship on helping: You don't always help the one you like. *Journal of Experimental Social Psychology*, 1980, *16*, 582–590.

Waldrop, M. F., & Halverson, C. G., Jr. Intensive and extensive peer behavior: Longitudinal and cross-sectional analysis. *Child Development*, 1975, *46*, 19–28.

Wright, B. A. Altruism in children and the perceived conduct of others. *Journal of Abnormal and Social Psychology*, 1942, *37*, 218–233.

Youniss, J. *Parents and peers in social development*. Chicago: University of Chicago Press, 1980.

Part III

Value internalization and moral development

8 Culture as a cognitive system: differentiated rule understandings in children and other savages

Deborah L. Pool, Richard A. Shweder,
and Nancy C. Much

For more than a century, from the early writings of Tylor (1871), Lévy-Bruhl (1910), and Hobhouse (1906) to more recent accounts by Lévi-Strauss (1966), Horton (1967, 1968), Gellner (1973), and Goody (1977), a contrast has been drawn between the savage (or primitive) mind and the modern (or domesticated) mind. There are striking parallels between these descriptions of a savage versus modern mind contrast and descriptions within cognitive developmental literature of a contrast between the child and the adult mind (Kohlberg, 1963, 1969, 1971, 1973; Piaget, 1954, 1932/1965, 1967; Werner & Kaplan, 1956). Unlike the differentiated, abstract, taxonomically minded, and concept-driven Western adult, both children and savages, it has been proposed, view the world in an undifferentiated, concrete, functional, and percept-driven way. Savage and child seem to provide reciprocal metaphors for one another.

Although the savage versus modern mind contrast has been drawn in various terms, the image of a conflated, undifferentiated mind shared by savage and child (or characteristic of the savage as child or the child as savage) is one of the most pervasive in the literatures of both cultural evolution and cognitive development. In this chapter we raise some doubts about the usefulness of "cognitive differentiation" as a general parameter for describing age-related, historical, and cross-cultural variations in social thought. We discuss evidence that young children possess quite differentiated criteria for distinguishing and identifying moral versus conventional versus prudential rules; indeed, we present evidence that

An earlier version of this chapter was presented at the symposium on Relations Between Symbolic and Psychological Anthropology, 78th Annual Meeting of the American Anthropological Association, Cincinnati, Ohio, November 27–December 1, 1979. The research was made possible by a grant from the Spencer Foundation.

the criteria possessed by children for classifying different elements of culture are as differentiated as the criteria possessed by adults. We then discuss the implications of this evidence for the understanding of savage cultural systems.

We advance an ancient Greek conception of cognition as "auto-normative" processing (Collingwood, 1972): "Any piece of thinking, theoretical or practical, includes as an integral part of itself the thought of a standard or criterion by reference to which it is judged a successful or unsuccessful piece of thinking. Unlike any kind of bodily or physiological functioning, thought is a self-critical activity." Thus, "the science of mind . . . must describe the self-judging function which is part and parcel of all thinking and try to discover the criteria upon which its judgments are based" (pp. 107–108).

Collingwood (1972, p. 109) labels this approach to cognition "criteriological," and it is this criteriological approach that we assume when discussing culture as a cognitive system. Following Geertz (1973), we view culture as a "historically transmitted body of meanings embodied in symbols, a system of inherited concepts expressed in symbolic forms by means of which men communicate, perpetuate and develop their knowledge about and attitudes towards life" (p. 89). Following Collingwood (1972), however, we emphasize that "the business of thinking includes the discovery and correction of its own errors" and that in every act of thought the thinker himself judges the success of his own act (pp. 109–110). By combining the "symbols and meanings" approach to culture with the "criteriological" approach to cognition we seek to bring back to center stage the self-critical activities of the schemer (child and savage) behind the interpretive scheme.

An autonormative, or criteriological, approach to cognition thus emphasizes the self-evaluative activities of the thinker. People's abilities to "communicate, perpetuate, and develop their knowledge about and attitudes toward life" (Geertz, 1973) presuppose the psychological processes of self-awareness and self-criticism by which one particular system of concepts, rather than others, is sustained. Or as Hallowell (1955) has written:

Any human society is not only a social order but a moral order as well. A moral order being one that is characterized by the fact that not only norms of conduct exist but organized or unorganized social sanctions to reinforce them [sic], an inevitable conclusion must be drawn: the members of such an order are expected to assume moral responsibility for their conduct. Such an assumption, in turn, implies self-awareness of one's own conduct, self-appraisal of one's conduct with reference to socially recognized standards of value, some volitional control of one's behavior, a possible choice of alternative lines of conduct, etc. (p. 83).

The very existence of norms for conduct and thinking presupposes actors' abilities to evaluate themselves in light of those norms; self-evaluations, in turn, presuppose evaluative criteria (e.g., the canons of propositional calculus, the rules of grammar, and in the case of the moral, prudential, and conventional judgments to be discussed in this chapter, evaluative criteria such as "obligation" and "importance").

If culture is to be viewed as a cognitive system, then an adequate "cultural account" must reveal the extent to which inherited concepts get partitioned, by the native, of course, into criteriological subsystems. Encouraged by recent evidence that the self-judging function of young children can be segmented into moral versus conventional versus prudential modes of appraisal, we suggest that the undifferentiated savage may exist more in the eyes of the ethnographer than in the mind of the primitive.

Cognitive differentiation: the savage and the child

Cognitive differentiation refers to the extent to which domains of knowledge or discourse are distinguished. Kant (1785/1959), for example, promoting a "cognitive division of labor" (Gellner, 1973, p. 169) with which we are all familiar, distinguished moral rules, which he viewed as "categorical," unconditional, and impersonally binding, from rules of skill (technical imperatives) and counsels of prudence (pragmatic imperatives), which were said to be "hypothetical," that is, conditional on variable purposes peculiar to particular individuals. For Kant, at least, efficiency and duty were not to be confused.

Gellner (1973), perhaps thinking of Kant, credits the modern mind with having accomplished the partitioning of knowledge or the uses of language into distinct types:

These types are generally defined in terms of the criteria of validity employed within each of them. . . . Propositions are classified into those which stand or fall in virtue of factual checking, those which stand or fall in virtue of formal calculation, those which stand or fall in virtue of consonance with the speaker's feelings, and those which have no basis or anchorage at all (p. 173).

Gellner (1973) suggests that an absence of such differentiation characterizes the magically enchanted world vision of the savage mind. A "lower functional specificity," he argues, is mirrored in the "systematic conflation of the descriptive, evaluative, identificatory, status-conferring, etc. roles of language." With modernity comes disenchantment and an irreversible "sense of the separability and fundamental distinctness" of the various functions of discourse.

Horton's (1968) influential account of cultural evolution likewise characterizes the savage mind by the absence of a cognitive division of labor. For the savage, the aims of science are interwoven or confused with nonscientific aims such as those of politics and esthetics. In modern societies, in contrast, the realms of the empirical, the normative, and the transcendent are distinct; science and religion, morals and politics, and truth and power are potentially independent enterprises. A variety of separate criteria exist by which objects and actions are explained and assessed; empirical truth is segregated from moral rightness, esthetic value, or technical efficiency.

Many scholars, perhaps most notably Piaget (1932/1965) and Kohlberg (1963, 1969, 1971, 1973), have characterized social-cognitive development in these same terms. Young children, it is argued, lack moral understandings per se in that they confuse moral and nonmoral (scientific, prudential, conventional) forms of appraisal. Piaget (1932/1965), for example, characterizes the young child's respect for rules as "heteronomous": Any act in obedience to rules set down by adults is judged to be good, whereas any act that does not conform is judged to be bad. In the stage of "moral realism," the child views rules as sacred, unchangeable, and inherent in the universe, much like physical laws. This attitude toward rules, Piaget suggests, applies equally to all kinds of imperatives; in moral realism, the child applies the same criteria of validity to the rules of marbles and the rules of morality.

In a second, "autonomous" stage, Piaget proposes, the child differentiates the natural from the social world. The child realizes that rules are the formulations of people, not given in nature but rather the products of mutual agreement. The older child sees that rules are changeable, not rigid duties but instruments through which the purposes and ideals of cooperating equals become realized. In autonomy, "what ought to be," the ideal, becomes differentiated from "what is," the body of custom received from adults. Existing rules may be wrong if they violate ideals; their status as rules no longer ensures them unconditional respect. Piaget identifies the ideal of justice as the principle around which an autonomous moral orientation is formed.

Thus, according to Piaget, the sense of justice as a moral imperative grows out of the heteronomous respect for all kinds of rules. Young children have no sense of the greater importance or superiority of some rules over others; they do not appreciate the special authority of moral imperatives, or conversely, they do not appreciate the conditional or hypothetical status of the purposes behind other imperatives. Only in autonomy, Piaget proposes, does the child adopt a distinctively deontological approach, whereby moral rules, framed in the name of justice, become distinct from, and superior to, pragmatic, technical, or conventional rules established in the service of efficiency, prudence, or custom.

Kohlberg's (1963, 1969, 1971, 1973) theory of moral development expands upon the Piagetian view. Early undifferentiated forms of understanding are replaced by increasingly differentiated forms. Kohlberg identifies three, rather than two, levels of moral understanding; each level is divided into two stages. Thus, individuals move from a preconventional morality (Stages 1 and 2), in which moral judgments are based on prudential considerations (punishment and reward), through conventional morality (Stages 3 and 4), in which judgments are oriented toward conformity and maintenance of the rules of society, to a postconventional or principled morality (Stages 5 and 6), in which principles of justice and respect for persons displace prudence and conformity as grounds for moral understanding. Hence for Kohlberg, moral development is viewed as a process of differentiation and replacement in which moral criteria are distinguished from prudential and conventional criteria and then supersede them. For both Piaget and Kohlberg, it is only at the most advanced developmental stages that the distinctions between physical law, convention, utility, and morality are mastered.

The image of a conflated, undifferentiated mind (an "enchanted" mind by some accounts, a "confused" mind by other accounts) shared by savage and child has not gone unresisted in the anthropological literature; resistance, however, has been fitful and not entirely successful. Both the romantic's article of faith that at least other cultures are enchanted and the developmentalist's article of faith that we possess what others lack add substantial ideological force to the view that what we separate, the savage blends, where we partition, the savage merges. Nonetheless, powerful objections to the image of a conflated savage mind have been raised. More than half a century ago Malinowksi (1926/1976) criticized Hobhouse and other developmentalists for their failure to partition the domain of "savage custom" into such subsets as "law," "morals," "manners," and "practical utility." Discriminations of this type were routinely made, Malinowski argued, not only by Oxford dons and Continental philosophers but also by any Melanesian savage.

Malinowski addressed the question "Why are rules obeyed in savage society?" Criticizing past accounts for what he viewed as excessive emphasis on the habitual, traditional, and sentimental bases of social order (an emphasis also found in Piaget's characterization of "heteronomy"), Malinowski (1926) remarked that global noncognitive motives such as the "desire to satisfy public opinion" or "the force of habit" or "conformism" or "the love of tradition" "account but to a very partial extent for obedience to rules" (pp. 50–54).

Malinowski offered ethnographic case material documenting the ability of Melanesian savages to think about and critically appraise the injunctions, prescriptions, and taboos of their culture according to a limited number of distinct criteria of validity. Thus some rules are obeyed, Malinowski argued, "because their practical utility is recognized by reason and testified by experience." Other rules are obeyed "because any deviation from them makes a man feel and look, in the eyes of others, ridiculous, clumsy, socially uncouth." Some rules are governed by self-interest; others are not. The rules for a game are appraised differently than the rules for a magical rite. Norms pertaining to things sacred are judged differently from norms pertaining to things profane. The rules of "law" are "one well-defined [i.e., differentiated] category within the body of custom"; if we attend to the criteria of validity, or principles, employed by natives for deciding whether or not to respect a rule, other well-defined categories, such as morals and manners, can be identified.

Malinowski's approach to savage culture implies that no single metaphor (society as ritual, society as a game, society as a marketplace, society as a church) is apt for all social life. Contrary to the predilections of some culture theorists, Malinowski argued that there may be no master plan or integrating code for a culture as a whole. Melanesian savages, like the Englishmen who study them, are differentiated in their orientation to rules. Ritual is not confused with sport, just as teatime etiquette is not confused with the rules of cricket.

More than thirty years after the publication of *Crime and Custom in Savage Society,* a position akin to Malinowski's was articulated in an important but curiously overlooked paper by Whiting and Whiting (1960). Two features of the Whitings's paper are noteworthy. First, like Malinowski, they argue for a partitioned view of "custom"; the Whitings propose that techniques, ethics, and beliefs constitute three symbolic or cognitive subsystems of culture. Second, the Whitings offer a prescient symbolic approach to the study of culture. Although best known for their emphasis on behavior observations and the noncognitive origins of culture, in this remarkable paper the Whitings seem to anticipate later developments in cognitive and symbolic anthropology (e.g., D'Andrade & Romney, 1964; Schneider, 1968). "The essential feature of the concept of culture," the Whitings (1960) argue, "is in the formulation of the shared symbolic determinants of behavior":

Although . . . this concept is often used to include overt behavior, and even the products of behavior such as artifacts, we feel that its essential contribution lies in providing a method for coding and classifying the shared ideas of the members of a society or group, rather than in describing norms [i.e., regularities] of behavior. (p. 918)

An emphasis on the cognitive or symbolic aspects of culture led the Whitings to propose cognitive criteria or tests of validity (e.g., efficiency, coherence, correspondence) for the partitioning of "custom" into subsystems; these criteria are, in addition, native criteria. Thus, according to the Whitings (1960), customs are "not a simple list of items but systems of techniques, beliefs, and values, each integrated with respect to its own principles" (p. 921). The rules of a culture, if they are to persist, must seem valid to the members of a culture, and no single test of validity will do.

A similar rebellion against the image of a conflated mind seems to be occurring in recent developmental literature (e.g., Nucci & Turiel, 1978; Turiel, 1979, 1980). Malinowski (1926/1976) suggested that distinct criteria of validity (moral, pragmatic, conventional, etc.) are equally available to both the Oxford don and the Melanesian savage. Recent developmental evidence suggests that an equally differentiated repertoire of cognitive criteria may also be available to the don's children. Both the intellectual world of the savage and the intellectual world of the child may be less enchanted and less confused than previously supposed.

Results of recent developmental studies on children's rule understandings suggest much earlier differentiation than proposed by Piaget and Kohlberg. American children as young as 5 years of age seem to distinguish moral versus conventional versus prudential rules; moreover, the distinctions they make seem to reflect patterns of formal features hypothesized to underlie these rule domains. Children's differentiation of the domains will be discussed later. First, a set of dimensions along which such differentiation seems to take place will be described. Several authors (see, e.g., Black, 1962; Collett, 1977; Kohlberg, 1971; Much & Shweder, 1978; Nucci & Turiel, 1978; Shweder, Turiel, & Much, 1981; Whiting & Whiting, 1960) have suggested criteria by which rules are differentiated and have hypothesized how moral, conventional, and other rules are perceived to differ on these dimensions. The set of dimensions or criteria in the following outline is thus a synthesis and elaboration of these various proposals.

Prescriptivity

Prescriptivity refers to the fact that rules recommend or require that conduct proceed in one way rather than another. Prescriptivity implies a cultural preference, either implicit or explicit; where rules are found, neutral attitudes are not. As Berlin (1956) has written, rules are general instructions "to act or refrain from acting in certain ways, in specified circumstances, enjoined upon persons of a specified kind" (p. 305). Insofar as rules are "enjoined," they presuppose the possibility that one could defy the injunction; and, insofar as rules enjoined can be rules defied, they implicate the practices associated with sanctioning: accusing, criticizing, scolding, and punishing.

Moreover, insofar as rules are enjoined "upon persons of a specified kind," they entail that principle of appraisal known as generality, equity, fairness, or justice (i.e., "Treat like cases alike and different cases differently," Hart, 1961, p. 155). As Berlin (1956) aptly remarks:

> To fall under a rule is *pro tanto* to be assimilated to a single pattern. To enforce a rule is to promote equality of behavior or treatment. This applies whether the rules take the form of moral principles or laws, or codes of positive law, or the rules of games or of conduct adopted by professional associations, religious organizations, political parties. . . . The rule which declares that tall persons are permitted to cast five times as many votes as short ones creates an obvious inequality. Nevertheless, . . . it ensures equality of privilege within each of the two discriminated classes – no tall man may have more votes than any other tall man, and similarly with short men (pp. 305–306).

The criterion of prescriptivity, its presupposed possibility of breach and sanction, and its entailed principle of justice distinguishes the "rules of conduct" from the "laws of nature," or what ought to be from what is. Natural regularities either do not require normative regulation or cannot be subject to it, which is one reason why (in this culture) a proscription such as "thou shalt not dream" is felt to be an absurdity.

The criterion of prescriptivity is, however, an exceedingly general criterion. It does not distinguish a moral rule ("Promises should be kept") from a conventional rule ("Do not eat rice with your hands") from a prudential rule ("Do not take freshly painted articles out in the rain"). The criterion also does not distinguish rules of wide application ("Promises should be kept") from rules with narrow application ("When playing bridge the dealer bids first"); the principle "treat like cases alike and different cases differently" implies neither that all cases are alike in relevant respects nor that they should be treated in like fashion (see Hart, 1961; Perelman, 1963).

Obligation

The criterion of obligation refers to the idea of duty: Some rules are perceived to be binding or required regardless of what anyone happens to want to do. Insofar as a rule is judged to be obligatory, it is perceived as *external* (impersonal or supraindividual), *unalterable,* and *ahistorical.*

A rule is perceived as external (impersonal or supraindividual) in that what is right or wrong to do is thought to be right or wrong independent of one's existence as a moral agent and regardless of whether one recognizes it as such. Just as, for example, shape or mass are thought to inhere in an object irrespective of the presence of human perceivers, so too certain actions (e.g., committing incest) seem to be thought inherently right or wrong independent of human recognition of them as such. A rule is perceived as unalterable in that it is believed that what is right or wrong cannot be changed by consensus or legislation, and it is perceived as ahistorical in that, although the date of its recognition may be identifiable, it is believed that there is no point in secular time at which the validity of what is right or wrong changes (Shweder, Turiel, & Much, 1981).

The criterion of obligation is independent of, and cuts across, the criterion of prescriptivity. Thus both "laws of nature," or "truths" about what is (e.g., $E = mc^2$), and moral strictures about what ought not to be (e.g., "Thou shalt not kill") seem to be viewed as external, unalterable, and ahistorical. The criterion of obligation does, however, distinguish among different rules. Many rules (e.g., the convention "Don't wear white clothing to a funeral") are perceived as canons created rather than discovered and are thus viewed as relative, potentially alterable, and historical. What if, for example, everybody decided that the color white is to represent sorrow? Would that be all right? Many would probably say "yes." What if long ago, in the future, or in another country today there was, will be, or is a people whose mourning color was or is white? Was that, is that, would that be okay? Again many would probably say "yes." Thus, whereas some rules (e.g., the incest taboo) may evoke a sense of inherent rightness, others do not.

Importance

The criterion of importance has two aspects. First, it refers to the extent to which one can decline an interest in the conduct covered by a rule. Second, it refers to the extent to which a breach of a rule is considered *serious*. Thus, in the United States one can disclaim an interest in fashions, and it is considered rather a minor transgression to wear a dress 10 inches too long for the times. Disclaiming interest in harm to other people, on the other hand, is quite a different matter.

Prescriptivity, obligation, and importance: the child's view

American children seem to distinguish and identify moral versus prudential versus conventional rules using these same formal criteria of validity, and they seem to agree with the adults of their culture about the moral versus prudential versus conventional status of particular rules.

Much and Shweder (1978), for example, conducted a sociolinguistic analysis of children's excuses in "situations of accountability" (i.e., when accused of wrongdoing). Much and Shweder did not directly ask children about their breaches but rather observed and recorded naturally occurring breach episodes in nursery school and kindergarten and then later analyzed children's excuses within those episodes. Episodes were classified as breaches of five rule types: morals (ethics), conventions (customs), regulations (school rules), instructions (prudential rules), and truths (beliefs). These five rule types were derived from Black's (1962) logicogrammatical analysis of adult language use. Episodes were classified according to various criteria of validity including obligation (namely, alterability and historicity) and prescriptivity (namely, the relevance of truth criteria). The classifications were treated as mutually exclusive, although it was sometimes disputable whether a breach event belonged to one category or another. Nevertheless, interjudge reliability was satisfactory (.83 for 171 cases; kappa coefficient of agreement, Cohen, 1960).

Much and Shweder (1978) found that preschoolers and kindergarteners excuse and justify their breaches differently for violations of the different types of rules. When violating regulations and conventions, for example, kindergartners most frequently make reference to "circumstances," "consequences," and "precepts." In attempting to be excused from the classroom regulation that everyone goes outdoors at a specified time, one child cited a competing precept: "If you're sick you can't go out." Moral breaches, in contrast, were associated with direct references to the "act," denials that the breach had occurred, attempts at redefinition to remove blameworthiness, or justification in terms of retribution for someone else's prior moral transgression. When accused of "stealing" a chair, for example, one child countered, "Nobody was in it and I sat in it," thereby disputing a "theft" interpretation of her action. As Much and Shweder (1978; also see Shweder, Turiel, & Much, 1981) suggest, the kinds of accounts given by children in moral breach (denial, redefinition, retributive justice) imply a perception of moral rules as unalterable, intrinsically valid, beyond negotiation. Similarly, the lack of reference to consequences and competing precepts also suggests the unconditional authority and respect that moral rules command.

Other researchers have directly probed children about the formal criteria of validity applicable to various types of rules. This method provides evidence whether or not, for example, moral rules, in contrast to conventional rules, are perceived to be external, unalterable, and important.

Obligation has been examined by asking children about the legitimacy of a behavior in the absence of an announced rule and by means of questions concerning the "relativity" and "changeability" of rules. Nucci and Turiel (1978) asked preschool children and adults to judge a set of 72 observed transgressions. Preschoolers were asked: "What if there weren't a rule in the school about (the observed act); would it be all right to do it then?" Adults were asked to classify the transgressions as moral or conventional using substantive definitions of the two domains. Preschoolers and adults agreed in their classifications 83% of the time: The preschoolers answered "yes" with regard to those acts that adults classified as conventional and "no" to those that adults classified as moral.

In another study by Turiel (1979), subjects were questioned about such matters as stealing (a moral issue), dress codes (a conventional issue), use of titles in school (a conventional issue), and so on. Queries were posed concerning the perceived relativity of various moral and conventional prescriptions ("Suppose there is another country in which no families have that rule. Is that all right?"). At all ages, from 6 to 17 years, subjects were discriminating in their responses and tended to agree with each other about which rules did or did not require unconditional respect. Although conventional and game rules are perceived as relative, a proscription about stealing is not. Damon (1977) also found that by age 8 or 9 the moral rule prohibiting stealing is regarded as inherently worthy of respect, whereas conventions are perceived as more optional. If conventions are governed by announced rules (e.g., a school rule that requires eating with a fork), they become more mandatory in the eyes of children, but the child continues to distinguish between "small rules," or "manners," and "real rules," or "laws."

Findings regarding the alterability of rules are somewhat more complicated. First, although a significant number of Turiel's (1979) subjects viewed both conventional and game rules as changeable, a majority of subjects also viewed all moral rules as changeable. Lockhart, Abrahams, and Osherson (1977) have reported similar findings: The first-, third-, and fifth-graders in this study were significantly less willing to change moral than conventional rules, but by fifth grade a majority viewed a rule prohibiting the taking of others' toys as changeable. These results suggest that the difference between moral and conventional rules may be not that one type is changeable whereas the other is not, but rather that a change in a moral rule is limited in the form it may take (i.e., a moral rule may be altered but not done away with entirely). The phrasing of the question "Can we change that rule?" leaves ambiguous the nature of the change; subjects who answer affirmatively may have in mind small changes (e.g., you can take people's toys but not their clothes), and subjects who answer negatively may be thinking of changes at a different level (e.g., can we do away entirely with the idea of private property?). Thus, although indicative of differences in the perceived changeability of moral and conventional rules, the Turiel (1979) and Lockhart, Abrahams, and Osherson (1977) studies also suggest that more in-depth investigation is needed.

Finally, Turiel (1979), Damon (1977), and Shantz (in press) have all examined children's views about the importance of moral and conventional rules. Turiel discovered that at all ages from 6 to 17 years subjects judged all moral rules to be significantly more important than conventional rules regarding dress, forms of address, or game rules. Damon (1977) likewise reports that by age 6 the rule against stealing is viewed as more important than rules concerning table manners and sex roles.

Shantz (in press) examined first- and second-graders' rankings of the seriousness of moral and conventional rule violations. Shantz found that, using mean rankings, all moral rule violations (hitting, not sharing, and stealing) were ranked significantly worse than convention violations (boys playing with dolls, not combing your hair). The childrens' rank ordering matched that of a group of undergraduates. In examining the consistency with which individual children ranked the violations, however, Shantz found that only 18 of the 48 children ranked all three moral violations as more serious than the two conventional violations. Thus Shantz warns that the consistent distinction between moral and conventional rules may not be typical for this age group. Damon's (1977) work indicates that indeed the sixth and seventh year may be transitional in this regard: 60% of the 6-year-olds, but 84% of 7-, 8-, and 9-year-olds in Damon's study viewed stealing as worse than poor table manners. Turiel (personal communication), however, discovered that his results hold up even at the individual level of analysis.

The extent to which the criteria of prescriptivity, obligation, and importance are sufficient to characterize perceived distinctions among rules is an empirical question; although the evidence just discussed suggests that American children do differentiate rules along these dimensions, this research has also suggested that the cultural domains underlying rules may be more complex or heterogeneous than researchers have imagined. Findings that, for example, some moral rules are perceived as alterable whereas others are not clearly indicate the need for more in-depth understanding of various domains. What beliefs or presuppositions about the nature of persons and their social interactions, for example, inform judgments about the relativity or alterability of rules regarding private property, the incest taboo, or the proper way to dress for ritual occasions? Finally, whereas some rules seem to be clearly identifiable as moral, conventional, or prudential, others seem to overlap domains: Is wasting one's resources only one's own business (and imprudent), or is it also denying others (present and future) their due? The boundaries between various domains do not seem clear-cut.

Detecting schemata differentiation: the intuitive versus reflective knowledge parameter

Piaget's (1932/1965) and Kohlberg's (1963, 1969, 1971, 1973) accounts of moral development seem to conflict sharply with the evidence that children as young as 5 years of age distinguish moral versus conventional versus prudential rules, using adultlike formal criteria of validity. That conflict, however, may be more apparent than real.

Piaget and Kohlberg, for the most part, have examined the ability of subjects to articulate the formal criteria of validity that define the moral domain and distinguish morality from prudence and convention. Piaget and Kohlberg have traced the ontogenesis of reflective knowledge: They have equated "knowing" with the ability to propositionalize and argue. In contrast, recent moral development research suggests that to grasp a distinction, to have knowledge of a concept, is not necessarily equivalent to the ability to state what one knows (also see Nisbett & Wilson, 1977, on "knowing more than one can tell").

There are diverse ways of demonstrating that one has knowledge (and diverse ways of acquiring knowledge). By one standard, the modulation of excuse patterns when accused of wrongdoing, schemata differentiation appears relatively early (roughly 4 to 6 years). By a second standard, the ability to be systematically discriminating in one's answers to direct probes about obligation (alterability, historicity, etc.) and importance, schemata differentiation appears slightly later (roughly 6 to 9 years). By a third standard, consistently explicating a justification or self-reflectively volunteering a formal criterion of validity as a rationale for one's decisions, schemata differentiation develops quite late and often not at all. But no single one of these standards has a privileged status. Each standard gives us a different portrait of social-cognitive development. Each tells us about "knowing" in a different sense of "knowing." Children are not moral philosophers; nevertheless, their "intuitive" knowledge of rule types respects the distinctions between efficiency, duty, and consensus.

Recently, we have experimented with a fourth standard of knowing, the ability to apply ordinary language terms to appraise rule violations.

Any competent adult speaker of English employs a "vocabulary of appraisal," a set of terms and phrases for condoning and condemning conduct. This vocabulary of appraisal is exemplified by such terms as impolite, rude, disobedient, inefficient, impractical, unfair, immoral, cruel, unreasonable, and unauthorized. Such terms are applied when explicit or tacit prescriptions for conduct are breached or transgressed. It is the assumption of our recent research that the distinctions between, for example, morality, convention, and prudence are encoded in our natural language and are expressed in discriminated patterns of language use.

To what extent are children and adults differentiated in the way they apply adjectives of appraisal (rude, unfair, stupid, unauthorized, etc.) to evaluate breach episodes? And to what extent, and in what ways, are childhood and adult patterns of appraisal alike or different? To answer these questions we asked 10 children (7 to 9 years of age) and 10 adults to appraise 15 breach episodes using a corpus of 17 adjectives of appraisal. The 17 "adjectives" are listed in Tables 1 and 2. The 15 breach episodes were derived from observations of children's transgressions in a preschool setting (Much & Shweder, 1978) and were selected from a larger corpus to "represent" apparent breaches of moral versus conventional versus prudential versus "legal" norms. For example:

1. At snack time children are saying: "More milk, more cookies."
   Philip: "More poo-poo." (laughs)
   Rebecca: "Don't say 'more poo-poo,' dummy."
2. Michael and Alice are sitting at a table coloring. Michael presses very hard on his crayons and colors furiously. Soon Michael says: "My crayon broke."
   Alice: "That's because you used it too hard."
   Michael and Alice keep coloring. In a while Michael says: "*Another* crayon broke."
   Alice: "You use them too hard."
3. Linda has made a bouquet of paper flowers and placed them in a milk-carton vase. Billy walks over to the flowers, takes the bouquet and puts the flowers upside down on his head.
   Linda: "Stop it Billy. Look what you did, I'm telling teacher." (To teacher:) "Billy took my flowers and put 'em on his head."
   Billy in the meantime is rearranging the flowers in the vase.

For each of 15 such episodes subjects were asked to judge on a 10-point scale the degree of applicability of each of the 17 adjectives of appraisal. Philip's behavior in Episode 1, for example, might be given a scale value of 8 for rude, 2 for unfair, 0 for cruel, and so on. Seven-year-old children had no difficulty using the scale; some, in fact, seemed to find the exercise mildly intriguing.

Having collected judgments on all 17 adjectives of appraisal for all 15 breach episodes from all of our subjects (10 children and 10 adults), we then constructed, for each subsample (child and adult), an aggregated 17 (adjectives) × 15 (breach episodes) matrix. In each cell of the matrix was placed the average score (between 0 and 10), representing the collective judgment of the subsample about the extent to which the breach described in each episode was rude, unfair, cruel, stupid, and so on.

For each subsample (child and adult) a 17 × 17 correlation matrix for all possible pairs of adjectives was then derived by treating the 17 columns of the original 17 (adjectives) × 15 (breach episodes) matrix as variables and the 15 rows as subjects. This 17 × 17 matrix represents in correlational form the degree of covariance of each pair of adjectives (e.g., rude–impolite) in their application across the 15 breaches. This derived correlation matrix for adjectives was then cluster-analyzed using the hierarchical cluster program described by Johnson (1967).

Using this method, adjectives are grouped together or differentiated in relationship to the degree of equivalence (i.e., correlation) of their distribution of scores across breach episodes. The primary clusters for children and adults and the pair-wise correlations for all adjectives are displayed in Tables 1 and 2. (Note: the correlation coefficients in Tables 1 and 2 have been scaled down to the nearest coefficient.) To measure the degree of similarity of childhood and adult patterns of language use in appraising breach episodes, the 17 × 17 adjective-correlation matrices for children (Table 1) and adults (Table 2) were directly compared by intercorrelating (Pearson *R*) the 136 *parallel* cells (e.g., rude–unfair) of the two tables.

The cluster analyses in Tables 1 and 2 reveal that both children and adults partition the adjectives of appraisal into subsets; this information on differentiation makes it possible to examine in some detail the structure of childhood and adult understandings of rule types and to compare childhood and adult understandings. The cognitive structures of children (Table 1) and adults (Table 2) are noteworthy in several respects.

1. Both children and adults are differentiated in their evaluations of rule violations. Children distinguish among six relatively coherent patterns of appraisal; adults distinguish among four patterns of appraisal. The childhood clusters seem to represent manners (inconsiderate, bad manners) versus morality (mean, cruel, etc.) versus convention (rude, impolite) versus school rules (not allowed, etc.) versus prudence-intelligence (not reasonable, stupid, etc.) versus doesn't make sense. The adults distinguish convention (inconsiderate, rude, impolite, bad manners, not nice) versus morality (mean, unkind, etc.) versus prudence-intelligence (doesn't make sense, stupid, etc.) versus school rules (not allowed, etc.).

2. Childhood and adult rule understandings substantially overlap, at least as reflected in the ordinary language use of adjectives of appraisal. The

Table 1. *Hierarchical cluster analysis of children's use of adjectives of appraisal showing differentiation of adjectives into six clusters and intercorrelations (Pearson R) among adjectives*

	In	BM	Me	Cr	Unk	NN	Ru	Im	NA	BR	Unf	NO	NR	St	NB	Ha	DMS
Inconsiderate	100	86	84	82	62	74	74	72	36	52	46	22	14	30	00	14	-20
Bad manners	86	100	60	62	34	56	68	56	46	46	32	00	26	54	26	20	-20
Mean	84	60	100	88	82	80	58	64	22	54	64	28	12	16	-12	18	-18
Cruel	82	62	88	100	72	68	64	68	30	52	6	22	06	24	-12	16	-10
Unkind	62	34	82	72	100	84	68	76	04	18	44	26	-06	-18	-44	-04	16
Not nice	74	56	80	68	84	100	72	76	32	44	48	34	-12	-06	-34	00	-10
Rude	74	68	58	64	68	72	100	86	16	10	12	16	-06	10	-28	-12	-14
Impolite	72	56	64	68	76	76	86	100	16	18	10	-02	04	-44	-14	-02	-02
Not allowed	36	46	22	30	04	32	16	16	100	72	60	44	28	44	24	08	14
Breaking a rule	52	46	54	52	18	44	10	18	72	100	72	34	10	36	24	34	-18
Unfair	46	32	64	56	44	48	12	18	60	72	100	30	30	22	10	-06	16
Not obeying	22	00	28	22	26	34	16	10	44	34	30	100	10	-30	-24	-10	02
Not reasonable	14	26	12	06	-06	-12	-06	-02	28	10	30	10	100	54	50	-02	16
Stupid	30	54	16	24	-18	-06	10	04	44	36	22	-30	54	100	74	46	-10
Not using your brains	00	26	-12	-12	-44	-34	-28	-14	24	24	10	-24	50	74	100	44	-06
Harmful	14	20	18	16	-04	00	-12	-02	08	34	-06	-10	-02	46	44	100	-32
Doesn't make sense	-20	-20	-18	-10	16	-10	-14	-02	14	-18	16	02	16	-10	-06	-32	100

	In	Ru	Im	Bm	NN	Me	Unk	Cr	NR	Unf	DMS	St	Ha	NB	NA	BR	NO
Inconsiderate	100	82	80	86	86	84	84	72	60	70	44	34	56	-16	28	20	12
Rude	82	100	90	86	88	84	86	72	60	54	36	16	34	-36	20	16	08
Impolite	80	90	100	96	90	66	70	56	42	42	32	08	24	-38	18	12	04
Bad manners	86	86	96	100	92	68	70	60	42	46	30	12	36	-36	26	18	08
Not nice	86	88	90	92	100	82	84	76	62	58	52	30	50	-22	24	14	06
Mean	84	84	66	68	82	100	98	90	78	70	48	32	54	-18	20	14	04
Unkind	84	86	70	70	84	98	100	90	78	62	50	32	52	-20	12	08	-02
Cruel	72	72	56	60	76	90	90	100	78	50	60	46	66	-08	18	04	-06
Not reasonable	60	60	42	42	62	78	78	100	44	76	72	56	32	-10	-20	-26	
Unfair	70	54	42	46	58	70	62	50	44	100	34	16	36	-16	44	48	50
Doesn't make sense	44	36	32	30	52	48	50	60	76	34	100	72	48	36	-04	-20	-18
Stupid	34	16	08	12	30	32	32	46	72	16	72	100	68	64	-06	-24	-22
Harmful	56	34	24	36	50	54	52	66	56	36	48	68	100	28	44	22	12
Not using your brains	-16	-36	-38	-36	-22	-18	-20	-08	32	-16	36	64	28	100	-48	-62	-56
Not allowed	28	20	18	26	24	20	12	18	-10	44	-04	-06	44	-48	100	94	90
Breaking a rule	20	16	12	18	14	14	08	04	-20	48	-20	-24	22	-62	94	100	96
Not obeying	12	08	04	08	06	04	-02	-06	-26	50	-18	-22	12	-56	90	96	100

Note: Column headings are abbreviations of the items listed in the left-hand column.

intercorrelation of the two correlation matrices in Tables 1 and 2 is .52 (Pearson R). Both children and adults seem to distinguish roughly similar clusters for morality, convention, prudence-intelligence, and school rules.

3. Children seem to distinguish between bad manners (probably table manners) and other varieties of conventional breach (politeness, rudeness). Adults, on the other hand, merge these two patterns of appraisal. Thus, in this evidence at least, children seem slightly more differentiated than adults!

The results of this vocabulary of appraisal analysis tend to converge with sociolinguistic analyses of children's excuse patterns (Much & Shweder, 1978) and cognitive-developmental examinations using direct interview probes (Nucci & Turiel, 1978). By investigating ordinary language use, in particular the application of adjectives of appraisal to breach events, we discover the existence in 7-year-old children of differentiated, adultlike schemata for classifying rule types and for distinguishing among morality, convention, and prudence.

Culture as a cognitive system: a challenge for ethnographers

Malinowski (1926/1976) warned us against an undifferentiated view of savage custom and called our attention to the cognitive side of an individual's respect for collective canons. "First of all," he noted,

if the rules of custom are obeyed by the savage through sheer inability to break them, then no definition can be given of law, no distinction can be drawn between the rules of law, morals, manners, and other usages. For the only way in which we can classify rules of conduct is by reference to the motives and sanctions by which they are enforced. So that with the assumption of an automatic obedience to all custom, anthropology has to give up any attempt at introducing into the facts order and classification, which is the first task of science (p. 50).

Despite Malinowski's admonitions, much contemporary ethnography is written as though the savage adult were Piaget's heteronomous child. The culture of the primitive is portrayed as a bloated normative order in which the claims of technical reason (prudence and efficiency), the claims of moral reason (duty and importance), the claims of conventional reason (consensus, constitutive process, and arbitrary code), and the claims of positive science are either denied autonomous status or comingle in an undifferentiated respect for "received wisdom," subserving an undifferentiated "symbolic function."

For some theorists (e.g., Firth, 1951), it is the moral category that is stretched to encompass all rules about what is right or wrong, thus obscuring the difference between morality, convention, and prudence. That distinction is obscured as effectively by those theorists (e.g., Sahlins

1976) for whom "utility" and "belief" are dismissed as folk concepts peculiar to the modern Western mind. The distinction is overlooked as well by those theorists (e.g., Harris, 1968) for whom all aspects of culture (morality, convention, belief) are merely prudence in disguise. In each case the pluralistic coexistence of multiple modes of appraisal in the mind of the native is either denied or transformed into a monolithic conception of culture as *either* moral order, free will, communication, false consciousness, or tool. Take your pick!

The "heteronomous child," as we have seen, is probably a myth. Recent research on social-cognitive development suggests the early appearance of the distinction between morality, convention, and prudence. And given the intuitive ability of young children to appraise untoward conduct using formal criteria such as prescriptivity, obligation, and importance, it is not too fanciful to hypothesize that the distinction between various types of rules is universally available and that it is available because it is important. Indeed, it is worth considering the possibility that the undifferentiated savage is to be found more in the eyes of the ethnologist than in the mind of the primitive.

The issue, of course, is an empirical one, but it is an issue that will not get resolved unless native criteria of validity become objects of systematic ethnographic inquiry. More strongly, one might argue that no ethnography is adequate if it fails to explain why rules are obeyed, how they are appraised, how they are tested, and, "taking the native point of view," how they are validated. Taking the native viewpoint here means taking the perspective of self-monitoring individual others; it is self-critical others who make their way in the world by means of the collective ideational inheritance we call "culture," the same self-critical others who appraise their symbolic inheritance and either grant it or deny it the kind of respect ideas require if they are to persist. Not until we can explain the persistence of ideas will we have arrived at a satisfactory theory of culture, and to explain the persistence of ideas we have to link them to the patterns of reason that lend them authority. "The business of thought includes the discovery and correction of its own errors" (Collingwood, 1972, p. 110).

Finally, as ethnographers and students of culture, we need not be discouraged by the oft-reported lack of reflective awareness (Horton, 1967; Levy, 1973) in many savage societies. Young children cannot necessarily tell us about their knowledge of the formal criteria of validity that distinguish morality, convention, and prudence. They simply "know more than they can tell" (Nisbett & Wilson, 1977), and they display this knowledge in ways that are available to ethnographers of any primitive society, that is, vis-à-vis excuse patterns, ordinary language applications of adjectives of appraisal, and so on. Complex cognitive structures preexist their own reflective representation. What the savage knows he may not be able to tell us, but what the savage himself is unable to say about what he knows is not necessarily a secret and is certainly not beyond our deliberate grasp.

References

Berlin, I. Equality. *Proceedings of the Aristotelian Society* (1955–56), 1956, N.S. *56*, 301–326.

Black, M. The analysis of rules. In M. Black, *Models and metaphors.* Ithaca, N.Y.: Cornell University Press, 1962.

Cohen, J. A coefficient of agreement for nominal scales. *Educational and Psychological Measurement,* 1960, *20,* 37–46.

Collett, P. The rules of conduct. In P. Collett (Ed.), *Social rules and social behavior,* pp. 1–27. Totowa, N.J.: Rowman and Littlefield, 1977.

Collingwood, R. G. *An essay on metaphysics.* Chicago: Regnery, 1972. (Originally published, 1939.)

Damon, W. *The social world of the child.* San Francisco: Jossey-Bass, 1977.

D'Andrade, R. G., & Romney, A. K. Summary of participants' discussion. In A. K. Romney & R. G. D'Andrade (Eds.), *Transcultural studies in cognition.* Report of a conference sponsored by Social Science Research Council Committee on Intellective Processes Research. *American Anthropologist,* 1964, *66,*(3), Part 2, 230–242.

Firth, R. Moral standards and social organization. In R. Firth, *Elements of social organization.* London: Watts, 1951.

Geertz, C. *The interpretation of cultures.* New York: Basic Books, 1973.

Gellner, E. The savage and the modern mind. In R. Horton & R. Finnegan (Eds.), *Mode. of thought,* pp. 126–181. London: Faber & Faber, 1973.

Goody, J. *The domestication of the savage mind.* Cambridge: Cambridge University Press, 1977.

Hallowell, A. I. *Culture and experience.* Philadelphia: University of Pennsylvania Press, 1955.

Harris, M. *The rise of anthropological theory.* New York: Cromwell, 1968.

Hart, H. L. A. *The concept of law.* London: Oxford University Press, 1961.

Hobhouse, L. T. *Morals in evolution.* London: Chapman & Hall, 1906.

Horton, R. African traditional thought and Western science, Part 2. *Africa,* 1967, *37,* 159–87.

Horton, R. Neo-Tylorianism: Sound sense or sinister prejudice? *Man,* 1968, *3,* 625–634.

Johnson, S. Hierarchical clustering schemes. *Psychometrika,* 1967, *32,* 241–254.

Kant, I. *Foundations of the metaphysics of morals.* (L. W. Beck, trans.) Indianapolis: Library of Liberal Arts Press, 1959. (Originally published, 1785.)

Kohlberg, L. The development of children's orientation toward a moral order. 1. Sequence in the development of moral thought. *Vita Humana,* 1963, *6,* 11–33.

Kohlberg, L. Stage and sequence. The cognitive-developmental approach to socialization. In D. A. Goslin (Ed.), *Handbook of socialization theory and research,* pp. 347–380. New York: Rand McNally, 1969.

Kohlberg, L. From is to ought: How to commit the naturalistic fallacy and get away with it in the study of moral development. In T. Mischel (Ed.), *Cognitive development an epistemology,* pp. 151–236. New York: Academic Press, 1971.

Kohlberg, L. The claim to moral adequacy of a highest stage of moral judgment. *Journal of Philosophy,* 1973, *70,* 630–646.

Lévi-Strauss, C. *The savage mind.* Chicago: University of Chicago Press, 1966.

Levy, Robert I. *Tahitians.* Chicago: University of Chicago Press, 1973.

Lévy-Bruhl, L. *Les fonctions mentales dans les sociétés inférieures.* Paris: Alcan, 1910.

Lockhart, K., Abrahams, B., & Osherson, D. Children's understandings of uniformities in the environment. *Child Development,* 1977, *48,* 1521–1531.

Malinowski, B. *Crime and custom in savage society.* Totowa, N.J.: Littlefield, Adams, 1976. (Originally published, 1926.)

Much, N. C., & Shweder, R. A. Speaking of rules: The analysis of culture in the breach. In W. Damon (Ed.), *New directions for child development,* Vol 2: *Moral development,* pp. 19–39. San Francisco: Jossey-Bass, 1978.

Nisbett, R. E., & Wilson, T. D. Telling more than we can know: Verbal reports on mental processes. *Psychological Review,* 1977, *84,* 231–259.

Nucci, L. P., & Turiel, E. Social interactions and the development of social concepts in preschool children. *Child Development,* 1978, *49,* 400–407.

Perelman, C. *The idea of justice and the problem of argument.* New York: Humanities Press, 1963.

Piaget, J. *The construction of reality in the child.* New York: Basic Books, 1954.

Piaget, J. *The moral judgment of the child.* New York: Free Press, 1965. (Originally published, 1932.)

Piaget, J. *Six psychological studies.* New York: Random House, 1967.

Sahlins, M. *Culture and practical reason.* Chicago: University of Chicago Press, 1976.

Schneider, D. *American kinship: A cultural account.* Englewood Cliffs, N.J.: Prentice-Hall, 1968.

Shantz, C. Children's understanding of social rules and the social context. In F. C. Serafica (Ed.), *Social cognition and social relations in context.* New York: Guilford Press, in press.

Shweder, R. A., Turiel, E., & Much N. C. The moral intuitions of the child. In J. H. Flavell & L. Ross (Eds.), *Social cognitive development: frontiers and possible futures.* Cambridge: Cambridge University Press, 1981.

Turiel, E. Distinct conceptual and developmental domains: Social convention and morality. In C. B. Keasy (Ed.), *Nebraska Symposium on Motivation,* 1977 (Vol. 25). Lincoln: University of Nebraska Press, 1979.

Turiel, E. Domains and categories in social cognitive development. In W. Overton (Ed.), *The relationship between social and cognitive development.* Hillsdale, N. J.: Erlbaum, 1980.

Tylor, E. B. *Primitive culture: Researches into the development of mythology, philosophy, religion, language, art and custom.* London: Murray, 1871.

Werner, H., & Kaplan, B. The developmental approach to cognition: Its relevance to the psychological interpretation of anthropological and ethnolinguistic data. *American Anthropologist,* 1956, *58,* 866–880.

Whiting, J. W. M., & Whiting, B. B. Contributions of anthropology to the methods of studying child rearing. In P. H. Mussen (Ed.), *Handbook of research methods in child psychology.* New York: Wiley, 1960.

9 Development of interpersonal values

Walter Emmerich and Karla Shepard Goldman

There is a long-standing paradox regarding the role of interpersonal values in human conduct. If interpersonal values are important for guiding conduct, why do they appear not to do so in many instances? Because the covariation of professed values and actual behaviors is neither strong nor consistent, many psychologists are skeptical about the power of the value construct in explaining individual behavior, although there are notable exceptions (Feather, 1975; Heider, 1958; Kohlberg, 1969; Rokeach, 1973). This criticism fails to consider the underlying basis for the value paradox, namely, that value and behavior refer to different realms of experience that may or may not be coordinated. Behavioral information is processed as knowledge about the actual social world, whereas an evaluation relates such knowledge to an ideal social world. People ordinarily distinguish between the worlds of fact and value, and they tend to maintain boundaries between them. On the other hand, it would be difficult to imagine how an individual or a society could function in the absence of value-guided behaviors. The value paradox does not imply that the study of value ends when it is shown that values fail to guide behaviors. Rather, it sets the stage for investigating those conditions that produce or fail to produce value-guided behaviors.

We shall examine certain implications of this view for the study of socialization. One implication is that value development and behavioral development involve distinct processes. Knowledge about value development is distinct from knowledge about behavioral development, and both are required before we can understand their coordination. Particular attention shall be given here to the development of substantive interper-

The reported study was supported in part by Grant MH 29458 from the National Institute of Mental Health. We wish to thank Debra Dash Friedman, Henrietta Gallagher, and Rina Pianko for their assistance and Dorothy Thayer and Kirsten Yocum for conducting the analyses. Special thanks are extended to the New York City schools that cooperated in the research. We also wish to thank Nina S. Feldman for her helpful comments on an earlier draft of this chapter.

214

sonal values (e.g., kindness, independence) that may be of sufficient specificity to control their corresponding behaviors.

The analysis also will consider certain distinctions within the value domain that have received relatively little attention in the study of value development. One such distinction is that between value and obligation. Following Sesonske (1964), we suggest that the value one holds is conceptually and functionally distinct from an obligation to act in accordance with the value. In this formulation, value does not become binding on action unless the individual also assumes a commitment (obligation) to act accordingly in particular circumstances (Kiesler, 1971). We shall suggest that his formulation applies to the mature end state, and that it is probably preceded by a series of developmental steps in understanding and applying the value-obligation distinction. The nature of these steps will be considered, as will their possible implications for developmental changes in value-behavior relationships.

Because the cognition of behavior and the evaluation of behavior engage distinctive processes, the question arises as to how they become linked in the course of development. One might expect the perceived quantity of a given attribute (intensity, frequency, duration) to be monotonically related to the strength of its value, but there is some evidence to the contrary (Coombs & Avrunin, 1977), and there are grounds for believing that moderate quantities of a personal attribute are especially likely to be valued by mature individuals. Though we might value the trait of independence, for example, the individual who is extremely independent is likely to be disvalued relative to the individual who is independent but not extremely so. Mature interpersonal evaluations are moderated by such factors as situational norms and judgments regarding balance in personality organization. Moreover, interpersonal evaluations are multidimensional, so that too much of an otherwise desirable trait, or too little of an otherwise undesirable one, are likely to be disvalued on another dimension of value. For example, the extremely independent person may be seen as asocial, and the person who cannot withhold kindness may be perceived as weak. However, it probably requires considerable maturity to fully understand and apply such modulating principles. Consequently, we might expect a developmental trend toward a decreasing monotonic relationship between the quantity of a trait and its judged value. Initial evidence on this hypothesis will be examined.

If interpersonal values are multidimensional, by what timetable do these dimensions develop? Research evidence on this question is scanty, but there is evidence that children value interpersonal characteristics that enhance social acceptance, whereas adolescents also value attributes that enhance individual autonomy within interpersonal relationships (Beech & Schoeppe, 1974; Douvan & Adelson, 1966; Emmerich, 1974). Additional evidence for this developmental trend will be presented. We shall also consider whether this trend is more consistent with a sociocultural or a cognitive-developmental interpretation of change in value development. From a sociocultural standpoint, age-graded changes in social experiences would be expected to strengthen autonomy values during adolescence (Higgins & Parsons, this volume). From a cognitive-developmental standpoint, however, specific changes in social experience, whether age-graded or not, are processed in relation to overarching concepts of social reality that change qualitatively in the course of development (Kohlberg, 1969). From this perspective the relationship between age-graded social inputs and interpersonal values would be less direct, but there could be a more direct relationship between individual differences in rate of general cognitive development and the timing of the shift toward an autonomy value orientation.

A developmental study

To provide an empirical base for examining these issues in greater depth, we now turn to a study of the development of interpersonal values during late childhood and adolescence. A key feature of the study was elicitation of separate evaluations of several behavioral traits under each of three frequency conditions: when the trait is implied to be present, when it is "absent," and when it is "sometimes present and sometimes absent." Together with an assessment of the child's general level of intellectual development, these evaluations of interpersonal traits were used to examine the value-obligation distinction, growth of value orientations, developmental changes in attribute-value relationships, and sociocultural versus cognitive-developmental interpretations of shifts in value development.

Procedure

Using a paper-and-pencil format, subjects evaluated each of the following interpersonal traits separately under each of the three frequency conditions: kindness, cooperation, sociableness, leadership, independence, forcefulness, conformity, self-centeredness. In most instances, items included a brief trait description, as reported elsewhere (Emmerich, 1974, Table 1). Each item also specified the gender of the target ("boy" or "girl"), yielding a total of 48 items (8 traits × 2 gender targets × ?

frequency conditions). There were four response alternatives, scored as follows: (4) like very much, (3) like a little, (2) dislike a little, (1) dislike very much.

To facilitate engagement of judgmental processes that relate a trait's quantity to its value strength, the format grouped and sequenced the three frequency conditions for a given trait-target combination in the following manner, illustrated for kindness toward the girl target: "Would you like a kind *girl* who cares about others?" "Would you like a girl who sometimes is kind and sometimes is not?" "Would you like a girl who is *not* kind?" The 16 trait-target subsets (3 items each) were presented in the reverse sequence to approximately half the subjects. Present interest is in commonalities across targets differing in gender. We computed each subject's mean score across the 2 targets within each combination of a trait and frequency condition. The resulting 24 scores (8 traits averaged across 2 targets under each of 3 frequency conditions) were used in the analyses.

Data were collected in school classrooms from urban subjects in grades 4 through 12. The sample included males and females, blacks and whites, and a distribution of socioeconomic backgrounds (excluding extreme poverty). The total sample of whites varied from 699 to 716 (depending upon missing data), and the total sample of blacks varied from 516 to 538. To increase cell sizes and facilitate interpretation of developmental trends, grade levels were combined to form *Late Childhood* (grades 4–6), *Early Adolescence* (grades 7–9), and *Late Adolescence* (grades 10–12) age groups.

During a second testing session, subjects were administered the Vocabulary, Verbal Analogies, and Non-verbal Figure Classification subtests from the Cognitive Abilities Test, Form 1 (Thorndike & Hagen, 1971). As expected, these three subtests were moderately intercorrelated. Intercorrelations within grades and races ranged from .19 to .74, with a median of .49. Consequently, each individual's three subtest scores could be summed to form a composite index of general intellectual functioning. This index was used to divide samples into two additional subgroups. Based upon median splits within grades and races, each subject was placed into a "More Cognitively Advanced" or a "Less Cognitively Advanced" subgroup.

Each of the 24 value scores was subjected to a sex (2) × age group (3) × cognitive level (2) analysis of variance, conducted separately by race. For whites, the smallest cell sizes varied from 35 to 39 and the largest varied from 77 to 81. For blacks, the smallest cell sizes varied from 15 to 7 and the largest varied from 60 to 64.

The analyses of variance yielded only scattered significant interactions and sex main effects for both races. Consequently, we shall consider only age group and cognitive level main effects. Because our aim here is to identify general societal trends, a particular effect for a value score will be called significant only when $p < .05$ for both races (18 instances), or when $p < .05$ for one race with marginal statistical significance for the other (4 instances). Of the 44 specific outcomes that met these criteria, 27 were statistically significant at $p < .001$ and 8 at $p < .01$. All figures report the means of racial group means. In all figures except Figure 2, a scale mean of 2.50 represents the neutral point between a positive evaluation (upper scale limit of 4.00) and a negative evaluation (lower scale limit of 1.00).

Value-obligation distinction

Our first (and most tentative) look at findings considers the value-obligation distinction. The value of a trait's absence is not necessarily symmetrical (opposite and equal) to the value of the same trait's presence. Consider, for example, the case where a trait's presence is positively valued, but where its absence is negatively valued to a considerably lesser degree. This case appears to signify a situation in which obligation is at least partially differentiated from value, because the weaker negative evaluation under the "absent" condition makes action in accordance with the value less mandatory. We shall refer to this situation as "deviation from polar symmetry."

As seen in Figure 1, polar symmetry (flat slope) generally occurred, although trait evaluations were at least slightly stronger under the "present" condition than under the "absent" condition. Of course, presence of a trait is palpable, and so it may engage a stronger evaluation than the trait's absence. One might also seek more information about a target's behavior, immediate state, and/or circumstances before evaluating the trait's absence to an equal and opposite degree. But despite such possible influences, polar symmetry generally prevailed, as might be expected if obligation were undifferentiated from value. The one trait that deviated considerably from symmetry (leadership) also happened to be the only trait, among those investigated, that was easily recognizable as nonobligatory, as not all individuals are expected or encouraged to assume leadership positions.

Such evidence is only suggestive, however. More direct measures of the value-obligation distinction are needed, as are broader samplings of interpersonal traits. Until such measures are formulated and used in developmental studies, we cannot be sure that the value-obligation distinction is either as difficult or as late in developing as our initial data suggest.

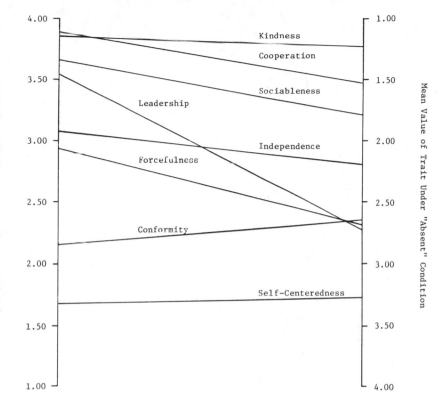

Figure 1. Deviations from polar symmetry across age groups.

Value development

Development of a trait's value could be indexed by an age-related change under either the "present" condition (Emmerich, 1974) or the "absent" condition (opposite direction). To utilize both sources of information we derived a value polarity index, based upon the difference between a trait's value under the two conditions. Developmental trends in trait polarities are given in Figure 2. Adopting a strong criterion, requiring that evaluations develop significantly in the opposite direction under the "present" and "absent" conditions, conformity, forcefulness, and self-centeredness were found to exhibit growth of polarity well into adolescence. In the case of self-centeredness, such growth was continuous with that which already had occurred during middle childhood, revealing an especially long period of development for this disvalued trait. In the cases of conformity and forcefulness, however, growth of polarity did not begin until

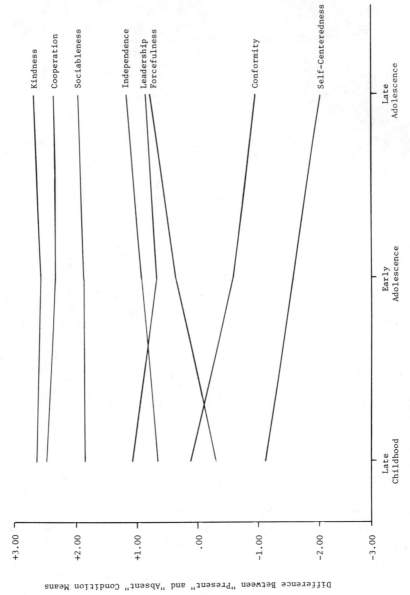

Figure 2. Development of value polarities.

after childhood (Figure 2). The poles for these traits may even undergo reversals between middle childhood and adolescence, an inference also supported by previous findings (Emmerich, 1974). There was weaker but definite evidence for growth of polarity in the case of independence, a result primarily of the significant developmental increase in this trait's value under the "present" condition, again replicating a previous finding (Emmerich, 1974). There was little evidence for a developmental shift in polarity for sociableness, and the significant developmental shifts for cooperation, kindness, and leadership were too small in magnitude and/or too complex in form to warrant inferences regarding their development after middle childhood.

These variations in the timing of value development support the view that children value traits that enhance social acceptance, whereas adolescents also value traits that enhance the individual's autonomy within interpersonal relationships (Douvan & Adelson, 1966; Emmerich, 1974). It is important to note that this developmental shift was not one in which the value of autonomy *displaced* the value of social acceptance. Rather, values signifying autonomy were selectively added to social-acceptance values in the course of development. For such traits as cooperation, kindness, and sociableness, the late childhood polarities were sustained throughout adolescence, and self-centeredness became increasingly disvalued during adolescence despite whatever positive connotations self-centeredness might have for increased autonomy.

The possible developmental reversal of polarity for conformity and forcefulness may be explained by the fact that the poles of these traits line up with the two value orientations in mutually exclusive fashion, with children placing greater value on the social-acceptance pole and adolescents placing greater value on the autonomy pole. This possibility suggests the importance of conflict resolution in value development, a theme that will become increasingly central to the discussion.

With the exception of self-centeredness, individual differences in rate of general cognitive development did not influence growth of polarity. Of course, one could argue that the growth of early formed polarities (cooperation, kindness, leadership, sociableness) would not be cognitively mediated during late childhood and adolescence, because these were not the primary growth periods for these particular values. However, cognitive mediation also failed to occur in the cases of conformity, forcefulness, and independence, indicating that rate of shift toward an autonomy orientation was unrelated to individual differences in rate of general cognitive development. Moreover, in the case of self-centeredness, more cognitively advanced individuals polarized this trait more as a negative value than did less cognitively advanced individuals. The direction of this effect was opposite to that expected if general cognitive development produces a value shift from social acceptance to autonomy.

Value in relation to trait quantity

We have suggested that modulating factors assign special value to a moderate amount of a personal attribute, producing deviations from a monotonic relationship between a trait's value and its perceived amount. In the present study the monotonic assumption was considered to be violated to the extent that evaluation of a given trait under the "sometimes" condition deviated from the midpoint of the trait's value under the "present" and "absent" conditions. The rather steep slopes of Figure 3 reveal considerable deviation from this assumption. For most traits the value of "sometimes" was closer to the same content's value under the "present" condition than under the "absent" condition. Similar to our earlier interpretation for polarities, this general effect could be due to the greater palpability of a content's meaning when it is "sometimes present" than when it is "sometimes absent."

More striking, however, were the marked variations among trait contents in their deviations from the monotonic assumption. Indeed, this assumption was so severely violated in the cases of conformity, forcefulness, and independence that "sometimes" became the most valued condition for these traits! Clearly, then, the usual assumption that attribute-value relationships are monotonic cannot be taken for granted (Coombs & Avrunin, 1977).

It is probably not coincidental that the monotonic assumption was most dramatically violated by those traits that defined the autonomy value orientation discussed earlier. The individual who values autonomy also is likely to perceive its extreme as "too much of a good thing," because this orientation in its extreme form directly conflicts with the complex of values governed by the social-acceptance orientation. To illustrate, the individual who rarely conforms is likely to be considered antisocial.

In our society the effectively socialized individual is able to sustain interpersonal ties *and* pursue individual goals within interpersonal contexts. Because these two sets of values will conflict under certain circumstances, it is also an important task of socialization to achieve an optimal balance between them. It is this latter function of socialization that would be served by the tendency to dampen one value orientation in relation to another through violations of monotonic attribute-value relationships.

From this perspective, findings on the growth of polarity suggest a kind

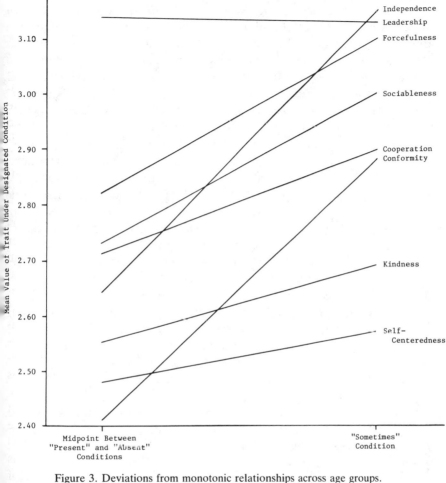

Figure 3. Deviations from monotonic relationships across age groups.

of imbalance during childhood, when social-acceptance values were more fully developed than autonomy values. The development of autonomy values during adolescence corrected this childhood imbalance, and the dampening tendency applied to autonomy values prevented an abrupt swing in the opposite direction. A residual imbalance in favor of social-acceptance values remained during the adolescent period, however. Several of the social-acceptance contents did deviate considerably from the monotonic assumption (Figure 3), but, unlike the autonomy-related contents, the former were consistently valued more under the "present" condition than under the "sometimes" condition. If extreme efforts to seek social acceptance (e.g., gratuitous kindness) were to be perceived as ingratiating, overbearing, or even as violations of equity norms, then such traits also would be valued more under the "sometimes" condition than under the "present" condition. Perhaps such a change occurs later in development. If so, then we would expect the two orientations to form a new kind of balance during adulthood, a balance in which both value orientations are dampened.

This interpretation implies that the growth of autonomy-related polarities during adolescence will be accompanied by increased dampening, manifested by significant growth of these values under the "sometimes" condition. As seen in Figures 4 and 5, this expectation generally held. Moreover, under the "sometimes" condition there was a significant tendency for cognitively advanced individuals to value each of these three traits more than less cognitively advanced individuals (irrespective of age). The resulting difference in value structure as a function of cognitive maturity can be seen by comparing Figures 4 and 5.

For the remaining traits, it would not be inconsistent with our interpretation to find similar decreases with age in the monotonic relationship. However, because these traits were more closely related to the social-acceptance value orientation, such evidence for increased dampening should be relatively weak, at least prior to adulthood. In fact, there were significant, but small, developmental increases in value under the "sometimes" condition for cooperation, leadership, and sociableness. This developmental trend was cognitively mediated only in the case of leadership. Figure 6 presents the overall developmental trend for the five traits combined. Comparisons of Figure 6 with Figures 4 and 5 indicate that the developmental decrease in the monotonic relationship for this value orientation was weaker than for the autonomy value orientation.

Implications

Attribute-value relationships

The exceptions we found to the monotonic assumption were striking but not mysterious, because different quantities along an attribute dimension can elicit different kinds of evaluational judgments. Findings suggested that extreme behaviors that are consistent with one value orientation tend to conflict with a different value orientation also held by the individual. For all practical purposes, however, the monotonic assumption *did* hold for social-acceptance traits from late childhood through adolescence, so

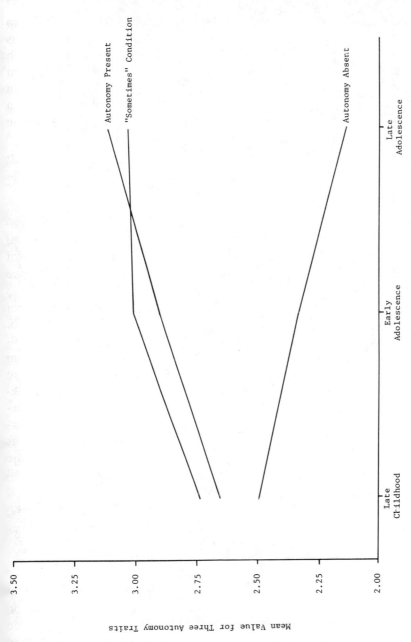

Figure 4. Value development by condition for autonomy traits in less cognitively advanced subjects.

225

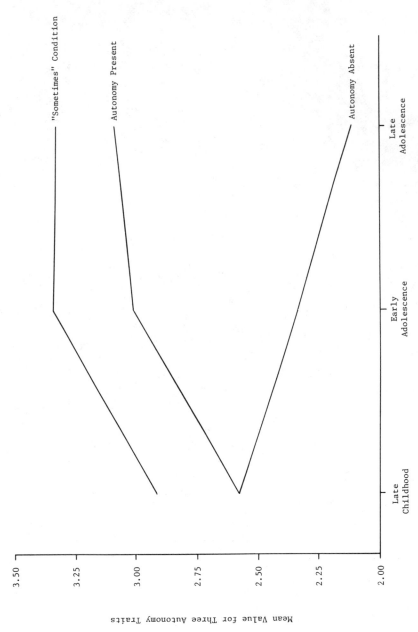

Figure 5. Value development by condition for autonomy traits in more cognitively advanced subjects.

226

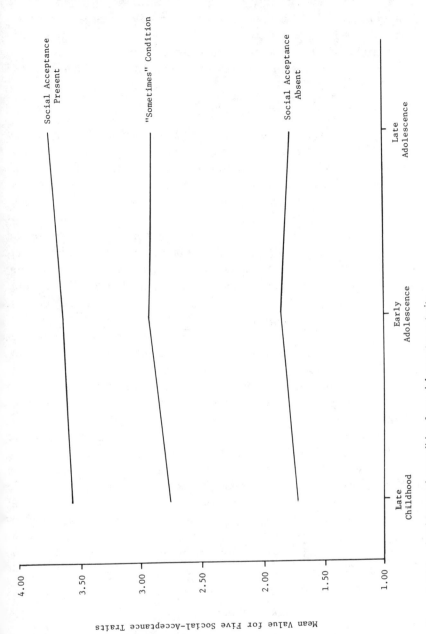

Figure 6. Value development by condition for social-acceptance traits.

227

one should be cautious in regarding the observed exceptions as the rule. Nevertheless, our developmental formulation implies that greater maturity increases the likelihood that judgmental processes will be engaged that aggregate value away from the extremes of attribute dimensions.

Social versus cognitive mediation

An earlier study, which indicated that the development of interpersonal values is cognitively mediated (Emmerich, 1974), did not incorporate the distinction between value acquisition and conflict resolution. Present findings indicate that accelerated cognitive growth serves as a catalyst, or ego resource, for resolving conflicts among value orientations (Emmerich, Goldman, & Shore, 1971; Haan, 1977; Maccoby, 1968) but not in defining the substantive direction of value development, at least after middle childhood. It would appear that the developmental shift in which social-acceptance values are supplemented by autonomy values is induced by age-graded changes in social experience during adolescence (Douvan & Adelson, 1966; Higgins & Parsons, this volume), and that such changes in social inputs occur generally across the sexes and races in our society. Broadly speaking, then, our findings are consistent with a cognitive-developmental interpretation of value conflict resolution and with a socio-cultural interpretation of the substantive direction of value development.

There is an important caveat, however. Our primary aim here is to highlight developmental continuities and change in how the *contents* of interpersonal traits are evaluated. The conclusion that cognitive growth does not directly influence the direction of value development after middle childhood is probably limited to this matter of valued contents. The same conclusion need not apply to the reasoning underlying value judgments, nor to the development of the value-obligation distinction. Indeed, there are many ways that cognitive growth can deepen interpersonal values and influence their differentiation and patterning. There is evidence, for example, that cognitive growth mediates developmental trends in the application of sex-role and age-graded concepts to interpersonal evaluations (Emmerich, 1974; Emmerich, Goldman, & Shore, 1971).

Structural change in value development

Our analysis suggests that social factors produce developmental shifts in value orientations, which, in turn, may stimulate value conflicts. Such conflicts had certain structural properties. First, they involved a choice between alternatives, each of which was valued by the individual. Consequently, neither alternative could be easily ignored. Second, conflict was evoked even when the stimulating condition did not force a direct choice between competing value orientations. Consequently, value conflict appeared to be an attribute of the individual that generalized beyond a narrow band of eliciting conditions. Third, the individual sensed that the values represented by each alternative could not be simultaneously maximized. Some form of compromise (balanced solution) was called for. Fourth, the form of compromise that was selected subordinated the emerging orientation to the better-established orientation, a point we shall pursue a little further.

Because we are dealing with conflicts between substantive values (contents), and not with the reasoning that underlies value statements or conflict resolutions, the above structural properties are not strictly comparable to those usually applied by cognitive-developmental theory to the value domain (Damon, 1977; Kohlberg, 1969; Turiel, 1974). Nevertheless, it is of interest that the observed developmental trend in value orientations reversed the usual account of structural change within cognitive-developmental theory. Ordinarily a structural change is said to occur when an emergent organizing principle restructures the organizing principle of the previous stage. The new integrating principle is considered to be more advanced on logical, philosophical, and/or adaptive grounds. However, because the childhood social-acceptance orientation dampened the emerging adolescent autonomy orientation, it was the earlier-formed value system that structured the newly formed one, rather than vice versa. Also, greater cognitive maturity ordinarily would facilitate movement toward a state in which the new organizing principle predominates, but we found that general cognitive growth facilitated the process of dampening the developmentally new value orientation in terms of the old. At least with regard to the resolution of substantive value conflicts, then, structural change appears to yield a more developmentally conservative solution than that typically noted by cognitive-developmental theory. Specifically, the personality and social influences that maintain social-acceptance values appear to operate continuously throughout the life-span.

Does socialization tame values?

Socialization often is viewed in Hobbesian terms as an effort to tame children and youth so that their behaviors come into line with adult society's prevailing norms. But does socialization also involve the taming of interpersonal values? Our findings suggest not, at least after middle childhood. An autonomy orientation serves societal as well as individual needs, and a social-acceptance orientation serves individual as well as group needs. If one were to force equations in which autonomy signifies self-enhancement and social acceptance signifies other-enhancement, then the observed developmental shift in value orientations would contradict the Hobbesian sequence for socialization. The dampening function assigned to violations of the monotonic relationship in the case of autonomy-related values does represent a kind of taming, but the contradiction would remain that it is the earlier developed value orientation that "tames" the later one.

It should be noted that the present study does not rule out the possibility that value socialization involves taming. Subjects were asked to evaluate each trait for a hypothetical "girl" and a hypothetical "boy," but not for the self. If subjects also were asked to evaluate the same traits for the self, we could then separate the substance of the two value orientations from their social referents (self vs. peers). This step would provide the sharp opposition between self-enhancing and other-enhancing tendencies called for by the Hobbesian view of socialization. Nevertheless, it is questionable whether this interpretation is applicable to interpersonal values. There is evidence, for example, that the social-acceptance standards that children and adolescents attribute to themselves in their peer relationships are as high if not higher than the standards they attribute to peers (Emmerich, Goldman, & Shore, 1971).

More fundamentally, the Hobbesian view of socialization typically bypasses consideration of the child's *values* and tries to explain how the child's *behaviors* are brought into line with adult values. However, when attention is given to value development as distinct from behavioral development, children's social-acceptance values appear to be more socialized than their behaviors. Children's values are tame probably for the same reason that adult values are tame, namely, interpersonal values refer to desired qualities (ideals) and not just to behavioral descriptions (actualities). We might even expect the values held by children and adolescents to be more idealized than the values held by adults. Indeed, the relatively late growth of autonomy values and the developmental trend toward a more optimal balance among value orientations probably reflect progressive losses of childhood innocence in the domain of interpersonal values. All these points are consistent with the alternative view that value socialization after childhood modulates and reality-tests the individual's value repertoire, rather than taming it (Brim, 1966).

Socialization of value-behavior discrepancies

Given that value development is distinct from behavioral development, an important task of socialization is to facilitate the individual's coordination of internalized values with actions (within limits imposed by the value paradox). Because there is little direct evidence on developmental changes in value-behavior discrepancies from the standpoint of the individual, we can speculate only on how the socialization process might produce better matches between internalized values and behaviors. Perhaps better matches between values and behaviors are built up separately within each interpersonal area. For example, the process of learning to moderate aggressive behaviors may parallel, but occur quite independently of, the process of acquiring prosocial behaviors. The same or similar principles of social learning could apply to both areas, but different learning experiences might be required to produce value-behavior convergences within each area.

But we have seen how specific interpersonal contents form superordinate value orientations, and how these value orientations are adjusted to one another in the course of development. Insofar as behaviors are "pulled" toward existing values in the individual's repertoire, a variety of related actions might be expected to converge in unison on their respective values. This process could apply to the social-acceptance value orientation, because in this case values formed early would serve as a continuous source of control over the individual's own behaviors during late childhood and adolescence. Here the task of socializing agents would be to help recognize connections between internalized values and their corresponding behaviors, exemplified by the application of induction techniques (Hoffman, 1977; Sigel, 1960; Staub, 1979).

By contrast, autonomous behaviors develop during childhood but are not explicitly valued until adolescence. Here the task of socialization would be to help the individual engage and extend existing behaviors in the service of the newly emerging value orientation. This task would be rather complex. First, the individual would attribute increased value to autonomous behaviors, presumably induced by the changing nature of interpersonal expectations during the adolescent period. Second, the individual would need to increasingly mobilize those behavioral tendencies called for by the autonomous value orientation. Third, the emerging value orientation would be acquired in such a way that its behavioral consequences do not conflict with the early formed social-acceptance orientation, accomplished by dampening the value of autonomous behaviors so that their moderate expression becomes the preferred mode. The net effect of these steps would be a developmental reduction of value-behavior discrepancies in the area of autonomy.

The third step just noted may also occur in adults with regard to social-acceptance values. With increased social experience there should be increased recognition that maximizing social-acceptance values carries unacceptable individual and/or social costs, leading to dampening of this value orientation and a closer match between the desirable and the actual in this area of behavior.

Value and obligation

The patterning of value-behavior discrepancies also could be influenced by how the individual differentiates and integrates value and obligation. In the mature case, a value-behavior discrepancy will be large if the individual values a behavior but does not assume an obligation to act in accordance with the value in a particular instance. On the other hand, the value-behavior discrepancy is likely to be reduced if the individual takes on a commitment (obligation) to act in accordance with the value in a particular instance. In the mature case, then, extent of match between value and behavior would vary considerably, but ordinarily would be regulated by a volitional component (decision as to whether or not to take on the obligation).

Because children may not fully understand or apply the value-obligation distinction, they may be less likely than adults to exhibit variations in value-behavior discrepancies that are regulated by this volitional component. Much has been made of the immature individual's tendencies to exhibit "unsocialized" behaviors (e.g., antisocial acts), on the one hand, and/or "oversocialized" evaluations (e.g., moralistic blame or guilt), on the other. Both tendencies may have a common origin, namely, incomplete understanding, or engagement, of commitment processes in assuming or not assuming an obligation, as distinct from holding a value. It is worth reiterating that this formulation differs sharply from the view that a "value deficit" produces deviant responses in the typical child, a view that our findings do not support.

As development proceeds, value and obligation may become differentiated and integrated, perhaps as aspects of structural shifts in moral or social reasoning (Damon, 1977; Kohlberg, 1969, 1973; Turiel, 1974, 1977). At least two and perhaps three or more steps would be involved. First, one would recognize that a behavior's value is distinct from a person's obligation to act in accordance with the value under all circumstances (differentiation). Analyses of postconventional moral development and identity formation suggest that value and obligation become polarized, producing conflicts between them (Erikson, 1959; Gilligan & Kohlberg, 1978). If so, then we can expect a phase in which the relationship between value and obligation becomes charged with ambivalence, leading in some instances to denials that interpersonal values regulate conduct (overdifferentiation?). Subsequently, the individual would assume specific obligations by making action-binding commitments to particular interpersonal values in selected instances (integration).

Because of a host of complicating factors, movement through the above steps could require long periods of time, even decades. Some and perhaps many adults may never attain the postulated end state. Indeed, certain variations in adult moral character could be linked to phase-related problems in handling the value-obligation distinction. For example, some individuals may only weakly internalize this distinction, yielding impulsively based value-behavior discrepancies. Others may overdifferentiate to the point where interpersonal values are denied as regulators of conduct (nihilism, psychopathy). Still others may confuse obligation with value, leading to unrealistic expectations regarding the self or others (compulsive autonomy, naive idealism).

Our findings on polar symmetry suggested tentatively that value and obligation do not become fully differentiated until adulthood, but the matter requires more thorough investigation. And quite apart from this unresolved issue on developmental timing, basic questions remain to be answered regarding obligation development as distinct from value development. For example, how do cognitive, social, motivational, and affective processes enter into the production of obligatory commitments, and how do these change in the course of development? By what rules do individuals meet, nullify, and abrogate their obligations, and how are conflicting obligations resolved? Do obligations to the self differ fundamentally from obligations to others?

Toward a value network

Thus far we have given relatively little attention to social norms as distinct from interpersonal values and obligations. Social norms modulate the strength and patterning of values in accordance with perceived situational requirements. For example, children and adolescents are known to alter their interpersonal evaluations in relation to the status characteristics (gender and generation) of social targets and reference figures (Emmerich, Goldman, & Shore, 1971). Because social norms modulate value in relation to situational requirements, they are also linked to obligations. But an obligation also produces a strong force to act in accordance with selected social norms under delimited circumstances.

We have suggested that once the value-obligation distinction begins to operate, obligation development can be expected to follow a distinctive course. Carrying this theme one step further, we also suggest that social norms as well as interpersonal values and obligations are best regarded as distinct aspects of the value domain, each developing in its own right. It is especially clear that the development of social norms is distinct from the development of interpersonal values, at least after middle childhood (Emmerich, Goldman, & Shore, 1971). Perhaps social-acceptance values develop earlier than social norms, and social norms develop earlier than obligations. However, there is probably considerable developmental overlap, and the suggestion that interpersonal values, social norms, and obligations represent three aspects of the value domain does not depend upon whether they form a strict developmental sequence.

In addition to representing distinct aspects of the value domain, interpersonal values, social norms, and obligations can be seen to form a three-tiered network for translating values into action. At the first level, interpersonal values are broadly applicable to action, but they do not take situational requirements into account. Nor do values provide strong behavioral motives. At the second level, social norms differentiate value in accordance with situational requirements, but they do not necessarily motivate action. At the third level, obligatory commitments are more selective, and they produce a strong force for action. Of course, this formulation in terms of three levels represents only a first approximation. It may be important, for example, to distinguish between social obligations and personal obligations, the latter representing even more selective and deeper commitments than the former.

By using a value network of this type, the individual may be able to translate value from its broad (universal) but weak form into its narrow (particularistic) but strong form. Such a translation both accepts the constraint on maximizing value-guided behaviors (value paradox) and makes it possible to produce value-guided behaviors in a selective and circumscribed fashion.

We have emphasized the role of cognitive-developmental factors in fleshing out the value network so that it might be utilized optimally in producing value-guided behaviors. However, there is a larger sense in which sociocultural factors become no less important. Here as well as elsewhere in this chapter we have emphasized the central role of volitional choice in the production of value-guided behaviors. The present formulation thus presupposes a social environment in which socializing agents routinely attempt to engage and guide, rather than coerce, the individual's translations of values into actions.

References

Beech, R. P., & Schoeppe, A. Development of value systems in adolescents. *Developmental Psychology*, 1974, *10*, 644–656.

Brim, O. G. Socialization through the life cycle. In O. G. Brim & S. Wheeler (Eds.), *Socialization after childhood: Two essays*. New York: Wiley, 1966.

Coombs, C. H., & Avrunin, S. Single-peaked functions and the theory of preference. *Psychological Review*, 1977, *84*, 126–230.

Damon, W. *The social world of the child*. San Francisco: Jossey-Bass, 1977.

Douvan, E., & Adelson, J. *The adolescent experience*. New York: Wiley, 1966.

Emmerich, W. Developmental trends in evaluations of single traits. *Child Development*, 1974, *45*, 172–183.

Emmerich, W., Goldman, K. S., & Shore, R. E. Differentiation and development of social norms. *Journal of Personality and Social Psychology*, 1971, *18*, 323–353.

Erikson, E. H. Identity and the life cycle. *Psychological Issues*, 1959, *1* (Whole No. 1).

Feather, N. T. *Values in education and society*. New York: Free Press, 1975.

Gilligan, C., & Kohlberg, L. From adolescence to adulthood: The rediscovery of reality in a postconventional world. In B. Z. Presseisen, D. Goldstein, & M. H. Appel (Eds.), *Topics in cognitive development* (Vol. 2). New York: Plenum, 1978.

Haan, N. *Coping and defending: Processes of self-environment organization*. New York: Academic Press, 1977.

Heider, F. *The psychology of interpersonal relations*. New York: Wiley, 1958.

Hoffman, M. L. Moral internalization: Current theory and research. In L. Berkowitz (Ed.), *Advances in experimental social psychology* (Vol. 10). New York: Academic Press, 1977.

Kiesler, C. A. *The psychology of commitment*. New York: Academic Press, 1971.

Kohlberg, L. Stage and sequence: The cognitive developmental approach to socialization. In D. A. Goslin (Ed.), *Handbook of socialization theory and research*. Chicago: Rand McNally, 1969.

Kohlberg, L. Continuities in childhood and adult moral development revisited. In P. B. Baltes & K. W. Schaie (Eds.), *Life-span developmental psychology*. New York: Academic Press, 1973.

Maccoby, E. E. The development of moral values and behavior in childhood. In J. A. Clausen (Ed.), *Socialization and society*. Boston: Little, Brown, 1968.

Rokeach, M. *The nature of human values*. New York: Free Press, 1973.

Sesonske, A. *Value and Obligation: The foundations of an empiricist ethical theory*. New York: Oxford University Press, 1964.

Sigel, I. E. Influence techniques: A concept used to study parental behaviors. *Child Development*, 1960, *31*, 799–806.

Staub, E. *Positive social behavior and morality: Socialization and development* (Vol. 2). New York: Academic Press, 1979.

Thorndike, R. L., & Hagen, E. *Cognitive abilities test examiner's manual, form 1, levels A–H, grades 3–12*. Boston: Houghton Mifflin, 1971.

Turiel, E. Conflict and transition in adolescent moral development. *Child Development*, 1974, *45*, 14–29.

Turiel, E. Distinct conceptual and developmental domains: Social convention and morality. In H. E. Howe, Jr. (Ed.), *Nebraska Symposium on Motivation* (Vol. 25). Lincoln: University of Nebraska Press, 1977.

10   Affective and cognitive processes in moral internalization

Martin L. Hoffman

Psychologists have long been intrigued with moral internalization, probably because it epitomizes the age-old problem of how individuals come to
manage the inevitable conflict between personal needs and social obligations. The legacy of Freud and Durkheim is the agreement among social
scientists that most people do not go through life viewing society's moral
norms, many of which deal with such conflict, as external, coercively
imposed pressures to which they must submit. Though the norms may be
initially external and often at variance with one's desires, they may eventually become part of one's motive system and help guide one's behavior
even in the absence of external authority. Moral action may thus not be
merely a response to external social pressures; it may also be to some
extent the individual's attempt to achieve an acceptable balance between
egoistic and moral motives within the self.

In this chapter I will first summarize the various theories of moral
internalization. My own theoretical formulation will then be presented,
highlighting the role of parental discipline, which I believe accords better
with the recent work on information processing as well as the emerging
literature on the interaction between affect and cognition.

Theories of moral internalization

Moral internalization means different things in different theoretical contexts. Thus a given theory of what fosters moral internalization may deal
with a particular facet of morality (affective, behavioral, cognitive) and treat
a certain aspect of the child's experience that is ignored in other theories.

Psychoanalytic theory

In the psychoanalytic account, young children resolve the conflict between the urge to express hostile and erotic impulses and the anxiety over

losing parental love by repressing the impulses and avoiding behaviors associated with loss of parental love. Furthermore, to help master the anxiety and maintain the repression, as well as to offset punishment and elicit continuing parental affection, the child identifies with the parent and adopts the rules and prohibitions issued by the parent. These rules and prohibitions to a large extent reflect the moral norms of society. Children also adopt the parents' capacity to punish themselves when they violate a prohibition or are tempted to do so – turning inward in the process the hostility that was originally directed toward the parent. This self-punishment is experienced as guilt feelings, which are dreaded because of their intensity and resemblance to the earlier anxieties about punishment and abandonment. Children therefore try to avoid guilt by acting in accordance with incorporated parental prohibitions and by erecting various mechanisms of defense against the conscious awareness of impulses to act to the contrary. These basic moral internalization processes are accomplished by about 5 or 6 years of age, and they are then worked through and solidified during the latency period, the remaining, relatively calm years of childhood. Moral internalization, then, occurs early in life, before the child is capable of the complex cognitive processing of information. Consequently, the moral norms become part of a rigid, primarily unconscious, and often severe, yet fragile, impulse control system.

This view is widely accepted with minor variations in the psychoanalytic literature, although it lacks data support other than the unsystematic observations of adult patients on which it was based. Insofar as pertinent research exists, it tends to be nonsupportive. For example, the hypothesis that anxiety over loss of parental love contributes to moral internalization finds no support in the parent-discipline research, that is, as we shall see, the use of the love-withholding discipline does not appear to contribute to moral internalization. The hypothesis that parent identification fosters moral internalization receives limited partial support: Identification does correlate with certain visible moral behaviors like helping people in need or making moral judgments about others, but identification does not appear to contribute to guilt or to the use of moral standards as a basis for evaluating one's own behavior (Hoffman, 1971, 1975a).

More fundamental, it is difficult to see how the largely unconscious internalized control system depicted in psychoanalytic theory can be adaptive, let alone account for the complexities of moral behavior. From the standpoint of the individual, this control system, or superego, is a quasi-pathological concept, as Freud and others noted some time ago (e.g., Freud, 1930/1955; Lederer, 1964). Current writers, too, are aware of its limitations, and some have suggested that, though it may persist through childhood, it is disrupted in adolescence owing to hormonal changes, social demands, and new information about the world that may often contradict the internalized moral norms (e.g., Blos, 1976; Erikson, 1970; Settlage, 1972; Solnit, 1972). According to these writers, considerable anxiety results from the disruption of the early control system and the resulting threat to the close, dependent relation with the parents that provided the system's main support. The child is therefore compelled to find new and more mature grounds for a moral stance or to erect defenses to ward off uncontrollable impulses and maintain the earlier control system intact. These writers suggest various mechanisms by which a mature morality may come about in adolescence, but the definitions of the mechanisms are fuzzy and persuasive support data are not provided (see review by Hoffman, 1980).

Social-learning theory

Social-learning theorists typically avoid such terms as *moral internalization,* which pertain to internal psychological states that may be several steps removed from observable behavior, but they have attempted to explain a similar phenomenon: the presence of overt moral behavior (defined by cultural norms) or the absence of deviant behavior under conditions of temptation and nonsurveillance. One explanation is that owing to a history of experiences in which one has been punished for deviant acts, painful anxiety states may become associated with these acts, that is, with the kinesthetic and perceptual cues produced by the acts, as well as the cognitive cues associated with the anticipation of the acts (e.g., Aronfreed & Reber, 1965; Mowrer, 1960). This anxiety over deviation may subsequently be avoided by inhibiting the act, even when no one else is present. Individuals may thus appear to behave in an internalized manner, although they are actually responding in terms of a subjective fear of external sanctions. When the anxiety becomes diffuse and detached from any conscious fears of detection, as may sometimes happen, the inhibition of the deviant act may be viewed as a primitive form of internalization having much in common with the psychoanalytic conception described earlier.

Social-learning theorists have also dealt with the child's exposure to models who behave in a moral manner or who are punished for behaving in a deviant manner (e.g., Stein, 1967; Walters & Parke, 1964). In the case of exposure to morally behaving models, it is assumed that the child learns by observing the model and consequently tries to behave like the model in similar future situations when the model is not present. As for exposure to a deviant model who is punished, it is hypothesized that the child is punished vicariously or that the child anticipates the same fate as the model and so avoids acting in the deviant manner.

Social learning, unlike psychoanalytic theory, has inspired a great deal of research. Unfortunately, the research has serious problems (Hoffman, 1970b, 1976a, 1977b). For example, in experimental studies on the effects of punishment, the entire socialization process is usually telescoped into a single adult–child interaction, that is, the child's immediate response to a particular punishment by the experimenter is used to indicate the presence or absence of moral behavior. This use of compliance as the moral index blurs the distinction between moral action and compliance to an arbitrary request by authority and, besides, it is a questionable moral index to begin with, as evidenced by Milgram's (1963) finding that it may at times lead to immoral action. The research on models also has problems, and the findings do not provide clear support for the theory (see review by Hoffman, 1977b). Although observing models who deviate from a moral norm clearly increases the likelihood of deviant behavior in children, observing models who resist temptation and adhere to the norm does not appreciably increase the likelihood of moral behavior. This may indicate that the observation of models who act morally does not arouse motives powerful enough to overcome the child's egoistic tendencies. The research also suggests that whereas observing models who deviate and are not punished fosters deviant behavior in the child, observing models who are punished has relatively little effect. The relevance of the latter research to internalization may be questionable, quite apart from the findings, because the children may be using punishment to the model only as an index of what may happen to them if they behave in the deviant manner.

There is another, more subtle social-learning approach that derives from the notion that one may engage in an act to gain self-reward (e.g., Bandura, 1977). It follows that if children are socialized to act morally and to experience self-rewards afterward, they will come to guide their behavior in accord with the moral norms even in the absence of external authority. This conception of internalization seems plausible, although there is as yet no evidence for it and it does leave certain important questions unanswered. For example, why should self-reward contribute to moral action? People may reward themselves for any behavior, as Bandura (1977) states. But the behaviors they actually reward themselves for depend on the cultural norms guiding socialization, and in our highly individualistic society these norms are as apt to include competitive aggressive behavior as morally considerate behavior. Self-reward may thus not be a reliable mediator of moral action for most people in individualistic societies. More fundamental, the self-reward conception does not explain how the self that is rewarded develops in the first place and what the mechanisms are by which moral actions come to reward that self.

Cognitive developmental theory

Theorists like Kohlberg (e.g., 1976) have studied the development of the individual's ability to resolve competing moral claims and the way individuals invoke concepts of society and justice to deal with these claims. These writers, like social-learning theorists, tend to avoid such terms as *moral internalization* but for a different reason: The term seems to suggest something outside the child that becomes part of his or her internal structure. The child thus appears relatively passive in acquiring moral norms (norms about rights, duties, and justice in human relationships) rather than active in constructing them. Though these writers avoid the term, they do appear to have an implicit moral internalization concept that might be described as follows: (a) When people are exposed to morally relevant information that is more comprehensive and in keeping with a level of moral thought optimally higher than their own, they engage in active mental efforts to process this information and integrate it with their prior view; (b) the normal human tendency is to move toward the higher level; (c) the highest levels are autonomous and principled, and one may be said to have internalized them by virtue of having constructed them oneself. This notion of internalization has appeal because the individual is viewed as thinking matters through and accepting the moral concepts on rational grounds.

The cognitive-developmental theory (see Rest, in press, for a review of concepts, methods, and findings) has been criticized on many grounds (e.g., Hoffman, 1970b, 1980; Kurtines & Greif, 1974). Most important for present purposes is the lack of empirical support for the notion that there are a certain number of homogeneous, invariant stages and that people advance through the stage sequence by being exposed to levels of moral reasoning that are moderately higher than their own. The theory may also have limited relevance to moral internalization development apart from the lack of evidence. Although it deals with moral conflict – how individuals resolve multiple competing moral claims made by others – it ignores the conflict between the individual's egoistic desires and the moral demands of a situation. It presupposes, rather than comes to grips with, what may be the central problem in early moral internalization: How children gain control of their egoistic desires and achieve a proper balance between these desires and the moral demands of situations.

This is perhaps the appropriate place to mention Piaget's views on the topic, although, despite being the father of cognitive-developmental theory, his views on moral development are as social as they are cognitive. According to Piaget (1932), unsupervised interaction with one's peers is essential for moral development in children. The reason, briefly, is that because of the absence of gross differentials of power among children, interactions with peers provide children with the kind of experiences needed to develop moral norms based on mutual consent and cooperation among equals. These experiences – taking the role of others, participating in decision making about rules and how to enforce them – are unlikely to occur in interactions with adults. The evidence, unfortunately, both experimental and observational, does not appear to bear Piaget out (see review by Hoffman, 1982b), although, as noted later, these views may apply in certain conditions.

Attribution theory

The earliest attributional explanation of moral internalization was simply this: If the pressure put on children is just enough to get them to comply with a moral norm but not enough for them to notice the pressure, they will then attribute their compliance to their own will rather than to the pressure (Festinger & Freedman, 1964). Although this formulation has an elegant simplicity, it bypasses the question of why children should subordinate their desires and alter their behavior against their will when they are unaware of any pressure to do so. And, like some of the experimental paradigms mentioned earlier in connection with social-learning theory, it equates compliance with moral internalization.

A more recent formulation by Dienstbier (1978) is unusual in that it attempts to deal with affect and motivation. According to Dienstbier, the child is emotionally aroused when disciplined by the parent. The aroused emotion is at first undefined but is then given meaning as the child attributes it either to the punishment the child expects to receive (if the parent has made punishment salient) or to the deviant act and its harmful effects (if explanation is used and punishment is mild). At a later date, when the temptation to behave in a similar deviant manner again occurs, the emotional discomfort that the child feels when contemplating the deviant act will likewise be attributed either to the anticipated punishment or to the deviant act. If no authority is present and detection is unlikely, attributing the aroused emotion to anticipated punishment –

likely in the child for whom punishment has been made salient – is irrelevant to the situation, and the child has no reason to resist temptation and refrain from the deviant act. Attributing the emotion to the act itself, however – likely in the child frequently exposed to explanations – is "relevant" even when no one is present and may be expected to play a role in facilitating the child's resistance to temptation. The use of explanations and mild punishment therefore contributes to moral internalization.

This explanation, too, is elegant and simple, but, as with its predecessor, the elegance may have been gained at the cost of ignoring certain important details. According to the theory, if punishment is salient, the child attributes the aroused emotion to punishment; if explanation about the act is salient, the child attributes the aroused emotion to the act and the harm done. That is, the particular attribution made by the child is isomorphic to the aspect of the situation made salient by the parent's behavior. The attribution may thus be little more than a labeling of the emotion according to the stimulus highlighted by the parent's behavior. What is lacking is an explanation of how the emotion is aroused in the first place and how it contributes to moral internalization. We may also ask just what it means for the emotion aroused in discipline encounters to remain in an undefined state until appropriate attributions are made? Another limitation of the theory is that it views moral internalization as nothing more than compliance without awareness of the external pressure that led to the compliance. Compliance without awareness may be part of the moral internalization process but surely not all of it. Although attribution theory is considered cognitive, the only cognitive process in Dienstbier's theory is that of viewing the more salient of two stimuli (act or punishment) as the cause of the emotion aroused in discipline encounters.

Although these theories may not account for the full complexity of moral internalization, some of their concepts have a bearing on important aspects of moral internalization and may represent processes that coexist in varying degrees in most individuals. Modified versions of these processes are included in my own theoretical formulation, which I began developing in the early 1960s and which encompasses both affect and cognition to a greater extent than the theories just described. My approach has been to select a particular moral norm and to identify the setting and the child's socialization experience in that setting that may be necessary to internalize that norm. The current version, still incomplete, which I will present here, is a focused and systematic information-processing analysis that highlights the affects and cognitions generated in discipline encounters, speculates about how these affects and cognitions are retained in memory, and suggests the implications of all this for moral motivation and moral action.

First I will briefly define what I mean by moral internalization, explain why I think discipline is especially important in its development, and summarize the pertinent research. Then I will present my theoretical formulation and, finally, I will attempt to show how the concepts previously discussed may fit into this formulation.

Moral internalization and moral motivation

The moral norm at issue here, simply defined, is that people should act out of consideration for the needs of others, as well as their own needs. Examples of morally prescribed acts are telling the truth, keeping a promise, and helping. Examples of proscribed acts are deceiving others, lying, stealing, betraying a trust, inflicting physical harm, and hurting a person's feelings. A moral norm is usually viewed as internalized when the person feels an obligation to act in accord with it even in the absence of any concern about being caught and punished for doing otherwise. That is, the initial motivation to act in accord with the norm, which may have been to avoid punishment or loss of love or to placate and maintain harmony with the parent, has lost its force and the appropriate action is motivated because the child accepts the norm.

This formulation is fine as far as it goes, but without further elaboration it may obscure the fact that in most moral encounters, or temptation situations, not only is a moral norm evoked but there is also a motive to behave in an egoistic, self-serving way (e.g., one is excited about going to a new movie but then remembers one's promise to visit a sick friend). For the moral norm to have an effect, it must be able to compete with the egoistic motive. This means the norm, too, must have motive force, which is often overlooked. The activation of a moral norm, or motive, does not guarantee moral action, because the egoistic motive may be more powerful. It does assure the existence of a moral conflict, however. And if the moral norm, or motive, loses out, the person very likely pays the price of feeling guilty. Moral action is thus not simply the expression of a moral motive but the attempt to achieve an acceptable balance between one's egoistic and moral motives.[1] People may also feel guilty in the absence of conscious moral conflict, as when they harm someone accidentally, through an oversight (e.g., not meeting expectations that they have inadvertently built up) or in the context of an argument or fight.

In addition to the affective and motivational component, moral norms also have a cognitive component that becomes increasingly complex with age. Included in the cognitive component are one's representations (visual or symbolic) of the consequences that one's actual or anticipated behavior may have for someone else, one's awareness of prohibitions against acting in ways that may harm others physically or psychologically, and one's judgments about the rightness or wrongness of particular acts and the reasons for these judgments. Also included are cognitive elaborations, such as the idea that it is especially wrong to harm someone smaller, weaker, and more helpless than oneself, or to harm someone without provocation or justification, or to retaliate for a hurt if the other person was only trying to help, or to retaliate excessively.

A final characteristic of moral internalization is that the activation of a moral norm is usually experienced as deriving autonomously from within the self. That is, the cognitive dimensions of the norm that come to mind are thought of as one's own idea; and the associated affect (usually guilt) and the disposition to act in accord with the norm are also experienced as coming from within the self. The original source of the norm – the particular socialization settings and the people from whom it was acquired – may be forgotten.

To summarize, when the norm in question has been internalized it is activated when the person contemplates acting in a way that may harm another. The norm has (a) a cognitive dimension and (b) a compelling, obligatory quality that is not based on fear of punishment and thus may be considered a moral motive. In addition, these cognitive and motivational properties of the norm (c) usually are experienced as deriving from oneself, with little or no recollection of their origins. The question for developmental psychology is: What prior socialization experiences are central in the development of such a complex network of moral cognition, feeling, and motivation? My answer: the child's experiences in discipline encounters with parents.

Why should discipline be important?

It seems obvious that parents should have an important influence on children's early moral development, but why single out discipline? Parents also take care of their children, love them, play with them, interpret the world for them, and serve as models of acceptable behavior. The special importance of discipline for moral internalization can be derived from a consideration of what people who have internalized the norm of considering others do when the moral requirements of a situation are in conflict with their desires of the moment. To the degree that one has internalized the norm, one will weigh one's desires in relation to the welfare of others without regard to external sanctions. And when one violates the norm, one will have the unpleasant affective reaction of guilt. The central conflict in the moral encounter, then, is between the person's desires and the moral norm applicable in the situation. As an illustration, consider the dilemma posed by wanting to see a movie and a promise to visit a sick friend. To the extent that one has internalized the norm, one will not only want to see the movie but will also feel an urge to visit the friend. One may feel some anticipatory guilt in the course of contemplating going to the movie. And if one does go to the movie, one will almost certainly feel guilty.

The developmental question is: What past experiences make a person vulnerable to such a conflict? What past experiences provoke activation of a moral norm when one contemplates acting in a way that deviates from it? An obvious answer is the kind of experiences one had as a child when faced with the same type of conflict, that is, between one's desires of the moment and the requirements of the norm. The norm was then, of course, external; it was embedded in the many physical and verbal messages from the parent regarding how the child should act, that is, in the parent's discipline techniques. Information pertinent to the cognitive dimensions of moral norms is also communicated to the child outside the discipline encounter, for example, in table conversation, stories, television programs, and by the parent's own actions (e.g., toward people in need). It is only in the discipline encounter, however, that the connection is often made between the norms, the child's egoistic desires, and the child's behavior. Furthermore, it is only in discipline encounters that children may have the earliest experience of being expected to control their deviant actions for reasons that derive from their own active consideration of these norms (as I will describe later).

Aside from these reasons for expecting discipline to be important in moral internalization, there is also evidence that discipline is a recurrent salient feature in the child's daily life. Though parents rarely discipline children in the first year (Moss, 1967; Tulkin & Kagan, 1972), by 2 years of age about two-thirds of the parent–child interactions have been found to involve attempts by parents to change children's behavior against their will (Minton, Kagan, & Levine, 1971). And, in more than 60% of these instances the children obeyed or were compelled by the parent to obey. Comparable data have been obtained with preschool-age children and with children up to 10 years of age (Lytton, 1979; Schoggen, 1963; Simmons & Schoggen, 1963). Stated differently, young children appear to experience pressures from parents to change their behavior on the average of every 6 to 7 minutes throughout their waking hours, and in most of these instances they end up complying.

To summarize the connection between discipline and internalization: In pertinent discipline encounters, the child acts or is tempted to act in a way that will have an adverse effect on someone else. The parent intervenes to change the child's behavior in accordance with the victim's or potential victim's needs. In moral encounters, too, the child acts or is tempted to act in a way that will have an adverse effect on someone else. The similarity is obvious, which is why what happens in discipline encounters should relate to what happens in moral encounters. The difference, of course, is that intervention is not necessary in the moral encounter if the norm has been internalized, that is, if the child is internally motivated to take the other's welfare into account. The processes mediating the shift from the discipline encounter, in which intervention is necessary, to the moral encounter, in which intervention is not necessary – the shift from compliance to internalization – is the focus of the remainder of this chapter.

Generalizations from research

A rather large body of research indicates that (a) a moral orientation characterized by independence of external sanctions and by high guilt is associated with the frequent use of induction (Hoffman, 1970b). Inductions, which are discipline techniques that point up the effects of the child's behavior on others, vary in complexity with age. In the earliest inductions, simple, direct effects may be included ("If you keep pushing him, he'll fall down and cry"). Later the parent may explain why the child's act was not justified, for example, by clarifying the victim's intentions ("Don't yell at him. He was only trying to help"). With further cognitive development, more subtle psychological effects may be pointed up ("He feels bad because he was proud of his tower and you knocked it down"). And, in any of these cases, reparative acts of some kind may also be suggested by the parent. (b) A moral orientation based on fear of external detection and punishment, on the other hand, is associated with the frequent use of power-assertive discipline, that is, physical force, deprivation of possessions or privileges, direct commands, or threats. There is evidence, however, that (c) the occasional use of power-assertion as a means of letting the child know that the parent feels strongly about a particular act or value, or as a means of controlling the behavior of a child who is acting in an openly defiant manner – by parents who usually employ inductions – may make a positive contribution to moral internalization (Hoffman, 1970a; Zahn-Waxler, Radke-Yarrow, & King, 1979). Finally, (d) there appears to be no relationship between moral internalization and love-withdrawal – techniques in which the parent simply gives direct, but nonphysical, expressions to anger or disapproval of the child for engaging in some undesirable behavior (e.g., ignores the child, turns his or her back on the child, refuses to speak or listen to the child, explicitly states a dislike for the child, isolates or threatens to leave the child). The bulk of this research was done with children ranging from about 4 to 12 years of age. There is recent evidence, however, that the generalizations hold up for children as young as 2 years (Zahn-Waxler, Radke-Yarrow, & King, 1979). The generalizations also receive support from recent experimental research (Kuczynski, 1980; Sawin & Parke, 1980).

The argument has been advanced that the correlational nature of the findings prevents the determination of causal inferences (Bell, 1968). Although the general point is beyond dispute, I have argued on theoretical, logical, and empirical grounds that the weight of the evidence in this particular body of research is far more favorable to one causal inference – that the type of discipline affects moral internalization – than the reverse (Hoffman, 1975c) and that it is therefore scientifically indefensible to assume that we know nothing about causality in this domain. I will mention only one part of my argument here. It is that parents have enormous power over their children and that they use this power. That is, they exert far more constraint on the child than the child exerts on them. The evidence for this lies in the finding mentioned earlier that parents frequently compel their children to change their behavior against their will, whereas children rarely attempt to control their parents' behavior (they try about one-fourth or one-fifth as often as do their parents) and such attempts are usually unsuccessful (Wright, 1967).

Three recent findings have been offered in rebuttal. The finding that altering the child's behavior can affect the disciplinelike behavior of an adult experimenter (Keller & Bell, 1979) is irrelevant, because the experimenter was a stranger who had no power over the child. The other two findings – that parental discipline techniques are influenced by both the nature of the child's deviant behavior and the extent to which the child is distracted (Chapman, 1979; Grusec & Kuczynski, 1980) – are irrelevant for another reason. That the child's deviant behavior has an effect on the parent misses the point of my argument. The point is that, given a particular deviant act, parents can use whatever discipline technique they choose.

The same argument can be made regarding genetic influences. Suppose it were found that parents of children who were temperamentally less abrasive from birth used more inductions than parents of more abrasive children. This would certainly be evidence that temperament affects the use of induction. It would not be evidence, however, against the view that induction contributes to moral internalization. Many factors, genetics possibly included, may affect the parent's choice of induction or any other discipline technique, but this does not negate the immediate ("proximal") impact of the parent's discipline on the child's behavior and internal states. Nor does it affect the possible long-range implications for moral internalization, as will now be discussed.

An information-processing approach to discipline and moral internalization

I will now present my current theoretical analysis of how inductive discipline contributes to moral internalization. There are two parts to the theory. One deals with the child's affective and cognitive processes in the discipline encounter, especially when inductions are used. The other deals with what happens between the discipline encounter, in which the parent intervenes, and later moral encounters or temptation situations in which moral motives may be aroused in the child in the absence of the parent or any other authority figure.

The child's affective and cognitive responses in the discipline encounter

I have elsewhere speculated as follows about the child's affective and cognitive responses in the discipline encounter that might account for the relationship between discipline and moral internalization (Hoffman 1970b, 1977b).

Optimal level of arousal. Though the research describes discipline techniques in terms of the three categories mentioned earlier, the techniques actually used by parents are usually multidimensional. Thus all techniques are apt to have some power-assertive and love-withdrawal properties because they all interrupt the child's ongoing act and communicate both a dissatisfaction with it and a desire that the child do something else. Furthermore, even if power-assertion and love-withdrawal are not explicit in a particular discipline technique, the technique nevertheless may have an implicit power-assertive or love-withdrawal component, owing to past situations in which parents may have made their displeasure more appar ent. And some techniques also contain the informational content characteristic of inductions.

The multidimensionality of discipline techniques also may be assumed because they usually have a nonverbal, emotional, as well as a physical and verbal, dimension. The parent can communicate anger, disapproval, hurt, or disappointment, for example, by changes in volume or tone of voice, facial expression, gaze, or posture. The parent can also communicate concern for the victim of the child's action by comforting the victim. These expressions of feeling may interact with the verbal message and add another dimension to it; for example, a raised voice may add a note of urgency – and perhaps a power-assertive overtone – to a verbal induction, and a hurt look may add an inductive dimension to a demand. Conversely, the emotion communicated to the child may be influenced by the verbal component. For example, it seems likely that an expression of moral outrage by the parent is more apt to be received as hostility toward the child's act rather than rejection of the child if it is accompanied by an explanation of what aspect of the child's behavior is being criticized (assuming of course that the child comprehends the explanation).

Power-assertion and love-withdrawal together comprise what I call the motive-arousal component of the technique, which is hypothesized as necessary to motivate the child to change behavior and, more important for present purposes, to pay attention to the parent. Having attended, the child may often be expected to be influenced cognitively and affectively by the information contained in the inductive component that may also be present, in a manner that I will describe soon. First, it must be noted that too little arousal may prompt the child simply to ignore the parent. Too much arousal, that is, if the love-withdrawal/power-assertion is salient, may provoke several reactions that may interfere with the processing of information in the inductive component.

1. To the degree that the power-assertive component predominates, the child may perceive a clear threat to freedom of action. This may arouse the motive to restore freedom – or "reactance" (Brehm, 1972) – as well as anger. But it also may arouse fears of punishment if the child refuses to comply or expresses the anger. As a result, the child may comply reluctantly and perhaps displace the anger toward less powerful figures outside the home (Bandura & Walters 1959; Hoffman, 1960).
2. The predominance of the love-withdrawal component may not heighten the will conflict between parent and child as clearly as does the predominance of power-assertion. Nor does it seem as likely to arouse anger in the child. It may be expected, however, to arouse anxiety – at times an intense, lingering anxiety – over the possible loss of the parent's love. A powerful motive, this anxiety often leads the child to comply to avoid the loss and restore harmony with the parent. (Techniques with pronounced

love-withdrawal components are often used when the child has expressed anger toward the parent Hoffman, 1970a. The association between anger and anxiety that presumably results may explain why love-withdrawal appears to contribute to the inhibition of anger, if not to moral internalization [Hoffman, 1963; Hoffman & Saltzstein, 1967].)

3. In either case – predominant power-assertion or predominant love-withdrawal – the child's attention may be presumed to be directed to the consequences of deviant behavior for the self. Whether the child complies or not, the importance of the desired behavior must be weighed against the anticipated punitive reaction of the parent. This should intensify the sense of opposition the child feels between desires and the moral standards reflected in the parent's demands and thus accentuate the child's view of these standards as external to the self. More important for present purposes, the combination of reactance, anger, fear, and anxiety – which I will call deviation anxiety – that is aroused may prevent the child from effectively processing the information in any inductive component that also may be present in the technique. This is in keeping with the research on attention showing that high emotional arousal generally disrupts cognitive processing in complex tasks like deriving meaning from verbal and other cues (Kahneman, 1973), and, more specific, that it directs a person's attention to the physical features of verbal communications to the relative neglect of semantic content (Mueller, 1979).

Thus there should be an optimal range of arousal for processing the information in the inductive component of a technique. Techniques with salient power-assertive and love-withdrawing properties will often exceed the optimal level for the reasons just mentioned. What happens when the inductive component predominates? First, the child's attention is directed to the consequences of deviant behavior for someone else rather than for the self. Second, the explanation given by the parent may lessen the arbitrary quality of the demand and hence diminish the likelihood of a reactance response by the child. Third, the punitive element should be considerably diminished. For example, the explanation helps make it clear that the parent is not rejecting the child but criticizing the child's act; this should reduce the likelihood of an intense anxiety response. In short, techniques with pronounced inductive components focus on the child's action and its consequences, and thus allow the pressure put on the child and the source of the pressure to be relatively low in salience. Although these techniques may arouse some concern over punishment and approval, this concern is apt to be far less intense than the deviation anxiety aroused by predominantly power-assertive and love-withdrawal techniques. Indeed, inductions may sometimes fall short of the optimal arousal level although in general they should not fall exceedingly short, for, as noted virtually all discipline techniques are motive arousing to some extent, and furthermore, a certain amount of motive arousal derives from the parent-child relationship itself and the child's desire to maintain harmony and good feeling with the parent. (That parents who often use inductions also tend to be highly affectionate outside the discipline encounter [Hoffman, 1970a] might be a contributing factor here.) All things considered, the optimal level of arousal for processing information should more likely be achieved by inductions than by other discipline techniques.

In some instances – emotionally charged situations and emergencies, for example – excessive arousal may be avoided and the optimal arousal level achieved by delaying the inductive component of the discipline technique. For example, the parent may be highly power-assertive because there is no time to do otherwise, but afterward, when things have quieted down, the parent may bring up the matter again and add an explanation. The child may process the information at that time or later in private. The cognitive and affective responses to inductions, which I will now describe, may thus be part of the child's reaction during the discipline encounter, or they may occur later.

Cognitive response to induction. Given an optimal level of arousal, the child may often be expected to attend and process the information contained in the inductive portion of the discipline technique. As a result, the causal connection between the child's action and the physical or psychological state of the victim should be more easily perceived than with other techniques. The child should also, depending on the particular content of the induction used, gain information about the other dimensions of the norm against harming others that I mentioned earlier. The causal connection and the dimensions of the norm may be totally new to the child in any given instance or they may be a reminder of something previously known but overlooked.

It is necessary, of course, if the child is to respond appropriately, that the inductions be cast in terms that are within the child's cognitive and linguistic capabilities. Common sense tells us that parents would tend to do this, and there is at least some evidence that parents are attuned enough to the child's age to use more induction and less power-assertion as children get older (Chapman, 1979).

Affective response. For a norm to have an obligatory quality, it must be associated with affect – not the affect aroused in connection with the motive-arousal component of a discipline technique, which, as I noted, concerns the well-being of the self, but an affect that derives from the inductive component and concerns the well-being of the victim of the child's actions. Because inductions direct the child's attention to the victim's pain or distress, they may frequently enlist just such an affect – a motivational resource that exists in the child from an early age, namely, the child's capacity for empathy, defined as a vicarious affective response to others. There is abundant evidence that children as well as adults typically react with empathic distress to another's pain or discomfort. And, furthermore, the arousal of empathic distress operates like a positive social motive, that is, it predisposes the observer to help the victim (Hoffman, 1977b).

Inductions also indicate that the child's action caused the other's pain or discomfort. This is important because very young children might simply empathize and cry along with the victim without realizing that they caused the victim's distress. There is evidence that even highly empathic preschoolers may not be empathically aroused spontaneously in a competitive context because their attention is directed toward other aspects of the situation such as task demands (Levine & Hoffman, 1975). Older children too may often not see their own causal role for a different reason: Many situations in which they harm others are ambiguous as regards who is to blame. The assignment of blame would be easy if one harmed another intentionally and without provocation, but this is rare. (Blame is obviously ambiguous when the harm is accidental and in fights and arguments as well, because it may often seem as reasonable to blame the other person as the self.) Owing to the ambiguity, it is easy for the child to project, rationalize, or use other cognitive strategies that facilitate blaming the other or perceptual strategies like turning away from the other.

Inductive techniques are thus most likely to arouse both empathic distress and an awareness of being the causal agent of the other's plight. I have suggested elsewhere that the combining of empathic distress and the awareness of being the causal agent produces a feeling of guilt. This is not Freudian guilt, which is based on repression of unacceptable impulses in the past and results from the transformation of the anxiety over loss of parental love associated with these impulses. Rather, it is a feeling of guilt that is based on the awareness of actually harming someone in the present and the realization that this is wrong (Hoffman, 1976b, in press). I am suggesting further that this integration may not occur spontaneously in the young child and that intervention in the form of inductive discipline may be necessary. (This analysis is most applicable to those instances in which the victim of the child's act exhibits clear signs of being sad and downcast, hurt or otherwise distressed. If the victim is angry and retaliates, the child may feel anger or fear rather than empathic distress and guilt.)

Suggestive evidence for the hypothesized contribution of empathy to guilt-arousal was obtained in a study by Thompson and Hoffman (1980). The subjects – first-, third-, and fifth-grade boys – were shown stories or slides, which were also narrated by the experimenter, in which a story character does harm to another person. For example, a boy who accidentally bumps another boy, scattering his newspapers, does not stop to help because he is in a hurry. Two guilt measures were used: (a) The subject is asked how he would feel if he were the story character who committed the transgression, and (b) the subject completes the story, and guilt scores are derived from the amount of guilt attributed to the culprit. Before administering the guilt measures, half the subjects were asked to tell how the *victim* in each story felt. The subjects in this empathy-arousing condition produced higher guilt scores than a control group who were not asked to think about the victim.

As for the motivational or obligatory property of guilt, I have presented the evidence in detail elsewhere (Hoffman, 1976b, 1980, 1982a). Briefly, there is considerable experimental research showing that the arousal of guilt feeling in adults leads to altruistic or reparative action, not only to the victim of their actions but to other people as well. Furthermore, in the story-completion research and the interview studies of the social activists of the 1960s there is evidence for long-range effects of guilt arousal in children and adolescents. That is, guilt arousal appears not only to contribute to immediate and future moral action but seems at times to lead to a self-examination and reordering of one's priorities, including a resolution to act less selfishly and to consider the needs of others more often.

To summarize thus far, all discipline techniques arouse some concern about punishment and parental approval. If there is a pronounced power-assertive or love-withdrawal component, this concern is heightened and the child may feel intense fear or anxiety. The child's attention will in either case be directed to the consequences of such action for the self, and the child will have to consider whether to comply with the parent's wishes or risk the consequences of noncompliance. When techniques having salient inductive components are used, these concerns are allowed to be less salient and, together with the child's desire to maintain harmony and good feeling with the parent, they may help assure that the child attends and processes the informational content of the technique. In this processing the child may perceive the causal connection between such action and the victim's physical or psychological state as well as any additional information about the dimensions of the moral norm against harming others that may be communicated. These cognitions, which may result from the child's attending directly to the cues of distress from the victim, as well as from the child's understanding of the parent's words, may trigger feelings of empathy and empathy-based guilt that give these cognitions a motivational quality.

There are thus three types of motives that may be aroused in discipline encounters: (a) motives pertaining to the implications for the child of the child's deviant act – the fear and anxiety that are direct responses to the power-assertive and love-withdrawal components; (2) motives that bear on the implications of the child's deviant act for the victim – the empathy and empathy-based guilt that result from the processing of information in the inductive component; and (3) the desire to maintain harmony with the parent, a desire that may be ever present, though heightened somewhat in discipline encounters owing to the parent's expression of displeasure. It may be worth noting that a change in behavior in response to inductions is not a clear instance of compliance in the sense of submitting to someone but rather a change in perspective resulting from the semantic processing of information. This leads to our next concern.

What happens between discipline encounters and moral encounters?

The children's affective and cognitive responses to inductions just described may be necessary but insufficient for the development of an internalized moral orientation. From the earlier discussion of the definition of moral internalization, it is clear that we must explain how, from countless discipline encounters involving all sorts of actions, verbal communications, and emotional expressions (from the parent, the child, and the child's victim), children acquire (a) a reasonably coherent set of cognitive dimensions that make up the norm of considering others and (b) an internal, autonomous motive to act in accord with this norm. How do children's cognitive and affective responses to the parent's inductions in early discipline encounters become transformed into internally generated moral motives that operate in later discipline encounters and eventually in temptation situations and moral encounters when the parent is absent? How do children generate their own guilt feelings and a cognitive awareness of the norm they are violating in response to distress cues (actual or anticipated) from victims or potential victims of their actions? How do these affective and cognitive responses become integrated and dissociated enough from the original discipline encounters to be experienced by children as their own?

   Some time ago I suggested casting these problems in memory terms (Hoffman, 1970b). That is, when harming someone is contemplated, previous inductive content may occur to the child as an appropriate reason for refraining from the harmful act, and the associated affect (guilt) may be evoked, although the origination of the parental disciplinary prohibition may not be. This selective memory may occur because the inductive technique, as discussed earlier, unlike other discipline techniques, focuses on the child's action and its harmful consequences and allows parental pressure to be low in salience. The child should therefore not only notice but also remember the causal connections between such actions and their effects on others while perhaps forgetting the external pressure. The informational aspect of inductions is also more easily represented in language, which facilitates memory, than are the relatively weak power-assertive or love-withdrawing components of inductions. This formulation may have some bearing on a recent explanation of the "sleeper effect" in attitude-change research, in which persuasive arguments but not their source are recalled (Cook et al., 1979). According to Cook and his associates, the sleeper effect is the result of forces that lead to an enhancement of the message content, to a discrediting of the source, or to some combination of the two. Under any of these conditions, the message may become dissociated from its source. The source is then soon forgotten, whereas the message is remembered.

It may be useful, in the interest of making a conceptual link between attitude-change and discipline research, to expand this formulation as follows: Anything that decreases the salience of the source and/or increases the salience of the message will lead to a progressive dissociation of the message from its source. The salience of the source may be decreased by discrediting it, as in the sleeper effect, or it may be decreased – and the salience of the message increased – when induction is used. In both cases there is a problem of accounting for the differential memory for the source and the message. I have already suggested in this connection that Tulving's (1972) distinction between episodic and semantic memory may be useful (Hoffman, 1976c, 1977b). In the remainder of this chapter I will enlarge upon that earlier formulation, and, to a greater extent than previously, attempt to incorporate the affective and motivational dimensions that have been neglected in memory as well as moral development research.

Memory and the acquisition of moral cognitive dimensions. For those unfamiliar with the distinction between semantic and episodic memory (Tulving, 1972), here is a brief summary. Episodic memory refers to the receiving and storing of information about temporally dated episodes and events and the temporal–spatial relations among them. The events are often stored in terms of their perceptual attributes and may have no special meaning or reference to anything outside the particular episode. Examples are memory of whether a word occurred in an experimental list, its position in the list, or its exact spelling. Semantic memory is concerned with the storage and utilization of knowledge. Whereas episodic memory refers to when, where, and how an item occurred, semantic memory about an event is independent of the event's actual occurrence in a particular situation or its temporal co-occurence with other events. Semantic memory also does not ordinarily register perceptual properties of inputs but rather their cognitive referrents, which are then stored and integrated with the organized knowledge a person has, for example, about words and their meanings, about concepts and relationships among concepts, and about rules and when they can be generalized and applied.

Semantic memory may be quite independent of episodic memory, because the items recorded and stored in semantic memory represent facts, concepts, and relationships among them and their referrents, all of which are to some degree detached from the particular situation. Information about the physical properties of the input signal itself are stored separately in episodic memory.

It is also of interest for our purposes that semantic memory appears to be more enduring than episodic memory. Because information stored in episodic memory is temporally dated, access to it is made difficult in real life by the many other inputs that may interfere with the temporal coding. Information in semantic memory, on the other hand, is usually incorporated into a complex structure of concepts and their relationships. Such embeddedness in the person's organized knowledge protects the stored information from interference by other inputs. Indeed, under certain conditions semantic memory may actually improve with time (Piaget & Inhelder, 1973). Because the cognitive level limits the complexity of information that can be comprehended, the child's memory for a communication might improve over time if during the interim relevant experience allowed better organization of material. The child might then be able to reconstruct certain connections or central points that were not merely forgotten but unnoticed in the first place.

To illustrate the distinction between the two types of memory, Tulving (1972) uses the example of listening to a story. Information regarding the episode of hearing a story, which includes among other things the perceptual properties of the storyteller and the precise words used, is encoded in episodic memory and relatively soon forgotten. The story content, that is, the concepts and meanings, are registered in semantic memory, to a great degree stripped of their connection to the circumstances surrounding the storytelling, and become part of the individual's relatively enduring categories of knowledge.

There are obvious parallels between listening to a story and responding to an induction, such as that between storyteller and parent and between story content and informational content of induction. In both instances the child attends to a verbal communication. There are also differences. The main one is that inductions occur in the context of a discipline encounter, whereas stories are usually told in more relaxed settings in which the child's behavior is not the central issue. A basic similarity may remain, however, at least as regards memory, because, as I have argued, children are often optimally motivated to process the information contained in inductions, just as they are to process the information in stories.

It thus seems reasonable to assume that the informational content of inductions, which corresponds to the cognitive dimensions of the moral norm described earlier, is ordinarily encoded in semantic memory. Over time, in numerous discipline encounters, the cognitive dimensions are presumably organized cumulatively and integrated in an increasingly complex structure that comprises the child's emerging moral norm regarding how one should, and should not, act toward others.

This structure may be highly organized, perhaps hierarchically ordered, but more likely it is a loosely organized network, at least for the young child. Certain of the rules may be given more prominence than others, depending on which were highlighted in discipline encounters as important to the parent. The rules may also be represented in different ways. For example, some may be represented by abstract concepts alone (e.g., you shouldn't lie, steal, break a promise). Others may include representations of generalized "scripts" depicting actual interaction sequences in which one has harmed others in certain ways, for example, by hurting their feelings. And still others may include representations of a particular event in which the harmful consequences of one's act were clearly visible, which may serve as a "prototype" for organizing one's thoughts (and feelings) about the rule.

In any case, the other aspects of inductions that contribute little to their meaning, such as the exact words and sentence structure employed, the fact that they originated with the parent, and the physical setting in which they occurred, may, as in the storytelling example, be encoded separately in episodic memory and be forgotten relatively soon. Consequently, they may provide little or no interference with the cumulative organization of the child's cognitive-normative structure, and, furthermore, as this cognitive-normative structure develops it may become increasingly dissociated in the child's mind from its origins in discipline encounters. Consequently, in future situations in which the child harms another or contemplates harming another, he or she may be reminded of the norm whether or not the parent or anyone else is present to point it out.

An alternative to Tulving's (1972) dual-storage, semantic–episodic model has been suggested by Craik (1977) and Craik and Lockhart (1972). According to this theory, the extent to which a stimulus persists in memory depends on the level at which it was processed when initially presented. There are basically three levels of processing that operate successively. First, there is a simple level of sensory registration of the stimulus. This is followed by a perceptual level involving matching or pattern recognition of the stimulus, and finally a deep, semantic level in which the stimulus is enriched by being associated with past images and cognitive structures. The semantic level is ordinarily more apt to be called forth by relatively complex information-containing communications than by simple stimuli (although if the subject is given a semantic-organizational set it may be applied even to simple stimuli).

Craik and Lockhart argue that organisms are normally concerned primarily with the extraction of meaning from stimuli, and it is therefore more advantageous to store the products of deep, semantic analysis than the products of the relatively shallow sensory and perceptual analyses. It follows that the informational content of a communication that requires semantic organization should be retained longer than the aspects of the communication that do not. The implications of this depth-of-processing formulation for our purposes are basically no different from the implications of the semantic-episodic distinction, because inductions should provide more appropriate arousal conditions and stimuli more likely to require semantic organization than other types of discipline. The informational content of inductions may therefore be organized cumulatively into a coherent moral-cognitive structure, with little or no interference from those aspects of the discipline encounter that require shallower processing, and be retained in memory for a relatively long time.

Craik and Lockhart also introduce another concept useful for our purposes: the "awareness of potential for interpretation." According to Craik and Lockhart, the interpretation of a verbal message may be deferred although the person exposed to it recognizes that it has meaning. This concept is in keeping with my earlier suggestion that the child may at times process the information contained in inductions retrospectively, after the discipline encounter had ended.[2]

I will now briefly summarize the evidence for semantic organization in memory in children. Though the precise mechanisms are subject to controversy (e.g., Cermak & Craik, 1979) – whether semantic and episodic information are stored separately, whether information is processed in three successively deeper levels, or whether some other mechanism applies – memory research does support the view that young children as well as adults engage in spontaneous acts of inferential comprehension and semantic organization in memory. They recall events primarily in terms of semantically meaningful units; and verbal inputs and fragmentary details that do not contribute to meaning are either not encoded or soon forgotten (e.g., see review by Brown, 1975). Thus, children as young as 2 and 3 years appear to extract semantic meaning from simple words, as evidenced by their greater memory for words that are meaningfully related to each other (peach, apple) than for unrelated words and even words that are related phonetically (sun, fun) (Rossi & Rossi, 1965; Rossi & Wittrock, 1971). Five-year-olds show evidence of semantic organization in their recall of short sentence sequences and fairy tales. That is, they concentrate on the central ideas and often omit unnecessary details, such as sentence structure and word order, that contribute little to ideas (Barclay & Reid, 1974; Brown & Murphy, 1975; Paris & Carter, 1973; Yendovitskaya, 1971). Futhermore, preschool children exhibit long-term memory for material that is meaningfully related to their ongoing activity (e.g., DeLoache & Brown, 1979). This finding is relevant to my argument because a central feature of inductions is their meaningful relation to the child's ongoing activity, in contrast to the more arbitrary way that other types of discipline relate to the child's activity. And finally, 6-year-olds showed long-term (one week) as well as short-term memory for the ideas, including the consequences depicted in a narrative account, and less recall for the episodic features of the narrative, such as the setting (Stein & Glenn, 1979). The Stein and Glenn study also has special interest because it is in keeping with Tulving's extension of the semantic–episodic distinction to story listening, and thus provides support for my view that children are more likely to organize and remember the ideas communicated by inductions than that the source of the ideas was the parent.

Memory and acquisition of moral affect. Thus far my memory analysis is based only on the processing of the cognitive dimensions of the child's experience in the discipline encounter. This is in keeping with the memory literature, which has traditionally neglected affect. We have to deal with affect, as I noted, to account for the motivational dimension of internalized moral norms. And the affects I have suggested as important are the empathy and empathy-based guilt aroused by inductions in the manner I described earlier. That is, the child's acquisition of a growing, organized cognitive-normative structure about potentially harmful actions is linked to feelings of self-blame and guilt. Therefore, in situations in which the child is aware of harming someone, guilt feelings are apt to be aroused even when the parent is not present. More important, perhaps, is that the *con-*

templation of acting in a way that may harm another may often be expected to arouse anticipatory guilt feelings. And, in view of the evidence that guilt operates as a moral motive – the evidence that guilt arousal leads to moral action, summarized earlier – it seems reasonable to expect that anticipatory guilt will produce a tendency toward moral action. The arousal of guilt may thus serve as a possible deterrent to harmful action. This control function of guilt is not foolproof, of course. If the egoistic motives that provoked the contemplation of a harmful act prevail, the child may engage in it regardless; in that case, however, the child should at least continue to feel guilty. (On the other hand, children who frequently experience power-assertion are more likely to experience fear than guilt when they contemplate a harmful act. If no one is present, they may see there is nothing to fear and thus feel free to engage in the act.)

I will now offer some speculations about how the child's affective responses in the discipline encounter – especially guilt feelings – are encoded in memory and later evoked in moral encounters or temptation situations. Of the several possibilities, all are compatible with the hypothesis that guilt feeling derives, in part (empathy plays a role too), from the moral cognitions produced by the child's processing of inductive information. These speculations will be brief because the literature provides little on which to draw.

One possibility is that guilt feeling is encoded in memory in the discipline encounter together with the moral cognitions that gave rise to it. Later, in situations in which the child harms another or contemplates acting in ways that may harm another, these moral cognitions are evoked. The evoked moral cognitions trigger guilt feelings more or less in the same manner that they did in the discipline encounter. This sequence suggests a general model in which the memory for an affect is tied to the cognition that gave rise to it, a model that gives primacy to cognition.

Another possibility is that although guilt feelings may *derive* from a cognitive product of the child's information processing in the discipline encounter (from the awareness that the child's actions harmed someone), the guilt feeling may not be *encoded* together with that cognitive product. Though evoked as the result of cognitive processing, once evoked the guilt feeling may have a life of its own in regard to how it is stored and remembered. For example, the guilt feeling may be associated, hence encoded, not with the words and ideas that gave rise to it but with the kinesthetic cues associated with the child's deviant act or with a visual image of the event – perhaps the distress cues from the victim made salient by the parent's induction. Future moral encounters or temptation situations in which the child's action produces the same kinesthetic cues or which contain similar picture images (e.g., anticipated crying by a potential victim of one's actions) may then evoke the guilt feeling. The guilt feeling, in turn, may then contribute to "recall" of the associated moral cognitions. This might occur, for example, if the encoding and retrieval of kinesthetic cues or picture images are especially swift, as seems possible. (If considerable time elapsed between the arousal of guilt and the arousal of the moral cognitions that initially gave rise to it, we would have an interesting temporary phenomenon resembling the Freudian notion of free-floating guilt, though it would be different because it would not be based on repression.)

This second model, which implies an affective, rather than a cognitive, primacy, is in keeping with Zajonc's (1980) conclusion, based on a recent review of adult memory research, that affect is encoded more quickly and efficiently, stored separately, and retained in memory longer than cognition. The model is also in keeping with Bower's (1981) finding that the subject's mood in recall situations facilitates retrieval of cognitions pertinent to that mood that were acquired when the subject was previously in the same mood. If we think of guilt as a mood state, the guilt evoked in the moral encounter should bring to mind the cognitions that were pertinent to the guilt aroused in discipline encounters.

A third possibility, and the one that makes most sense to me, is that the guilt feeling and moral cognitions are not encoded separately. Instead, once guilt feelings are aroused in discipline encounters, the accompanying moral cognitions are suffused with guilty affect and become emotionally charged or "hot" cognitions whose affective and cognitive features are inseparable. The emotionally charged cognitions are then encoded in memory and eventually experienced in temptation situations as an affective-cognitive unity.

Although these three models of the encoding of moral affect and cognition in discipline encounters and their retrieval and utilization in moral encounters may not exhaust the possibilities, they do suggest directions for research. It may be that only one model applies or they all may operate, with individuals differing as to which is predominant. It is also possible that the processes described in all three models are employed by everyone, with situational factors determining which one or more are called into play at any given time. For example, if distress cues from the victim are salient, then guilt may be evoked first. If, on the other hand, the moral conflict is articulated verbally, the pertinent moral cognitions may be evoked first. Obviously, research is needed before we can speak with authority on this topic.

Moral internalization and "self-attribution." Owing to the power of semantic organization in memory, children not only may remember the
moral norm and feel some compulsion to act in accord with it when they
contemplate a potentially harmful act even in the parent's absence, they
may also forget the many settings of discipline-encounters in which they
were first exposed to the norm. We may ask whether similar processes
can explain the fact noted earlier that children are often unaware that
their parents, rather than themselves, are the source of the norms they
internalize. It may seem strange that children often forget that their parents are the source, because parents probably are the major invariants
across discipline encounters as well as being so affectively important to
the child. We might therefore expect the parental image to be perma-
nently connected to the inductive content in the child's memory.

It must be noted, however, that the relation between parental image
and inductive content is simple association. The parental image is not
semantically related to the inductive content, which pertains to the causal
relation between the child's action and the well-being of others. Although
the parent provides the information and the motivation for the child to
process it, it is typically not the parent but the inductive content that is
made salient, as noted in our earlier discussion. Ordinarily, therefore, the
parental image may not be part of the semantic content of a child's
discipline encounters.

Because the parent's affective value to the child is high in all interactions, not just discipline encounters, the parental contribution to making
discipline encounters particularly salient and memorable, especially when
inductions are used, is minimal. The child's image of the parent may
therefore lack not only a semantically meaningful connection to the moral
ideas but also a distinctive affective tie to the discipline encounters in
which the moral ideas were generated. Consequently, although the child
remains fully aware of the parent's existence, there may eventually be
little or no connection in the child's mind between the parent and the
inductive content, or moral norm, and as the child gets older, an external
referent to the norm may disappear altogether.

In the absence of an external agent, to whom should the child attribute
the norm? One possibility is that children, who are known to have a
tendency to externalize (they often externalize blame, for example), will
show great ingenuity in creating some other external agent to account for
the norm. As already noted, however, a characteristic of internalized
norms is that they are often experienced as emanating from the self.
Self-attribution theory suggests a reason for this: If the external sources

of one's actions and thoughts are salient, unambiguous, and sufficient to explain them, the person attributes them to these external agencies. But if the external sources are not perceived, or if they are unclear or invisible, it is assumed that children as well as adults will attribute their actions and thoughts to themselves (e.g., Bem, 1972; Kelley, 1967; Lepper & Greene, 1975). Similarly, without an external agent to whom to attribute the moral norm, the child may then be expected to experience it as originating from within the self.

There is another, perhaps more compelling, reason for expecting the child to attribute the norm to the self. The child's mental activity – semantically organizing the inductive content – is apt to make such internal processes highly salient. The mental activity is also semantically related to the inductive content, that is, the child is thinking about the connection between the act and the victim's condition or the way in which the act relates to some cognitive dimension of the moral norm. Under these conditions it seems reasonable to expect the child over time not only to loosen the connection between the parental image and the inductive content but also eventually to perceive the self, rather than the parent, as the source of the information in inductions, hence as the source of the norm. I do not mean here that the child consciously attributes the origin of the norm to the self. Meta-cognitive operations like these apparently come fairly late in development – around 6 years or so. Even after that, however, children may not think about where the cognitions came from but simply experience them as thoughts that pop into their heads.

Introduction of the moral dimension in early discipline encounters

Thus far I have described discipline encounters and their subsequent influence. To speculate intelligently about origins, that is, the earliest instances in which children are exposed to inductions before they can be said to have internalized any moral norm, we need to know the cognitive and affective capabilities that young children bring to disciplinary encounters. At what age is the child capable of processing and storing information in the manner described? When does the child possess the necessary developmental prerequisites of guilt – the capacity for empathy, the sense of the other as distinct from the self, the causal schemas? And how does the parent relate the inductive information to the child?

The research suggests that by 2 years of age the child has an empathic capability, an awareness of others as physical entities distinct from the self, and an emerging awareness that others have inner states (thoughts, feelings, perceptions) independent of one's own (Hoffman, 1977a). As for the necessary causal schemas, children as young as 3 years are apparently capable of using information about the covariation of events in making causal attributions of simple physical phenomena (Mendelson & Shultz, 1976). They are apparently not bound by strong assumptions about temporal order, however, as they sometimes see the later-occuring event as the causal one, which is in keeping with Heider's (1958) primitive level of causality in which only a rough temporal order of events is needed for a causal inference to be made. This research suggests that 3 years may be the lower limit for inductions to work, but, according to Piaget (1976), the child's attainment of causal schemas for objects is preceded by the attainment of schemas for the effects of one's own actions, which are more pertinent to our concern with induction and guilt. In Piaget's view, children at the age of a few months can discover simple causal connections through their own physical action (by 4 years they can follow instructions to do complex things like throwing a ball so that it hits another ball, which then hits the target, although they cannot explain what happened). I have presented elsewhere anecdotal evidence that children under 2 years, when in natural settings and properly motivated, are clearly aware of the impact of their actions on others and can use this awareness in helping or manipulating others (Hoffman, 1975b). And, finally, there is evidence that 1-year-old children respond to objects with different emotions, depending on whether or not they can control the movement of the object (Gunnar, 1980), and thus indicate that they have some sense of having an impact on the physical environment. Although none of these findings is definitive, it appears reasonable to conclude tentatively that children have the requisite schemas for processing the information in simple inductions and responding cognitively and affectively, as I hypothesized earlier, by about the same time that parents begin to discipline their children in earnest, which, as noted, is sometime in the second year. Perhaps this explains the finding that the use of inductions relates positively to consideration for others in children under 2 years of age (Zahn-Waxler, Radke-Yarrow, & King, 1979).

   We can now speculate about those early discipline encounters. First, it is safe to assume that for an induction to be effective at that early age it must be very simple, perhaps nothing more than pointing up the harmful physical effects of the child's behavior on someone. If the explanation is something the child can comprehend, and assuming of course that the child is properly aroused and attends, we may then expect the content (e.g., the cause–affect relation between the act and the well-being of another person) to be integrated into the child's causal schema. The newly enriched schema has the beginnings of a moral-cognitive dimension that it previously lacked. The child may also be expected to react with feelings of empathy and empathy-based guilt, feelings that may sometimes be further enhanced by exposure to direct distress cues from the victim. As a result, the newly emerging, rudimentary moral schema is infused with these moral affects. It is then presumably encoded in memory and activated in the next discipline encounter, and the process is repeated. In this way, children's simple, at first nonmoral, cognitive structures and causal schemas may be gradually transformed through experiences in countless discipline encounters into structures having the moral-cognitive dimensions and affective-motivational quality that characterize internalized moral norms.

A general model for discipline and internalization

The preceding analysis obviously does not apply to highly arousing power-assertive or love-withdrawing techniques. In these cases, there is little or no information to organize semantically. And if such information were included, it might not be organized semantically because of the intense "deviation anxiety" aroused, as discussed earlier. Yet we know, from research done in past decades on learning to avoid responses that provoke punishment (e.g., Mowrer, 1960), that avoidance-learning is often extremely difficult to extinguish. Early punishment can very likely result in the classic conditioning of emotions, the establishment of links that are not easily extinguished over many years. Although the memory literature does not deal with this phenomenon, it is clearly a memory matter: Anxiety and anxiety-avoidance behavior are "remembered" for a long time. Punitive power-assertions, for example, may result in the storage not of semantically organized materials but of conditioned responses and primitive associations between kinesthetic and perceptual cues produced by the child's deviant acts, images of the punishment, and feelings of deviation anxiety. In future situations the child may begin to experience anxiety in the initial stages of engaging in a deviant act, perhaps even when only anticipating it. The anxiety may then operate as a seemingly internal motive for avoiding deviant action (which is in keeping with Freud's notion of the function of the superego).

We are now in a position to consider an overall model for discipline and moral internalization, a model that encompasses power-assertion and love-withdrawal as well as induction. The analysis thus far suggests that an overall model must encompass the differential storage in memory of these four items: (a) representations of moral-cognitive structures pertaining to deviant behaviors; (b) representations of external demands by parents pertaining to the deviant behaviors; (c) guilt feelings derived from the moral-cognitive structures; (d) deviation anxiety aroused by the external demands. The model must also encompass two types of information processing and long-term memory: (e) the semantic organization and long-term retention of meaningful information and associated affects, and (f) a simple associative memory pertinent to retention of anxiety and avoidance responses. The discussion to this point suggests two basic processes:

1. The frequent use of inductions increases the likelihood that (a) and (c) and the connection between them are stored in long-term memory through process (e).
2. The frequent use of power-assertion and love-withdrawal increases the likelihood of long-term retention of (b) and (d) and the connections between them through process (f).

Because children are exposed to different techniques – even the most inductive parents sometimes use power-assertion (Hoffman, 1970a) – both processes may be assumed to operate in varying degrees in most children. We may therefore expect that thoughts about moral norms and images of past discipline encounters (individual prototypic encounters or scripted versions), along with feelings of guilt and deviation anxiety, may often be evoked in most children when they engage in deviant actions or anticipate doing so. Thus it may not be an all-or-none matter. The question is, to what extent does each process operate? Children for whom induction is the mode may have the appropriate moral cognitions and feelings, although they may also have images of past discipline encounters and perhaps feel some deviation anxiety. The more powerful motive for them, however, should often be the empathy or empathy-based guilt that is aroused. Children of highly power-assertive or love-withdrawing parents should be less likely to have the appropriate moral cognitions and affects and more likely to experience deviation anxiety.

It may be possible for this general model to encompass the several different types of moral internalization included in the theories summarized earlier. Children of highly power-assertive or love-withdrawing parents, for example, may have images of past discipline encounters stored in memory, as just noted, and the relatively intense deviation anxiety associated with these images may operate as a motive for them to avoid deviant behavior even in the absence of witnesses. This is in keeping with the concept of moral internalization advanced by social-learning theorists such as Mowrer (1960) and Aronfreed and Reber (1965). Furthermore, if the mere anticipation of the deviant act were to produce intense anxiety in children and if this led them to avoid anxiety by employing perceptual and cognitive strategies designed to avoid thinking about the act in the first place, social-learning theory would be exemplified as well as Freud's notion of the superego. Our focus on the child's active role in processing the information contained in inductions and on the importance this may have for acquiring the necessary cognitive moral structures has something in common with the views of Kohlberg (1976) and other cognitive developmentalists. And, finally, attribution theory has a role in our explanation of how the moral norm may come to be experienced as deriving autonomously from oneself.

A note on "retrieval" processes. In real life, moral dilemmas or conflicts are not usually labeled as such, as they are in the research. Rather, they tend to be embedded in a welter of words, feelings, and thoughts, often in the context of an interpersonal interaction. An important question neglected in the research is this: How does a person know that a given situation is an instance in which the moral norm applies? One advantage of a motivational theory, such as I have presented, is that it suggests a way of answering this question. Included in most interpersonal interactions are verbal and nonverbal cues that to some degree reflect the thoughts and feelings of the participants. Also present are cues bearing on the causal relationship between one's own action and the thoughts and feelings of others. These cues should all be especially salient to children who have frequently experienced discipline encounters in which inductions were used and who are therefore motivated to consider the needs of others and to guide their own actions accordingly. That is, the child should be more likely to attend to and process the cues signifying the internal states of others and how their internal states are affected by the child's actions. It is not necessary that the child label the situation as a moral one. The child simply responds – for example, with empathy and empathy-based guilt if the child has harmed someone or, in the case of a contemplated act, by taking into account the probable consequences of the act for that person.

Concluding remarks

This chapter began with a critical review of moral internalization theories and ended with a presentation of my own information-processing approach that incorporates some concepts of the other theories. I will now summarize the assumptions and major point of my formulation. First, I assume that in individualistic societies like ours most people have pronounced egoistic needs, which are often in conflict with the needs of others, and a major dimension of a person's moral life is the extent of the internal motivation to consider the needs of others. Second, I define an internal moral motive as having a cognitive dimension as well as a compelling, obligatory quality that is not based on fear of punishment. To the degree that this motive operates, a person considers the needs of others in situations in which the person's needs and the needs of others are in conflict; the person also feels guilty if the other's needs are ignored. Internal moral motives are also usually experienced as deriving from oneself. My theory is an attempt to account for the development of this internal moral motive. Third, I assume that the child's experiences in discipline encounters are crucial in the development of an internal moral motive and, as the research indicates, it is the frequent use of inductive discipline that is of central importance.

The analysis of what happens in discipline encounters and afterward and the special role played by inductions, the heart of the theory, is as follows: (a) Most discipline techniques have power-assertive and love-withdrawing properties, which comprise the motive-arousal component needed to get the child to pay attention to the inductive component that may also be present. (b) Too little arousal may prompt the child to ignore the parent; too much arousal and the resulting fear, anxiety, or resentment may prevent the effective processing of the inductive component and direct the child's attention to the consequences of the action for the self. A salient inductive component should ordinarily achieve the best balance and direct the child's attention to the consequences of the action for the victim. (c) The child may then process the information in the inductive component. The cognitive products of this processing constitute knowledge about the cognitive dimensions of the moral norm against harming others. (d) Processing the information in the inductive component should also often arouse empathy and empathy-based guilt, affects known to have prosocial motivational properties. (e) The cognitive products of the information processing are hypothesized as being semantically organized, encoded in memory, and activated, modified, and integrated with similar information provided by inductions in countless discipline encounters over time. The source of the information – the setting of the discipline encounter – is organized separately in a shallower mode. It interferes minimally with the semantic organization and may be soon forgotten. (f) The prosocial affects, which continue to be associated with the cognitive products in one or more ways, are seen as providing the necessary internal motive base. (g) Owing to the child's active role in processing the information, as well as the differential memory for idea content and setting, the child may eventually experience the moral cognitions and affects generated in discipline encounters as deriving from the self.

I also suggested how the young child's simple, initially nonmoral cognitive structures and causal schemas may be gradually transformed through the processing of information in many discipline encounters into structures having the moral-cognitive and affective-motivational properties of internal moral motives. And, finally, I advanced an overall model for the internalization of moral motives through discipline, a model that encompasses power-assertion and love-withdrawal as well as induction. This model may accord well with the real world in which both internal and external moral motives and egoistic motives may coexist in each individual and in a different balance among individuals.

Stated most generally, this theory suggests that it is (a) the mix of parental power, love, and information, (b) the child's processing of the information in discipline encounters and afterward, and (c) the cognitive and affective products of that processing that determine the extent to which the child acquires an internal motive to consider others.

Though my focus has been on the central role of early parental discipline, the child's interactions with adults and peers outside the home may also contribute to moral development. For example, given the early motivational base discussed here, the child may be receptive to inductionlike communications from teachers and other authorities. And, despite my earlier pessimistic appraisal of the effects of unsupervised peer interaction, it is possible that interactions among peers from homes in which inductions are frequently used may have the constructive effects hypothesized by Piaget. This may be especially likely when there is some indirect adult supervision, stage setting, or "coaching," as I have suggested elsewhere (Hoffman, 1980). Such peer interactions and inductions from adults may reinforce the trend begun in early discipline encounters with parents in which inductions were used, and the result may be to expand the domain in which the child's moral motive is applied. This domain may also be expanded as the child acquires language and social-cognitive (e.g., role-taking) skills of increasing sophistication, so that the effects of actions on others can be comprehended long after the immediate situation or anticipated beforehand. Although social cognition and language are neutral skills that bear more directly on moral competence than on moral motivation, that is, they can be useful in manipulating as well as benefitting others, a child who has developed a motive to consider others may be expected to employ these skills more often in the service of benefitting others. The same may be true of children's increasing ability to learn by observing others. If children are motivated to consider others, they should be selective in their observational learning, that is, more apt to adopt ways of acting morally than immorally.

Insofar as the motive to consider others persists into adolescence, the individual may be more receptive to certain moral, as well as political and economic, ideologies – perhaps those pertaining to victims and other distressed people. In adopting these ideologies, another, as yet unmentioned, internalization mechanism may come into play. According to Erikson (1970) and other contemporary psychoanalytic writers (see review by Hoffman, 1980), some adolescents, in the face of overwhelming evidence from the adult world, may become disillusioned with the moral beliefs and values acquired in childhood. They may then become strongly motivated to search for moral concepts or an ideology that resolves the conflict. I would suggest that to the extent that a person is morally motivated and actively involved in constructing such an ideology, he or she may be expected to feel personally bound to it, to try to act in accord with it, and thus to internalize it. The individual's new moral viewpoint may be considered an advancement because it incorporates certain social realities previously ignored. Although this mechanism may appear to be the same as Kohlberg's view about how people advance morally, it lacks Kohlberg's assumptions that the contradiction is between "structural" elements of the person's moral schemas rather than between moral values and social reality and that the newly gained perspective fits a predetermined sequence. These individually constructed ideologies thus become part of a person's moral motive system, rather than adopted as abstract modes of thought lacking a motive base. In other words, the simple moral motive treated in this chapter may provide a motive base for ideological commitment. (See Hoffman, 1980, for an extended discussion of this point.)

In short, what I have suggested in this chapter are the antecedent factors that may lead to the development of an early moral motive to consider others. Later experiences of various kinds may expand this motive to other areas of life, provide skills and competencies that serve the motive and build upon it to create complex moral ideational structures. The theory does have limitations. Although empathy and empathy-based guilt may explain why some people act morally and feel bad when they harm others, no theory of moral motive development can by itself explain how children learn to negotiate to achieve a proper balance between the motive to consider others and egoistic motives. And although a moral motive may make one receptive to certain moral ideologies, as suggested above, it alone cannot explain how people formulate such ideologies and apply them in situations. A similar limitation may be revealed in situations involving moral judgments, especially when several behaviors must be compared or competing moral claims evaluated. To be objective in such situations may require recourse to moral principles that go beyond showing consideration to others. The developmental link between the simple moral motive discussed here and the complex cognitive processes involved in building ideologies and establishing moral priorities is a worthy topic for research.

Notes

1 Our theoretical model assumes that people frequently experience conflict between their own needs and the needs of others. There are, to be sure, individual differences in how sharply people differentiate their own needs from the needs of others, and for some, perhaps overly socialized, individuals the needs of self and other may merge or they may be unaware of their own needs (see Hoffman, 1970a, for discussion of this syndrome and its possible socialization antecedents). For most people in stratified individualistic societies like ours, however, though perhaps not in simpler more traditional societies, frequent conflicts between the needs of self and other are likely to be inevitable.
2 Two things should be said about the dual-storage and depth-of-processing models: (1) Neither assumes a deliberate attempt to remember information, and (2) both assume that given the set to organize information semantically, a person might apply the set even to simple stimuli. For example, a child might infer the reasons underlying an unqualified power-assertion. Generally, however, and with young children especially, semantic organization is far more likely to be applied to semantically meaningful information than to information that lacks semantic meaning.

References

Aronfreed, J., & Reber, A. Internalized behavioral suppression and the timing of social punishment. *Journal of Personality and Social Psychology,* 1965, *1,* 3–16.
Bandura, A. *Social learning theory.* Englewood Cliffs, N.J.: Prentice-Hall, 1977.
Bandura, A., & Walters, R. H. *Adolescent aggression.* New York: Ronald Press, 1959.
Barclay, J. R., & Reid, M. Semantic integration in children's recall of discourse. *Developmental Psychology,* 1974, *10,* 277–281.
Bell, R. Q. A reinterpretation of the direction of effects in studies of socialization. *Psychological Review,* 1968, *75,* 81–95.
Bem. D. J. Self-perception theory. In L. Berkowitz (Ed.), *Advances in experimental social psychology* (Vol. 6). New York: Academic Press, 1972.
Blos, P. The split parental image in adolescent social relations. *Psychoanalytic Study of the Child,* 1976, *31,* 7–33.
Bower, G. H. Mood and memory. *American Psychologist,* 1981, *36,* 139–148.
Brehm, J. W. *Responses to loss of freedom: A theory of psychological reactance.* Morristown, N.J.: General Learning, 1972.
Brown, A. L. The development of memory: Knowing, knowing about knowing, and knowing how to know. In H. W. Reese (Ed.), *Advances in child development and behavior* (Vol. 10), pp. 103–152. New York: Academic Press, 1975.

Brown, A. L., & Murphy, M. D. Reconstruction of arbitrary versus logical sequences by preschool children. *Journal of Experimental Child Psychology,* 1975.

Cermak, L. S., & Craik, F. I. M. *Levels of processing in human memory.* Hillsdale, N.J.: Erlbaum, 1979.

Chapman, M. Listening to reason: Children's attentiveness and parental discipline. *Merrill-Palmer Quarterly of Behavior and Development,* 1979, *25,* 251–263.

Cook, T. D., Gruder, C. L., Henningan, K. M., & Flay, B. R. History of the sleeper effect. *Psychological Bulletin,* 1979, *86,* 662–679.

Craik, F. I. M. Depth of processing in recall and recognition. In S. Dornic (Ed.), *Attention and performance* (Vol. 6). Hillsdale, N.J.: Erlbaum, 1977.

Craik, F. I. M., & Lockhart, R. R. Levels of processing: A framework for memory research. *Journal of Verbal Learning and Verbal Behavior,* 1972, *11,* 671–684.

DeLoache, J., & Brown, A. L. Looking for big bird: Studies of memory in very young children. *LCHC Newsletter,* 1979, *1,* 4.

Dienstbier, R. A. Attribution, socialization, and moral decision making. In J. H. Harvey, W. Ickes, & R. F. Kidd (Eds.), *New Directions in attribution research* (Vol. 2). Hillsdale, N.J.: Erlbaum, 1978.

Erikson, E. H. Reflections on the dissent of contemporary youth. *International Journal of Psychoanalysis,* 1970, *51,* 11–22.

Festinger, L., & Freedman, J. L. Dissonance reduction and moral values. In P. Worchel and D. Byrne (Eds.), *Personality change,* New York: Wiley, 1964.

Freud, S. *Civilization and its discontents.* London: Hogarth Press, 1955. (Originally published, 1930.)

Grusec, J. E., & Kuczynski, L. Direction of effect in socialization: A comparison of the parent's vs. the child's behavior as determinants of disciplinary techniques. *Developmental Psychology,* 1980, *16,* 1–9.

Gunnar, M. R. Control: warning signals, and distress in infancy. *Developmental Psychology,* 1980, *16,* 281–289.

Heider, F. *The psychology of interpersonal relations.* New York: Wiley, 1958.

Hoffman, M. L. Power assertion by the parent and its impact on the child. *Child Development,* 1960, *31,* 129–143.

Hoffman, M. L. Parent discipline and the child's consideration for others. *Child Development,* 1963, *34,* 573–588.

Hoffman, M. L. Conscience, personality, and socialization techniques. *Human Development,* 1970, *13,* 90–126. (a)

Hoffman, M. L. Moral development. In P. H. Mussen (Ed.), *Carmichael's manual of child psychology* (3rd ed., Vol. 2). New York: Wiley, 1970. (b)

Hoffman, M. L. Identification and conscience development. *Child Development,* 1971, *42,* 1071–1082.

Hoffman, M. L. Altruistic behavior and the parent–child relationship. *Journal of Personality and Social Psychology,* 1975, *31,* 937–943. (a)

Hoffman, M. L. Developmental syntheses of affect and cognition and its implications for altruistic motivation. *Developmental Psychology,* 1975, *11,* 607–622. (b)

Hoffman, M. L. Moral internalization, parental power, and the nature of parent–child interaction. *Developmental Psychology,* 1975, *11* (2), 228–239. (c)

Hoffman, M. L. A critique of experimental research on discipline and moral behavior. *Development Report No. 86,* University of Michigan, 1976. (a)

Hoffman, M. L. Empathy, role-taking, guilt, and development of altruistic motives. In T. Likona (Ed.), *Moral development: Current theory and research.* New York: Holt, Rinehart and Winston, 1976. (b)

Hoffman, M. L. Parental discipline and moral internalization: A theoretical analysis. *Developmental Report N. 85*, University of Michigan, 1976. (c)

Hoffman, M. L. Empathy, its development and prosocial implications. In C. Keasey (Ed.), *Nebraska Symposium on Motivation* (Vol. 25). Lincoln: University of Nebraska Press, 1977. (a)

Hoffman, M. L. Moral internalization: Current theory and research. In L. Berkowitz (Ed.), *Advances in experimental social psychology* (Vol. 10). New York: Academic Press, 1977. (b)

Hoffman, M. L. Moral development in adolescence. In J. Adelson (Ed.), *Handbook of adolescent psychology*. New York: Wiley Interscience, 1980.

Hoffman, M. L. Development of prosocial motivation: Empathy and guilt. In N. Eisenberg-Berg (Ed.), *Development of prosocial behavior*. New York: Academic Press, 1982. (a)

Hoffman, M. L. Social and emotional development in children. In *The five-year outlook: Problems, opportunities, and constraints in science and technology*. Washington, D.C.: National Science Foundation, 1982. (b)

Hoffman, M. L. Empathy, guilt, and social cognition. In W. Overton & J. Gallagher (Eds.), *Knowledge and development*. New York: Plenum, in press.

Hoffman, M. L. & Saltzstein, H. D. Parental discipline and the child's moral development. *Journal of Personality and Social Psychology*, 1967, *5*, 45–57.

Kahneman, D. *Attention and effort*. Englewood Cliffs, N.J.: Prentice-Hall, 1973.

Keller, B. B., & Bell, R. Q. Child effects on adult's methods of eliciting altruistic behavior. *Child Development*, 1979, *50*, 1004–1009.

Kelley, H. H. Attribution theory in social psychology. In D. Levine (Ed.), *Nebraska Symposium on Motivation* (Vol. 15). Lincoln: University of Nebraska Press, 1967.

Kohlberg, L. Moral stages and moralization: The cognitive-developmental approach. In T. Likona (Ed.), *Moral development: Current theory and research*. New York: Holt, Rinehart and Winston, 1976.

Kuczynski, L. *Reasoning, prohibitions and motivations for compliance*. Unpublished manuscript, Laboratory of Developmental Psychology, National Institute of Mental Health, 1980.

Kurtines, W., & Greif, E. B. The development of moral thought: Review and evaluation of Kohlberg's approach. *Psychological Bulletin*, 1974, *81*, 453–470.

Lederer, W. Dragons, delinquents, and destiny. *Psychological Issue*, 1964, *4*.

Lepper, M. R., & Greene, D. Turning work into play: Effects of adult surveillance and extrinsic rewards on children's intrinsic motivation. *Journal of Personality and Social Psychology*, 1975, *28*, 129–137.

Levine, L. E., & Hoffman, M. L. Empathy and cooperation in four-year olds. *Developmental Psychology*, 1975, *11*, 533–534.

Lytton, H. Disciplinary encounters between young boys and their mothers and fathers: Is there a contingency system? *Developmental Psychology*, 1979, *15*, 256–268.

Mendelson, R., & Shultz, T. R. Covariation and temporal contiguity as principles of causal inference in young children. *Journal of Experimental Child Psychology*, 1976, *22*, 408–412.

Milgram S. Behavioral study of obedience. *Journal of Personality and Social Psychology*, 1963, *67*, 371–378.

Minton, C., Kagan, J., & Levine, J. Maternal control and obedience in the two-year old. *Child Development*, 1971, *42*, 1873–1894.

Moss, H. Sex, age, and state as determinants of mother-infant interaction. *Merrill-Palmer Quarterly of Behavior and Development*, 1967, *13*, 19–26.

Mowrer, O. H. *Learning theory and behavior*. New York: Wiley, 1960.
Mueller, J. H. Anxiety and encoding processing in memory. *Personality and Social Psychology Bulletin*, 1979, *5*, 288–294.
Paris, S. G., & Carter, A. Y. Semantic and constructive aspects of sentence memory in children. *Developmental Psychology*, 1973, *9*, 109–113.
Piaget, J. *The moral judgment of the child*. New York: Harcourt, 1932.
Piaget, J. *The grasp of consciousness*. Cambridge, Mass.: Harvard University Press, 1976.
Piaget, J., & Inhelder, B. *Memory and intelligence*. New York: Basic Books, 1973.
Rest, J. R. Morality. In J. Flavell & E. Markman (Eds.), *Cognitive development*, in P. Mussen (General ed.), *Carmichael's manual of child psychology* (4th ed.). New York: Wiley, in press.
Rossi, E. L., & Rossi, S. I. Conceptualization, serial order and recall in nursery school children. *Child Development*, 1965, *36*, 771–778.
Rossi, S. I., & Wittrock, M. C. Developmental shifts in verbal recall between mental ages 2 and 5. *Child Development*, 1971, *42*, 333–338.
Sawin, D. B., and Parke, R. D. Empathy and fear as mediators of resistance-to-deviation in children. *Merrill-Palmer Quarterly*, 1980, *26*, 123–134.
Schoggen, P. Environmental forces in the everyday lives of children. In R. G. Barker (Ed.), *The stream of behavior: Explorations of its structure and content*. New York: Appleton-Century-Crofts, 1963.
Settlage, C. F. Cultural values and the superego in late adolescence. *Psychoanalytic Study of the Child*, 1972, *27*, 57–73.
Simmons, H., & Schoggen, P. Mothers and fathers as sources of environmental pressure on children. In R. G. Barket (Ed.), *The stream of behavior: Explorations of its structure and content*. New York: Appleton-Century-Crofts, 1963.
Solnit, A. J. Youth and the campus: The search for a social conscience. *Psychoanalytic Study of the Child*, 1972, *27*, 98–105.
Stein, A. H. Imitation of resistance to temptation. *Child Development*, 1967, *38*, 157–169.
Stein, N. A., and Glenn, C. An analysis of story comprehension. In R. O. Freedle (Ed.), *New directions in discourse processing*. Norwood, N.J.: Ablex, 1979.
Thompson, R., & Hoffman, M. L. Empathy and the arousal of guilt in children. *Developmental Psychology*, 1980, *15*, 155–156.
Tulkin, S. R., & Kagan, J. Mother-infant interaction in the first year of life. *Child Development*, 1972, *43*, 31–42.
Tulving, E. Episodic and semantic memory. In E. Tulving & W. Donaldson (Eds.), *Organization of memory*, pp. 381–403. New York: Academic Press, 1972.
Walters, R. H., & Parke, R. D. Emotional arousal, isolation and discrimination learning in children. *Journal of Experimental Child Psychology*, 1964, *1*, 163–173.
Wright, H. F. *Recording and analysing child behavior*. New York: Harper and Row, 1967.
Yendovitskaya, T. V. Development of memory. In A. V. Zaporozhets, & D. B. Elkonin (Eds.), *The psychology of preschool children*, pp. 89–110. Cambridge, Mass. MIT Press, 1971.
Zahn-Waxler, C., Radke-Yarrow, M., & King, R. M. Childrearing and children's prosocial initiations toward victims of distress. *Child development*, 1979, *50*, 319–330.
Zajonc, R. B. Feeling and thinking: Preferences need no inferences. *American Psychologist*, 1980, *35*, 151–175.

11 The internalization of altruistic dispositions: a cognitive analysis

Joan E. Grusec

The mature member of society must show concern for the rights and welfare of others. If it is assumed that no innate predisposition for altruism exists and that the young child's behavior is governed by selfish desire for immediate gratification, then some effort is required to effect a change from self-interest to interest in others. Thus, to comply with demands that others be comforted, helped, or shared with, children must be encouraged to give up a certain degree of physical and psychological comfort. This chapter focuses primarily on how altruism can be encouraged. However, the analysis proposed is applicable to the whole domain of moral development where the growing child is required to substitute societal demands for personal desires. The analysis is cognitive in orientation, focusing on changes in children's thinking about concern for others and the implications of this thinking for subsequent altruistic behavior. In keeping with the intent of this volume I stress the crucial importance of the specific learning experiences to which children are exposed in the formulation of a concept of concern for others. Although some degree of concern for others may naturally emerge with increasing cognitive capacities (e.g., the ability to understand the perspective of others), the focus here is on some specific socialization practices that appear to promote the development of thinking about altruism. This thinking presumably mediates the actual practice of concern for others.

Those responsible for the development of altruism have as their goal the internalization of a general principle of concerns for others. This goal has two aspects, that of internalization and that of a general principle of concern for others. By internalization is meant that concern for others must be displayed independently of fear of punishment or hope of reward by external agents, that children must take over a set of attitudes from others and make them their own. Internalization, in fact, may be a mythical concept, made necessary in a middle-class society where property rights are important and where individuals are given important responsi-

275

bilities with minimal surveillance (Hoffman, 1970a). Nevertheless, to achieve as much independence of external constraint as possible seems a worthy goal.

The second aspect of socialization is the acquisition of a general principle of concern for others. Acquisition of this general principle would mean that an individual could be characterized as having an altruistic disposition and that such an individual would behave altruistically across a wide variety of settings and under a wide variety of circumstances. Although the argument continues about whether or not behaviors subsumed under such labels as altruism are, or are not, interrelated (see Rushton, Jackson, & Paunonen, 1981, for a recent statement), we should not be prevented from looking for those conditions of socialization that would be most likely to produce a generalized disposition of concern for others. Bem and Allen (1974) have argued, for example, that it is possible to divide individuals into those who are consistent across settings on a particular trait and those who are not. Thus they found that subjects who reported themselves to be cross-situationally consistent in friendliness and conscientiousness did, in fact, display less variability across situations than subjects who reported their behavior to be more variable. This could well be the case with altruism. Perhaps some individuals are more generally altruistic than others, with the source of this difference lying in the techniques used by teachers and parents to promote altruism. Some techniques may be more likely to facilitate a generalized disposition or trait of altruism, whereas others may be more likely to develop only specific instances of altruistic behavior. It is the former set of techniques that should be of greatest interest to students of socialization. I shall argue in this chapter that the most effective techniques for the promotion of a general trait of altruism are those that most easily facilitate the development of a cognitive structure that would enable the child to recognize the importance and appropriateness of altruism across a wide variety of situations.

Reinforcement, punishment, and modeling

Reinforcement, punishment, and modeling – the major techniques of behavior change in social-learning theory – have received substantial attention as ways of facilitating the growth of moral development. If one assesses their efficacy in promoting the dual goals of socialization, however, they cannot be considered all that successful. Reinforcement increases the probability of occurrence of the response that it follows, and punishment decreases the probability of occurrence of the response that it follows. When removed, however, both consequences reverse the response of interest to its base-line level. Clearly, then, they are not good candidates for the task of fostering internalization, for when socializing agents are no longer present to administer them altruism disappears. Although the effects of reinforcement and punishment may well generalize to a wide variety of situations, depending on such things as magnitude of consequence and motivational level of the individual being socialized, this attribute is of little help if it is not accompanied by the ability to promote internalization.

Now to modeling. It has been amply documented that children will imitate models who are altruistic (Bryan, 1975; Grusec, 1981; Mussen & Eisenberg-Berg, 1977; Rushton, 1976). Is modeling effective for the internalization of a generalized principle of altruism? Let us consider first the problem of internalization. If children who imitate an altruistic model do not appear to feel that they have been coerced to do so, then this would be an indication that the altruism they exhibit had indeed been internalized. Evidence that such an outcome results from observation of a model comes from two studies.

In the first study (Dix & Grusec, 1981) we read stories to children and adults about children who helped others after they had seen helpful behavior modeled. Subjects were asked to indicate whether children in the stories had helped because they wanted to (an indication of internalization) or because they thought their mothers wanted them to (an indication of lack of internalization). In addition, they were asked to indicate how helpful the protagonist in the story would be in the future. Subjects were more likely to say children had helped because they wanted to and to indicate that these children would be helpful in the future. This outcome, then, indicates that modeled behavior is indeed perceived by both children and adults to result from the internalization of a norm for helping. In a second study (Grusec et al., 1978) children either were told to donate half their winnings from a game to less fortunate children or they observed a model engage in this behavior. Subsequent to this, all children donated half their winnings from the game. We hypothesized that children who donated because they had been told to do so would identify their behavior as coming from an external source, whereas those who donated because they had seen someone else do it might be more likely to believe that their altruism had been self-generated. Support for this belief was provided in the next step of the study. After they had shared, children were provided with reasons for their behavior – they were told either that they had shared because they were the kind of people who liked to help others (an internal attribution) or that they had shared because they were expected to (an external attribution). These attributions affected the subsequent sharing only of children in the modeling condition. After the internal attribution they shared more than they did after the external attribution, whereas children in the direct instruction condition were unaffected by the attributions provided by the experimenter. Thus we concluded that direct instruction makes the external control of behavior salient, whereas modeling is a much more subtle influence technique in which the perceived causes of behavior can more easily be manipulated. Examples of prosocial behavior, therefore, should help children to internalize societal values. In fact, one of the more frequently cited mechanisms for the acquisition of moral standards has been that of identification with (or imitation of) the parent (Freud, 1936; Mowrer, 1960; Sears, Maccoby, & Levin, 1957).

Modeling fares less well, however, when it comes to generalization. It is true that the effects of even one exposure to an altruistic model show great durability, revealing themselves in retests over a two- to four-month period (Rice & Grusec, 1975; Rushton, 1975). And the results of modeling do generalize to slightly different situations, for example, sharing candy and sharing pennies, donations of candy solicited by two different adults in two different settings (Elliot & Vasta, 1970; Midlarsky & Bryan, 1972). Generalization to more distant situations, however, does not seem to occur. Children trained to share candies did not give up a preferred toy to a stranger (Elliot & Vasta, 1970), and children who imitated a model's donation of game winnings to poor children were no more likely to share pencils with fellow schoolchildren or to collect craft materials for sick children than children who had not observed an altruistic model (Grusec, Saas-Kortsaak, & Simutis, 1978). In a study by Yarrow and Scott (1972) preschoolers observed warm and friendly (nurturant) and nonnurturant adults who modeled either gentleness and warmth or roughness and punitiveness to play animals. The children imitated the friendliness of the nurturant model when they were with the play animals, but there was no evidence that these effects generalized to the children's helpful interactions with their peers.

All this is not to discount the great effectiveness of example in encouraging altruism. Children need to know the exact form that concern for others might take, and there seems no better way of learning this than by observing another engaged in a specific example of altruistic behavior. No words, no matter how eloquent, could teach so adequately how to verbally and physically comfort a person in distress as someone's actual actions. Moreover, it is no doubt safe to assume that most children see a great many examples of a variety of altruistic behaviors and that this would then result in a variety of imitated altruistic acts. Still, modeling seems an inefficient way of trying to promote an altruistic disposition. Surely many adult altruistic acts are hidden from children (after all, a major characteristic of "true" altruism is that the behavior be carried out in private and anonymously). It may be that children are eventually able to extract some generalized principle of concern for others after they have viewed a series of altruistic behaviors. But at what point? And is there not a more efficient way of making this occur?

Certainly modeling is an important socialization technique. Moreover, Hoffman's (1970a) argument that children are more likely to imitate antisocial than prosocial models seems not to be the case. When the actions of antisocial and prosocial models are made equally salient, the latter can be as effective, and sometimes even more effective, than the former (Grusec et al., 1979; Perry, Bussey, & Perry, 1975). But the true effectiveness of modeling may lie in its combination with other techniques. Note, for example, Friedrich and Stein's (1975) finding that children who observed a prosocial television show helped more in real life but only when the modeling was combined with playing the role of the individual in need of help. Similarly, Yarrow, Scott, and Waxler (1973) found that children imitated altruistic models: The model, however, accompanied her examples of altruism with statements of awareness of, and sympathy for, the animal or person she was helping; she described the aid that was necessary and the pleasure she felt in providing that aid, and she used the word *help* to summarize what had been done. In some conditions, moreover, an adult confederate who was helped provided approval for the model's altruism. And finally, Grusec and her associates (1979) asked 5- to 8-year-old children to carry out a boring card-sorting task and not to play with some attractive toys. Children took longer to deviate only when they had observed a model who not only resisted temptation but who also accompanied her resistance with a rationale, a statement that she was there to sort cards and that she always tried to do what was right whenever she could.

Response consequences and internalization reconsidered

In the immediately preceding section it was argued that reinforcement and punishment are not effective techniques for promoting the internalization of altruistic values and behavior. I shall now maintain, however, that although they are not sufficient to achieve such a goal, they *are* necessary. Without fear of punishment or hope of reward, that is, without motivation, altruism will not emerge. If impulsivity and self-centeredness are the natural state of affairs, then anti-social behavior will exert itself unless there is reason to suppress it. The reason lies in the manipulation by agents of socialization of response consequences – social and material reward for the display of acceptable behavior and punishment in the form of social disapproval, verbal and physical intervention, and withdrawal of privileges and material rewards for the display of unacceptable behavior.

If response consequences manipulated by an external agent are necessary, then one must ask how altruism might ever occur independently of external coercion and, therefore, how internalization might ever be achieved. The following possibilities have been suggested (e.g., Dienstbier, et al., 1975; Lepper, this volume; Walters & Grusec, 1977). People attribute causes of behavior to internal dispositions when external causes are not immediately obvious (Kelley, 1967). Let us suppose that the external cause is, in reality, fear of punishment. If the role of punishment could be made less salient in the socialization process, children would feel anxious when they were about to deviate (because of earlier punishment) but would attribute this anxiety to some inner desire to be good because they could not identify an external source of compulsion. *One* way to minimize the salience of punishment would be to accompany it with reasoning or some kind of verbal statement that would draw the child's attention away from the baldness of the punitive consequence. Hoffman (1970b) has suggested that punishment is necessary for the voice of reason to be noticed. The present approach suggests that the voice of reason is necessary so that punishment will not be noticed.

Indeed, there is evidence that parents who are most successful at socialization are those who employ some form of response consequence with reasoning. Baumrind (1973) identifies authoritative parents – those most likely to produce children who are high in both conformity to parental demands and social responsibility – as individuals who both exhibit firm control in their demands and reason. Hoffman (1970b) found that parents who produced children with an altruistic orientation were those who employed both reasoning and some form of power assertion in their discipline encounters. Zahn-Waxler, Radke-Yarrow, and King (1979) report that young children who showed the greatest amounts of altruism were those whose mothers responded to their deviations (i.e., situations in which they caused distress to others) with explanations as to why they should not have done what they did. Zahn-Waxler and her associates describe these explanations as having a strong affective component, with the most effective being those with a large element of moralizing (e.g. "You made Doug cry. It's not nice to bite"). Certainly mothers report that they frequently combine reasoning and punishment when they respond to their children's misdemeanors (Grusec & Kuczynski, 1980). An so I conclude that a socializing agent who makes firm demands for appropriate behavior and accompanies these demands with reasons will be successful in promoting the internalization of altruism: These reasons, which often involve reference to internally oriented desires and obligations ("you want to make other people happy," "you'll feel good if you help out"), induce children to find an internal reason for their good behavior.

But what about a generalized disposition for altruism? Whereas the effects of reinforcement and punishment may generalize, particularly if they are of high magnitude, their use does not seem to be an efficient way of inducing a generalized disposition to be altruistic. The socializing agent has little control over which responses increase, or decrease, in their probability of occurrence. And the more intense the response consequence, the more difficult it would be to reattribute the causes of behavior to an internal disposition. In the case of punishment and concern for others, the child must actively, rather than passively, avoid punishment. High levels of arousal, caused by high intensities of punishment, would interfere with the effective execution of helpful acts. The content of the verbal message that accompanies the response consequences, then, must bear the responsibility for ensuring development of a generalized tendency toward altruism. In the material that follows I shall attempt to show how various kinds of reasoning might function to ensure the development of an altruistic disposition. I shall suggest how the concept of a cognitive structure or schema might help to explain how children move beyond specific experiences to generalized dispositions, dispositions brought into play by the anticipation of response consequences but with the underlying motivation made less salient by attention being directed toward the content of a verbal message.

Schemata or scripts for altruism

In addition to being motivated to show concern for others, children (and adults) must come to understand that a situation demands concern for others and to know how that concern for others should be put into effect. Cognitive psychologists have used such notions as scripts, schemata, frames, and rules to explain the existence of such understanding. Schank and Abelson (1977) define a script as a structure that describes an appropriate sequence of events in a particular context. Thus a script consists of "slots" and requirements about what can fill these slots. Scripts consist of a predetermined, stereotyped set of actions that define a well-known situation or, as Schank and Abelson put it, they are, in effect, "a very boring little story." Understanding, in Schank and Abelson's view, involves the fitting of new information into a previously organized view of the world.

Although the construct of script was developed primarily to deal with language processing, it offers a way of understanding how children could develop a generalized tendency to behave altruistically across a variety of situations. Some mechanism must exist to separate altruistic acts from the concreteness of their initial occurrence. Whereas many scripts for altruism are no doubt about concrete acts, the scripts we should want to teach to encourage a generalized altruistic disposition would be those that are general enough to accommodate a wide variety of altruistic acts. It is these sorts of scripts that will be of particular interest in the following discussion.

Children must be taught scripts for altruism. Agents of socialization must teach the appropriate sequences of events in a situation involving altruism, that is, they must teach boring little stories. When a new situation arises, children would then be able to incorporate it into an existing script and thereby understand what was required or possible in that situation.

The following sketch of a script for altruism is based on the model of Schank and Abelson.

script: showing concern for others
roles: helper, helpee
reason: help others so as to reduce anxiety about not having behaved morally
scene 1: observing someone apparently in need of help (crying, falling down, asking for money)
scene 2: inferring their thoughts or needs (they want help, they don't want help, they are drunk, they are lonely) *or* recalling that one's self-concept demands a response to need in others
scene 3: deciding that help is appropriate and the form it should most appropriately take (hugging, pep talk, physical aid)
scene 4: offering help

The concept of script, of course, resembles the Piagetian notion of a scheme. As a baby incorporates a rattle into its sucking scheme, one would strive to produce individuals who would incorporate cancer victims, refugees, and orphans into their altruism scheme. In fact, it does not matter whether one employs the concept of a script or a scheme or any other term that designates some kind of cognitive structure. To understand fully the growth of altruism, there must merely be provision in one's explanatory apparatus for a framework or a set of rules that organizes past material and provides a place into which new material can fit.

Note again that scripts designed to promote generalized altruism must be independent of specific events. Certainly scripts develop from concrete, specific happenings (e.g., observing a teacher tie someone's shoe-lace, discovering that mother is pleased when you offer to put away the groceries). To encourage more generalized behavior, however, scripts need to be more abstract in nature (e.g., listening to father talk about how those who are more fortunate have an obligation to help those who are less fortunate). Tulving (1972) has differentiated episodic from semantic memory, that is, memories of specific events from knowledge produced by the event, with the latter not tied to the situation in which it was first acquired. In the moral domain, this is the difference between knowing that you were punished this morning for hitting your sister and knowing that it is wrong to behave aggressively. Consequently, the most effective techniques for socialization make the principles of morality abstract rather than having them tied to a specific situation.

The development of scripts for altruism

In this chapter the role of socialization techniques in the growth of scripts for altruism is being emphasized. Nevertheless, changing cognitive capabilities must also play an important role. It has been repeatedly emphasized (e.g., Hoffman, 1976) that altruism based on empathy for the affliction of others cannot appear until the child is capable of understanding the emotional perspective of others. Altruism that relies on a child's self-concept as a good and helpful person cannot develop until children see themselves as persons having enduring and stable personality characteristics and begin to act in accord with these images of themselves. Until certain cognitive capacities have matured, then, no adequate script or scheme can develop.

The development of generalized scripts is fostered by socialization techniques that encourage the processing of information into semantic memory and produce knowledge not about single acts but about general principles of behavior. Two approaches that appear to satisfy these criteria will be described: verbal exhortation about the importance of concern for others and the encouragement of self-attributions of morality. Certainly these are only examples from a larger class of socialization techniques that could promote general altruistic scripts.

Verbal exhortations. General scripts for altruism should develop much more speedily and efficiently if they are described verbally by socializing agents. Consider the following. Schank and Abelson (1977) describe one very simple script: how to obtain a meal in a restaurant. Certainly such a script might be learned through extensive observation of the behavior of others or through reinforcement of appropriately occurring behavior. But it is surely better learned through verbal means. I have never been served a piece of bad meat in a restaurant and so have never had the occasion to return one. Nor have I ever seen anyone else do so. And, so far as I can remember, I have never heard or read of anyone returning such an item. Should an off-color steak ever come my way, however, I shall understand what to do with it. And this I have learned through hearing the repeated exhortation that when one pays high prices for restaurant food one is entitled to decent fare. (Whether I put my understanding into action, of course, depends on my relative levels of anxiety about potential arguments with the waiter and about having to live with the knowledge that I paid good money for bad food and never had the fortitude to complain.)

It has been argued that verbal exhortation or the preaching of morality is an ineffective way to promote prosocial behavior (e.g., Bryan, 1975). In fact, the evidence seems to suggest that extensive exhortations are at least as effective as modeling, whereas short ones are not (Midlarsky & Bryan, 1972; Rushton, 1975; Staub, 1972; Yates, 1974). Presumably short exhortations do not contain sufficient information from which to develop a suitable script. For present purposes, of course, verbal exhortations must be shown under certain conditions to be *more* effective than modeling. Such evidence is provided in the following study (Grusec, Saas-Kortsaak, & Simutis, 1978).

Children observed an adult who donated half his winnings from a game to poor children whereas other children were merely exhorted by the adult to share their winnings because it would make the poor children happy (an appeal to their empathic feelings). Still others were exposed to a combination of preaching and example. Finally, two forms of preaching were used: a specific one that emphasized the fact of donation and a general one that emphasized the fact of helping others in any way one can. Not only were children's immediate donations to poor children measured but also their behavior in a variety of situations involving altruism. In this way we could discover which method was most effective in producing a generalized disposition to be altruistic.

The results of this experiment are summarized in Table 1. Briefly, the model's example was more effective than the model's exhortations on an immediate test of donation to poor children, although exhortation was more effective than no treatment alone. After a one- to two-week period, however, the difference between example and exhortation declined. Other data suggest that this decline occurred because children had forgotten the form in which they had learned that donation was appropriate in the situation. In a pilot study children had been asked, immediately after

Table 1. *Number of children donating (N = 16 per group) in immediate and delayed tests, picking up dropped items, mean number of pencils shared, and number of children returning paintings and craft items in each condition*

Preaching	Example			No Example		
	Specific	General	None	Specific	General	None
Donation, immediate	13	12	11	4	6	0
Donation, delayed	5(15)	3(14)	4(14)	2(13)	3(13)	0(15)
Helping	7	4	2	3	4	9
Sharing, boys	3.62	1.62	2.25	3.50	1.37	2.62
Sharing, girls	2.50	3.00	2.37	1.37	2.37	2.62
Paintings and craft items	5	3	4	5	9	4
Craft items	4	2	3	4	9	2

Note: Figures in parentheses indicate number of children available for the follow-up.
Source: Adapted from Grusec, Saas-Kortsaak, and Simutis (1978).

training, to recall what the model had said or done in the various treatment conditions. Whereas children accurately recalled the model's behavior in the example conditions, significantly more of them incorrectly recalled that the model had donated when in actuality he had not. Because some children forgot immediately, it seemed likely that the distinction between words and deeds would blur even more after the passage of several days.

Of greater interest for the development of generalized scripts were the effects of example and exhortation beyond the specific training situation. At one point during the procedure the experimenter "accidentally" knocked over a box containing a great many small items. Exhortation, in fact, depressed helping relative to the control group, a possible indication of reactance, that is, an unwillingness to be helpful after being the recipient of moral exhortation. Helping was also depressed in the example condition, however, so that some factor other than reactance may have been operative. Children were also asked to share some pencils they had been given with other children in the school who would not be able to participate in the research and thereby win prizes. Here specific exhortations facilitated the altruism of boys. (Note that the model's exhortation had emphasized sharing, and children in this test of generalization were again being asked to share.) Finally, three weeks after their training children were visited in their classrooms by an experimenter they had never seen before. He asked them to make paintings and collect craft items for sick children who were hospitalized. In the group that had received only a general exhortation about the virtues of helping others whenever possible produced the greatest number of positive responses.

These data are complex and they pose a number of questions. Why did fewer children in the example condition than in the control condition help the experimenter pick up the items she had dropped? Why did only boys share more pencils? Why did children who had been exposed to both example and exhortation not collect more craft materials for the sick children? Nevertheless, the data do suggest that exhortation may be more effective than example in promoting altruism beyond the training situation. To produce altruistic dispositions, then, it appears better to provide children with general principles of concern for others than to leave them to abstract these principles themselves. Moreover, these exhortations need to be of a particular kind. Exhortations that are specific to the situation in which they are used will not be especially effective in contributing to scripts for generalized altruism. An effective way of developing altruistic dispositions is to employ messages that subsume a wide range of acts.

Any part of an altruistic exhortation can elaborate on the variety of ways in which altruism could be performed. Consider the following basic and specific exhortation: "When your sister has trouble doing up the zipper on her snowsuit, zip it up for her. That way she won't cry." Such an exhortation can be divided into three components: those conditions that ought to elicit altruism, those actions that are required to be altruistic, and the reactions of the helper or the person helped. Now consider the statement in a more general form: "When your younger siblings (or when anybody younger or less experienced than you) are having trouble getting dressed (or doing any demanding task) then help them (either do it for them or show them how to do it). That way they avoid being frustrated and will be grateful to you, and you will feel good that you have done something nice." Obviously some background of specific information is necessary for general exhortations to be meaningful. Children must have learned – through observation or direct tuition – how to effect some helpful acts. But not all specific helpful acts need be taught. A child may be able to show another how to get her scarf untangled, even though this specific helpful behavior has never been experienced before. I am simply suggesting that some general statements (against a background of specific experiences that will have eventuated in specific scripts for behavior) should facilitate general scripts. Although children themselves can produce some of these general scripts, the process can be aided by the verbalization of socializing agents.

Attributions of goodness. Earlier some attempts at an attributional analysis of moral behavior were described. Causal inferences about behavior either can be self-generated or supplied by others. In one study (Lepper, 1973) in which these inferences were assumed to be self-generated, children received either a mild or a severe threat designed to keep them from playing with a particular toy. All children complied, but in a subsequent test of honesty, children who had been mildly threatened cheated less than those who had been severely threatened. Lepper suggested that children in the mild-threat condition had attributed their original compliance to inner causes. Because they now had a concept of themselves as honest, they behaved more honestly in a subsequent test. Such a change in self-concept, in fact, was evidenced by the fact that children tended to rate themselves as more honest in the mild-threat than in the severe-threat condition.

Causal attributions provided by external agents also produce changes in moral behavior (e.g., Grusec et al., 1978; Miller, Brickman, & Bolen, 1975; Toner, Moore, & Emmons, 1980). The study by Grusec and her associates was discussed briefly earlier in this chapter. Recall that children who had donated tokens to poor children to help buy them toys were told that they must have done so because they were the kinds of people who liked to help others whenever possible. Other children were told that they must have done it because they thought the experimenter had expected them to. In addition to looking at the effects of these attributions on the donation of tokens to poor children, we also assessed their effects on other acts of altruism. Children in the first group subsequently shared more pencils with other children in their school than did children in the second group, regardless of how they had been induced to share in the first place. The difference between these groups could also have been mediated by changes in self-concept, with the first group now seeing themselves as helpful persons and acting in accord with that self-concept, although there is not, as yet, any direct evidence that would support this hypothesis. But it should also be noted that attributions of internal goodness immediately take attention away from a specific act and focus it, instead, on a *class* of behavior. Depending on what is contained in the child's concept of a good person, then, further material is provided for the developing script of altruism. Children learn that good people help others whenever possible and that they are members of that class of good people. When a subsequent opportunity for altruism arises, the child understands that, being a good person, it is appropriate to be helpful.

It could be argued, of course, that the attribution of goodness is merely a form of social reinforcement. As such it should be effective only in increasing the occurrence of the specific act toward which it is directed and should do nothing to promote a script or a set of general rules for altruism. Sharing tokens and sharing pencils may have been similar enough that the latter did not provide an adequate test of generalization. In a study designed to test this possibility (Grusec & Redler, 1980), 8-year-old children were induced to donate tokens to poor children and were then told either that they must have done so because they were nice people who liked to help others whenever possible (attribution condition) or that donating tokens was a nice and helpful thing to do (social-reinforcement condition). In essence, children were labeled as having altruistic dispositions in one condition, whereas their specific act of altruism was praised in the second condition. A few days later they were given a similar message after helping another experimenter. The results of this study are summarized in Table 2. Both attribution and social reinforcement increased the subsequent donation of tokens to poor children, the altruistic act that had set the occasion for treatment. On a variety of generalization tests, however – sharing pencils with other children in the school, folding cards for the experimenter instead of playing with an attractive toy, and making drawings and collecting craft materials for sick children – children in the attribution condition helped more, whereas those in the social-reinforcement condition helped no more than children in the control condition who had merely been thanked for their altruism. It would appear, then, that labeling a child as helpful contributes more to a general altruism script than does reinforcement of the act.

It must be pointed out, however, that this pattern of results only holds for children within a fairly narrow age range. When we attempted to replicate the findings with 5-year-olds we found no generalized effects of attribution (or social reinforcement). We assumed this was because 5-year-olds may not yet think of themselves as having stable dispositional characteristics; consequently, it is difficult for them to develop a script in which they see themselves as behaving consistently across situations. In fact, there appears to be a quite abrupt shift, at approximately 8 years of age, between thinking of one's self and others in terms of surface traits and thinking in terms of dispositional traits (Livesley & Bromley, 1973; Peevers & Secord, 1973).

When we compared attribution and social reinforcement in a sample of 10-year-old children, we found yet another change. The two techniques were *equally* effective in promoting both the altruistic behavior with

Table 2. *Mean number of marbles donated, pencils shared, cards sorted, and drawings returned in each condition*

	Attribution	Reinforcement	Control
Marbles	7.7	6.4	3.3
Pencils	5.8	2.8	2.3
Cards	4.6(16)	1.8(9)	2.1(10)
Drawings	2.7	1.6	1.4
Craft material	(9)	(2)	(4)

Note: Figures in parentheses indicate the number of children in each condition who folded cards and returned craft materials. $N = 10$ per group.
Source: Grusec and Redler (1980).

which they had been originally associated and a generalized altruism. Whereas 8-year-olds discriminated between statements about their acts and statements about their dispositions, 10-year-olds seemed willing or able to extrapolate from evaluations of their actions to more general inferences about their own characteristics. Nelson and Nelson (1978) shed some light on this particular result. They noted that children's concepts develop through a series of stages in which they swing from a great breadth of inclusion to a rigid inflexible application of rules to a more flexible extension of rules. In the area tapped by our studies 8-year-olds appear to be in the rigid stage, whereas 10-year-olds have moved to the stage of flexible extension.

This latter finding, of course, means that social reinforcement is a candidate at certain points in the developmental process for yet another technique that would facilitate the development of scripts for altruism. At times this technique may be successful in encouraging the growth of rules to govern generalized altruistic behavior. It may seem paradoxical that reinforcement, which we saw earlier was not conducive to internalization of societal values, has properties that satisfy the second criterion for socialization, that is the development of a generalized concern for others. It may, in fact, be less harmful to internalization than material reinforcement. Smith and her associates (1979) found that children who received social consequences (praise or rebuke) for sharing or failure to share attributed their behavior to a desire to help or to concern for another child. On the other hand, children given material consequences (penny rewards or fines) were more likely to attribute their altruism to external sources.

Adult reactions to moral transgressions

Some behaviors that adults want to suppress seem more important, or more moral, than others. Taking out the garbage and sitting still at the dinner table are qualitatively different activities from stealing or harming others. It is presumably the latter that are deemed worthy of both internalization and generalization to a wide variety of situations. That parents have an understanding of the difference between the two classes of activities might be reflected in their different reactions to them.

Nucci and Turiel (1978) have made some observations that suggest this is the case. They recorded the occurrence of two types of events in a preschool setting. The event they labeled as "moral" included such behaviors as hitting another child and failing to share. The event they labeled "social conventional" included behaviors such as eating a snack while standing rather than sitting. These investigators found that teachers more frequently provided rationales and references to the feelings of others when they were dealing with moral transgressions, and that they more frequently commanded, threatened sanctions, specified rules, or indicated that the behavior was creating a mess when they were trying to enforce social conventions. Similarly, Grusec and Kuczynski (1980) asked mothers to report what they would do in response to a variety of misdemeanors in which their children might engage. Stealing and making fun of a senile man were responded to with reasoning, whereas misdemeanors such as arguing about turning off the television set were responded to with a withdrawal of privileges and a demand that the child engage in appropriate behavior. As in the Nucci and Turiel study, our mothers appeared to distinguish between moral behaviors and those that are situation-specific. I have argued that rationales, reasoning, and references to the feelings of others promote the learning of scripts, or frameworks, for given classes of behaviors, whereas commands, threats, material punishment, and specific rules do not. Apparently adults, in their everyday dealings with children, act as though my argument has some merit.

Conclusion

Social-learning theory has traditionally portrayed the development of morality as the acquisition of specific patterns of behavior, first learned, perhaps, through observing the behavior of others and subsequently strengthened through reinforcement or avoidance of punishment. Certainly this approach is cognitive in orientation. Bandura (1977), for example, stresses the function of models in conveying information to observers and introduces the notions of self-reinforcement and self-punishment as devices to explain how behavior can become independent of external sanctions. In this chapter it has been argued, however, that one must go further in developing an adequate theory of moral development by taking into account how children reinterpret and structure events in the external world. I have suggested that how events are interpreted and structured depends to some extent on how agents of socialization attempt to train concern for others. Morality does not emerge, it is acquired – in part, at least – through the direct teaching strategies employed by teachers and parents.

Two issues have been addressed: internalization and generalization. It has been maintained that internalization is encouraged by techniques of socialization that encourage children to minimize the influence of external events on their behavior, although I have also argued that these external influences are crucial. Socializing agents, then, can take advantage of the human tendency to seek explanations for behavior by using techniques that encourage children to see their behavior as internally motivated. Here we have, then, the impetus to take part in moral behavior. The form of the morality, however, is dictated by those cognitive structures that provide a framework or an outline for action. To facilitate a wide-ranging concern for others, it has been suggested that these structures should be as broad as possible. The well-socialized child, then, must have adequate scripts for altruism available, as well as be encouraged to participate in these scripts.

References

Bandura, A. *Social learning theory*. Englewood Cliffs, N.J.; Prentice-Hall, 1977.

Baumrind, D. The development of instrumental competence through socialization. In A. D. Pick (Ed.), *Minnesota Symposia on Motivation* (Vol. 7). Minneapolis: University of Minnesota Press, 1973.

Bem, D. J., & Allen, A. On predicting some of the people some of the time: The search for cross-situational consistencies in behavior. *Psychological Review*, 1974, *81*, 506–520.

Bryan, J. H. Children's cooperation and helping behaviors. In E. M. Hetherington (Ed.), *Review of child development research* (Vol. 5). Chicago: University of Chicago Press, 1975.

Dienstbier, R. A., Hillman, D., Lehnhoff, J., Hillman, J., & Valkenaar, M. C. An emotion-attribution approach to moral behavior: Interfacing cognitive and avoidance theories of moral development. *Psychological Review*, 1975, *82*, 299–315.

Dix, T., & Grusec, J. E. *Parental influence techniques: An attributional analysis*. Unpublished manuscript, University of Toronto, 1981.

Elliot, R., & Vasta, R. The modeling of sharing: Effects associated with vicarious reinforcement, symbolization, age, and generalization. *Journal of Experimental Child Psychology*, 1970, *10*, 8–15.

Freud, A. *The ego and the mechanism of defense*. London: International Universities Press, 1936.

Friedrich, L. K., & Stein, A. H. Prosocial television and young children: The effects of verbal labeling and role playing on learning and behavior. *Child Development*, 1975, *46*, 27–38.

Grusec, J. E. Socialization processes in the development of altruism. In J. P. Rushton, & R. M. Sorrentino (Eds.), *Altruism and helping behavior*. Hillsdale, N.J.: Erlbaum, 1981.

Grusec, J. E., & Kuczynski L. Direction of effect in socialization: A comparison of the parent vs. the child's behavior as determinants of disciplinary techniques. *Developmental Psychology*, 1980, *16*, 1–9.

Grusec, J. E., Kuczynski, L., Rushton, J. P., & Simutis, Z. M. Modeling, direct instruction, and attributions: Effects on altruism. *Developmental Psychology*, 1978, *14*, 51–57.

Grusec, J. E., Kuczynski, L., Rushton, J. P. & Simutis, Z. M. Learning resistance to temptation through observation. *Developmental Psychology*, 1979, *15*, 233–240.

Grusec, J. E., & Redler, E. Attribution, reinforcement, and altruism: A developmental analysis. *Developmental Psychology*, 1980, *16*, 525–534.

Grusec, J. E., Saas-Kortsaak, P., & Simutis, Z. M. The role of example and moral exhortation in the training of altruism. *Child Development*, 1978, *49*, 920–923.

Hoffman, M. L. Moral development. In P. H. Mussen (Ed.), *Carmichael's manual of child psychology*. New York: Wiley, 1970. (a)

Hoffman, M. L. Conscience, personality, and socialization techniques. *Human Development*, 1970, *13*, 90–126. (b)

Hoffman, M. L. Empathy, role-taking, guilt, and development of altruistic motives. In T. Lickona (Ed.), *Moral development and behavior*. New York: Holt, Rinehart and Winston, 1976.

Kelley, H. H. Attribution theory in social psychology. In D. Levine (Ed.), *Nebraska Symposium on Motivation*. Lincoln: University of Nebraska Press, 1967.

Lepper, M. R. Dissonance, self-perception, and honesty in children. *Journal of Personality and Social Psychology*, 1973, *25*, 65–74.

Livesley, W. J., & Bromley, D. B. *Person perception in childhood and adolescence*. London: Wiley, 1973.

Midlarsky, E., & Bryan, J. H. Affect expressions and children's imitative altruism. *Journal of Experimental Research in Personality*, 1972, *6*, 195–203.

Miller, R. L., Brickman, P., & Bolen, D. Attribution versus persuasion as a means for modifying behavior. *Journal of Personality and Social Psychology*, 1975, *31*, 430–441.

Mowrer, O. H. *Learning theory and the symbolic processes*. New York: Wiley, 1960.

Mussen, P. H., & Eisenberg-Berg, N. *Roots of caring, sharing, and helping*. San Francisco: Freeman, 1977.

Nelson, K. E., & Nelson, K. Cognitive pendulums and their linguistic realization. In K. E. Nelson (Ed.), *Children's language* (Vol. 1). New York: Gardner Press, 1978.

Nucci, L. P., & Turiel, E. Social interaction and the development of social concepts in preschool children. *Child Development*, 1978, *49*, 400–407.

Peevers, B. H., & Secord, P. F. Developmental changes in attribution of descriptive concepts to persons. *Journal of Personality and Social Psychology*, 1973, *27*, 120–128.

Perry, D. G., Bussey, K., & Perry, L. C. Factors influencing the imitation of resistance to deviation. *Developmental Psychology*, 1975, *11*, 724–731.

Rice, M. E., & Grusec, J. E. Saying and doing: Effects on observer performance. *Journal of Personality and Social Psychology*, 1975, *32*, 584–593.

Rushton, J. P. Generosity in children: Immediate and long-term effects of modeling, preaching, and moral judgment. *Journal of Personality and Social Psychology*, 1975, *31*, 459–466.

Rushton, J. P. Socialization and the altruistic behavior of children. *Psychological Bulletin*, 1976, *83*, 898–913.

Rushton, J. P., Jackson, D. N., & Paunonen, S. V. Personality: Nomothetic or ideographic. *Psychological Review,* 1981, *88,* 582–589.

Schank, R. C., & Abelson, R. P. *Scripts, plans, goals, and understanding.* Hillsdale, N.J.: Erlbaum, 1977.

Sears, R. R., Maccoby, E. E., & Levin, H. *Patterns of child rearing.* New York: Harper, 1957.

Smith, C. L., Gelfand, D. M., Hartmann, D. P., & Partlow, M. E. Y. Children's causal attributions regarding help giving. *Child Development,* 1979, *50,* 203–210.

Staub, E. Effects of persuasion and modeling on delay of gratification. *Developmental Psychology,* 1972, *6,* 166–177.

Toner, I. J., Moore, L. P., & Emmons, B. A. The effect of being labeled on subsequent self-control in children. *Child Development,* 1980, *51,* 618–621.

Tulving, E. Episodic and semantic memory. In E. Tulving & W. Donaldson (Eds.), *Organization and memory.* New York: Academic Press, 1972.

Walters, G. C., & Grusec, J. E. *Punishment.* San Francisco: Freeman, 1977.

Yarrow, M. R., & Scott, P. M. Imitation of nurturant and nonnurturant models. *Journal of Personality and Social Psychology,* 1972, *23,* 259–270.

Yarrow, M. R., Scott, P. M., & Waxler, C. Z. Learning concern for others. *Developmental Psychology,* 1973, *8,* 240–260.

Yates, G. C. R. Influence of televised modeling and verbalization on children's delay of gratification. *Journal of Experimental Child Psychology,* 1974, *18,* 333–339.

Zahn-Waxler, C., Radke-Yarrow, M., & King, R. A. Child rearing and children's prosocial initiations toward victims of distress. *Child Development,* 1979, *50,* 319–330.

12 Social-control processes and the internalization of social values: an attributional perspective

Mark R. Lepper

> To internalize: to incorporate (as values, patterns of culture, motives, restraints) within the self as conscious or unconscious guiding principles through learning or socialization
> To comply: to conform or adapt one's actions (as to another's wishes)
>
> Webster's Third New International Dictionary

Among both social and developmental psychologists there is a long history of concern with the distinction between "internalization" and "compliance" and the factors that promote both processes. Equally long, however, is the history of isolation that has existed between researchers considering these issues within the two camps. The goal of this chapter is to consider some points of convergence and divergence between these historically distinct research traditions. Its particular focus is on the implications of recent social-psychological research on the potentially adverse effects of functionally superfluous social controls for our understanding of the socialization process.

Processes of attitude change

Consider first the distinction between different processes of social control, or attitude change, in the social-psychological literature. Although

Preparation of this chapter was supported, in part, by Research Grants HD-MH-09814 from the National Institute of Child Health and Human Development and BNS-79-14118 from the National Science Foundation. The report was begun during the author's term as a Fellow at the Center for Advanced Study in the Behavioral Sciences, Stanford, California, and financial support for this Fellowship from National Science Foundation, Grant BNS-78-24671, and the Spencer Foundation is gratefully acknowledged. In preparing this chapter the author benefited greatly from conversations with John Condry, Tom Gilovich, and Eleanor Maccoby and from insightful and detailed comments graciously provided by Joan Grusec and Diane Ruble.

294

the basic distinction can be easily traced to some of the earliest experimental demonstrations in Kurt Lewin's group dynamics laboratory (e.g., Lewin, Lippitt, & White, 1939), the most analytic treatment of the issue arises in Kelman's (1958, 1961) discussion of three processes of attitude change: compliance, identification, and internalization. Although each process may produce apparent attitude change, Kelman suggested, the three may be distinguished by the range of subsequent situations in which the individual will voice, or behave in accord with, these same attitudes. In the case of "mere" compliance, the individual will voice a given value or opinion only when it is instrumentally relevant to do so, that is, when the individual expects to attain particular rewards or avoid particular punishments by adopting that specific attitude. In later situations in which the behavior is no longer seen as instrumental, however, the individual will be expected to respond quite differently. In the case of identification, attitude change and congruent behavior will persist so long as the agent of social influence whom the individual wishes to emulate remains salient to the person but will dissipate when the link between "source" and "action" is no longer obvious or salient. By contrast, internalized attitudes may be expected to influence behavior across a variety of situations, exerting effects on behavior and values that are independent of momentary changes in the instrumental value of the behavior or the salience of the source. Such attitudes, therefore, may influence behavior even when the individual is seemingly free from external surveillance or coercion.

Behavioral changes of the third category, of course, form the conceptual goal of the socialization process. Parents seek to promote children's acceptance of values and patterns of behavior that will lead them to behave in an appropriate manner not only at home, or under the watchful eyes of other adults, but also in other settings in which they alone are present to monitor and judge the appropriateness of their actions. Indeed, it is the shift from initially external forms of control to later internalized social-control mechanisms that is the hallmark of successful socialization (Aronfreed, 1968; Kohlberg, 1969, 1971; Maccoby, 1980).[1]

Internalization versus compliance: some theoretical considerations

A central implication of this analysis is that the conditions that may be optimal for producing compliance and immediate functional control over another's behavior may not be the same as those most likely to produce subsequent internalization. In fact, these two goals may sometimes stand in conflict. Both the use of unnecessarily powerful, functionally superfluous techniques of social control to produce compliance and the use of functionally inadequate social-control techniques that fail to produce initial compliance may frequently have long-term consequences contrary to the aims of the agent seeking to induce compliance. Let us consider the data relevant to such claims in terms of three interrelated classes of experimental paradigms: the effects of psychologically "insufficient," objectively insufficient, and psychologically "oversufficient" social-control attempts.

Psychologically "insufficient" justification

The term *insufficient justification* was initially presented within the cognitive dissonance tradition to describe the results obtained in studies of "forced compliance" (Festinger, 1957), which compared the effects of different levels of incentives, or threats, employed to induce compliance with a request to engage in some action that subjects would find initially unpleasant, aversive, or otherwise contrary to their personal attitudes (Aronson, 1966, 1969). The rubric included two basic paradigms yielding conceptually analogous results.

The first of these involved the basic paradigm first developed by Festinger and Carlsmith (1959), in which subjects were offered either quite minimal or substantially more attractive incentives to defend a position at variance with their prior attitudes. Here the basic dissonance prediction, and finding, was that subjects induced to engage in this counterattitudinal behavior in the face of rather minor external inducements were more likely to report subsequent attitudes in line with their public behavior than subjects induced to engage in this same behavior in the face of more desirable and salient external incentives. Subjects induced to behave in a manner inconsistent with their personal beliefs in the presence of psychologically "insufficient" justification for their actions, it was argued, would be motivated to provide further justification on their own for their attitude-discrepant behavior. One prime means of doing so, particularly under circumstances in which it would be difficult to "retract" one's overt actions, would be to revise their private attitudes to be more consistent with their public actions. By contrast, subjects induced to engage in the same actions in the presence of clearly sufficient and highly attractive incentives should find sufficient justification for their actions in these external pressures and consequently should have minimal motivation to change their initial attitudes. Over the years, a large number of studies consistent with this general model have been generated (cf. Fazio, Zanna, & Cooper, 1977; Wicklund & Brehm, 1976; Zanna & Cooper, 1976) and have made reasonably clear the conditions under which these "reverse incentive" effects are most likely to occur: conditions in which individuals consider themselves to have had free choice in engaging in the action and to be personally responsible for the consequences of that action (Calder, Ross, & Insko, 1973; Collins & Hoyt, 1972; Wicklund & Brehm, 1976).

The second basic "insufficient justification" paradigm examined the other side of the coin: the case in which the agent of influence is attempting to induce compliance with a request *not* to engage in an inherently unattractive or unpleasant activity. The initial prototypic study in this area, reported by Aronson and Carlsmith (1963), involved the "forbidden toy" procedure. In this study children were prohibited from playing with a particularly desirable toy under threat of either a relatively mild or a considerably more severe punishment for transgression. Again, the prediction was quite clear: Subjects complying with this request in the face of only rather minimal external pressure would be more likely to "internalize" this prohibition. They should express more negative attitudes toward the activity itself and should avoid the activity in later settings in which it was no longer explicitly prohibited. In this initial experiment, as well as a variety of further studies along these lines (e.g., Freedman, 1965; Lepper, 1973; Lepper, Zanna, & Abelson, 1970; Pepitone, McCauley, & Hammond, 1967; Zanna, Lepper, & Abelson, 1973), such effects were observed. Children who had initially resisted the temptation to engage in this desirable activity under mild threat proved more likely on later testing to express negative evaluations of the activity and to avoid engaging in the previously forbidden activity even in subsequent situations in which the prohibition was no longer in force. This effect appears reliable, robust, and reasonably durable over intervals of several weeks.

In both cases the data suggest an inverse relationship between the salience of the external pressures applied and the likelihood of subsequent attitude change congruent with the presumed intent of the agent of influence. The basic findings from these two paradigms are represented schematically by the *solid lines* on either side of Figure 1, where the two "X's" along the abscissa represent the hypothetical points at which the external pressures applied to induce the person either to engage in a particular action (on the far right-hand side of the figure) or to refrain from engaging in a particular action (on the far left-hand side of the figure) would be *just sufficient in a specific setting* to elicit compliance from the individual (or, in the experimental studies, from the entire group). Beyond this point, the model suggests, increases in the amount or salience of external pressure will result in less private attitude change, or internalization of the values or attitudes underlying the initial request –

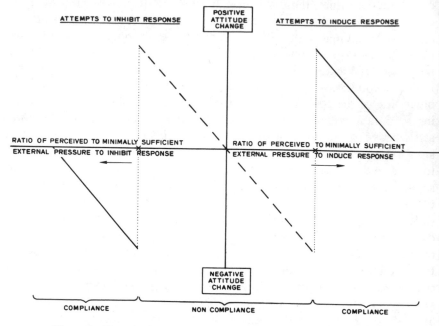

Figure 1. Hypothesized relationship between the salience of external pressures employed in an attempt to induce compliance, relative to the amount of pressure minimally sufficient to produce compliance, and resultant attitude change, as a function of actual compliance versus noncompliance. The right half of the figure refers to cases in which the goal of the influence attempt is to elicit a given response; the left half refers to cases in which the goal of influence is to suppress a given response. The dashed diagonal lines in the center of the figure represent the hypothesized relationship between external pressure and subsequent attitude change under conditions of objectively insufficient justification (i.e., in which the individual does not comply). The solid diagonal lines to the sides of the figure represent the hypothesized relationship between external pressure and subsequent attitude change under conditions of objectively sufficient, but psychologically "insufficient," justification (i.e., in which the individual does comply). The two points marked on the abscissa with "X's" represent the hypothetical points at which the external pressure applied in a particular case is just sufficient to produce actual compliance.

that is, less positive change in the case of induced action and less negative change in the case of induced restraint.[2]

Objectively insufficient justification

These effects of psychologically "insufficient" justifications, of sufficient objective power to produce actual compliance with the initial request, may be contrasted with the effects of social-influence attempts that are objectively insufficient – that is, that are not successful in producing initial compliance. For these cases, the model predicts quite opposite effects, illustrated schematically by the *dotted lines* in Figure 1. Here the more pressure one applies, without success, to induce initial compliance, the more likely that influence attempt is to have effects opposite to those intended, producing changes in attitudes (and presumably in related behaviors) in the other direction. Again, there are two basic cases: The first involves attempts to persuade an individual to engage in an activity he or she would not spontaneously approach, and the second attempts to dissuade the individual from engaging in an activity he or she would be likely to approach in the absence of external pressures. Again, there are some, although considerably fewer, experimental findings to support these theoretical contentions.

In this instance, the experiment best approximating the paradigmatic case represented in the inside left half of the figure – involving the effects of the introduction of external "costs" to engagement in an activity of initial interest to subjects – is well known, though perhaps not in this context. It is the early study by Aronson and Mills (1959) on the effects of severity of initiation on subsequent attitudes toward the group. In this experiment, subjects motivated to engage in a particular action (i.e., to join a particular group) find themselves faced with either relatively mild or considerably more substantial external pressures that would lead them not to undertake this action (i.e., the requirement that they undergo either a mild or a severe initiation in order to be able to join this group). Here, in contrast to the preceding studies, these external pressures are in both cases objectively insufficient to deter subjects, who proceed to undergo the initiation procedure and become members of the group. In this case, the effect of the presence of relatively more powerful or salient external pressures is, of course, to increase the inconsistency of subjects' actions. The result was the predicted enhancement of subjects' personal evaluations of the activity in the severe initiation condition relative to the mild initiation condition, a finding that is conceptually the opposite of that obtained when objectively sufficient, but psychologically "insufficient," external deterrents to action are employed. Although early discussions focused on methodological difficulties with this initial study, the basic finding appears to be replicable, even when the alleged deficiencies are corrected (e.g., Gerard & Mathewson, 1966).

Turning to the dotted line on the right half of Figure 1, by contrast, readers familiar with the early history of this research will notice a "missing cell": the case in which external incentives are employed to induce the person to engage in an activity that would otherwise be avoided, but in which the attempt is unsuccessful. Only recently has this remaining case received investigation in a study reported by Darley and Cooper (1972). Briefly, these authors attempted to induce students to engage in a counter-attitudinal behavior (i.e., writing an essay discrepant with their attitudes) through the offer of either a quite small or a relatively larger financial reward (i.e., 50 cents vs. $2.50). These inducements were offered in a context, however, in which all subjects refused to engage in the activity, choosing to forgo the proffered reward. Consistent with the analysis underlying the previous studies, these investigators found that subjects who had refused to comply with the request in the face of an external inducement to do so showed an adverse effect of this attempt to influence their behavior. Subjects' attitudes retreated from the position they had been asked to advocate and did so significantly more the greater the external incentive they had forgone by refusing to comply.

Certainly, the experimental evidence in this area is much more scanty than in the case of the classic "insufficient justification" paradigms. It seems sufficient to indicate, however, that increases in the external pressures employed to induce initial compliance have very different effects on later attitude change or internalization, as a function of whether the attempt to influence subjects' behavior is initially successful or unsuccessful.

These basic paradigms all derived initially from a cognitive dissonance model. Over the last decade, however, it has become clear that these findings could also be reinterpreted in terms of an attributional, or self-perception, framework (Bem, 1967, 1972; Kelley, 1967, 1973). In this model, the results just described are seen as the result of an attributional process in which subjects may be led to conceptualize their reasons for engaging, or refusing to engage, in a particular action in terms of either intrinsic versus extrinsic or endogeneous versus exogeneous motives (cf. Kruglanski, 1978; Lepper & Greene, 1978c).

To the extent, this reanalysis suggested, that the external constraints and incentives controlling one's actions are salient, unambiguous, and sufficient to explain those actions, the person will be likely to attribute those responses to these compelling external pressures. If, by contrast, the external contingencies and pressures in a particular setting are seen as weak, unclear, or psychologically "insufficient" to account for one's actions, the person will be likely to attribute those actions to personal attitudes, dispositions, or interests. Hence, under low justification conditions, subjects will be likely to view prior compliance as reflective of their own preferences, standards, or dispositions but noncompliance as a "natural" response to minimal external incentives. Under high justification conditions, however, subjects will be more likely to see prior compliance as a response to strong extrinsic constraints and pressures inherent in the situation but noncompliance as indicative of personal preferences and dispositions.

Psychologically "oversufficient" justification

Without entering the continuing debate concerning the relative merits of the dissonance and attribution accounts of these prior studies (cf., Fazio, Zanna, & Cooper, 1977; Greenwald 1975) it seems clear that this attributional account has had the important heuristic advantage of suggesting that conceptually analogous effects might be observed in a third set of cases, those involving the use of overly sufficient justification. As detailed elsewhere (Lepper, 1981; Lepper & Greene, 1978b, 1978c), this account suggested that the use of unnecessarily powerful or salient (i.e., functionally superfluous) extrinsic constraints might undermine subsequent intrinsic interest in the activity to which those constraints had been applied.

More specifically, in our own work, this analysis suggested the following hypothesis: If a child could be induced to view his or her engagement in an activity of initial intrinsic interest as an explicit means to some ulterior goal, the child's subsequent intrinsic interest in the activity, in the later absence of further extrinsic pressures or constraints, may be undermined by the prior imposition of salient, but functionally superfluous, extrinsic constraints. To emphasize the conceptual parallels between this hypothesis and the previous work considered earlier, we termed this proposition the *overjustification* hypothesis.

In our intitial paradigmatic study in this area (Lepper, Greene, & Nisbett, 1973) we sought to test this hypothesis in an ecologically representative classroom setting that provided an appropriate laboratory for assessing "intrinsic" interest behaviorally. To do so, we began by observing covertly (from behind a one-way mirror) children's approach to a particular experimental activity in their regular preschool classrooms during a series of explicitly designated "free-play" periods in which children were allowed and encouraged to choose freely from among some 30 or 40 available alternatives. We selected as subjects for our study only those children showing an initial interest in our target activity. These children were then seen in individual experimental sessions in a different setting and were asked to engage in this same activity under one of three conditions. Expected Award subjects were first shown a sample extrinsic reward – a "Good Player" certificate – and were asked if they would like to win such a prize. These subjects were then informed that to win this award they would have to engage in the target activity;

all these children agreed to undertake this activity in order to obtain the extrinsic reward. To control for the effects of the association of the activity with a reward and the receipt of a reward per se, Unexpected Award subjects were asked to engage in the activity without promise or mention of any tangible reward but subsequently received the same reward and feedback from the experimenter unexpectedly. Finally, children in a Control condition were simply asked to engage in the same activity without knowledge or receipt of any tangible reward. Several weeks later, children's intrinsic interest in the target activity was again observed in their classrooms under conditions in which subjects had no knowledge that their behavior was being monitored and no expectation of further extrinsic rewards or external pressures contingent upon task performance. In this setting, children who had previously undertaken the activity to obtain a reward showed significant decreases in intrinsic interest, relative both to their own behavior during the base-line period and the behavior of subjects in the other two conditions. The use of unnecessarily salient extrinsic incentives, it appeared, had undermined children's intrinsic interest in the activity per se.

Over the last five years these findings have received considerable experimental scrutiny, and a rather substantial body of research is now available that provides evidence concerning the conditions under which such detrimental effects are, and are not, likely to occur (Condry, 1977; Lepper, 1981; Lepper & Greene, 1978b). Briefly, there is a good deal of data to suggest that such effects depend to a large extent on whether the child perceives his or her actions as being extrinsically controlled (Lepper, 1981). Thus, detrimental effects appear likely to occur only when the child's actions can be reasonably seen as having been directed toward the attainment of some extrinsic goal – when the proffered rewards are, for example, expected in advance but not when they are unexpected (e.g., Enzle & Look, 1980; Lepper & Greene, 1975; Lepper, Greene, & Nisbett, 1973; Lepper, Sagotsky, & Greene, 1982a, 1982b; Smith, 1976) or when the rewards are contingent upon task engagement but not when task engagement is merely incidental to reward attainment (e.g., Ross, Karniol, & Rothstein, 1976; Swann & Pittman, 1977). Similarly, cognitive "set" manipulations that focus the subjects' attention on the instrumentality of their actions appear to enhance the probability that detrimental effects will be observed, whereas manipulations that focus subjects' attention on the inherent value of the activity even in the face of an expected reward appear to decrease the likelihood of such effects (Johnson, Greene, & Carroll, 1980; Pittman, Cooper, & Smith, 1977.)[3]

Adverse effects of superfluous extrinsic constraints on subsequent intrinsic interest, moreover, do not seem to depend upon the use of rewards per se but can also be shown to occur following the imposition of other forms of external constraint, such as unnecessarily close surveillance (e.g., Lepper & Greene, 1975; Pittman, Davey, Alafat, Wetherill, & Wirsul, 1980), expectation of external evaluation (Amabile, 1979; Maehr & Stallings, 1972), or functionally superfluous temporal deadlines (Amabile, DeJong, & Lepper, 1976). Indeed, even the imposition of a purely nominal contingency – for example, "You must do x, in order to be able to do y" – between two activities of equal and high initial intrinsic interest appears to decrease later interest in the activity presented as a "means" to obtaining a chance to play with the other (Lepper, Sagotsky, Dafoe, & Greene, 1982).

As with the preceding literatures on psychologically "insufficient" and objectively insufficient justification, however, these studies represent only one of two salient prototypes involving the use of overly sufficient external pressure: the case in which one is attempting to induce the subject to engage in a particular behavior. On theoretical grounds, of course, it should also be possible to observe detrimental effects of psychologically "oversufficient" justification in contexts in which one is attempting instead to prevent the person from engaging in a particular action or activity.

In contrast to the relatively large literature just described, this second possibility has received virtually no experimental attention. Only one study from our own laboratories seems to speak even obliquely to this issue (Lepper, 1973). In this study, our principal concern was with the potentially generalized effects of prior resistance to temptation, under either a mild or a severe threat of punishment for transgression, on later resistance to temptation in a quite different setting. This interest arose initially from anecdotal observations of a curious tendency for children who had undergone the mild threat procedure in the traditional "forbidden toy" paradigm outlined earlier to engage in overtly self-congratulatory or self-justificatory statements following the temptation period (i.e., to offer spontaneous comments on the fact that they had "been good" or had done "just what" the experimenter had asked them to do).

To investigate the possibility that such responses might reflect a process of self-justification that would have consequences for their behavior in a very different subsequent situation, we first exposed children to a version of the Aronson and Carlsmith (1963) procedure, in which they were prohibited from playing with a highly attractive toy under either mild or severe threat of punishment for transgression or, in a control condition, were not exposed to a temptation situation at all. When children's attitudes toward the previously forbidden toy were assessed following the temptation period, the standard finding of greater devaluation of the prohibited activity under mild threat conditions was replicated. To examine the more generalized effects of exposure to this procedure, however, these same children were also observed in a second experimental setting, several weeks later. This session took place in a different location and involved a different and ostensibly unrelated experimenter and a different set of activities. In this second session, the children were presented with a quite different, but traditional, measure of resistance to temptation. Specifically, they were asked to play a game in the experimenter's absence to see if they could attain a sufficiently high score to obtain their choice of a set of highly attractive prizes. The game, of course, was secretly preprogrammed so that all children would receive a score that fell slightly short of that needed to win a prize. The measure of interest in this second setting was the likelihood that children in the different conditions would falsify their scores so as to claim a prize. In contrast to the first experimental session, in which care was taken to ensure that all subjects would actually comply with the experimenter's prohibition, this second session was deliberately designed to provide a sufficiently attractive set of rewards and a sufficiently minimal probability of detection so that a substantial proportion of the subjects would actually transgress.

The study, therefore, allowed us to examine the effects of prior compliance with an adult prohibition, under either minimal or unnecessarily powerful and salient extrinsic pressures, on later compliance with a quite different prohibition in a functionally separate setting. The results, from the present perspective, were quite informative. Children who had previously resisted temptation in the face of only relatively mild extrinsic pressures proved significantly more likely than control subjects to resist temptation as well in this later dissociated context. Children who had initially resisted temptation in the face of overly powerful, and functionally superfluous, extrinsic pressures tended to show quite the opposite effect, that is, to be less likely than control subjects to resist temptation in this later different setting. Prior compliance in the face of sufficient, but relatively minimal, extrinsic pressures, in more general terms, seemed to increase subsequent internalization or private acceptance of the standards implicit in the adult's initial request; prior compliance in the face of more salient extrinsic pressures seemed to decrease later internalization.

These findings concerning the potential deleterious effects of the use of overly powerful social-control techniques on later intrinsic interest or internalization in the subsequent absence of further extrinsic constraints, however, suggest an extension of our initial model. Although the representation is not precisely accurate (e.g., if the action one wishes to induce is one that subjects would already display spontaneously in the absence of any external pressures, virtually any request should be sufficient to produce initial compliance),[4] this extension is illustrated – again, in highly schematic terms – in Figure 2. At least in terms of the experimental literature, this figure suggests that the use of either objectively insufficient or functionally superfluous and psychologically oversufficient social-control techniques may prove counterproductive. The use of objectively effective, but psychologically "insufficient," social-control procedures, on the other hand, appears likely to promote subsequent attitudes and behaviors that appear to reflect "internalization" of the values or standards underlying the initial social-influence attempt.

The minimal sufficiency principle: applications to socialization

These data, and the attributional model that underlies them, have potentially significant implications for our understanding of the socialization process and the ways in which different sorts of social-control techniques may influence the child's internalization of adult and societal values and standards of conduct. The following section will examine this argument in greater detail to explore both the possible strengths and the obvious deficiencies of such an analysis.

Clearly, the most straightforward derivation from this analysis is what I have termed elsewhere the *minimal sufficiency principle* of social control (Lepper, 1981). Techniques of social control that are successful in producing compliance, but are at the same time sufficiently subtle (rather than obviously coercive) to prevent the individual from viewing such compliance solely as a function of those extrinsic controls, will be most likely – other things being equal – to promote subsequent internalization. Figure 3 casts the present model in these broader terms and illustrates the parallels between attempts to induce and to inhibit response in terms of a common criterion of internalization. Here the ordinate has been reoriented so that "high" values in all cases represent change consistent with the aims of the social-influence attempt (i.e., more positive attitudes when the intent is to induce action, but more negative attitudes when the intent is to inhibit action).

The thesis, it should be noted, is purely relative. It does not lead one to expect that the use of overly powerful control techniques will always, or typically, produce adverse effects in any absolute sense. This model would not predict, for instance, that even the use of blatantly coercive social-control techniques to induce a child to learn to read or to play the

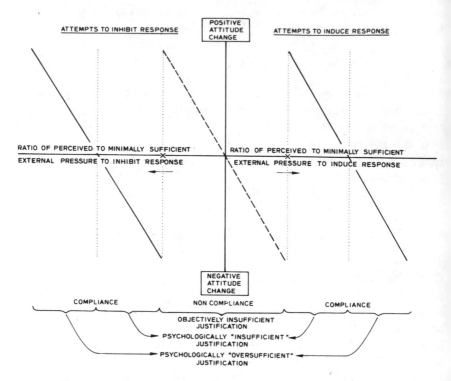

Figure 2. Hypothesized relationship between the salience of external pressures employed in an attempt to induce compliance, relative to the amount of pressure minimally sufficient to produce compliance, and resultant attitude change, under conditions of objectively insufficient justification, objectively sufficient, but psychologically "insufficient," justification, and psychologically "oversufficient" justification. The center of this figure is identical to Figure 1. The additional segments added to the extreme left and right of the figure represent the addition of the case of overly sufficient justification, in which the individual complies in the face of functionally superfluous and psychologically "oversufficient" external pressures.

piano would necessarily produce less interest in those activities than would have been the case had the child never attempted these activities. Other factors, such as the skills that children may acquire in the process of engaging in the activity itself or changes in children's perceptions of their own competence at the activity, will obviously also influence the absolute outcome of such a situation. The argument, more simply, is that *if* it were possible to elicit the same behavior from that child through the use of less salient or coercive techniques of control – that is, if the extrinsic pressures applied were truly unnecessarily powerful or salient – then those more subtle techniques of control would be expected to produce

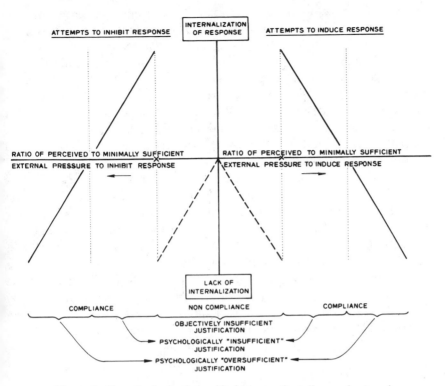

Figure 3. Hypothesized relationship between the salience of external pressures employed in an attempt to induce compliance, relative to the amount of pressure minimally sufficient to produce compliance, and subsequent internalization of the intent of the agent attempting to elicit compliance, under conditions of objectively insufficient justification, psychologically "insufficient," and psychologically "over-sufficient" justification. High values on the ordinate at any point in this figure represent changes in attitudes or behavior consistent with the initial intent of the social-influence attempt.

more subsequent interest in the activity in the later absence of further extrinsic pressures or constraints.[5]

Stated in terms of these broader issues of social control, it seems evident that this model ought to have some application to traditional concerns in developmental psychology regarding the nature of discipline and control techniques that promote or impede internalization of adult moral and social values. Equally evident, however, is the fact that there has been virtually no contact between these two streams of research. Before considering the implications of this analysis for the study of socialization more fully, it may be worth taking a moment to consider the sources of this relative insulation. In part, there seems to have been confusion among some developmental researchers concerning the quite different predictions one would make as a function of whether an influence attempt has been successful or not (e.g., Biaggio & Rodrigues, 1971). To a larger extent, however, this insulation also seems to stem from the fact that the particular experimental paradigms that have been most thoroughly studied are often quite far removed from their possible socialization analogues. Typically, these studies have employed highly complex and ecologically atypical experimental settings, have relied on attitudinal, rather than behavioral, measures of subsequent effects, and have focused on adult subject populations.

Moreover, in two cases, the studies presented earlier as illustrative examples clearly do not represent the most obvious or direct test of the specific hypotheses of interest to students of socialization. Instead, they involve the most clearly related paradigms to have received experimental investigation. In the case of the Aronson and Mills (1959) "severity of initiation" paradigm, for example, it is clear that subjects did not perceive the experimenter as desiring to inhibit them from engaging in an otherwise attractive activity. A much more direct test of the effects of objectively insufficient justification for response inhibition, therefore, might involve a study in which children were explicitly offered either a relatively small or a somewhat more substantial incentive not to engage in a particular activity, but in which the activity itself was sufficiently attractive so that neither incentive would be sufficient to induce the children to resist the temptation to engage in it. Similarly, the Lepper (1973) study does not represent the most obvious example of the use of oversufficient justification to inhibit a response. A more direct analogue to previous overjustification research, for the case in which one wishes to inhibit a particular response, might involve instead a comparison of the effects of mild versus severe threats of punishment for engaging in an activity that the child would already prefer to avoid. In both cases, the proposed analysis implies that the results of these more direct studies should be comparable to those obtained in the experiments discussed. Whether this is true is, of course, an empirical question. One function of this chapter is to indicate the sorts of data one might need to collect to support this argument. For the moment, however, let us accept these implicit assumptions in the model and consider its possible applicability to the study of socialization processes.

Applications to previous socialization research

Perhaps the most obvious previous literature to which the present analysis should be relevant is that concerning the effects of different types of parental disciplinary or social-control techniques on children's internalization of social and moral values, as indexed by their behavior and attitudes outside the home situation in which these control techniques were initially applied. The simpleminded prediction, from an attributional perspective, is that the use of unnecessarily powerful and salient techniques of control to produce compliance with parental demands at home should result in less internalization of the values underlying those demands. As a result, children should be less likely to behave in accord with those demands in other settings in which the child's behavior is no longer perceived to be under direct parental surveillance or control. An examination of the relevant socialization literature provides some evidence consistent with such a claim.

Consider first the elegant research on children's internalization of moral values that has been carried out over the last dozen years by Hoffman and his colleagues (Hoffman, 1970a, 1970b, 1975a, 1975b; Hoffman & Salzstein, 1967). In this work, Hoffman and his associates have distinguished three sorts of disciplinary techniques that parents might apply in training children to behave in socially or morally acceptable ways at home: power-assertion, love-withdrawal, and induction. Power-assertion includes physical punishment, deprivation of material objects or privileges, and other direct applications of force or authority. Love-withdrawal involves the use of techniques of social control that express parental disapproval or anger directly but nonphysically, such as ignoring, isolating, or stating a dislike for the child. Induction involves techniques in which the child is presented with explanations or reasons why the behavior is unacceptable, including procedures that make clear to children the consequences of their actions for others involved. The most general conclusion to emerge from the study of these different disciplinary practices (cf. Hoffman, 1970b) is that the use of highly controlling, power-assertive techniques appears to decrease subsequent internalization; whereas the use of more subtle and less punitive inductive techniques seems to promote later internalization. The effects of love-withdrawal techniques, representing a theoretically intermediate case, seem somewhat more varied, frequently showing no relationship to later internalization but sometimes showing small positive effects on subsequent attitudes or behavior in other settings.

Though obtained in a quite different and considerably more complex setting, these findings are consistent with the attributional model described here. Although these studies do not provide direct data on the ways in which children view these different sorts of control techniques, it is clear that there are several reasons why power-assertive techniques should be most likely, and inductive techniques least likely, to promote extrinsic attributions for compliance. First, it seems generally clear that social-influence attempts that rely on verbal persuasion will be less likely to provoke perceptions of constraint than influence attempts that rely upon more tangible and visible incentives or sanctions (Lepper, 1981). Second, inductive techniques frequently seem to imply a belief on the parent's part that the child would not have behaved, or want to behave, in an undesirable manner if the consequences of such actions or if the reasons underlying the rules and standards imposed were fully understood. Conversely, power-assertive techniques often appear to include explicit statements that indicate that the reason for complying with an adult request is to avoid arbitrary and external sanctions (e.g., "You'll do that because I told you to, and if you don't . . ."). Love-withdrawal techniques, by contrast, appear somewhat more variable along all these dimensions and therefore form a theoretically more ambiguous case. Hoffman's data, therefore, would support the conclusion that more direct, salient, and psychologically unambiguous techniques of control appear to produce less subsequent internalization of the standards and values they were initially designed to promote.[6]

A similar analysis might also be applied to the extensive observational studies conducted by Baumrind and her associates (1967, 1971a, 1972, 1973; Lamb & Baumrind, 1978) on the effects of different parenting styles on children's social responsibility, as indexed by their behavior outside the home situation in which these practices are implemented. To simplify, once again, a complex typology, Baumrind distinguished three parenting styles: authoritarian, authoritative, and permissive. In this analysis, the authoritarian parent "values obedience as a virtue and favors forceful, punitive measures to curb self will"; the permissive parent favors a strategy of few demands or restrictions on the child's behavior and believes the parent should "behave in an affirmative, acceptant, and benign manner"; whereas the authoritative parent "attempts to direct the child's activities in a rational, issue-oriented manner," generally employing firm, but fair and less overtly punitive, techniques of discipline (Baumrind, 1972). In terms of children's later social responsibility, the effects of these practices were clear: Children from authoritative homes showed significantly greater social responsibility than children from homes in which parents employed either authoritarian or permissive practices.

The difference between the effectiveness of authoritarian and authoritative practices, of course, conceptually parallels the results obtained by Hoffman on the relatively positive effects of inductive disciplinary techniques and the relatively adverse effects of power-assertive control techniques. In an attributional model, both are seen as reflective of the difference between the use of objectively sufficient and necessary techniques of control and the use of overly salient and psychologically "oversufficient" control techniques. The relative ineffectiveness of permissive parenting styles, by contrast, more closely resembles the case in which objectively insufficient social-control procedures are attempted, at least to the extent that these parents do have values and standards that they wish their children eventually to acquire. Again, these results are generally consistent with an attributional analysis.

These findings, and the results of other naturalistic studies suggesting that the use of unnecessarily powerful or salient social-control techniques may prove ultimately dysfunctional (e.g., Lytton, 1977; Sears, Maccoby, & Levin, 1957; Sears, Rau, & Alpert, 1965), provide evidence supporting the potential relevance of the proposed attributional analysis to traditional socialization research. At the same time, it is evident that the sorts of complex child-rearing patterns examined in these studies involve a considerable array of potentially significant differences in parental behavior. Indeed, it seems highly likely that the long-term effects of these patterns are the result of the joint operation of a number of conceptually differentiable processes (Hoffman, 1970b). Thus, the argument is not that the present analysis provides a comprehensive account of the effects observed in these naturalistic studies. Instead, the argument is simply that attributional processes may form one important class of factors that contribute to these effects.

To obtain more direct support for such an analysis, obviously, requires a return to a more experimental research approach in which potentially confounding factors can be held constant by experimental design. In part, the research reviewed earlier, at least in those cases where the possible socialization analogs are clear (e.g., Lepper, 1973), may serve this function. Let us consider, however, another line of recent experimental work that has examined the consequences of more direct manipulations designed to induce children to label their behavior either in terms of salient external pressures to which it was a response or as a reflection of internalized standards or attitudes.

Although this literature is quite recent, there are now several studies that suggest that inducing children to think about their actions in internalized, instead of external, terms may make it more likely that they will subsequently show behavior change in accord with the intent of the initial influence attempt in later situations in which those controls are no longer present. Dienstbier, Hillman, Lehnhoff, Hillman, and Valkenaar (1975), for example, showed that labeling a child's emotional reaction following an unavoidable transgression as either an indication of the child's upset at being caught or an indication of the child's upset at failing to do the assigned task properly led to significant differences in children's subsequent behavior in a later, comparable situation in which the possibility of detection of any transgression was eliminated. Labeling the child's previous response as a reaction to detection led to less subsequent internalization than labeling that prior response as an indication of an internalized reaction to transgression. In a similar vein, Grusec and her colleagues (Grusec, this volume; Grusec, Kuczynski, Rushton, and Simutis, 1978) have shown that providing children with a self-attribution for their altruistic behavior produced enhanced internalization and generalization of altruistic behavior to a different setting, compared to groups given no specific attributional set or given an external attribution for their behavior. Other studies of the effects of labeling the individual's behavior in internal terms (e.g., Kraut, 1973; Miller, Brickman, & Bolen, 1975; Perry, Perry, Bussey, English, & Arnold, 1980; Toner, Moore, & Emmons, 1980) suggest similar conclusions.

Taken together, these findings suggest that the effectiveness of different socialization techniques in producing later internalization of the standards and patterns of behavior parents are attempting to teach children may depend, in part, on the manner in which different social-control procedures affect children's perceptions of their reasons for having engaged in related actions or activities in the past.

Implications for further research

Perhaps the most general implication of this analysis is simply that the study of socialization processes may benefit substantially from a more direct focus on children's interpretation of social-control techniques applied to them and the attributions they make about their own behavior. To assess these processes more directly will require considerable ingenuity; indeed, some might argue that the task is inherently intractable (e.g. Nisbett & Wilson, 1977). More direct analyses of this sort may well reveal, however, attributional processes involved in the socialization process on many levels. As children mature, for example, it may become important not only whether they see their particular actions in internal versus external terms but also why they perceive their parents or others as attempting to control and modify their behavior. It may make a considerable difference whether the child views a particular request or prohibition as an arbitrary attempt to make the parent's own life easier or as a legitimate response dictated by the parent's perception of the child's own best interests. Such effects are likely to depend, moreover, on the impor tant developmental changes Damon (1977) has shown to occur in children's perceptions of adult authorities and the factors that legitimize their rules and requests. In addition to this general focus on children's interpretation of social-control techniques in the socialization context, however, there are a number of other, more specific issues that the present approach raises.

Escalation and de-escalation of social control. Consider, for example, the effects of a child's initial compliance or noncompliance with a particular request on the course of later attempts to induce the child to comply with the same or some similar request. Initial compliance, the present analysis suggests – unless the extrinsic pressures applied to induce that compliant response are overly powerful or salient – should make subsequent compliance along similar lines more probable. Conversely, initial noncompliance should make subsequent compliance with the same request less probable. Put in somewhat different terms, a successful attempt at social control should make the parent's subsequent task easier – that is, less pressure should be required on the next occasion to produce further compliance – whereas an unsuccessful attempt at control should make the parent's subsequent task harder – that is, even greater extrinsic pressures will be required to produce compliance with a further request of the same sort (cf. Mills, 1958).

Consistent with the first half of this analysis, that initial compliance breeds further compliance, are some of the data already described. Recall, for instance, the finding (Lepper, 1973) that children who initially resist temptation in the face of a relatively mild threat of punishment are more likely than control subjects to subsequently resist temptation in a different setting in the face of even less obvious external pressures. Additional support for this proposition can also be found in the social-psychological literature on what has been termed the *foot-in-the-door* effect (cf. DeJong, 1979). In these studies, with adult subjects, it has been repeatedly shown that inducing compliance, using minimal external pressure, with a small and seemingly trivial initial request may substantially enhance the probability that subjects will later comply with a much larger request along similar lines, even in a different context and from a different individual (e.g., Cann, Sherman, & Elkes, 1975; Freedman & Fraser, 1966; Pliner et al., 1974; Snyder & Cunningham, 1975; Uranowitz, 1975; Zuckerman, Lazzaro, & Waldgeir, 1979). Moreover, such effects are less likely to appear, as one would predict, when more powerful justifications are employed to produce initial compliance (Lepper, 1973; Uranowitz, 1975; Zuckerman, Lazzaro, & Waldgeir, 1979).

Much less attention has been devoted to the other side of this argument – that initial noncompliance may enhance resistance to further compliance – although the phenomenon is one of considerable relevance to the socialization context and illustrates clearly the fine line that parents continually walk. Examples of the basic effect are easy to generate. The parent approaches the child with a relatively simple request and the child refuses to comply; to press the issue and obtain compliance from the child, at this point, the parent will theoretically be forced to use significantly more powerful control techniques than would otherwise (i.e., in the absence of a prior refusal on the part of the child) have been sufficient to produce initial compliance. Experimental evidence concerning this predicted escalation of social coercion following the initial use of objectively insufficient external pressure is sparse (cf. Cann, Sherman, & Elkes, 1975; Snyder & Cunningham, 1975), but the process seems anecdotally familiar from naturalistic studies of children's obedience in the home (e.g., Minton, Kagan, & Levine, 1971; Patterson, in press) or at school (Landauer, Carlsmith, & Lepper, 1970). Clearly, however, this process deserves more systematic experimental attention.[7]

The exercise of subtle social control. In a related vein, a second general focus of the present analysis concerns the issue of how to achieve control over a child's behavior without leading the child to see such behavior as exclusively attributable to external forces – the study, in a sense, of the psychology of subtle social control. In an early analysis of the manner in which classic "insufficient justification" studies achieve this effect, Kelley (1967) has pointed to a number of typical strategies employed to this end by experimental social psychologists: the labeling of a subject's behavior as the consequence of a "free choice," the use of diffuse social pressures instead of tangible rewards and punishments, and so on. No doubt such techniques have their appropriate analogs in the social exchanges between parents and children. Mahoney (1974), for example, describes the use of a strategy for producing compliance by creating an "illusion of choice" (e.g., asking a child whether he wished to take his shower in the upstairs or the downstairs bathroom, presuming compliance in either case, rather than directly asking him to take a shower) that may be familiar to parents of many young children. One might expect, however, that the effectiveness of such explicitly manipulative procedures will diminish rapidly with their repeated use or with increased sophistication on the part of the child.

Perhaps more useful, and more significant, are strategies of social influence that involve providing children with increased levels of actual choice and control. Frequently, the introduction of even a small amount of actual choice into a request for compliance (e.g., allowing children to decide when, but not whether, to do their homework) may often produce a greater sense of internal control, without sacrificing parental goals, than an unadorned request permitting no latitude of discretion (Condry & Chambers, 1978; Lepper & Greene, 1978c). In related contexts, there is some evidence that a "suggestive" approach may prove more effective than a more explicitly "directive" approach in producing behavioral persistence and an internal locus of control (e.g., Bee, 1967; Condry & Chambers, 1978; Loeb, 1975; Maccoby, 1980, and this volume; Rainey, 1965). Similarly, modeling a desired response, as opposed to simply dictating it, may often prove to have more positive effects on subsequent indices of internalization (cf. Rosenhan, 1969). Indeed, a direct examination of relative perceptions of choice and control produced by exposure to adult models versus direct requests might well prove useful in understanding when modeling procedures are, and are not, likely to prove superior to comparable direct instructions (e.g., Grusec, et al., 1978; Lepper, 1981; Lepper, Sagotsky, & Mailer, 1975). Finally, the technique of offering to share a task with the child (e.g., to help in cleaning up the child's room) would seem most likely to minimize the child's perception of external constraint.[8]

Other strategies for inducing initial compliance but minimizing perceptions of external constraint are more complex. Lepper and Gilovich (1982), for example, examined the effects of one such strategy – the use of what they termed activity-oriented requests – as a means of enhancing children's later compliance to other adult demands. Activity-oriented requests involve attempts to structure a task the child is asked to undertake in ways designed to emphasize the attractiveness of the activity itself. Thus, one might attempt to enhance interest in the task of doing long-division problems by presenting them in a context of greater intrinsic interest – computing, for instance, the batting averages of the school's baseball team. Or, one might attempt to increase the attractiveness of a household clean-up job by presenting it to children as a detective game or as part of a race. To the extent that such techniques may effectively focus children's attention on the activity itself and not its instrumental value, the present analysis would predict enhanced compliance in subsequent situations among children exposed to such techniques for eliciting prior compliance in a different setting. Lepper and Gilovich (1982) found that children exposed to such activity-oriented requests were more willing to comply with later requests by a different adult than children in appropriate control conditions in which initial compliance was produced with comparable more direct requests.

These issues deserve further investigation in more naturalistic contexts as well. What are the strategies that particularly effective parents, or teachers, use to elicit compliance without producing resistance and perceptions of constraint? Studies of the techniques that superior teachers use to sustain the learning and practice of repetitious tasks necessary for the acquisition of basic academic skills (cf. Bruner, 1962, 1966) may provide other suggestions for further research. In an analogous vein, it would be of great interest to study further the social histories of Baumrind's (1971b) "harmonious" families, in which social control is apparent but is seldom the source of controversy or even discussion.

Explicit training in self-control techniques. As a final example of the potential implications of the present analysis, let us consider a quite different set of issues raised by recent work in the area of contingency management: research concerning techniques for supplanting initially powerful external contingency systems with self-imposed contingency systems (e.g., Drabman, Spitalnik, & O'Leary, 1973; Turkewitz, O'Leary, & Ironsmith, 1975).

Consider a paradigmatic demonstration by Turkewitz, O'Leary, and Ironsmith (1975). In this study, highly disruptive children attending a tutorial class were first placed under a traditional token economy – a systematic extrinsic reward system in which appropriate academic and social behavior earned the children tokens that could later be redeemed for attractive tangible rewards. Subsequently, this extrinsic reward system was gradually modified and withdrawn. Initially, the tokens children earned were made contingent upon their own self-evaluations, but only when those self-evaluations corresponded to evaluations of their behavior made by adult raters. Subsequently, this "accuracy of evaluation" contingency was gradually faded out until the children had complete control over their earning of rewards. Finally, the entire system of tangible rewards was gradually eliminated. The results, compared to findings obtained in previous research employing only the tangible token economy, suggested greater generalization of behavior change to a setting in which rewards were not contingent upon the target behaviors as a function of the introduction of this training program.

Although generated, quite obviously, within a very different theoretical framework, research along these lines seems also consistent with the general analysis presented in this chapter. Indeed, the parallels with our own work on the potential detrimental effects of unnecessarily powerful extrinsic incentives on subsequent intrinsic interest is illustrated by findings in our own laboratories (Lepper, Sagotsky, & Greene, 1982b) and elsewhere (Brownell, Colletti, Ersner-Hershfield, Hershfield, & Wilson, 1977; Enzle & Look, 1980; Weiner & Dubanoski, 1975) that suggest that providing children with some measure of control over the application of an extrinsic contingency system to their own behavior will result in greater maintenance of later intrinsic interest.

Again, there are a large number of interesting questions yet to be explored. In a sense, one might view this applied work as an attempt to program and explictly accelerate the "normal" developmental shift from a reliance on external constraints and criteria of evaluation to self-imposed standards and self-generated evaluations that will later affect one's behavior even in the absence of further external surveillance or extrinsic pressures. The introduction of more "cognitive" manipulations into such a procedure in an attempt to enhance the generalization of behavior changes obtained even further would appear a rich field for additional study.

Limitations of the present model

The foregoing speculations indicate some of the directions in which an attributional analysis might have implications for traditional issues in the study of socialization. It is equally important to be clear, however, about some of the more evident limitations of the present analysis.

Specific versus general concepts of internalization. In the first place, as emphasized throughout this chapter, an attributional analysis does not pretend to provide a complete account of the processes that contribute to children's internalization of social standards and values. To make this point more salient, however, it is important to recognize the difference between the "internalization" of specific attitudes or responses in the sense used in the present chapter and "internalization" in the broader sense of the development of a coherent and interrelated set of values and principles (cf. Kohlberg, 1969, 1971). Certainly the model presented in this chapter does not provide an analysis of the long-term developmental processes by which children do come to develop consistent value systems and moral ideologies. There can be no doubt, for example, that there is more to the use of inductive disciplinary techniques than the absence of salient coercion and constraint. Providing the child with information about, and drawing attention to, the consequences of one's actions for other persons and to issues of fairness, justice, or consideration must, in and of itself, have important effects on the child's attitudes and later behavior. The use of power-assertive techniques, likewise, involves a number of potentially significant components: the provision of parental models of aggression and the arousal of strong emotional reactions, in addition to feelings of external control. The present thesis is simply that other factors, particularly children's attributions concerning the reasons for their actions, may also contribute to the relative effectiveness or ineffectiveness of such techniques.

Reward versus punishment. Similarly, for purposes of exposition, the present analysis has emphasized the parallels between the effects of promise of reward and threat of punishment, as well as the parallels between attempts to induce a child to display a particular pattern of behavior and attempts to prevent a child from displaying a particular response. In so doing, it has glossed over some potentially significant differences between these different techniques and goals of social control (cf. Lepper, 1981). One might argue, for instance, that situations involving attempts to instigate a particular response are inherently more complex than situations involving attempts to inhibit a particular response. Inevitably, the former case entails a variety of issues concerning the nature, intensity, and frequency of the response produced that often do not arise in the latter case. In like fashion, one can easily point to a number of differences generally associated with the use of rewards versus punishments: the affective tone of the interaction, the social models provided, or the extent to which children are provided with information concerning their relative competence. Probably there are important differences, as well, in the contexts in which each of these forms of social control is likely to be used (cf. Lewin, 1935). Nor has this chapter provided a detailed analysis of the factors that are likely to produce attributions of behavior to either intrinsic or extrinisc sources, although it seems likely that there are important differences in the conditions under which the use of rewards and the use of punishment will be likely to produce attributions of control or constraint. In any more complete analysis, such differences would require further attention (cf. Lepper, 1981; Lepper & Greene, 1978).[9]

The reciprocality of social interactions. A third simplifying assumption inherent in the present chapter involves a focus on the effects of parental practices on the child and a relative inattention to the effects of the child's behavior on the parent. Although one might argue that such a focus is not without justification (cf. Hoffman, 1975b), it is evident that the reciprocal and interactive nature of social exchanges between parent and child requires further consideration (Bandura, 1978; Bell, 1968).

Consider the definition of a child's response to an adult request or demand as either compliant or noncompliant. In this chapter I have treated the distinction as self-evident; but, in many cases, the seeming simplicity of this judgment may be misleading. Often, the definition of whether a child has satisfactorily complied with a request (e.g., to practice the piano or to clean one's room) will involve more complex decisions about what constitutes "substantial compliance." Does pushing everything under the bed or into the closet constitute cleaning up one's room? Can a board game in progress be left on the floor? And so forth. The answer to questions of this sort may depend not only on the parent's initial intentions and goals but also on a complex and interactive process of negotiation and compromise between parent and child – a process that will clearly have important consequences for the child's feelings and perceptions of personal control and external constraint.

Perhaps more important, this chapter has touched only briefly – in terms of the escalation and de-escalation of social controls – on the ways in which previous patterns of interaction between parents and children may have a persistent influence on the nature of the social-control techniques that will prove sufficient to obtain initial compliance from the child. Presumably, the hypothetical level of external pressure that will be minimally sufficient to induce compliance will vary, across families and across situations within a family unit, as a function of a number of obvious individual and situational variables. These factors would include chronic or temperamental differences in children's general willingness to comply with parental requests, the child's mood at the time of the request, the inherent attractiveness or aversiveness of the behavior requested of the child, and the salient alternatives to compliance at that time, as well as the child's expectations concerning the immediate consequences of compliance versus noncompliance. It may also vary, however, as a function of the general emotional relationship between parent and child. Maccoby (1980, and this volume) and others (Matas, Arend, & Sroufe, 1978) suggest that an early history of secure attachment and positive interaction in the first years of life may make it more likely that he child will later comply more readily with parental requests in the face of relatively minimal external pressures. The presence and strength of early affective bonds, in this view, may predispose families toward entry into longer-term patterns either of relatively harmonious social interactions or of cycles of escalating mutual coercion.

The role of identification. This last possibility brings us to the final, and perhaps most significant, limitation of the present analysis. In essence, his chapter has ignored the role of "identification" – the third of Kelman's (1958) processes of attitude change and the subject of an enormous amount of developmental research (e.g., Bronfenbrenner, 1960; Hoffman, 1971; Kagan, 1958) – and has focused instead on the two "extreme" cases of compliance versus internalization. The present approach, therefore, deals only tangentially with issues of the relative effectiveness of different techniques of social control as a function of the broader context of the affective atmosphere of the home and the history of interaction patterns in the family.

There is also, however, a second important limitation posed by our lack of attention to processes of identification. Even within the more limited realm of experimental research considered in this chapter, one cannot ignore the fact that social-control attempts typically carry implications about the evaluation placed upon the behaviors in question by the socializing agent. To take a simple example from our own research concerned with the conditions under which the use of superfluous extrinsic rewards can be shown to produce decrements in subsequent intrinsic interest (Lepper, Sagotsky, & Greene, 1982a), we have found that the consequences of exposure to a systematic reinforcement program will appear to be quite different as a function of the setting in which the child's subsequent behavior is observed. In this study, we observed the behavior of children who had been previously exposed to a differential-reward system or to a variety of nondifferential-reward or control procedures in two subsequent settings after the reward system had been withdrawn. When children's behavior was observed unobtrusively in their regular classrooms, without their knowledge that their responses were being monitored and in the absence of further social pressures, significant decreases in intrinsic interest in the previously rewarded activity were observed for subjects in the differential-reward condition. When these same children were observed instead in an experimental context in which they knew that their responses were being observed (and in which we had independent evidence that the children perceived that differential social demands were associated with the target activity), they showed higher levels of engagement in the activity for which they had previously been rewarded.[10]

The present analysis, then, is incomplete in a number of important respects. The point of presenting it, despite these difficulties, is to suggest both the directions in which further research would need to go to refine this general analysis and some of the potential heuristic benefits of such an approach to the study of the socialization process.

Internalization as a criterion of socialization: a postscript

To extend this final point one step further, it may be useful to close this chapter with a brief consideration of some potential developmental and societal limitations to the general concept of internalization as a hallmark of successful socialization. The basic argument, simply stated, is that there may be contexts in which issues of internalization, in both the narrow and the broad senses in which we typically use them, are potentially irrelevant.

This is perhaps most obvious when one thinks about internalization in the more specific sense – the internalization of specific values, goals, or prohibitions. Many tasks that parents set for children, whether for the benefit of parent or child, are inherently dull and boring; and in no sense is the parent's goal to induce the child to enjoy or cherish the task. The child need not learn to love mowing the lawn; it is simply a task that requires doing periodically. In such cases, mere compliance is satisfactory; immediate functional control over the child's behavior is quite sufficient.

These sorts of issues become considerably more interesting, however, when one considers internalization in the broader sense. Implicit in the central role we typically assign to internalization as a criterion for evaluating the effectiveness of the socialization process are two basic presuppositions. The first is that children will frequently be exposed to different, and often conflicting, attitudes, values, or patterns of behavior in different situations and in their interactions with different individuals. We tend to think of internalized values and standards as serving the function, in short, of maintaining particular patterns of response in the face of conflicting social pressures and examples. Perhaps more important, we also implicitly presume that children will often be faced with situations and contexts in which they are not under the direct or immediate control of adult socializing agents or the larger society in which they live. Were this not the case – were a parent, or a policeman, constantly by the child's side – our concern with the child's personal acceptance of parental or societal standards would surely be lessened. Indeed, it is precisely this distinction that is illuminated by much of the experimental work discussed in this chapter. Systems of social control that may be perfectly sufficient to control children's behavior within the settings in which the system is operative do not necessarily produce comparable effects, and may produce opposite effects, on behavior in other settings in which those controls are no longer functional (Lepper & Greene, 1978a, 1978b).

In our own culture, of course, it is easy to document the applicability of both these presuppositions. A central focus on the processes that underlie internalization of social and moral values seems highly appropriate. Similar considerations should also apply to other complex and pluralistic societies. The question of interest, however, concerns the applicability of such an analyis to contexts in which these conditions are not met or are at least less important.

To dramatize the case, imagine a society in which children (or adults, for that matter) are under constant "surveillance" and rarely, if ever, face situations in which they believe they could violate societal standards without detection and retribution. Under such circumstances, a student of socialization might be considerably less interested in the process of internalization than in the process by which surveillance and functional control are maintained. Of course, there are no societies in which this is completely true; some, however, may approximate this template more than our own society does. On the one hand, one might consider small and reasonably self-sufficient societies in which each member is known to all other members of the society and in which the behavior of any member is the joint concern of the entire community (cf. Gadlin, 1978; Morgan, 1956; Whiting & Whiting, 1975). On the other, one can imagine more complex and industrialized societies – perhaps the Soviet Union or the People's Republic of China (Bronfenbrenner, 1970; Kessen, 1975) would be examples – in which relatively more pervasive systems of institutional control and mutual monitoring are employed to maintain a generally accepted ideological structure. In such contexts, it might be the case that the use of social-control techniques hypothesized to promote internalization – even if the principles underlying the present analysis were entirely general – would prove less important than the use of techniques that would promote identification with shared societal values or simple compliance with those values in the face of continued external surveillance and control.[11]

Similar issues may also be relevant in considering potential differences in the effectiveness of different socialization techniques at different ages within a given culture. There is, for example, some experimental evidence to suggest that harsh physical punishment for transgressions by 2-year-olds in our own society may have positive rather than negative effects on the "internalization" of self-control (cf. Lytton, 1977; Lytton & Zwirner, 1975). Such findings contrast sharply with the results of studies with older children considered earlier. Such differential effects of disciplinary techniques as a function of the age of the child, however, make some sense if one considers the fact that the average 2-year-old both spends very little time in settings outside the surveillance and control of adult socializing agents and may lack the cognitive capacity to distinguish clearly between settings in which it is possible to "get away" with something without being caught and those in which detection is unavoidable (cf. Piaget, 1932; Solidus 1965).

The important point, in both these cases, is that the relevance of internalization as a criterion of socialization may vary as a function of the larger social and societal context in which we can observe the effects of different socialization techniques. One cannot sensibly examine questions concerning the potential differential effects of different socialization techniques without attention to the cultural context in which those techniques are employed.

Notes

1 This proposed analogy between the processes that underlie attitude change with adults in a short-term persuasive communication context and the processes that may underlie the formation and internalization of more general social values and patterns of behavior in the context of parent–child relationships entails a number of assumptions regarding the continuity of social-influence processes across large differences in the scale of interventions, outcomes, and social relationships involved. A number of these issues will be considered more fully in later sections of this chapter.

2 Several comments may be helpful in understanding this figure and those following. First, it should be noted that the abscissa involves an inherently relative scale in which the perceived sufficiency of external pressures is assumed to depend both on the salience and amount of external pressure actually applied and the amount of external pressure that would have been necessary, in that situation, to produce the response that one is attempting to elicit or suppress. Thus, the points at which the external pressure applied will be just barely sufficient to produce compliance – i.e., the two points indicated as "X's" in Figure 1 – will have different absolute values as a function of the inherent aversiveness or attractiveness of the response requested of the person in that setting. Finally, the diagonal lines used to represent the relationship between external pressure and attitude change are intended to represent only monotonic (and not necessarily linear) relationships between these two variables.

3 Even the use of expected and contingent tangible rewards in such contexts, however, will not always lead to decreases in later intrinsic interest. Of perhaps greatest interest, "performance-contingent" rewards (i.e., rewards presented as contingent upon some specifiable standard of excellence of performance, in either absolute or relative terms) frequently appear less likely to undermine subsequent intrinsic interest than "task-contingent" rewards (i.e., rewards that are presented as contingent upon task engagement per se) (cf. Boggiano & Ruble, 1979; Karniol & Ross, 1977). More detailed discussions of this distinction and other limiting conditions of this phenomenon appear elsewhere (Lepper, 1981; Lepper & Gilovich, 1981; Lepper & Greene, 1978b).

4 Again, it should be emphasized that the definition of any particular set of extrinsic pressures as either objectively insufficient, psychologically "insufficient," or psychologically "oversufficient" will depend upon the response being requested. Figure 2 is presented in its current form, however, to illustrate the relevance of these three cases under conditions in which the agent of influence wishes to induce a response or to inhibit a response. Prototypic examples of the six different possibilities delineated by the vertical lines in Figure 2 would include, from the far left to the far right, Lepper (1973), Aronson and Carlsmith (1963), Aronson and Mills (1959), Darley and Cooper (1972), Festinger and Carlsmith (1959), and Lepper, Greene, and Nisbett (1973). As indicated in the text, however, neither the Aronson and Mills (1959) nor the Lepper (1973) study provides the most direct tests that might be designed to evaluate the present model.

5 Although these issues have received attention primarily with regard to the literature concerned with the effects of oversufficient justification, it should be clear that these same considerations, and accompanying *ceteris paribus* assumptions, apply in principle to

all the experimental paradigms discussed. Note, however, that there may be some inherent asymmetry between cases in which an attempt is made to induce a response and cases in which an attempt is made to prohibit a response. Inducing the child to engage in a particular activity, in particular, seems much more likely to introduce additional variables – e.g., potential differences in the nature of task performance, the acquisition of further skills, increased familiarity with the task, or changes in perceptions of personal competence or incompetence at the task – than prohibiting the child from engaging in a particular activity.

6 Two additional points regarding Hoffman's analysis should be noted. First, it should be made clear that any discussion of distinctive disciplinary styles represents a considerable simplification of a complicated topic. Not only is the categorization itself complex. There is, in addition, considerable evidence that parental practices are neither as simple nor as well differentiated as a straightforward reading of this typology might suggest (cf. Clifford, 1959; Grusec & Kuczynski, 1977; Hoffman, 1970b, 1971). Virtually all parents make some use of each of these techniques in particular situations and display different reactions to different classes of transgressions. Similarly, parents often use multiple techniques simultaneously in response to particular problematic behaviors. Differences across families, then, are clearly a matter of degree. Second, it should also be noted that these data on parental uses of different disciplinary techniques have typically been obtained in a context in which a transgression has already occured. Thus, the present analysis rests, in part, on the assumption that the techniques used by parents to attempt to induce compliance will be closely related to the techniques they employ in response to transgression or noncompliance.

7 Again, it should be made clear that the present argument is not that attributional processes are the only important determinants of the escalation and de-escalation of social-control exchanges. In many cases, depending upon the nature of the outcomes experienced by the parties involved, a straightforward reinforcement account can also be offered to explain such effects. Teasing apart these two possibilities would require analysis on a much more specific, and molecular, level.

8 Although I have attempted to distinguish here between techniques that involve enhancing "actual control" from those involving the production of a mere "illusion of control," it should be clear that this distinction will often be a matter of degree. Even differences between suggestive and directive techniques or between modeling and direct instruction may be "illusory" in the sense that equivalent levels of initial compliance would be obtained in both cases. On the other hand, the provision of seemingly minor choices to children may make a substantial difference in the extent to which they will actually find the activity aversive.

9 Other additional complexities are also likely. Presumably, in a long-term sense, it should make a considerable difference whether the parent's behavior, and use of incentives and sanctions, is consistent or inconsistent across time and situations. It would not be surprising, moreover, if consistency of response proved to be correlated with characteristics of persons or situations that would lead to a reliance on rewards versus punishments.

10 This, of course, is one major reason why one would not wish to draw conclusions concerning internalization from subsequent behavior exhibited in the same situation (e.g., the home or the classroom) in which tangible rewards and punishments were previously administered, unless one could independently demonstrate that the child no longer expected the target behavior to be instrumental in gaining either further tangible rewards or continued social reinforcement and approval.

11 It would be easy, and inappropriate, to overstate the point being made here. The claim is not that internalization will not occur in other cultures that differ along these dimen-

sions or that the examples cited are even close approximations to some hypothetical society in which dissent is nonexistent and surveillance ubiquitous. It is, rather, that the structure of our society makes issues of internalized controls over action particularly important in determining the individual's conduct in the face of frequent exposure to conflicting pressures and relatively ineffective sanctions for promoting compliance with societal standards. In the same sense, this analysis should make clear the relative irrelevance, within our own society, of the present approach to issues concerning the child's adoption of nearly universal social conventions (e.g., eating with utensils) that do not arouse salient conflicts–either between the individual's selfish interests and the interests of society or among different members or groups within the society.

References

Amabile, T. M. Effects of external evaluation on artistic creativity. *Journal of Personality and Social Psychology*, 1979, *37*, 221–233.

Amabile, T. M., DeJong, W., & Lepper, M. R. Effects of externally-imposed deadlines on subsequent intrinsic motivation. *Journal of Personality and Social Psychology*, 1976, *34*, 92–98.

Aronfreed, J. *Conduct and conscience: The socialization of internalized control over behavior.* New York: Academic Press, 1968.

Aronson, E. The psychology of insufficient justification: An analysis of some conflicting data. In S. Feldman (Ed.), *Cognitive consistency.* New York: Academic Press, 1966.

Aronson, E. The theory of cognitive dissonance: A current perspective. In L. Berkowitz (Ed.), *Advances in experimental social psychology* (Vol. 4). New York: Academic Press, 1969.

Aronson, E., & Carlsmith, J. M. The effect of the severity of threat on the devaluation of forbidden behavior. *Journal of Abnormal and Social Psychology*, 1963, *66*, 584–588.

Aronson, E., & Mills, J. The effects of severity of initiation on liking for a group. *Journal of Abnormal and Social Psychology* 1959, *59*, 177–181.

Bandura, A. The self-system in reciprocal determinism. *American Psychologist*, 1978, *33*, 344–358.

Baumrind, D. Child care practices anteceding three patterns of preschool behavior. *Genetic Psychology Monographs*, 1967, *75*, 43–88.

Baumrind, D. Current patterns of parental authority. *Developmental Psychology Monographs*, 1971, *4* (1, Pt. 2):1–103. (a)

Baumrind, D. Harmonious parents and their preschool children. *Developmental Psychology*, 1971, *4*, 99–102. (b)

Baumrind, D. From each according to her ability. *School Review*, 1972, *80*, 161–197.

Baumrind, D. The development of instrumental competence through socialization. In A. D. Pick (Ed.), *Minnesota Symposium on Child Psychology* (Vol. 7). Minneapolis: University of Minnesota Press, 1973.

Bee, H. Parent-child interaction and distractibility in nine-year-old children. *Merrill-Palmer Quarterly of Behavior and Development*, 1967, *13*, 175–190.

Bell, R. Q. A reinterpretation of the direction of effects in studies of socialization. *Psychological Review*, 1968, *75*, 81–95.

Bem, D. J. Self-perception: An alternative interpretation of cognitive dissonance phenomena. *Psychological Review*, 1967, *74*, 183–200.

Bem, D. J. Self-perception theory. In L. Berkowitz (Ed.), *Advances in experimental social psychology* (Vol. 6). New York: Academic Press, 1972.

Biaggio, A., & Rodrigues, A. Behavioral compliance and devaluation of the forbidden object as a function of probability of detection and severity of threat. *Developmental Psychology*, 1971, *4*, 320–323.

Boggiano, A. K., & Ruble, D. N. Competence and the overjustification effect: A developmental study. *Journal of Personality and Social Psychology*, 1979, *37*, 1462–1468.

Bronfenbrenner, U. Freudian theories of identification and their derivatives. *Child Development*, 1960, *31*, 15–40.

Bronfenbrenner, U. *Two worlds of childhood: U.S. and U.S.S.R.* New York: Basic Books, 1970.

Brownell, K., Colletti, G., Ersner-Hershfield, R., Hershfield, S. M., & Wilson, G. T. Self-control in school children: Stringency and leniency in self-determined and externally-imposed performance standards. *Behavior Therapy*, 1977, *8*, 442–455.

Bruner, J. S. *On knowing: Essays for the left hand.* Cambridge, Mass.: Harvard University Press, 1962.

Bruner, J. S. *Toward a theory of instruction.* Cambridge, Mass.: Harvard University Press, 1966.

Calder, B.J., Ross, M., & Insko, C. A. Attitude change and attitude attribution: Effects of incentive, choice, and consequences. *Journal of Personality and Social Psychology*, 1973, *25*, 84–89.

Cann, A., Sherman, S. J., & Elkes, R. Effects of initial request size and timing of a second request on compliance: The foot in the door and the door in the face. *Journal of Personality and Social Psychology*, 1975, *32*, 774–782.

Clifford, E. Discipline in the home: A controlled observational study of parental practices. *Journal of Genetic Psychology*, 1959, *95*, 45–82.

Collins, B. E., & Hoyt, M. F. Personal responsibility-for-consequences: An integration and extension of the "forced compliance" literature. *Journal of Experimental Social Psychology*, 1972, *8*, 558–593.

Condry, J. C. Enemies of exploration: Self-initiated versus other-initiated learning. *Journal of Personality and Social Psychology*, 1977, *35*, 459–477.

Condry, J., & Chambers, J. Intrinsic motivation and the process of learning. In M. R. Lepper & D. Greene (Eds.), *The hidden costs of reward.* Hillsdale, N.J.: Erlbaum, 1978.

Damon, W. *The social world of the child.* San Francisco: Jossey-Bass, 1977.

Darley, S. A., & Cooper, J. Cognitive consequences of forced noncompliance. *Journal of Personality and Social Psychology*, 1972, *24*, 321–326.

DeJong, W. An examination of self-perception mediation of the foot-in-the-door effect. *Journal of Personality and Social Psychology*, 1979, *37*, 2221–2239.

Dienstbier, R. A., Hillman, D., Lehnhoff, J., Hillman, J., & Valkenaar, M. C. An emotion-attribution approach to moral behavior: Interfacing cognitive and avoidance theories of moral development. *Psychological Review*, 1975, *82*, 229–315.

Drabman, R. S. Spitalnik, R., & O'Leary, K. D. Teaching self-control to disruptive children. *Journal of Abnormal Psychology*, 1973, *82*, 10–16.

Enzle, M. E., & Look, S. C. *Self versus other reward administration and the overjustification effect.* Unpublished manuscript, University of Alberta, 1980.

Fazio, R. H., Zanna, M. P., & Cooper, J. Dissonance vs. self-perception: An integrative view of each theory's proper domain of application. *Journal of Experimental Social Psychology*, 1977, *5*, 464–479.

Festinger, L. *A theory of cognitive dissonance.* Stanford, Calif.: Stanford University Press, 1957.

Festinger, L., & Carlsmith, J. M. Cognitive consequences of forced compliance. *Journal of Abnormal and Social Psychology*, 1959, *58*, 203–210.

Freedman, J. L. Long-term behavioral effects of cognitive dissonance. *Journal of Experimental Social Psychology*, 1965, *1*, 145–155.

Freedman, J. L., & Fraser, S. C. Compliance without pressure: The foot-in-the-door technique. *Journal of Personality and Social Psychology*, 1966, *4*, 195–202.

Gadlin, H. Child discipline and the pursuit of self: An historical interpretation. In H. W. Reese & L. P. Lipsitt (Eds.), *Advances in child development and behavior* (Vol. 12). New York: Academic Press, 1978.

Gerard, H. B., & Mathewson, G. C. The effects of severity of initiation on liking for a group: A replication. *Journal of Experimental Social Psychology*, 1966, *2*, 278–287.

Greenwald, A. G. On the inconclusiveness of "crucial" cognitive tests of dissonance versus self-perception theories. *Journal of Experimental Social Psychology*, 1975, *11*, 490–499.

Grusec, J. E., & Kuczynski, L. Teaching children to punish themselves and effects on subsequent compliance. *Child Development*, 1977, *48*, 1296–1300.

Grusec, J. E., Kuczynski, L., Rushton, J. P., & Simutis, Z. M. Modeling, direct instruction, and attributions: Effects on altruism. *Developmental Psychology*, 1978, *14*, 51–57.

Hoffman, M. L. Conscience, personality, and socialization techniques. *Human Development*, 1970, *13*, 90–126. (a)

Hoffman, M. L. Moral development. In P. H. Mussen (Ed.), *Carmichael's manual of child psychology* (Vol. 2). New York: Wiley, 1970. (b)

Hoffman, M. L. Identification and conscience development. *Child Development*, 1971, *42* 1071–1082.

Hoffman, M. L. Altruistic behavior and the parent–child relationship. *Journal of Personality and Social Psychology*, 1975, *31*, 937–943. (a)

Hoffman, M. L. Moral internalization, parental power, and the nature of parent–child interaction. *Developmental Psychology*, 1975, *11*, 228–239. (b)

Hoffman, M. L., & Saltzstein, H. D. Parent discipline and the child's moral development. *Journal of Personality and Social Psychology*, 1967, *5*, 45–57.

Johnson, E. J., Greene, D., & Carroll, J. S. *Overjustification and reasons: A test of the means–ends analysis.* Unpublished manuscript, Carnegie-Mellon University, 1980.

Kagen, J. The concept of identification. *Psychological Review*, 1958, *65*, 296–305.

Karniol, R., & Ross, M. The effect of performance-relevant and performance-irrelevant rewards on children's intrinsic motivation. *Child Development*, 1977, *48*, 482–487.

Kelley, H. H. Attribution theory in social psychology. In D. Levine (Ed.), *Nebraska Symposium on Motivation* (Vol. 15). Lincoln: University of Nebraska Press, 1967.

Kelley, H. H. The processes of causal attribution. *American Psychologist*, 1973, *28*, 107–128.

Kelman, H. C. Compliance, identification, and internalization: Three processes of opinion change. *Journal of Conflict Resolution*, 1958, *2*, 51–60.

Kelman, H. C. Processes of attitude change. *Public Opinion Quarterly*, 1961, *25*, 57–78.

Kessen, W. (Ed.) *Childhood in China.* New Haven, Conn.: Yale University Press, 1975.

Kohlberg, L. Stage and sequence: The cognitive-developmental approach to socialization. In D. A. Goslin (Ed.), *Handbook of socialization theory and research*. Chicago: Rand McNally, 1969.

Kohlberg, L. From is to ought: How to commit the naturalistic fallacy and get away with it in the study of moral development. In T. Mischel (Ed.), *Cognitive development and epistemology*. New York: Academic Press, 1971.

Kraut, R. Effects of social labeling on giving to charity. *Journal of Experimental Social Psychology*, 1973, *9*, 551–562.

Kruglanski, A. W. Endogenous attribution and intrinsic motivation. In M. R. Lepper & D. Greene (Eds.), *The hidden costs of reward*. Hillsdale, N.J.: Erlbaum, 1978.

Lamb, M. E., & Baumrind, D. Socialization and personality development in the preschool years. In M. E. Lamb (Ed.), *Social and personality development.* New York: Holt, Rinehart and Winston, 1978.

Landauer, T. K., Carlsmith, J. M., & Lepper, M. R. Experimental analysis of the factors determining obedience of four-year-old children to adult females. *Child Development,* 1970, *41,* 601–611.

Lepper, M. R. Dissonance, self-perception, and honesty in children. *Journal of Personality and Social Psychology,* 1973, *25,* 65–74.

Lepper, M. R. Intrinsic and extrinsic motivation in children: Detrimental effects of superfluous social controls. In W. A. Collins (Ed.), *Minnesota Symposium on Child Psychology* (Vol. 14). Hillsdale, N.J.: Erlbaum, 1981.

Lepper, M. R., & Gilovich, T. The multiple functions of reward: A social-developmental perspective. In S. S. Brehm, S. M. Kassin, & F. X. Gibbons (Eds.), *Developmental social psychology: Theory and research.* New York: Oxford University Press, 1981.

Lepper, M. R., & Gilovich, T. Activity-oriented request strategies for promoting generalized compliance from children: On accentuating the positive. *Journal of Personality and Social Psychology,* 1982, *42,* 248–259.

Lepper, M. R., & Greene, D. Turning play into work: Effects of adult surveillance and extrinsic rewards on children's intrinsic motivation. *Journal of Personality and Social Psychology,* 1975, *31,* 479–486.

Lepper, M. R., & Greene, D. Divergent approaches to the study of rewards. In M. R. Lepper & D. Greene (Eds.), *The hidden costs of reward.* Hillsdale, N.J.: Erlbaum, 1978. (a)

Lepper, M. R., & Greene, D. (Eds.), *The hidden costs of reward.* Hillsdale, N.J.: Erlbaum, 1978. (b)

Lepper, M. R., & Greene, D. Overjustification research and beyond: Toward a means–ends analysis of intrinsic and extrinsic motivation. In M. R. Lepper & D. Greene (Eds.), *The hidden costs of reward.* Hillsdale, N.J.: Erlbaum, 1978. (c)

Lepper, M. R., Greene, D., & Nisbett, R. E. Undermining children's intrinsic interest with extrinsic rewards: A test of the "overjustification" hypothesis. *Journal of Personality and Social Psychology,* 1973, *28,* 129–137.

Lepper, M. R., Sagotsky, G., Dafoe, J., & Greene, D. Consequences of superfluous social constraints: Effects on young children's social inferences and subsequent intrinsic interest. *Journal of Personality and Social Psychology,* 1982, *42,* 51–65.

Lepper, M. R., Sagotsky, G., & Greene, D. *Overjustification effects following multiple-trial reinforcement procedures: Experimental evidence concerning the assessment of intrinsic interest.* Unpublished manuscript, Stanford University, 1982. (a)

Lepper, M. R., Sagotsky, G., & Greene, D. *Self-determination, extrinsic rewards, and intrinsic interest in preschool children.* Unpublished manuscript, Stanford University, 1982. (b)

Lepper, M. R., Sagotsky, G., & Mailer, J. Generalization and persistence of effects of exposure to self-reinforcement models. *Child Development,* 1975, *46,* 618–630.

Lepper, M. R., Zanna, M. P., & Abelson, R. P. Cognitive irreversibility in a dissonance-reduction situation. *Journal of Personality and Social Psychology,* 1970, *16,* 191–198.

Lewin, K. *A dynamic theory of personality.* New York: McGraw-Hill, 1935.

Lewin, K., Lippitt, R., & White, R. Patterns of aggressive behavior in experimentally created "social climates." *Journal of Social Psychology,* 1939, *10,* 271–299.

Loeb, R. C. Concomitants of boys' locus of control examined in parent–child interactions. *Developmental Psychology,* 1975, *11,* 353–358.

Lytton, H. Correlates of compliance and the rudiments of conscience in two-year-old-boys. *Canadian Journal of Behavioral Science,* 1977, *9,* 242–251.

Lytton, H., & Zwirner, W. Compliance and its controlling stimuli observed in a natural setting. *Developmental Psychology*, 1975, *11*, 769–779.

Maccoby, E. E. *Social development: Psychological growth and the parent–child relationship.* New York: Harcourt Brace Jovanovich, 1980.

Maehr, M. L., & Stallings, W. M. Freedom from external evaluation. *Child Development*, 1972, *43*, 177–185.

Mahoney, M. J. Self-reward and self-monitoring techniques for weight control. *Behavior Therapy*, 1974, *5*, 48–57.

Matas, L., Arend, R. A., & Sroufe, L. A. Continuity of adaptation in the second year: The relationship between quality of attachment and later competence. *Child Development*, 1978, *49*, 547–556.

Miller, R. L., Brickman, P., & Bolen, D. Attribution versus persuasion as a means for modifying behavior. *Journal of Personality and Social Psychology*, 1975, *31*, 430–441.

Mills, J. Changes in moral attitudes following temptation. *Journal of Personality*, 1958, *26*, 517–531.

Minton, C., Kagan, J., & Levine, J. A. Maternal control and obedience in the two-year-old. *Child Development*, 1971, *42*, 1873–1894.

Morgan, E. S. *The puritan family.* Boston: Trustees of the Public Library, 1956.

Nisbett, R. E., & Wilson, T. D. Telling more than we can know: Verbal reports on mental processes. *Psychological Review*, 1977, *84*, 231–259.

Patterson, G. R. *Contexts and reactions: An interactive approach to coercive family processes.* Englewood Clffs, N.J.: Prentice-Hall, in press.

Pepitone, A., McCauley, C., & Hammond, P. Change in attractiveness of forbidden toys as a function of severity of threat. *Journal of Experimental Social Psychology*, 1967, *3*, 221–229.

Perry, D. G., Perry, L. C., Bussey, K., English, D., & Arnold, G. Processes of attribution and children's self-punishment following misbehavior. *Child Development*, 1980, *51*, 545–551.

Piaget, J. *The moral judgment of the child.* New York: Free Press, 1965. (Originally published, 1932.)

Pittman, T. S., Cooper, E. E., & Smith, T. W. Attribution of causality and the overjustification effect. *Personality and Social Psychology Bulletin*, 1977, *3*, 280–283.

Pittman, T. S., Davey, M. E., Alafat, K. A., Wetherill, K. V., & Wirsul, N. A. Informational vs. controlling verbal rewards, levels of surveillance, and intrinsic motivation. *Personality and Social Psychology Bulletin*, 1980, *6*, 228–233.

Pliner, P., Hart, H., Kohl, J., & Saari, D. Compliance without pressure: Some further data on the foot-in-the-door technique. *Journal of Experimental Social Psychology*, 1974, *10*, 17–22.

Rainey, R. G. The effects of directed vs. non-directed laboratory work on high school chemistry achievement. *Journal of Research in Science Teaching*, 1965, *3*, 286–292.

Rosenhan, D. Some origins of concern for others. In P. A. Mussen, J. Langer, & M. Covington (Eds.), *Trends and issues in developmental psychology.* New York: Holt, Rinehart and Winston, 1969.

Ross, M., Karniol, R., & Rothstein, M. Reward contingency and intrinsic motivation in children: A test of the delay of gratification hypothesis. *Journal of Personality and Social Psychology*, 1976, *33*, 442–447.

Sears, R. R., Maccoby, E. E., & Levin, H. *Patterns of child rearing.* Evanston, Ill.: Row, Peterson, 1957.

Sears, R. R., Rau, L., & Alpert, R. *Identification and child rearing.* Stanford, Calif.: Stanford University Press, 1965.

Smith, W. F. *The effects of social and monetary rewards on intrinsic motivation.* Unpublished doctoral dissertation, Cornell University, 1976.

Snyder, M., & Cunningham, M. R. To comply or not comply: Testing the self-perception explanation of the "foot-in-the-door" phenomenon. *Journal of Personality and Social Psychology,* 1975, *31,* 64–67.

Swann, W. B., Jr., & Pittman, T. S. Initiating play activity of children: The moderating influence of verbal cues on intrinsic motivation. *Child Development,* 1977, *48,* 1125–1132.

Toner, I. J., Moore, L. P., & Emmons, B. A. The effect of being labeled on subsequent self-control in children. *Child Development,* 1980, *51,* 618–621.

Turkewitz, H., O'Leary, K. D., & Ironsmith, M. Producing generalization of appropriate behavior through self-control. *Journal of Consulting and Clinical Psychology,* 1975, *43,* 577–583.

Uranowitz, S. W. Helping and self-attributions: A field experiment. *Journal of Personality and Social Psychology,* 1975, *31,* 852–854.

Weiner, H. R., & Dubanoski, R. A. Resistance to extinction as a function of self- or externally determined schedules of reinforcement. *Journal of Personality and Social Psychology,* 1975, *31,* 905–910.

Whiting, B. B., & Whiting, J. W. *Children of six cultures: A psycho-cultural analysis.* Cambridge, Mass.: Harvard University Press, 1975.

Wicklund, R. A., & Brehm, J. W. *Perspectives on cognitive dissonance.* Hillsdale, N.J.: Erlbaum, 1976.

Zanna, M. P., & Cooper, J. Dissonance and the attribution process. In J. H. Harvey, W. J. Ickes, & R. F. Kidd (Eds.), *New directions in attribution research* (Vol. 1). Hillsdale, N.J.: Erlbaum, 1976.

Zanna, M. P., Lepper, M. R., & Abelson, R. P. Attentional mechanisms in children's devaluation of forbidden activity in a forced-compliance situation. *Journal of Personality and Social Psychology,* 1973, *28,* 355–359.

Zuckerman, M., Lazzaro, M. M., & Waldgeir, D. Undermining effects of the foot-in-the-door technique with extrinsic rewards. *Journal of Applied Social Psychology,* 1979, *9,* 292–296.

Part IV

Commentary and overview

13   Interaction and development in social cognition

Elliot Turiel

There is a long-standing conflict in psychology between the cognitive approach and the socialization approach. Both traditions, apparent in social and developmental psychology, go back at least to the earlier part of this century. In the cognitive tradition, thought, or cognition, has been regarded as central to social development and behavior (Asch, 1952; Heider, 1958; Kohlberg, 1963; Kohler, 1938; Lewin, 1935; Mead, 1934; Piaget, 1932/1948; Vygotsky, 1962; Werner, 1948; Wertheimer, 1935). Although these researchers proposed different explanations of the origins and functions of social cognition, all focused on processes of thought in the social domains. Common to cognitively oriented researchers is the proposition that the individual's interactions with the social world entail descriptions and prescriptions, inferences and interpretations, the resolution of conflicts, and the formation of social theories. The socialization tradition, in which the specific explanations proposed by different researchers have also varied, is characterized by the view that nonrational processes govern behavior in the social domains (Aronfreed, 1968; Bandura & Walters, 1963; Dollard et al., 1939; Erikson, 1950; Freud, 1923/1960, 1930/1961; Miller & Dollard, 1941; Sears, Maccoby, & Levin, 1957; Skinner, 1948; Whiting & Child, 1953). Common to researchers oriented to socialization formulations is the proposition that social behavior is emotionally based and reflects a nonintellective accommodation, from an initially self-interested state, to the demands and expectations of other persons and the social system. Social development entails internalization of control over behavior, replacing external surveillance.

In developmental psychology, during the past 20 years or so, the opposition between the two approaches has centered on structural-developmental (e.g., Feffer & Gourevitch, 1960; Kohlberg, 1969; Selman, 1976; Turiel, 1969) and social-learning (e.g., Aronfreed, 1968; Bandura & Walters, 1963; Mischel, 1966) accounts. In recent years, however, among social-learning theorists there has been a movement away from the tradi-

333

tional rejection of a role for cognition in the social domains. For instance, efforts have been made to reconceptualize a cognitive social-learning analysis of personality (Mischel, 1973) and to consider the nature of *reciprocal interactions* between the individual and the social environment (Bandura, 1977, 1978). The essays in this volume, which were originally presented at a conference sponsored by the Committee on Social and Affective Development During Childhood of the Social Science Research Council, signal a distinctive shift in the traditional opposition between the socialization and cognitive approaches. Most of these researchers are centrally concerned with the development of social cognition. Differences still exist, however, between the approach taken by several of the authors in this volume and the approach represented by some of the cognitive perspectives, particularly those I am labeling structural-developmental. One central difference pertains to explanations of the influences of the social environment on the development of social cognition.

Indeed, one of the original motivations for the conference, which is reflected in part of the title to the volume (i.e., *A Sociocultural Perspective*), was a concern with social influence. This is stated in the conference proposal (Higgins, Ruble, & Hartup, 1979) presented to the Committee of the Social Science Research Council:

Recently there has been a considerable amount of empirical and theoretical interest generated in the topic of social cognition. . . . Curiously, however, with few exceptions research in the area of developmental social cognition has assumed a rather limited definition of the topic. Specifically, the field has been dominated by the "cognitive" side of social cognition and the more "social" aspects have been relatively ignored.

This point can perhaps be clarified by considering social cognition within the traditional S-O-R model of behavior, which can be labeled in more relevant terms as follows:

Social Information → Social Cognition → Social Behavior

That is, the influence of the social environment on children's social behaviors is assumed to be mediated by the way the information is construed. This mediating process is, in turn, affected by age-related changes in cognitive structures and information processing.

Our major point is that research in the area has been limited in the sense that it has focused almost exclusively on the cognitive mediating processes in the above model, such as: (1) describing the development of socially relevant cognitions per se (e.g., descriptions of persons) or (2) the interrelationship between cognitive variables (e.g., egocentrism or attention) and social perception (e.g., moral judgments). What is generally missing are the direct links to the more social aspects of social cognition: socialization or social situational forces on the antecedent side, and social behavior on the response side.

The purpose of the proposed conference is to focus on these social developmental links and, in doing so, attempt to redirect and redefine the theoretical foundations of research in the area of developmental social cognition. (pp. 1–2)

One reason for quoting at length from the proposal is to introduce my specific role and function as a commentator on this volume. It can be said that it is a committee assignment. My role is directly related to some of the statements in the conference proposal and to my membership on the Social Science Research Council committee that sponsored the conference. The committee deemed it desirable to include a commentary from the perspective of the "cognitive" approach, which has "assumed a rather limited definition of the topic." In short, I was perceived by my colleagues on the committee as one who fits the description and thus was requested to comment on the contributions from that perspective.

I have taken the committee's assignment to comment from the perspective of the "other" approach seriously because there is a need at the present time to identify as precisely as possible, and thereby clarify, some of the disagreements between different theoretical formulations on social-cognitive development. One aim of the commentary, therefore, is to clarify what has been proposed by structural-developmental theorists researching social cognition. A second aim is to comment, again from a "cognitive" perspective, on propositions put forth in this volume pertaining to the nature of social experience, social cognition, and their relationships. Such commentary must be viewed as stemming from my own construction and interpretation of structural-developmental theory. I note this obvious point to make clear that the label structural-developmental, as any other such label to identify a grouping of researchers, is used for the sake of convenience and should not be taken to imply that there is a monolithic view accepted by all researchers who might fit the label.

The passages quoted from the conference proposal highlight important issues that arise in several of the essays and are being increasingly debated in developmental and social psychology. In particular, the emphasis in the proposal on the need for greater attention to social experience and on the related concern with shortcomings in the treatment of social experience by structural-developmental research are reiterated in the volume itself. Implicit in some essays and explicit in others is the view that along with the insufficient concern with social environmental influences comes an overreliance on cognitive variables (e.g., see the Higgins & Parsons statements on the "bias" of cognitive approaches toward dispositional attributions). In this volume, the cognitive variables are characterized as skills, capacities, or abilities. In turn, the structural-developmental approach is characterized as proposing a cognitive-mediation (or a cognitive-maturational-mediation) explanation of social cognition. It is these two complementary issues – the role of experience and the way cognition is characterized – that I address in explicating the "cognitive" approach.

The central points of departure in the two approaches are in (1) explanations of the nature of the individual's interactions with the environment, (2) ways of characterizing social judgments, (3) proposed mechanisms of development, and (4) the epistemological categories guiding research and theory on social interaction and development.

Have the cognitive approaches paid inadequate attention to the social components of social cognition – or have they proposed a different explanation of social influence from those represented in this volume? Of course, the extent to which children's social experiences contribute to their social-cognitive development is an open question. We cannot a priori, without evaluating the evidence, dismiss or discount hypotheses that, for instance, either minimize the role of experience (as in Freud's [1905/1962] propositions regarding psychosexual development or ethological [Lorenz, 1966] and sociobiological [Trivers, 1971; Wilson, 1975, 1978] explanations of social behavior) or maximize the mediating role of cognitive skills and capacities. However, the role of the environment, including its social aspects, is central to structural-developmental theory. In fact, a recent debate between Piaget and Chomsky (Piattelli-Palmarini, 1980) produced the criticism that Piaget's explanation of cognitive development gives too much weight to environmental influences and insufficient weight to biological determinants of cognitive structures. As is evident in the following comments made by Piaget (1980) during the debate, the characterization of his position by those critics was not inaccurate:

Knowledge does not result from a mere recording of observations without a structuring activity on the part of the subject. Nor do any a priori or innate cognitive structures exist in man; the functioning of intelligence alone is hereditary and creates structures only through an organization of successive actions performed on objects. Consequently, an epistemology conforming to the data of psychogenesis could be neither empiricist nor preformationist, but could consist only of a constructivism, with a continual elaboration of new operations and structures. (p. 23)

Piaget has not proposed a "cognitive maturational" view of development. The functions of assimilation and accommodation are proposed to be hereditary, but cognitive structures are viewed neither as innately given nor as emerging through maturation. At the same time, Piaget stressed interaction and argued against an empiricist view of development. The hypothesis has been clearly stated in many of Piaget's writings: Cognitive structures are created or constructed through action, that is, through the individual's interactions with the physical and social environment.

Piaget's theory of development, as is well known, has undergone substantial modification and extension since the period during which he conducted research on children's moral judgments (Piaget, 1932/1948). His recent work has focused on what I will refer to as "nonsocial" cognitive (e.g., logical-mathematical and physical concepts) development. Nevertheless, his approach to moral judgment was generally consistent with the later notions of construction through interaction, as are recent analyses of social-cognitive development (Damon, 1977; Kohlberg, 1969, 1976; Nucci, 1981; Selman, 1975, 1976; Turiel, 1979, in press-b; Youniss & Volpe, 1978).

Piaget proposed a developmental sequence of moral judgments (from a heteronomous to an autonomous orientation) based on analyses of the interrelations of social experience, nonsocial cognitive components, and distinctively social-cognitive components. Piaget did not regard cognitive factors, or "intellectual ability," as mediating or underlying social judgments or social behavior. Rather, it was proposed that cognitive components (which at the time included the shift from egocentrism to perspectivism and from an objective–subjective fusion to their differentiation and coordination) contributed to the construction of distinctively moral judgments, that is, to an organization of judgment different from, and irreducible to, nonsocial cognitive skills, operations, or structures. In other words, Piaget's descriptions of the two levels of moral judgment represented systems of thought organized differently from those for nonsocial concepts. In each of the two levels Piaget attempted to characterize the child's thinking regarding authority relations, obedience, peer relations, cooperation, social rules, consequences of social transgressions, intentionality, punishment (retributive justice), and the social distribution of resources, rewards, and punishments (distributive justice). Data based on empirical investigations of children's concepts of each of these social issues were used to formulate the moral judgment levels.

It is not merely quibbling with words to say that Piaget described an organization of judgment pertaining specifically to social matters rather than a mediation of intellectual skills or capacities. The significance of this description is that it reflects Piaget's direct concern with the child's interactions with social experiences. In turn, distinctively social judgments constitute one of the bases for the child's involvement with social events, as manifested in behavior. For this reason, Piaget (1932/1948) conducted detailed analyses of children's social behaviors, proposing levels of the "practice" of rules that paralleled levels of "consciousness" of rules.

Piaget's research on moral judgments was, in large part, motivated by a concern with what he saw as a fundamental and far-reaching set of social experiences characterized by authority relations and peer relations. According to Piaget, young children's (3- to 7-year-olds) social experiences center on relations with adults in authority and predominantly entail social constraint. Relations of constraint are due to a combination of the way adults relate to children, to the developmental status of children, and to the way children interpret the status of adults. The adult exerts constraints because of the child's relative immaturity, which in turn produces an acceptance of the adult's commands, rules, and expectations (what Piaget referred to as unilateral respect and associated with the heteronomous orientation). Age-related changes in social experiences, akin to those discussed by Higgins and Parsons, were proposed by Piaget as a partial account for the change from one level to the next. A decreasing emphasis on authority relations in late childhood and early adolescence, along with increasing relations with peers entailing mutual respect, intersects with changes in cognitive level to stimulate changes in level of moral judgment. (These ideas have been elaborated and extended to nonmoral social domains by Damon, 1981; Youniss, 1980; and Youniss & Volpe, 1978.)

In more recent formulations we also see attempts to describe social judgments as different from, and irreducible to, nonsocial cognition but yet partially related to cognitive development (Damon, 1977; Kohlberg, 1969, 1976; Selman, 1975, 1976). Mention is made in this volume of Kohlberg's explanation of moral development as one taking a cognitive-mediation, or intellectual-ability, approach. Like Piaget, however, Kohlberg proposed that children's moral judgments are partially related to their nonsocial cognitive development.[1] He hypothesized that stages of cognitive development are necessary but not sufficient for stages of moral development. The insufficiency of cognitive stages stems from Kohlberg's proposition that moral judgment constitutes an organization of reasoning that is social in nature and different from reasoning about nonsocial events. Therefore, it is hypothesized that nonsocial cognitive structures contribute to the formation of social-cognitive structures but not that they serve a mediating function. Indeed, Kohlberg's moral-judgment stages are defined so as to characterize reasoning about such issues as law, affectional relations, authority roles, civil rights, contract, promise, punishment, life, property rights, rules, and sexual roles (Kohlberg, 1976; Kohlberg et al., 1978). Again, research has been conducted on social-experiential variables (e.g., group discussion, role-taking opportunities, and interpersonal conflict) associated with development (e.g., Blatt & Kohlberg, 1975; Kohlberg, 1971; Selman, 1975). Research has also been conducted on the relations of moral judgments and behavior (see Blasi, 1980, for a review of the voluminous literature on this topic).

Not all analyses of social concepts have presumed strong relationships between social and nonsocial cognition. Some recent research, including my own and that discussed by Pool, Shweder, and Much in this volume, has examined direct relationships between social interactions and social concepts. Unlike the Piaget and Kohlberg propositions regarding moral judgments, I (Turiel, 1975, 1978) have made a sharper differentiation between the organization of reasoning in social and nonsocial domains and proposed that social concepts, including the categories of concepts of persons, of systems of social relations and organizations, and of prescriptive judgments of moral necessity, develop autonomously from nonsocial concepts. Moreover, it has been proposed and substantiated by research in the United States (Much & Shweder, 1978; Nucci & Nucci, 1982; Nucci & Turiel, 1978) and the Virgin Islands (Nucci, Turiel, & Gawrych, 1980) that children's social interactions among themselves and with adults systematically differ according to the domain of the social events. Social interactions in the context of moral events are of a different type from interactions in the context of social-conventional events. This research has shown (a) that distinctions need to be made between qualitatively different types of social interactions experienced by children at varying ages, which intersect with different types of social concepts and (b) that there are age-related changes in the form of each type of social interaction (Nucci & Nucci, 1982).

The purpose of this brief review is to establish parameters of structural-developmental approaches, thus providing a basis for comparisons with the approaches represented in this volume. Although both approaches attempt to account for social experience and the social elements of social cognition, they do so in different ways. I believe it is accurate to say that one of the differences between the two approaches stems from the proposed modifiability of the individual's social cognitions by events in the social environment. In several of the chapters we see a reliance on internalization as a mechanism of acquisition of social knowledge; variations in social or cultural systems, or in subcultures (e.g., age-associated subcultures), produce variations in the development of social cognition. In several chapters, social experiences, as they relate to the child's development, are defined as (a) activities designed to control and/or shape the child's behavior and (b) prepackaged units communicated or transmitted to the child. Social development, in this view, includes the acquisition of mechanisms of control (see especially Costanzo & Dix, Grusec, Hoffman, Lepper) and the internalization of representations of the social environment and of previously experienced event sequences (Berndt, Higgins, & Parsons).

In the structural approach emphasis is placed on the structuring activities of the child. The co-occurrence of variations or changes in social experiences and variations or changes in social cognition is not assumed to demonstrate a causal relation of experience and knowledge. From the viewpoint of a reciprocally interactive process of development, it is proposed that the child interprets and transforms social experiences while being transformed by them. The social aspects of social cognition include the construction of inferences and propositional theories about persons, social relations, and social events. This is to say that children may form *social understandings* that are not restricted to a copy model of the representation of knowledge. Indeed, some of the metaphors used in social and developmental psychology, such as references to the individual as a moral philosopher (Kohlberg, 1971) or an intuitive social scientist (Nisbett & Ross, 1980; Ross, 1981; Shweder, Turiel, & Much, 1981; Turiel, 1979), are meant to reflect the view that social cognition goes beyond representation of what exists in the social environment to the generative aspects of inferences, theoretical constructs, and prescriptions of oughts, in addition to comprehension of what exists. Ross (1981), for instance, has described a model that "portrays the adult human as an *intuitive social scientist* who, like the formal scientist, employs data and theories, and a variety of inferential tools, in attempting to understand, predict and control the phenomena of everyday social experience" (p. 1).

The distinction I am drawing between the different ways of describing social cognition bears on what to me is a confusing reference in some chapters to the need to account for "social and cognitive factors." From such statements one gets the impressions that social factors are not cognitive and vice versa. Probably, this also accounts for the assertion that the "cognitive" approaches propose a mediational view of social cognition. In separating "social and cognitive" factors, cognition is regarded as processing ability (Berndt), strategies for processing social content (Collins), or capacities and skills (Higgins & Parsons). In the alternative formulations, social and cognitive factors are intertwined in that they are cognitions about social phenomena or "everyday social experiences." There is a realm of nonsocial cognition that has been proposed to be structurally interrelated with the realm of social cognition (e.g., Kohlberg, 1976; Selman, 1975) and that has also been proposed to be structurally distinct from domains of social cognition (Turiel, 1975, 1978). For the sake of clarity, the terms *social* and *cognitive* require referents, such as social environment, social experience, social cognitive, nonsocial cognitive.

I now turn to the second aim of this commentary and consider the concepts and research findings presented in the chapters in this volume, with particular emphasis on their epistemological and research strategies. I have said that the two approaches differ in propositions regarding the ways individual-environment interactions determine development. Moreover, in structural theories, analyses of social cognition and its development are guided by examination of the epistemological categories to which they are related. The study of any form of cognition or knowledge, including the social realms, needs to be informed by an explication of the domains in which the development occurs. Investigations of mechanisms of acquisition or development should be coordinated with systematic analyses of the type of knowledge acquired. In such a case, investigations of the development of social cognition would include a concern with definitions and classifications of social interactions and social knowledge. A course of research that accounts for the nature of the domain under investigation has been well characterized by Noam Chomsky (1975) in the following way:

> What is a theory of learning? Is there such a theory as *the* theory of learning, waiting to be discovered? Let us try to sharpen and perhaps take some steps toward answering these questions.
>
> Consider first how a neutral scientist – that imaginary ideal – might proceed to investigate the question. The natural first step would be to select an organism, O, and a reasonably well delimited cognitive domain, D, and to attempt to construct a theory that we might call "the learning theory for the organism O in the domain D." This theory – call it LT(O,D) – can be regarded as a system of principles, a mechanism, a function, which has a certain "input" and a certain "output" (its domain and range, respectively). The "input" to the system LT(O,D) will be an analysis of data in D by O; the "output" (which is, of course, internally represented, not overt and exhibited) will be a cognitive structure of some sort. This cognitive structure is one element of the cognitive state attained by O.
>
> For example, take O to be humans and D language. The LT(H,L) – the learning theory for humans in the domain language – will be the system of principles by which humans arrive at knowledge of language given linguistic experience, that is, given a preliminary analysis that they develop for the data of language. Or, take O to be rats and D to be maze running. Then LT(R,M) is the system of principles used by rats in learning how to run mazes. The input to LT(R,M) is whatever preliminary analysis of data is used by rats to accomplish this feat, and the output is the relevant cognitive structure, however it should properly be characterized as a component of the state achieved by the rat who knows how to run a maze. There is no reason to doubt that the cognitive state of which it is a constituent will be rather complex. . . .
>
> To pursue the study of a given LT(O,D) in a rational way, we will proceed through the following stages of inquiry:
> 1. Set the cognitive domain D.
> 2. Determine how O characterizes data in D "pretheoretically," thus constructing what we may call "the experience of O in D" (recall the idealization to "instantaneous learning").
> 3. Determine the nature of the cognitive structure attained; that is, determine, as well as possible, what is learned by O in the domain D.

    4. Determine LT(O,D), the system that relates experience to what is learned. (pp. 14–15)

According to this formulation, which seems to me an eminently sound research strategy, investigations of social-cognitive development would entail (1) identification and definition of the social domain under investigation, ideally including comparisons and contrasts with other related social domains, (2) descriptions of the cognitive state or states attained by the individual, (3) a determination of the individual's experiences or interactions with the environment that are related to the domain, and (4) proposition of a theory of development (or learning or acquisition) of the domain. The research strategies reflected in most of the present chapters are different. The starting point in these investigations is a set of assumptions about the psychological mechanisms of acquisition that are presumed to apply to the organism and, therefore, *across* domains of knowledge. Two factors are central to these analyses: (a) the identification of what exists in the child's social environment, which may *vary* from context to context or from one age period to another, and (b) specification of the mechanisms of acquiring social content and maintaining it, which are presumed to be *constant* from individual to individual and from one age period to another.

Using Chomsky's notations, the procedures used in these investigations can be characterized as follows. First, the organism, O, is selected and the learning theory, LT, is presumed to apply to O; then the attempt is made to apply LT to domain, D. Social cognition is presumed to be one general domain and the learning theory applied to it is taken from earlier socialization and social-psychological formulations. In these chapters social cognition has been linked to several mechanisms previously posited to explain social control and social influence. These include punishment, parental discipline, social comparison, and the general notion of internalization.

In starting with a proposed mechanism of acquisition that is applied to various topics of social cognition, the implicit assumption is made that the learning and functioning of the organism is similar across domains. For instance, Higgins and Parsons seem to apply the same analysis to cognitions about morality, regulation, authority, and attributional processes. I assume that in Grusec's analysis the central role attributed to punishment and its resulting anxieties in the process of internalization is not meant to be restricted to altruism or morality. Ruble maintains that social comparison is a basic process during early socialization. The implication of this statement is that social comparison is a basic process for a variety of areas of social-cognitive development (as I discuss in more detail later, Ruble's findings suggest that social comparison is a process associated with a particular type of social knowledge). Similarly, the Costanzo and Dix thesis reflected in their research agenda is that socialization, in the form of communications from adults or peers, has much influence on various social judgments, including moral reasoning and values, self-perception, and perception of other persons.

It is certainly plausible to hypothesize that the acquisition mechanism and type of reasoning is the same across domains, as long as it is recognized as a hypothesis. A determination of the validity of the hypothesis, however, requires comparative analyses of different types of social cognition, which would entail definitions of the types of knowledge under investigation. In other words, a system for categorizing and classifying domains of social knowledge is useful in empirical studies bearing on the validity of the hypothesis. In a similar vein, it could be plausibly maintained that social judgments are all in one domain (*the* social domain) and, therefore, that there is no need to be concerned with domain distinctions. (I do not mean to suggest that this is explicitly stated by anyone in this volume.) Such an assertion should also be regarded as a hypothesis requiring specification of the parameters of *the* domain of "social cognition" and concomitant research findings that demonstrate the unity of the domain. Whatever the hypothesis, identification and definition of categories of social domains are unavoidable in research on social cognition.

Recent research aimed at comparisons of different aspects of children's social judgments and evaluations has yielded a good deal of evidence indicating that social concepts are not of one kind and that qualitatively different types of social experiences are associated with distinct domains of social concepts. Much of this evidence with respect to the domains of morality and social convention is reviewed in this volume by Pool, Shweder, and Much. They report several studies showing that young children distinguish between moral and conventional forms of evaluation. I would add three comments to their review of the research. First, it should be noted that a series of studies using methods appropriate for young children have yielded a good deal of evidence demonstrating that by a very early age morality is distinct from social convention. The criteria used by children as young as 3 or 4 years of age to identify and evaluate moral issues differ from those used to identify and evaluate conventional issues (Nucci & Nucci, 1982; Nucci & Turiel, 1978; Nucci, Turiel, & Gawrych, 1980; Smetana, 1981). Therefore, the evidence for the presence in young children of systematic discriminations between domains of social judgment is now even stronger than that indicated by Pool, Shweder, and Much.

The second comment is to point out that the distinction between the moral and conventional forms of evaluation is found (Nucci, 1981; Weston & Turiel, 1980) to be constant across a wide age range (the studies have included subjects up to 19 years). Those findings serve to underscore the contention of Pool, Shweder, and Much that development is not adequately characterized as entailing increasing differentiations *between* fundamental domains of social judgment. This should not be taken to mean that there are no age-related changes in moral judgments or concepts of social convention. It is the distinction between the two domains that was found to be constant across age, indicating that at a very early age children begin to form social concepts within delimited domains. This proposition does not by any means preclude the possibility of analyses of developmental changes within a domain or in the ways in which domain-specific considerations are coordinated with each other in situations that require such coordinations. Developmental changes within a domain may indeed entail increased differentiations, as has been found in analyses of age-related changes in ways of organizing an understanding of social convention (Turiel, 1978). Moreover, development entails the construction of concepts, preceded and followed by processes of reevaluation of existing concepts. This process entails the types of self-critical activity and correction of errors in thought that Pool, Shweder, and Much discussed and that is part of Piaget's (1970, 1977) scheme of self-regulation in the equilibration process.

The third comment regarding this body of research is to reiterate my earlier statement that there are relations between forms of social judgment and types of social experiences. It has been found that social experiences are systematically associated with domains. For instance, communications among children and between child and adult occurring in the context of moral transgressions differ from those occurring in the context of transgressions of conventions.

The research findings, therefore, are not supportive of a view of social cognition as one domain largely determined by the content of social experiences. The findings indicate that explanations of social cognition need to account for the individual's domain-specific ways of conceptualizing social phenomena, as well as social-informational knowledge. Therefore, the minimal requirements of a framework for classifying social cognitions would include (a) a basis for distinguishing between methods of extracting or reproducing social information and systems of social-conceptual or inferential knowledge[2] and (b) delineation of the fundamental domains of social knowledge.

On the basis of the current evidence and as part of a working model, three fundamental and generally stated conceptual domains have been identified (Turiel, in press-a). These are (1) the domain of psychological knowledge, which refers to concepts of persons as psychological systems (e.g., concepts of personality, the self, the behavior of others), (2) the domain of societal or social-organizational knowledge, which refers to concepts of systems of social relations (e.g., concepts of social convention, groups, social institutions, authority, and social roles), and (3) the domain of morality, which refers to prescriptive judgments regarding how people ought to behave toward one another (e.g., concepts of justice, rights, and welfare). This is not the place to provide a rationale for the model or an extensive discussion of the evidence in its support. It is mentioned so as to provide a framework for further commentary on how some of the research discussed in this volume can be informed by a system for classifying and identifying social domains.

As a first example, consider the research discussed by Berndt. He proposed a general model of social-cognitive factors that includes attitudes toward acts, social norms, and personal norms. Conceived as a general model applicable across domains, Berndt applied it to other theoretical systems, such as Kohlberg's proposed stages of moral development, that include the components of consequences, social norms, and personal norms. Accordingly, Berndt has attempted to test the validity of the moral-judgment sequence proposed by Kohlberg through a study of children's responses to questions pertaining to how one would and should behave (e.g., with regard to sharing or helping) toward friends and acquaintances. Such a procedure, however, includes at least two components of judgment: friendship and morality. For this reason, Berndt's results may not be completely applicable to Kohlberg's formulations regarding *moral* judgments. Berndt also contends that the finding that young children show "a personal commitment to norms" supports the social-learning internalization hypothesis rather than the "cognitive-developmental" hypothesis. Even if the findings clearly pertained to the moral domain, this particular test of the relative merits of the two theories would be inappropriate, given that more than one structural-development explanation of morality (e.g., Damon, 1977; Piaget, 1932/1948; Turiel, 1978) proposes the emergence of personal norms by early childhood.

Berndt's review of research findings illustrates how the study of a broad topic like friendship and social behavior can be related to different aspects of social cognition. Berndt reviewed and reported studies showing that children share more with strangers than with friends when they believe the stranger is in greater need than the friend. It is likely that "friendship" behavior in these studies is closely related to children's moral judgments regarding distribution and need. If the child's behavior toward friends or strangers depends on the domain in question, then it is to be expected that in morally relevant situations friends and strangers would be treated equally so that need is taken into account. In other realms, however, it is surely the case that children's behavior would be influenced by relations of friendship. For instance, in questions of intimacy, such as in revealing or sharing personal information, it is likely that children do so to a greater extent with friends than with strangers (regardless of the other person's state of material need). As another example, behavior toward friends may be related to conventional regulation in the sense that there would be greater adherence to certain conventional norms in relations with strangers or acquaintances than in relations with friends. Although the proposed intersection between friendship and domain is speculative, just such an intersection has been found in studies of children's conceptions of social rules.

The research reported by Ruble is also consistent with the domain analysis in that her findings suggest that social comparison processes are associated with the development of psychological concepts. Although it appears that Ruble began with the assumption that social comparison processes are associated with social development in general, her attunement to the initial research findings correctly led to greater specificity, in subsequent research, in the types of social-cognitive factors that may be related to the social-comparison process. The initial, and unexpected, finding was that social comparison was not used by children under 7 years of age, in spite of the availability of prerequisite cognitive skills, motivations, and strategies. On the basis of Ruble's investigations as well as several other studies of children's concepts of self, other persons, and the causes of behavior, it is plausible to maintain that young children's failure to use social-comparison processes stems from their lack of stable concepts of internal psychological processes.

Ruble's findings are consistent with those of Josephson (1977), who examined the degree to which children predict the behavior of others on the basis of personal-dispositional or situational information. He found that children under 7 years of age relied on situational factors to a greater extent than older children (7- to 15-year-olds) and that older children used dispositional factors to a greater extent than younger children. The findings indicate that children do not form stable concepts of internal psychological processes until at least 7 years of age. Given that the social-comparison process entails comparisons with *other persons,* it then follows that it would not be used by children under 7 years of age. In other words, the use of social comparison presupposes the development of psychological concepts. Moreover, the ways in which the social-comparison process is used should be, in part, dependent on the type of psychological concepts developed by the child. Indeed, Ruble's description of age-related changes in social comparison refers to changes in the domain of psychological concepts. It should also be noted that Collins, too, found that psychological concepts influence interpretations of what is observed through the medium of television.

Distinctions between social domains are also relevant to Hoffman's explanation of moral internalization. In an effort to define the moral domain, Hoffman lists a set of norms that pertain to the behavior of one person toward another (e.g., considering the feelings of others, telling the truth, keeping a promise, lying, stealing, inflicting harm). However, the definition of morality contains some ambiguities because for Hoffman moral internalization is ultimately dependent upon how the child is disciplined by the parents. In Hoffman's view, moral norms represent social obligations that are in conflict with personal needs and that become internalized through the child's experiences "in discipline encounters with parents."

The nature of the definitional ambiguity can be illustrated by referring to a distinction Hoffman draws between moral action and arbitrary requests by authority. Hoffman stated that the index of avoidance of a forbidden toy used in some experiments is questionable as a moral index. I would agree that the measure of the extent to which a child plays with a forbidden toy is not a clearly moral one and that the Milgram (1974) experiment demonstrates the difficulty of defining morality through compliance with authority (cf. Turiel, 1978). By the same token, however, the emphasis on techniques of parental discipline blurs the distinction between moral and nonmoral norms. If parents were to use the appropriate discipline techniques with regard to playing with forbidden toys (supposing they considered it a moral norm), then would the child internalize it as a moral norm? The issue can be put another way. When parents intervene to change the child's behavior with discipline, how do they know that a violation of a "moral" norm has occurred? And what is the correspondence, if any, between the parents' form of knowledge and that of the child? To paraphrase Malinowski (as quoted by Pool, Shewder, and Much), if the acquisition of moral norms is based on what occurs in discipline encounters with parents, then no clear distinction can be drawn between the acquisition of moral norms, conventional norms, playing-with-toys norms, and other usages.

I believe the ambiguity stems from a reliance on one type of social experience (e.g., parental discipline or punishment) and that greater attention should be given to how individuals conceptualize those and other social experiences. As noted earlier, qualitative distinctions in social experiences are related to corresponding distinctions in social conceptual domains. Qualitative difference in social experiences is a focus of the Higgins and Parsons analyses. They have put forth an interesting set of proposals regarding changes in social experiences that are associated with age. These proposals are meant to be preliminary and speculative, thus leaving much room for interpretation. There are at least two ways of interpreting the relation of social-cognitive changes to social-experiential changes. One is that experiential changes occur for reasons largely independent of the child (e.g., they are arbitrarily determined; they are determined by societal-functional considerations external to the child) and that, assuming internalization as the developmental process, the variations will be reflected in the individual's social cognitions. Hence "stagelike" changes are observed because of the sequence of social changes. If the experiences were ordered differently (or are ordered differently in another place or time), then a stagelike sequence would appear reflecting that order of social-life experiences (this is essentially the position put forth by Bandura & McDonald, 1963, regarding Piaget's moral-judgment stages).

The other interpretation of social-experiential changes is that there is a coordination and complementarity between changes in the child's developmental status and the experiential changes. In such a case, experiences sought by the child, experiences presented to the child, and the child's social-cognitive state of development are all interrelated. Children seek out and interpret social experiences, but social experiences, reciprocally, serve to transform thinking. In this regard, it is important to keep in mind that, as research has demonstrated, children at different levels of development deal with objectively similar experiences in different ways. Interpreted as a "social × cognitive" interaction, the Higgins and Parsons formulation is consistent with Piaget's explanation of the development of moral judgments. Like Piaget, Higgins and Parsons attempted to account for the role of changes in social experiences in conjunction with cognitive changes.

I would suggest that the Higgins and Parsons analyses could benefit from further distinctions in types of social experiences. Attention should be given to specifying relations of different types of experiences to types of social concepts and to differentiating experiences that produce changes in informational knowledge from those that stimulate changes in conceptual knowledge. Finally, it seems to me that Higgins and Parsons need to delineate the mechanisms of response acquistion and modification in order for their analyses to better inform a systematic understanding of social-cognitive development. Specification of mechanisms of acquisition and change would serve to explain the processes by which the child's existing state is modified or transformed with shifts in social experiences.

A concern with mechanisms by which changes in attitudes and behavior occur is central to Lepper's careful analysis of social control and attributional processes. Lepper appropriately limits the scope of his attributional analyses to compliance and the internalization of specific attitudes and behavior patterns. I certainly concur with, and encourage, the stress Lepper places on the important distinction between short-term local changes in specific attitudes or behaviors and long-term developmental processes producing stable forms of knowledge. At the same time, however, the precise and detailed nature of Lepper's analyses serves to highlight potential discrepancies between processes applicable to the short-term, specific changes and those applicable to long-term, systematic social-cognitive changes. Furthermore, some of the same questions just raised regarding the Hoffman and the Higgins and Parsons analyses are also appropriate to the research discussed by Lepper.

A question corresponding to the one posed earlier regarding Hoffman's definition of moral norms is relevant to the attribution model and experimental paradigm. To which types of behaviors and attitudes does the "minimal sufficiency principle" of social control apply? Is it being proposed that the principle applies to all types of activities or is it limited in its scope? For example, it may be that the principle applies best to the types of activities used in the experiments reported (e.g., prohibitions on playing with toys) but not to the formation of broader concepts (e.g., justice and fairness or an understanding of social organization). An attempt to delinate the limitations of the scope of activities relevant to the minimal sufficiency principle would follow from Lepper's distinction between changes in specific behaviors and the development of "consistent value systems and moral ideologies." Correspondingly, it would be useful to specify the child's existing state of social-cognitive functioning in the relevant domain as it intersects with the experimental conditions. This would include an assessment of how the child perceives the authority of the experimenter, in conjunction with how the child views the activity in the experiment (e.g., is it viewed as moral or nonmoral?).

Given the assumption that children do form concepts of social relations, it is also important to consider how their interpretation of events and objects in the experimental situation may, at least partially, account for the findings. Although the attributional interpretation of the findings focuses on the subjects' conceptualization of their reasons for engaging in a particular action or refusing to engage in a particular action, it is possible to interpret the findings in terms of the subjects' conceptualization of the value of objects or activities and of the rules and expectations of the experimental situation. Elsewhere (Turiel, 1978) I have reinterpreted the punishment conditions (e.g., early and late timings of punishment) in forbidden-toy experiments (e.g., Aronfreed & Reber, 1965; Parke & Walters, 1967) as providing information to the subject regarding the experimenter's expectations and the rules of the situation. It is interesting that, according to Lepper, some children who had undergone the "mild threat" procedure in forbidden-toy attribution studies thought that they "had done 'just what' the experimenter had asked them to do."

Consider one example – the mild-threat and severe-threat conditions in the forbidden-toy paradigm – of how the findings can be given an interpretation based on the subject's inferences from the experimenter's implicit communications about objects, activities, and expectations. Recall that the standard finding is that subjects under mild threat of punishment for playing with a presumably highly attractive toy devalue the activity to a greater extent than subjects under a severe threat of punishment. First, it is not clear in these experiments that the subject assesses the value of the activity as high in a consistent or unambiguous way. The desirability of playing with the toy may not be fixed or strong in the child's mind. In turn, the experimental conditions may be interpreted as messages or communications regarding an authoritative adult's assessment of the desirability of playing with the toy. A severe threat is likely to be interpreted by the subject to mean that the experimenter regards the toys more desirable than ones meriting only a mild threat. Accordingly, the subject takes advantage of the opportunity, at a future time or in a different context, to play with a toy perceived to be valued by the adult.

Similar reinterpretations can be made of findings from the other experiments (this type of reinterpretation is certainly applicable to the Aronson and Mills [1959] finding that a severe initiation for group membership enhances the subjects' evaluations of the activity). A corresponding cognitive reinterpretation is also applicable to studies of parental techniques of social control and discipline. The discipline techniques of punishment, love-withdrawal, and reasoning with the child may all constitute implicit or explicit communications from parents to children. For instance, the use of physical punishment and withdrawal of affection, perhaps intended as disciplining techniques by parents, are also likely to provide the child with information about the expectations of others and the rules or conventions of social situations. It has generally been found, as noted by Lepper, that providing the child with reasons or explanations regarding the acceptability or unacceptability of behavior is the most successful of the methods of "discipline." The obvious advantages of reasoning are the greater clarity of the communication and the greater likelihood that it will stimulate changes in the child's way of thinking. Although reasoning on the part of parents is often regarded as a form of discipline (e.g., induction), another interpretation would be that the function of one person providing another with reasons or explanation is to communicate ideas, often in an attempt to influence the other person's thinking. Simply because it is a parent communicating with a child does not, in itself, render the process a form of discipline. If the process were reversed and a child or adolescent reasoned with the parents, thereby changing their ideas and/or behavior, we would not say that the child had disciplined the parents.

In experimental and naturalistic studies it would be useful to know more about the intersections of types of implicit and explicit communications provided by experimenters and parents, children's interpretations of those communications, and the domain of the prescriptions, rules, or prohibitions to which the communications pertain. My point is that social relations are reciprocal not only in the sense that children influence parents, but, more important, in the sense that children interpret parental behaviors, as well as the social situation of the family or school or the broader social system. In studies of social-cognitive development attention needs to be given to the complex nature of individual-environment interactions in the developmental process, including systematic differentiations in types of social concepts, age-related changes in social concepts, qualitatively different social experiences, and age-related changes within categories of social experience.

Notes

1 A cognitive-mediational approach to the development of sex-role concepts has been proposed by Kohlberg (1966). In this regard, Kohlberg's explanation of sex-role development is based on assumptions different from those used in his explanation of moral development.
2 One framework for identifying differences between social-conceptual and social-informational knowledge is the distinction between cognitive functions that form organized systems of thinking subject to qualitative changes in development and cognitive functions that do not form organized transformational systems (Turiel, in press-a,): "Systems of organization constitute means by which objects and events are *transformed*, are comprehended, interpreted and manipulated. . . . At the same time, individuals also utilize . . . *methods* for gathering information or data from the social environment. The individual extracts and reproduces information about people, about interactions between people, and about systems of social organization. Under the general category of social informa-

tion we may include knowledge about the behaviors and existing psychological states (thoughts and feelings) of specific persons, the composition of individuals within groups, the rules, laws, and regulations of social systems, the institutions existing within specific societies, etc. These forms of social information are extracted and reproduced through the use of methods, which include such activities as observation, communication, imitation, and symbolically taking the perspective of another (role taking). As methods of information gathering, these activities serve as means for representing social information, without directly producing conceptual transformations; through the use of methods the individual attempts to reproduce what is given in the external environment. The methods, therefore, do not form organized systems and do not undergo structural changes. With increasing age there may be *quantitative* changes in the methods, such as increments in their accuracy and scope" (p. 27).

References

Aronfreed, J. *Conduct and conscience: The socialization of internalized control over behavior.* New York: Academic Press, 1968.

Aronfreed, J., & Reber, A. Internalized behavioral suppression and the timing of social punishment. *Journal of Personality and Social Psychology,* 1965, *1,* 3–16.

Aronson, E., & Mills, J. The effects of severity of initiation on liking for a group. *Journal of Abnormal and Social Psychology,* 1959, *59,* 177–181.

Asch, S. *Social psychology.* Englewood Cliffs, N.J.: Prentice-Hall, 1952.

Bandura, A. *Social learning theory.* Englewood Cliffs, N.J.: Prentice-Hall, 1977.

Bandura, A. The self-system in reciprocal determinism. *American Psychologist,* 1978, *33,* 344–358.

Bandura, A., & McDonald, F. J. The influence of social reinforcement and the behaviors of models in shaping children's moral judgments. *Journal of Abnormal and Social Psychology,* 1963, *67,* 274–281.

Bandura, A., & Walters, R. *Social learning and personality development.* New York: Holt, Rinehart and Winston, 1963.

Blasi, A. Bridging moral cognition and moral action: A critical review of the literature. *Psychological Bulletin,* 1980, *88,* 1–45.

Blatt, M., & Kohlberg, L. The effects of classroom moral discussion upon children's level of moral judgment. *Journal of Moral Education,* 1975, *4,* 129–161.

Chomsky, N. *Reflections on language.* New York: Pantheon, 1975.

Damon, W. *The social world of the child.* San Francisco: Jossey-Bass, 1977.

Damon, W. Exploring children's social cognition on two fronts. In J. H. Flavell and L. Ross (Eds.), *Social cognitive development: Frontiers and possible futures.* Cambridge: Cambridge University Press, 1981.

Dollard, J., Doob, L. W., Miller, N. E., Mowrer, O. H., & Sears, R. R. *Frustration and agression.* New Haven: Yale University Press, 1939.

Erikson, E. *Childhood and society.* New York: Norton, 1950.

Feffer, M., & Gourevitch, V. Cognitive aspects of role-taking in children. *Journal of Personality,* 1960, *28,* 283–396.

Freud, S. *The ego and the id.* New York: Norton, 1960. (Originally published, 1923.)

Freud, S. *Civilization and its discontents.* New York: Norton, 1961. (Originally published, 1930.)

Freud, S. *Three essays on the theory of sexuality.* New York: Avon, 1962. (Originally published, 1905.)

Heider, F. *The psychology of interpersonal relations.* New York: Wiley, 1958.

Higgins, E. T., Ruble, D., & Hartup, W. W. *Social cognition and social behavior: Developmental perspectives.* Conference proposal submitted to the Committee on Social and Affective Development During Childhood, Social Science Research Council, 1979.

Josephson, J. *The child's use of situational and personal information in predicting the behavior of another.* Unpublished doctoral dissertation, Stanford University, 1977.

Kohlberg, L. The development of children's orientations toward a moral order: 1. Sequence in the development of moral thought. *Vita Humana*, 1963, *6*, 11–33.

Kohlberg, L. A cognitive-developmental analysis of children's sex-role concepts and attitudes. In E. E. Maccoby (Ed.), *The development of sex differences.* Stanford, Calif. Stanford University Press, 1966.

Kohlberg, L. Stage and sequence: The cognitive-developmental approach to socialization. In D. A. Goslin (Ed.), *Handbook of socialization theory and research.* Chicago: Rand McNally, 1969.

Kohlberg, L. From is to ought: How to commit the naturalistic fallacy and get away with it in the study of moral development. In T. Mischel (Ed.), *Psychology and genetic epistemology.* New York: Academic Press, 1971.

Kohlberg, L. Moral stages and moralization: The cognitive-developmental approach. In T. Lickona (Ed.), *Moral development and behavior: Theory, research and social issues.* New York: Holt, Rinehart and Winston, 1976.

Kohlberg, L., Colby, A., Gibbs, J., & Speicher-Dubin, B. *Standard form scoring manual.* Cambridge, Mass.: Center for Moral Education, Harvard Graduate School of Education, 1978.

Kohler, W. *The place of value in a world of facts.* New York: Liveright, 1938.

Lewin, K. *A dynamic theory of personality.* New York: McGraw-Hill, 1935.

Lorenz, K. Z. *On aggression.* London: Methuen, 1966.

Mead, G. H. *Mind, self, and society.* Chicago: University of Chicago Press, 1934.

Milgram, S. *Obedience to authority.* New York: Harper & Row, 1974.

Miller, N. E., & Dollard, J. *Social learning and imitation.* New Haven: Yale University Press, 1941.

Mischel, W. A social learning view of sex differences in behavior. In E. E. Maccoby (Ed.), *The development of sex differences.* Stanford, Calif.: Stanford University Press, 1966.

Mischel, W. Toward a cognitive social learning reconceptualization of personality. *Psychological Review*, 1973, *80*, 252–283.

Much, N., & Shweder, R. A. Speaking of rules: The analysis of culture in breach. In W. Damon (Ed.), *New directions for child development.* Vol 2: *Moral development.* San Francisco: Jossey-Bass, 1978.

Nisbett, R., & Ross, L. *Human inference: Strategies and shortcomings of social judgment.* Englewood Cliffs, N.J.: Prentice-Hall, 1980.

Nucci, L. The development of personal concepts: A domain distinct from moral or societal concepts. *Child Development*, 1981, *52*, 114–121.

Nucci, L., & Nucci, M. Children's social interactions in the context of moral and conventional transgressions. *Child Development*, 1982, *53*, 403–412.

Nucci, L., & Turiel, E. Social interactions and the development of social concepts in preschool children. *Child Development*, 1978, *49*, 400–407.

Nucci, L., Turiel, E., & Gawrych, G. E. *Preschool children's social interactions and social concepts in the Virgin Islands.* Unpublished manuscript, University of Illinois at Chicago Circle, 1980.

Parke, R., Walters, R. Some factors influencing the efficacy of punishment training for inducing response inhibition. *Monographs of the Society for Research in Child Development*, 1967, *32* (1).

Piaget, J. *The moral judgment of the child.* Glencoe, Ill.: Free Press, 1948. (Originally published, 1932.)

Piaget, J. Piaget's theory. In P. Mussen (Ed.), *Carmichael's manual of child psychology* (Vol. 1). New York: Wiley, 1970.

Piaget, J. *The development of thought: Equilibration of cognitive structures.* New York: Viking Press, 1977.

Piaget, J. The psychogenesis of knowledge and its epistemological significance. In M. Piattelli-Palmarini (Ed.), *Language and learning: The debate between Jean Piaget and Noam Chomsky.* Cambridge, Mass.: Harvard University Press, 1980.

Piattelli-Palmarini, M. (Ed.). *Language and learning: The debate between Jean Piaget and Noam Chomsky.* Cambridge, Mass.: Harvard University Press, 1980.

Ross, L. The "inituitive scientist" formulation and its developmental implications. In J. H. Flavell and L. Ross (Eds.), *Social cognitive development: Frontiers and possible futures.* Cambridge: Cambridge University Press, 1981.

Sears, R. R., Maccoby, E. E., & Levin, H. *Patterns of child rearing.* Evanston, Ill.: Row, Peterson, 1957.

Selman, R. L. Toward a structural analysis of developing interpersonal relations concepts: Research with normal and disturbed preadolescent boys. In A. Pick (Ed.), *Minnesota Symposium on Child Psychology* (Vol. 10). Minneapolis: University of Minnesota Press, 1975.

Selman, R. L. Social cognitive understanding: A guide to educational and clinical practice. In T. Lickona (Ed.), *Moral development and behavior: Theory, research and social issues.* New York: Holt, Rinehart and Winston, 1976.

Shweder, R. A., Turiel, E., & Much, N. C. The moral intuitions of the child. In J. H. Flavell and L. Ross (Eds.), *Social cognitive development: Frontiers and possible futures.* Cambridge: Cambridge University Press, 1981.

Skinner, B. F. *Walden two.* New York: Macmillan, 1948.

Smetana, J. Preschool children's conceptions of moral and social rules. *Child Development,* 1981, *52,* 4408–4411.

Trivers, R. L. The evolution of reciprocal altruism. *Quarterly Review of Biology,* 1971, *46,* 35–57.

Turiel, E. Developmental processes in the child's moral thinking. In P. H. Mussen, J. Langer, & M. Covington (Eds.), *Trends and issues in developmental psychology.* New York: Holt, Rinehart and Winston, 1969.

Turiel, E. The development of social concepts: Mores, customs and conventions. In D. J. De Palma and J. M. Foley (Eds.), *Moral development: Current theory and research.* Hillsdale, N.J.: Erlbaum, 1975.

Turiel, E. The development of concepts of social structure: Social convention. In J. Glick and A. Clarke-Stewart (Eds.), *The development of social understanding.* New York: Gardner Press, 1978.

Turiel, E. Distinct conceptual and developmental domains: Social convention and morality. *Nebraska Symposium on Motivation,* 1977 (Vol. 25). Lincoln: University of Nebraska Press, 1979.

Turiel, E. Domains and categories in social cognitive development. In W. Overton (Ed.), *The relationship between social and cognitive development.* Hillsdale, N.J.: Erlbaum, in press. (a)

Turiel, E. *The development of social knowledge: Morality and convention.* Cambridge: Cambridge University Press, in press. (b)

Vygotsky, L. *Thought and language.* Cambridge: MIT Press, 1962.

Werner, H. *Comparative psychology of mental development.* New York: International Universities Press, 1948.

Wertheimer, M. Some problems in the theory of ethics. *Social Research*, 1935, *2*, 353–367.

Weston, D., & Turiel, E. Act-rule relations: Children's concepts of social rules. *Developmental Psychology*, 1980, *16*, 417–424.

Whiting, J. M. W., & Child, I. L. *Child training and personality: A cross-cultural study.* New Haven: Yale University Press, 1953.

Wilson, E. O. *Sociobiology: The new synthesis.* Cambridge, Mass.: Harvard University Press, 1975.

Wilson, E. O. *On human nature.* Cambridge, Mass.: Harvard University Press, 1978.

Youniss, J. *Parents and peers in social development: A Sullivan-Piaget perspective.* Chicago: University of Chicago Press, 1980.

Youniss, J., & Volpe, J. A relational analysis of children's friendship. In W. Damon (Ed.), *New directions for child development.* Vol. 1: *Social cognition.* San Francisco: Jossey-Bass, 1978.

14   Let's not overattribute to the attribution process: comments on social cognition and behavior

Eleanor E. Maccoby

The chapters in this volume constitute an extraordinarily impressive effort to bring to bear the concepts and findings of social psychology and cognitive science upon the development of children's social cognitions. My comments will be selective, dealing primarily with those chapters that relate most directly to aspects of the socialization process.

The chapter by Collins reports a body of research on children's comprehension of the contents of TV shows and the inferences they make concerning cause-and-effect relationships and the motivations of characters. It is clear that analogous processes must occur when children observe the real-life interactions of other people, and the Collins work suggests a number of refinements to existing formulations concerning the role of observational learning in socialization. Specifically, the Collins work would lead us to expect that: (1) young children remember a limited portion of the information available from the behavior of others; (2) even when they do know the events that occurred, they are not clear about what events are the consequences of other events, particularly when events are separated in time by intervening occurrence; (3) often they mistake the motives of characters; especially, they miss or misinterpret the information that indicates another person has evil intent, and thus misplace their trust. The nature of the information children glean from an episode, and the nature of the inferences they make, seem to be heavily determined by the knowledge they bring to the encounter. They comprehend more when the actors and situations are familiar. And they come equipped with a set of scripts, some of which are powerful enough to override what actually happens. Thus children may report what they expected to see rather than what they actually did see. These findings add considerable weight to the current emphasis on the observer's cognitive processes as determinants of what will be learned through observational

356

learning. Clearly, "modeling" is far from an automatic process in which an item of behavior is transferred from the repertoire of a model to that of a young observer. The process is shot through with inference and other constructive processes, which reconcile new elements with material previously acquired, and which may involve considerable distortion as the new information is dealt with. We begin to see a child's social environment as the raw material from which social scripts are gradually built up, and the Collins work raises interesting questions concerning the nature and degree of transfer that takes place from one social environment to another.

The chapter by Pool, Shweder, and Much deals with children's knowledge about moral rules. It is consonant with the current wave of reaction against Piagetian–Kohlbergian thinking. Its basic thesis is that children's thinking is not nearly so different from that of adults as has been claimed. Specifically, Pool and her colleagues challenge the notion that children's moral thinking is comparatively undifferentiated. The facts of the matter are not yet clear. As the authors say, Damon (1977) and Shantz (in press) find that infractions of conventional rules and violations of moral injunctions tend not to be as clearly distinguished from one another by children under the age of 8 as they are in the minds of adults; Turiel and now Pool and her associates claim that children as young as preschoolers classify infractions in much the same way as do adults, if their knowledge is probed in age-appropriate ways. It may be that the resolution of this issue will lie, as Pool and her associates believe, in the distinction between what children know and what they are able to tell about their own thinking. However, there are some considerations that would lead us to believe that this cannot be the whole story. Even if one took the position that children's thinking is not qualitatively different from that of adults – that is, does not change structurally in ordered progression – one would expect that simple increases in knowledge about moral issues would result in increased differentiation and a more complex classification of rules. This is the familiar principle that leads us to expect that artists and biologists will each have more differentiated conceptual systems in their own spheres of knowledge than in the others' sphere. Considering the young child as a neophyte in all spheres, including the moral one, it would be surprising to find that children's moral conceptions are as differentiated as those of adults. If it were true, it would be a major exception to well-established principles about the growth of knowledge and its utilization. Clear differentiation of moral categories in preschoolers would suggest that the informational base underlying moral classification systems is acquired quite early and remains relatively unchanged throughout development. Such an assumption would have many challengers, including Higgins and Parsons in this volume, who place great stress on the changes brought about in children's moral thinking by age-graded changes that occur in their social milieu.

Nevertheless, future theorists of moral development will have to come to grips with the evidence presented by Pool and her colleagues that children do make distinctions, at a much earlier age than Piaget or Kohlberg would have led us to expect, between rule infractions that lie in the moral versus the merely conventional or prudential domains. At least, children can make these distinctions at an intuitive, if not a self-reflective, level. What do such distinctions imply? Students of socialization are immediately led to speculate about the reactions of significant others to these classes of infractions. Have parents reacted with power-assertion to one kind of infraction, with induction to another? Do children get stronger reactions from peers to one kind of infraction, from adults to another? Such distinctions in socialization experiences would presumably help children to differentiate between classes of moral infraction, but they may not be necessary for such differentiation.

Costanzo and Dix, too, argue that there are fewer limitations on young children's moral inferences than we have been led to expect. Specifically, they find that children of kindergarten age can judge certain events on the basis of the intent of the actors, but only under certain conditions. They are likely to judge that a prosocial action was intentional but that an antisocial action was not. And given an antisocial action, they may not use the actor's intent as a basis for verbal judgment, but they show that they are aware of intent when asked whether they want to work with various categories of other persons who are distinguished on the basis of their intent. Costanzo and Dix suggest that although the child is quite capable of the inference processes that are involved in appraising other people's intentions, these inference processes are not always called into play. When there is an obvious, salient external cause for another person's behavior (which Costanzo and Dix call constraint), there is no need for the child to engage in a search for intent. When such constraints are absent, the child does embark on a causal analysis. We could extrapolate that children who are dealt with primarily by power-assertive parents will be slower than others to develop a set of causal inferences concerning the behavior of others.

The Higgins and Parsons chapter brings into the foreground an issue that has been lurking behind the scenes of the conflict between cognitive-developmental theory and social-learning theory. Insofar as social-learning theorists do recognize age-related changes in thinking or behavior that occur according to a fairly predictable timetable in most children, they are likely to push these aside as reflecting differences in the way children of different ages are treated by socializing agents. On the other hand, if cognitive developmentalists find evidence that adults change their modes of interaction with children in ways that are closely related to children's age, or stage, of cognitive development, they are likely to interpret this as evidence that adults are adapting themselves to the cognitive level of the child, so that adult behavior is seen as a result, not a cause, of children's developmental change. (Obviously, influence of both kinds could be occurring!) The issue comes to a head in the interpretation of age changes in social cognition – changes that cognitive-developmental theorists have tended to interpret largely as reflections of a progressive restructuring of basic cognitive processes. Although they do not deny that cognitive change may place to some degree automonously, Higgins and Parsons claim a primary role for social-environmental factors. They do not focus upon socialization practices within the family but instead point to age-graded subcultures and argue that a child's passage through these subcultures provides opportunities for the acquisition of new forms of social cognition. Thus the transition from home to school is a crucial one for the child's learning opportunities, as is the transition from school to work. It would follow from this point of view that in cultures such as ours, which prolong adolescence and delay entry into the adult work force, young people experience a delay in the development of certain aspects of social cognition, as compared to youth growing up in cultures or subcultures where work begins in mid-adolescence.

The authors attempt to link the Kohlberg moral-judgment stages to major changes that occur in most children's lives in the nature of the social settings where they spend most of their time, implying that children shift from one Kohlbergian level to the next in response to the changes in external demands entailed in the shifts in social settings. Thus they say that Stage 3 moral thinking should predominate in the age period 7 to 10, when children are subjected to common standards of good behavior and expected to conform to them. They find similar consonance between Stage 4 thinking and the social milieu of children aged 10 to 15 and point to "a sharp increase" in the appropriate level of moral thought at each of these ages. We must be aware, however, that Kohlberg's longitudinal work has placed the ages for transitions between stages much later than was formerly claimed (Kohlberg, 1976). Consequently, it is difficult to support the claim that the consonance between children's subcultural setting and their moral-judgment stage is in fact a close one if the Kohlberg work is relied upon to establish the modal transitional ages. However, it may be argued that important elements of Kohlbergian stage-wise transitions can be detected earlier than Kohlberg finds them if one uses more familiar situations for assessing moral judgments (cf. Damon, 1977).

In assembling evidence for the influence of social-situation factors on moral judgment, Higgins and Parsons show that the competitiveness of the situation in which an infraction occurs influences children's weighting of intent versus objective outcome, and that the age curves for objective versus subjective judgments are not the same for competitive versus non-competitive settings. Cogently, they say that the same underlying cognitive developmental charges could hardly account for these distinctly different curves. It is unfortunate that they have chosen this particular Piagetian dimension as their outcome measure, as Kohlberg has shown that objective versus subjective judgment is an aspect of moral thought that does *not* have a robust, replicable development course. The argument would be more powerful if the Kohlbergian levels themselves could be shown to change in relation to social-environmental settings. Nevertheless, the Higgins–Parsons thesis is a reasonable one, and it leads us to think seriously about why and how societies do age-grade the social experiences of their children and what role children's levels of "readiness" for a new social setting play in (1) the ages cultures choose as transitional to new settings and (2) the impact of those settings.

We may find an analogy for this issue in some of the recent work on physical maturation at adolescence. It is known that there has been a secular trend toward earlier dating over the past 50 years in at least some Western industrialized societies. There is also a secular trend toward earlier sexual maturation. Is the kind and amount of interaction adolescents seek with the opposite sex primarily a function of the onset of new biological drives? Dornbusch and his colleagues (1980) have recently studied the relation between three variables: (1) chronological age, (2) age of beginning hetrosexual dating, and (3) Tanner stage of sexual maturation. They find that the age at which individual children begin to date is related to chronological age but *not* to level of sexual maturation once age has been partialed out. They interpret these findings as meaning that social expectations are geared to a child's place in the age-graded subcultures rather than to the child's individual state of readiness. However, the social expectation does reflect the *average* state of readiness. That it is now considered appropriate for eighth-graders to date, whereas at earlier times the onset of dating usually occurred later, may very well reflect the secular trend toward earlier sexual maturation (as well as other factors). Thus societies are not blind to developmental changes and establish their age-graded subcultures accordingly. But once these cultural expectations and structures are established, they beome powerful sources of influence in their own right. As Higgins and Parsons point out, individual states of readiness may have some bearing upon the pace at which children take on the intellectual trappings of a subculture when they do enter it; however, sufficient evidence to support this conclusion is not yet available.

Several other chapters that bear directly on the socialization process, specifically those by Hoffman, Lepper, and Grusec, deal with aspects of internalization. Two major themes emerge: (1) Although internalization involves children's acquisition of a cognitive understanding of moral rules and values, there is also a strong affective component; affect is indeed a *necessary* element in internalization; (2) children's attributions concerning the source of their own actions and emotions play an important role in determining whether they will internalize control processes, i.e., monitor their own behavior in the absence of surveillance.

Let us consider the affective issues first. Hoffman refers to parents' expression of anger, disapproval, hurt, or disappointment during disciplinary encounters as the "motive-arousal component" of parental influence attempts. These reactions by parents arouse anxiety in the child. Hoffman suggests that there is an optimum arousal level. Too much "deviation anxiety" interferes with the child's processing of the cognitive elements in the disciplinary message; too little leaves the child without motivation to change. According to Hoffman, emotion plays another part in the socialization process, namely, empathic emotional reactions to others' distress. Here again, the emphasis is on a negative emotional state, albeit a vicarious one. Empathic distress is pinpointed as a motivator for the child to behave prosocially. The role of anxiety in socialization is also heavily stressed by Grusec, who says: "Without fear of punishment, or some form of anxiety . . . there would be no motivation to be altruistic or to suppress undesirable responses."

I would not wish to deprecate the role of anxiety in socialization. It is clearly true that there must be some motivation for children to behave prosocially, and there is a venerable history of work on anxiety showing that it can indeed provide the necessary motivation. It is also true that parents do make extensive use of anxiety-arousing techniques. My question is: why the *exclusive* emphasis on negative emotional states as motivators? There is considerable evidence that positive affective states are influential as well. Consider the following examples:

1. Induction of positive moods increases the likelihood that a child will behave altruistically (Isen, How, & Rosehan, 1973; Moore, Underwood, & Rosenhan, 1973).

2. If a child has just been helped by another individual, the chances are increased that the child will be helpful if that other individual needs help (Cox, 1974).
3. Helpful behavior acquired through observation of an altruistic model will be more widely generalized to a variety of real-life opportunities for helpfulness if the model has a previous history of nurturant interaction with the child (Yarrow, Scott, & Waxler, 1973).
4. Both positive and negative empathic reactions can be conditioned and will motivate altruistic behavior (Aronfreed & Paskal, reported in Aronfreed, 1969).
5. Empathy based on perceived similarity to another person takes both positive and negative forms. That is, people experience both vicarious distress and vicarious pleasure when observing others similar to themselves and either emotion will serve to motivate subjects to sacrifice their own immediate gains to relieve another's distress or give another pleasure (Krebs, 1975).
6. Two-year-old children who display high frequencies of altruistic behavior have mothers with a history of empathic interaction wth the child; that is, in the course of daily life with the child, these mothers are responsive to the child's needs and emotional states and are skillful in anticipating difficulties the child may experience. Altruism in these very young children is also influenced by emotionally toned induction, which is probably anxiety arousing. Thus, either a positive affective relationship with a socialization agent or certain (not all) forms of anxiety arousal, or both, are conditions that appear to foster prosocial behavior in very young children (Zahn-Waxler, Radke-Yarrow, & King, 1979).
7. Young children with a history of secure attachment to their mothers show a willingness to accept direction from their mothers in mastering a new task, without negative maternal pressures (Matas, Arend, & Stroufe, 1978).

All these findings suggest that, even in very young children, positive emotional states operate as an alternative to anxiety as a source of motivation for prosocial behavior.

Both Hoffman and Grusec emphasize the role of anxiety in motivating children to pay attention to their parents' requirements. I would like to suggest that a history of playful and cooperative interactions with their parents also fosters childrens' cognition of their parents' signals. For example, it is a reasonable conjecture that children with such a history would more often be found looking at their parents, whereas children with a more negative history would more often be looking away. As Schaffer and Crook (1980) have shown, a mother can more easily obtain a young child's compliance with a task requirement if the child is already paying attention to her – a not surprising, but important, finding. If the mother tries to impose a task without first getting the child's attention, she is likely to fail to get compliance and may be impelled to escalate negative pressures; however, the mother of the attentive child can more often get cooperation on the first try. Thus, the presence of a positive emotional tie reduces the need to use anxiety-arousing forms of socialization pressure. We do not know how the positive and negative emotional states balance out in the lives of most children. Undoubtedly, all parents use anxiety-arousing techniques to some degree in the course of disciplinary encounters, and undoubtedly almost all rely on mutual affection to get the child's interest and cooperation when the occasion permits. Thus it could be argued that the use of positive versus negative emotional states as a means of getting compliance to socialization demands is determined, at least in part, by the strength of the preexisting affectional bond. The parent who has been responsive, comforting, and interesting to the child in the first 12 or 18 months, when parental demands are few, has put assets into the socialization bank – assets that can be drawn upon when the child has developed to the point when socialization pressures are necessary. Traditionally, we have thought of the affective bond in negative terms: we have assumed that when a child wanting to be liked by significant others, and wanting to please them, reflects a fear of *not* being liked. We have said that a warm and loving parent who has fostered attachment is in a position to use withdrawal of love as a technique of control, because the child is vulnerable to the fear of losing the established emotional support. I am emphasizing a different role for the early affective bond, namely, that it engenders attention to the parent and a readiness to become interested in, and cooperative with, an enterprise suggested by the parent. The parent who has established such a relationship has, in a sense, earned the opportunity to be a nonauthoritarian parent. In the absence of such attentiveness and positive motivation on the part of the child, the parent has little recourse but to resort to heavy-handed, power-assertive modes of control if the child is to be socialized.

If we may assume that both positive and negative emotional states are involved in the international process, we can ask further questions about the origins of these states. Grusec says: "I shall assume that no innate predisposition for altruism exists, that the young child's behavior is governed by selfish desires for immediate gratification, and that some effort is required to effect a change from self-interest to the interest in others." We cannot doubt that socialization agents play a considerable role in motivating this shift. Yet it may be that certain inborn biases foster the quick acquisition of empathic emotional responses. Shweder asked, during our conference, whether antisocial behavior could be taught as easily as prosocial behavior. If we consider the empathic responses, and the processes of simple classical conditioning whereby they can be acquired, it would seem that the answer to Shweder's question would be *no*. Given that young children are frequently in the presence of others who are in the same eliciting situation they are in, and experiencing matching emotions, it would follow that the signs of distress in others would become associated with the child's own distress and the signs of others' pleasure with the child's own pleasure without any deliberate teaching being required. We need not assume that children's emotional states are always matched by those of others around them; only that a match occurs more often than a countermatch. It would be an unusual environment indeed in which other people were commonly experiencing pain on those occasions when the child was experiencing pleasure. This condition would be required for a child to acquire "reverse empathy" (experiencing pleasure when others experience distress), which would then become a motivator for causing pain in others. It is reasonable to assume that almost all environments are biased toward a similarity of emotional states that co-occur in the child and other persons in the child's vicinity. In addition, presumably, the conditioning of the child's empathic reactions to signs of emotion in others will be strengthened if the parents are (1) emotionally expressive and (2) empathic with the child's emotional states, so that they initiate a match. But even without these parental responses, conditions normally exist for considerable conditioning of empathy. In this sense, an innate predisposition for altruism does exist if one accepts the propositions (1) that empathic emotional responses contribute to the motivation for altruism, and (2) that human beings are innately equipped with a readiness for classical conditioning of emotions.

Let us turn now to a consideration of the role of attribution in internalization. Lepper provides a review of the research on attitude change under conditions of over- or under-justification. He reminds us that if people can be made to act in a way contrary to their initial beliefs, without there being any salient external pressure to which they can attribute their actions, they will believe that they acted voluntarily and change their attitudes accordingly. On the other hand, if there is strong external pressure to act as they did, their initial attitudes remain unchanged. In a similar vein, if there is external pressure to behave in a certain way and the target persons resist the pressure, continuing to behave in a way contrary to what is being demanded by an external agent, the target persons' attitudes supporting the behavior are strengthened, so that they become even more convinced after the event than before about the rightness of their own behavior and the wrongness of the action or belief that the external agent is demanding. Lepper links attitude change to internalization in children, suggesting that mild pressure from socialization agents, *if it is effective* in bringing about the desired behavior, will result in the child's having a sense of having done the desired action voluntarily; the child will then value the behavior and come to adopt it voluntarily. If external pressure is strong and salient, however, and the child complies, the compliance is attributed to the external pressure, and the child neither values the behavior nor spontaneously adopts it; indeed, the behavior comes to be *dis*valued. If parental pressure is applied ineffectively, so that the child does not comply, the child will become more resistant than ever to parental demands, more addicted than ever to the behavior the parent is trying to change.

Although Lepper does not incorporate the attitude-change literature that deals with inoculation, it is relevant and supports his argument. It has been shown (Festinger & Maccoby, 1964; Roberts & Maccoby, 1973) that the acceptance of an advocated position is interfered with and belief in the opposed position is strengthened when an audience rehears counterarguments to a persuasive communication. The desired attitude change can be brought about only by either distracting the audience from rehearsal of counterarguments or dealing frontally with the counterarguments before introducing the persuasive arguments for the new position (as Mark Anthony did in his funeral oration for Julius Caeser). This salient parental pressure that does not promote compliance prompts the child to think about all the reasons for not complying and in the process strengthens oppositional attitudes as well as oppositional behavior.

In an elegant analysis, Lepper likens Baumrind's three major parenting styles to three positions on the degree-of-pressure and child-compliance diagram (Lepper's Figure 3). Permissive parenting involves "objectively insufficient justification" – that is, the pressure is insufficient to promote compliance. In this case, the child is poorly socialized. Not only does the child's behavior not change in a prosocial direction, but the original unsocialized behavior is consolidated and comes to be supported by the child's belief system. Although authoritarian parenting does obtain compliance, it does not foster the adoption of parental values or rationale because the salience of the external pressure felt by children subjected to such parenting leads them to believe that their prosocial behavior was forced upon them – not voluntary. (No doubt, they rehearse counterarguments as well.) Authoritative parenting is, then, the desired in-between: when sufficient, but not salient, pressure is exerted, children conclude that they behaved prosocially because they wanted to and thus adopt the desired values. Grusec takes a similar position, arguing that although punishment is necessary to motivate prosocial behavior, the salience of punishment must be minimized for internalization to occur. She concludes: "A socializing agent who applies negative consequences for misbehavior but who helps the child to make an attributional error by accompanying these consequences with verbal statements will be successful in producing internalization of altruism."

There are some difficulties with this formulation, not the least of which is that you probably can't fool very many of the children very much of the time. They develop uncanny skills at detecting the iron hand within the silken glove. Simply accompanying a spanking with verbal statements is unlikely to provide successful camouflage for the fact that the child is being made to conform through fear of external retribution. We must consider the possibility that the child's sense of having done something prosocial voluntarily would be fostered by providing real choices, in situations maximally conducive to prosocial behavior, so that when the child behaves prosocially, the action was in fact in large part voluntary. I am talking about the carrot rather than the stick and am assuming, as argued earlier, the existence of social motivation not based on fear.

The Lepper formulation places extraordinary emphasis on compliance. The implication is that on a parental-pressure scale of 1 to 10, there is some point on the scale when pressure will be just sufficient to bring about compliance. Let us assume, for illustration, that this point is 5. At pressure level 4, then, we have conditions that have deleterious effects upon the child's voluntary acceptance of parental values. At pressure point 5.5, they are maximally favorable. If "John, dear, wouldn't you like to eat your spinach?" (pressure only about 2) does not cause John to eat the spinach, a little increment has been added to his dislike for spinach. "John, I want you to eat your spinach *now*" (pressure 4) adds more dislike if the increased pressure does not succeed in producing the desired behavior. If the parents escalate to "If you don't eat your spinach this minute you can't go to see *Star Wars* tomorrow" (pressure 6) and the child finally complies, we should find John suddenly thinking "Hey! I *love* spinach!" There is something improbable about this scenario. We know full well that even though the pressure exercised was just sufficient to obtain compliance, the child will perceive it as external. It was a clear, easily comprehended threat to withdraw privileges, and it would be difficult for a child to make any other attribution. I would like to suggest that the flaw in the theory appears to lie in the assumption of a fixed compliance point. Some children, of course, comply with little pressure, whereas others comply only with considerable and very evident power-assertion. There is also situation-to-situation and day-to-day variability in how much parental pressure is needed to motivate a given child to comply. A modification of the right-hand side of Lepper's Figure 3 shows what is being proposed (my Figure 1). In this formulation I buy the idea that parental

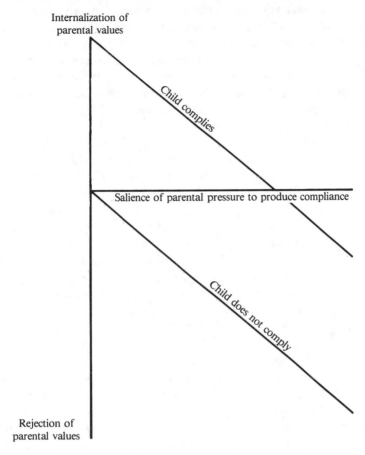

Figure 1. Effect of salient parental pressure (from left to right, low to high) on internalization under condition of child compliance or noncompliance.

pressure insufficient to produce compliance will not produce internalization; and indeed, that if the child does not comply, parental pressure is likely to move the child in a direction opposite from that intended by the parents. Thus, the importance of obtaining compliance is affirmed. (There is wisdom in the dictum that appears in an army officer training manual: "Never give an order if you have reason to believe it will not be obeyed.") Compliance, I assume, may happen under varying degrees of parental pressure. Whereas compliance with little pressure (another way of saying that there is a substantial voluntary element in the child's compliance) fosters internalization, compliance under conditions of strong external pressure does not. In the preceding example, a child who complies to "Wouldn't you like to eat your spinach?" might actually come to like it better. The child who complies to a strong threat would not, even though it was a just-sufficient pressure. This formulation is similar to Lepper's, except that it does not require a sudden reversal in the child's attitudes from maximally negative to maximally positive with a very small change in the degree of parental pressure. Nor does it assume that the effect of compliance will be the same regardless of the amount of pressure that was just sufficient to bring it about.

I believe that the power of socialization agents to manipulate the child's attributions has been overstressed. There is a certain heady excitement in being able to make contact with the body of elegant studies that constitute the attribution literature. Experimental social psychologists have been very skillful in locating the range where attribution can be successfully manipulated and have worked within this range. Their findings are real and important, and they do show (among other things) that children who think they have control over outcomes are more likely to persist after failure (Dweck), maintain intrinsic interest in activity (Lepper, this volume), and resist temptation in the absence of surveillance (Dienstbier et al., 1975). Also, it is reasonably clear that at least some forms of salient external pressure are associated with low internalization (see Hoffman, 1970), perhaps because the children cannot reasonably attribute their prosocial behavior to their own volition. However, under most circumstances, it seems probable that when children believe they did an expected prosocial act voluntarily, their belief is solidly grounded in fact: They *did* willingly cooperate and were not forced. Thus, I would argue that external manipulation of attribution is usually not the key to internalization. Finding a way of eliciting willing compliance with minimal external pressure is.

If we take the position that internalization calls for children's attributing efficacy to themselves, and that they are likely to do this when they have some real control over the outcomes that affect them, we are brought to some new issues in socialization theory and some possible contradictions with existing research findings. Although there is considerable evidence that a sense of control has positive effects on children's motivation (see Lepper, this volume; Seligman, 1975, on learned helplessness; Gunnar, 1978, on reduction of fear in 12-month-olds by providing them with control over aversive stimulation), there is equally clear evidence that firm parental control fosters various aspects of children's competence, self-esteem, and moral internalization (see Maccoby and Martin, in press, for a summary of this evidence). One does not want to buy a sense of efficacy for the child at the expense of the parent's efficacy, or vice versa. Clearly, what is needed is a system of mutual responsiveness (*A*'s responsiveness translates as *B*'s control) and mutual gratification. A bargain can be struck, in which the parent expects compliance with certain demands but also accepts the obligation to be responsive to certain of the child's needs. Of course, when children are very young, their cognitive understanding of reciprocal obligations is limited. Damon (1977) has provided an important account of the way in which this understanding develops during the middle-childhood years. But I would argue that Piaget (1948) was probably wrong in his contention that true reciprocation is not possible between adults and children, only between peers. Reciprocation is, of course, a matter of degree, but considerable amounts can be attained within families despite the manifest differences between adults and children in knowledge and power.

I have suggested that willing compliance by children implies their having accepted a kind of bargain with their parents for the exchange of favors. This is a reasonable description of situations in which the child wants one thing and the parent another. Willing compliance can occur in another kind of situation, however: when the child and the parent want the same thing, so that the parent has only to suggest "Wouldn't it be fun to . . . " or "how about if we . . . " to arouse the child's interest without the need for bargaining (see Baumrind, 1971, on harmonious families). It would be too much to expect that certain onerous tasks can be turned into fun. But a history of joint activity in pursuit of mutual goals, along with a parent's positive attitude toward tasks to be done, should contribute to the likelihood that the child and parent will have the same objective, so that disciplinary encounters are circumvented.

There are some conceptual problems in the formulation I have suggested, and there is no point in trying to duck them. I have transformed a rather neat antecedent–consequent relationship (parent atributes volition to the child, child internalizes) to a rather murky circular one (child complies readily, requiring parent to use only minimal pressure, and minimal pressure enables both parent and child to attribute volition to the child, which in turn fosters internalization). In such a system, we have lost the clarity of where the causal agency in the system lies. Nevertheless, I would argue that circular process is the name of the game in family interaction. We must find ways of conceptualizing it, rather than trying to understand it by dealing only with selected, unidirectional links.

Note

1 Attitude change that is brought about after overcoming counterarguments is highly stable and resistant to change, a fact that may help to explain why parental use of reasoning is associated with internalization in children.

References

Aronfreed, J. The concept of internalization. In D. A. Goslin (Ed.), *Handbook of socialization theory and research.* Chicago: Rand McNally, 1969.

Baumrind, D. Harmonious parents and their preschool children. *Developmental Psychology*, 1971, *4*, 99–102.

Cox, N. Prior help, ego development, and helping behavior. *Child Development*, 1974, *45*, 594–603.

Damon, W. *The social world of the child.* San Francisco: Jossey-Base, 1977.

Dienstbier, R. A., Hillman, D., Lehnkoff, J., Hillman, J., & Valkenaar, M. C. An emotion-attribution approach to moral behavior: Interfacing cognitive and avoidance theories of moral development. *Psychology Review*, 1975, *82*, 299–315.

Dornbusch, S., Carlsmith, M., Gross, R. T., Martin, J., Jennings, D., Rosenberg, N., & Duke, P. *Sexual development, age, and dating: A comparison of biological and societal influences upon one set of behaviors.* Unpublished report, Boys Town Center, Stanford University, 1980.

Festinger, L., & Maccoby, N. On resistance to persuasive communication. *Journal of Abnormal & Social Psychology*, 1964, *68*, 359–367.

Gunnar, M. Changing a frightening toy into a pleasant toy by allowing the infant to control its actions. *Developmental Psychology*, 1978, *14*, 157–162.

Hoffman, M. L. Moral development. In P. H. Mussen (Ed.), *Carmichael's manual of child psychology.* New York: Wiley, 1970.

Isen, A. M., Horn, N., & Rosenhan, D. L. Effects of success and failure on children's generosity. *Journal of Personality and Social Psychology*, 1973, *27*, 239–247.

Kohlberg, L. Moral stages and moralization: The cognitive-developmental approach. In T. Lickona (Ed.), *Moral development and behavior: Theory, research, and social issues.* New York: Holt, Rinehart & Winston, 1976.

Krebs, D. Empathy and altruism. *Journal of Personality and Social Psychology*, 1975, *32*, 1134–1146.

Maccoby, E. E., and Martin, J. A. Socialization in the context of the family: parent-child interaction. In E. M. Hetherington (Ed.), *Social Development*, Vol. III of *Mussen's Manual of Child Psychology*, 4th ed. New York: Wiley, in press.

Matas, L., Arend, R. A., & Sroufe, L. A. Continuity of adaptation in the second year: The relationship between quality of attachment and later competence. *Child Development*, 1978, *49*, 547–556.

Moore, B. S., Underwood, B., & Rosenhan, D. L. Affect and altruism. *Developmental Psychology*, 1973, *8*, 99–104.

Piaget, J. *The moral judgment of the child.* Glencoe, Ill.: Free Press, 1948.

Roberts, D. F., & Maccoby, N. Information processing and persuasion: Counterarguing behavior. In P. Clarke (Ed.), *New models for communication research*, pp. 269–307. Beverly Hills, Calif.: Sage, 1973.

Schaffer, H. R., & Crook, C. K. Child compliance and maternal control techniques. *Developmental Psychology*, 1980, *16*, 54–61.

Seligman, M. P. *Helplessness.* San Francisco: Freeman, 1975.

Shantz, C. Children's understanding of social rules and the social context. In F. C. Serafica (Ed.), *Social congition and social relations in context.* New York: Guilford Press, in press.

Yarrow, M. R., Xott, P. M., & Waxler, C. Z. Learning concern for others. *Developmental Psychology*, 1973, *8*, 240–260.

Zahn-Waxler, C., Radke-Yarrow, M., & King, R. A. Child-rearing and children's prosocial initiations toward victims of distress. *Child Development*, 1979, *50*, 319–330.

15   Five questions for research in social-cognitive development

William Damon

With the publication of this volume, it is clear that social scientists from a variety of approaches have found children's social cognition worthy of study. The variety includes developmental, cross-cultural, experimental, and social-psychological approaches, each of which has its own particular rationale in choosing goals and questions for empirical study.

Although there is some discussion of goals in this volume, rarely in such presentations as these do investigators make explicit the full rationale behind their research. I do not know all the goals and questions that researchers from these different approaches have for their studies of children's social cognition. But I can delineate my own goals for studying children's social cognition, goals that consist mostly of questions from a developmental orientation. By so doing, I shall be able to specify the ways in which I can profit from the present volume. Reciprocally, others with different orientations may decide for themselves whether the developmental questions I ask address the problems they find interesting in children's social cognition.

My own goals for studying children's social cognition can be summed up in five sets of research questions:

1. Are there age differences in children's understanding of social phenomena? If so, which phenomena consistently yield such differences? That is, where exactly are clear age trends to be found? These last two questions are closely related to the following: Which aspects of social reality pose the greatest conceptual difficulty for young children trying to make sense of the world?

2. If age differences in children's social understanding are established, how are they best characterized? For example, are the differences best described as quantitative in nature, reflecting continuous increases in basic abilities like language, information processing, or decentering (to name a few of the possibilities)? Or do these age differences signify qualitative changes in how children conceptualize social phenomena, re-

371

flecting the construction of conceptual principles specifically "social cognitive" in nature?

3. What are the social and developmental processes through which children improve their understanding of social phenomena? In part, the answer to this will be determined by the way in which Question 2 is answered, in the sense that the way age changes are characterized will lead to certain expectations concerning the processes that account for the changes. If we believe, for example, that it is really only children's memory that is changing with age, we will posit different sorts of developmental processes than if we believe that children must specifically reformulate their social thinking as they develop. But there are additional sides to the present question as well. These have to do with the developmental relations between social influence and social cognition. How does social interaction influence children's social understanding in developmentally progressive ways? In other ways, how do children benefit from their social experience with respect to their social understanding? Related to this is the intriguing question of whether specific types of social experience are necessary (or at least particularly facilitating) for particular gains in children's social knowledge.

4. What are the relations between developmental changes in children's social cognition and their everyday social conduct?

5. What is the role of affect in the development of social understanding? Does affect play a unique part in the acquisition of emotionally laden areas of social knowledge like moral judgment, self-evaluation, and sexuality? Or do all cognitive acquisitions – social or otherwise – draw upon identical "cold-blooded" reasoning processes like encoding, recall, and logical inference?

The current state of research on these five questions, prior to the work presented in this volume, varies in strength from question to question. Here I shall offer an encapsulated and personal view of developmental psychology's progress in this area, citing some work familiar to me as illustrative of what we do and do not know at the time of this writing (June 1980). I shall proceed question by question, beginning with Question 1. It will become clear that I have arranged these questions according to the degree of our present knowledge, with the state of our art strongest on Question 1 and weakest on Question 5.

1. By now it has been established beyond denial that there are age differences in children's social understanding. These age differences can be tapped by virtually any interview procedure, and the social phenomena that have been the focus of child interviews of one sort or another include people (Scarlett, Press, & Crockett, 1971; Lively & Bromley,

1973), social relations (Berndt, in press; Bigelow, 1977; Damon, 1977; Selman & Jacquette, 1978; Youniss, 1980), social and moral rules (Damon, 1977; Kohlberg, 1963; Turiel, 1978), societal institutions (Connell, 1971), and the self (Broughton, 1978; Furth, 1980; Keller, Ford, & Meachum, 1978; Lewis & Brooks-Gunn, 1980). Generally such studies have found strong and consistent empirical relations between age and the nature of children's statements about social phenomena.

As an illustration, children's conceptions of two common social relations, friendship and authority, have been found to change with considerable regularity between the ages of 4 and 10. Young children confine their statements about friendship to descriptions of friends as playmates-of-the-moment with whom one shares toys and activities. Older children recognize friends as long-term associates toward whom one feels admiration, loyalty, and commitment, and with whom one exchanges trust, common interests, secrets, and other forms of exclusive psychological intimacy (Berndt, in press, Bigelow, 1977; Selman & Jacquett, 1978; Youniss, 1980). During this same age period, children's statements about authority evolve from considering obedience as a deferral to superior persons possessing special powers (such as the power to spank) to considering obedience as a voluntary and situationally specific submission between equals, serving the welfare of both leader and follower (Damon, 1977, 1980).

Now these are only two of many social-cognitive changes associated with age during the childhood years. Many more have been established, in and beyond the social relations of friendship and authority (see Damon, 1977; Maccoby, 1980; Shantz, 1975, in press, for compendia of such changes in these and other areas of children's social understanding). The question at this point no longer is whether age changes of this sort are common in children as they grow but rather how best to describe and explain them. This brings us to Question 2 and will require a more extended discussion.

2. Currently there is widespread disagreement about how best to describe psychological development in general. The major focus of this disagreement is whether to use stagelike models that emphasize discontinuities during development or whether to use quantitative notions that emphasize continuities. To date, most developmentalists studying children's social understanding have generated stagelike models for their descriptive accounts. This is not accidental, nor is it merely a convenient following of scientific tradition and convention. There are properties of age-related social-cognitive change that have proven difficult to capture without the use of constructs associated with stage models. On the other hand, not all aspects of social-cognitive change are amenable to a stage

analysis, and some connotations of the stage notion have proved unhelpful and even misleading. This has led many to reject the use of stage descriptions altogether. The problem is that such total rejection does not in itself help us find alternative means of analyzing those features of development for which stage models are well suited.

Among such features, I would select two as being both critical to the phenomenon of development and resistant to description by models that do not include some stagelike language. These two critical features are qualitative change and sequentiality. Qualitative change means that there are different modes of understanding that emerge in the course of development. These different modes are not increases in specific abilities (such as the ability to store more information or speak more words) but rather are fundamentally new ways of apprehending, interpreting, and knowing the world and one's experience in it. Sequentiality means that the qualitatively different modes of understanding emerge in some rational order as the child develops. That is, there are reasons for expecting some modes to develop before others.

Briefly, the case for qualitative description is that any careful analysis of differences between older and younger children's social reasoning will indicate that such differences cannot be characterized only as quantitative increases along specified dimensions. The changes noted in children's friendship and authority conceptions, for example, cannot simply be called increases in dimensions like reciprocity, even though it might be tempting to do so. To say that older children are more reciprocal than younger children is not only an inadequate analysis, it is also somewhat inaccurate. The exchange of commitment and psychological intimacy in friendship is a different kind of reciprocity than the exchange of goods and play, but it is not exactly more reciprocal. Similarly, the reciprocal exchange of compelled obedience for an authority figure's expression of superior power is different from reciprocal exchange of voluntary obedience for an authority figure's expression of concern and special leadership competence. These are only two examples of social-understanding differences that defy any quantitative analysis that I have ever seen or imagined. A reading of the literature on children's social-cognitive development will reveal that such examples permeate data collected by virtually any interview procedure.

As for sequentiality, there are both rational and empirical grounds for believing it to be a critical feature of children's social-cognitive development. The rational grounds are (1) that some notions are conceptually more difficult than others and (2) that children typically encounter some types of social experiences later than others. For example, notions like commitment, intimacy, trust, leadership competence, and voluntary submission are harder to conceptualize than notions like sharing goods and deferring to physical threats, partly because the former notions are relatively complex and partly because they deal with psychologically subjective aspects of experience. This is one reason to expect that conceptions of friendship and authority reflecting the former notions will emerge somewhat after those reflecting the earlier ones. The second reason, which in some ways goes hand in hand with the first, is that children (at least in our society) are treated differently by both peers and adults as they grow older. Therefore, they have different kinds of experiences with friends and authority figures, experiences that in fact coincide closely with the qualitative changes in their understanding of friendship and authority. This, too, is an indication of rational sequence, although the source is social-contextual rather than cognitive-developmental.

The empirical reasons to expect sequentiality in social-cognitive development have been established by both cross-sectional as well as longitudinal data, the latter, of course, being by far the more convincing evidence. The only condition that I would add to the published reports (see Damon, 1983, for a summary) is that empirical sequentiality does not mean lock-step, invariant change from day to day. Any system of measurement will reveal temporary "regression," unevenness, and a great deal of flux and momentary instability during the process of change. This is in the very nature of developmental transitions. Children do not change their thinking patterns overnight. When they begin to add new ideas and to reformulate old ones, it is initially with considerable uncertainty and back-and-forth reasoning. Despite the qualitative nature of the shift that will ultimately take place, the change process itself is gradual and continues in many respects. As an example of the type of sequentiality to be expected in children's social cognition, I offer a summary figure of two-year longitudinal data that I have collected on children's authority reasoning. The 34 children, initially ages 4 through 10, were interviewed on three separate occasions, each one year apart, so that by the end of the study their ages were 6 through 12. As can be seen from this figure, there was movement both up and down the developmental levels from year to year.[1] But when the two-year period is taken as a whole, the overall movement is markedly upward: Almost all children were higher by one or two levels in Year 2 than in Year 0.

Developmental data such as this helps us resist expectations of sudden, wholistic transformations in children's social understanding. Such expectations have also proved empirically unfeasible in a range of cognitive domains beyond just the social concepts that I have studied (Flavell,

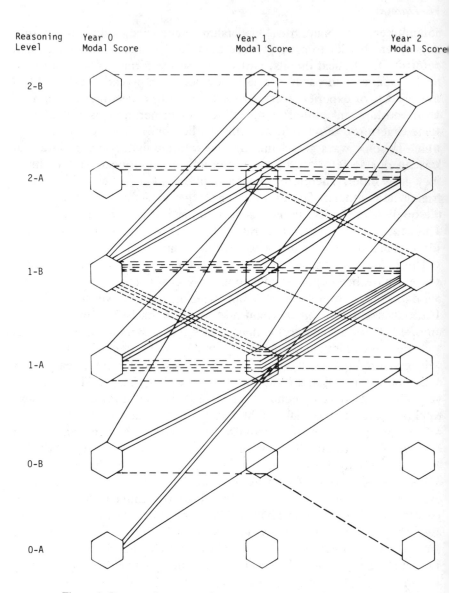

Reasoning Level	Year 0 Modal Score	Year 1 Modal Score	Year 2 Modal Score
2-B			
2-A			
1-B			
1-A			
0-B			
0-A			

Figure 1. Pattern of two-year change in children's justice reasoning. (*Note:* Each line represents one subject's progress from Year 0 to Year 2. Solid portions of the lines indicate upward movements from one year to the next, and broken portions of the lines indicate lateral or downward movements.) (From W. Damon, The nature of social-cognitive change in the developing child, in W. Overton (ed.), *The relationship between social and cognitive development.* Hillsdale, N.J.: Erlbaum, 1983. By permission.)

376

1980). There is little reason to believe that a few "underlying" structures determine the nature of all thinking or that sudden or discrete changes in these structures lead to across-the-board changes in understanding the world. Unitary-structure notions like egocentrism, for example, must be modified, because many studies have shown that, whatever their cognitive deficits, children at all ages show some awareness of others' perspectives (Borke, 1975; Flavell, 1977; Garvey & Hogan, 1973; Shatz & Gelman, 1973). Even if some aspects of young children's behavior may be described as egocentric, other aspects defy this description. Similar problems have been found with other attempts at wholistic structural description, including Piaget's logical-mathematical stages and Kohlberg's moral-judgment stages (Brainerd, 1978; Kurtines & Greif, 1974).

Stage-model connotations aside, why should we expect cognitive development to follow a pattern of wholistic transformation? The world is full of diversities, and for optimal functioning, thinking must be organized to deal with these diversities. For example, I have argued elsewhere that the social world is quite different from the physical world: Among other things, people are able to conduct mutually intentional interactions and relations with one another unlike anything remotely possible between a person and the physical world (Damon, 1979). This means that understanding the social world requires notions that are not appropriate for understanding the physical world. Social cognition, therefore, must be organized to some extent around principles different from those of logical or physical cognition, and this already negates the possibility of a unitary cognitive structure. But to go further along these lines, even within the social world there are multiple diversities. There are interactions with a range of meanings and intentions, relations built upon different assumptions, rules and regulations serving different social purposes, and so on. Thus social cognition itself must reflect not one but many systems of cognitive principles. Turiel (1978) has made this point in distinguishing moral from social-conventional reasoning. My own work has begun with the assumption that there are fundamental conceptual issues that separate friendship from authority, justice from social rules, and the self from others, to cite a few examples from my studies of social relations, social regulations, and social objects, respectively (Damon, in press-b).

The point I have been making is that there is both a developmental and a functional reason to doubt that children's thinking undergoes wholistic, discrete, or sudden changes with age. The developmental reason is that transitions are gradual and uneven from day to day, reflecting the flux and uncertainty of trying out new ideas. The functional reason is that thinking can never be wholistic if it is to cope with the varieties of human experience. Because thinking is thus comprised of diverse cognitive systems, there is no reason to expect that it develops all of a piece. Depending upon a child's particular experience in the world, and perhaps also upon a child's own inherent pattern of abilities, some cognitive systems will no doubt advance more rapidly than others and along different dimensions. There will be considerable individuality to the total process and an infinity of final possibilities.

With the notion of wholism discarded, can we still speak usefully of stages? Flavell has suggested substituting the word *sequences* (Flavell, 1980), but this still does not preserve all the developmentally critical features of cognition captured by stage models. A fuller alternative would be "ordered sequences of qualitatively distinct modes of knowing," implying (1) that the sequence is ordinal, but not interval, in nature and (2) that the sequence's progression is defined by qualitative distinctions that are not reducible to quantitative differences. I believe that such a phrase would serve adequately as a model for describing social-cognitive development, though I do find it linguistically awkward. I would greatly prefer using words like stage or level, with the understanding that such usage does not bring with it claims of wholism or sudden developmental leaps. But I cannot say whether such a moderate and restricted use of these overextended words is at this time possible.

The preceding discussion is intended to indicate my belief that substantial progress is being made in describing age changes in children's social cognition. We are moving away from earlier, unitary models of cognition to more specific analyses that chart the development of children's social understanding in a number of areas. Simplistic and wholistic notions of change have been discarded without blurring the difference between children at different periods of development. Much refinement and further taxonomic work is needed, but some tangible beginnings have already been made.

3. About Question 3 – accounting for the processes of change in children's social cognition – we have less current enlightenment, and most of that available is somewhat vague and ambiguous. On this question theory and assumption predominate, and empirical studies with operationalized concepts have been rare. Theoretically, almost all of us have assumed a social-interactionist position to account for social-cognitive development. This means that, each in our own way, we all try to recognize that a child's knowledge owes a debt both to the child's social experience and to the child's always-changing capacities to make sense out of this experience. But we have done little to document this debt or to analyze the nature of the interaction between children's cognitive capacities and their social experience.

How does a child develop new ways of understanding the social world? We believe that social influence is somehow crucial to this process, but it is not easy to understand how a child makes use of such influence. We know too much about children to believe any longer in the process of direct transmission of information or values. Not only are children cognitively limited in what they can comprehend, but they also actively resist attempts at direct indoctrination. If developmental psychology has made any progress in the past 50 years, it is in gaining respect for the active role of children in their own socialization: It is not easy these days to find child psychologists who believe that children may be simply molded like clay into well-socialized citizens.

We are then forced to look for more subtle and indirect mechanisms of social influence. This is where social cognition in the second sense of the term comes in. Beyond its use to denote the understanding of social phenomena, social cognition also may signify the processes by which social experience is apprehended. It is through social cognition, therefore, that social influence is realized. In this sense it "mediates" between the child and the socializing agents of the world, although mediation is an improper metaphor because it suggests that there is a chronology in which social cognition comes after the socializing agent's initiation and before the ultimate effect upon the child. In actuality, the processes of social influence follow no such sequence. They are as much initiated by social-cognizing on the part of the child as by the actions of others in the social world, because the latter has no meaning and no influence upon the child without the former. For the child, psychologically and developmentally, there is no social experience without social cognition.

What, then, are the social-cognitive processes that account for the developmental impact of social influence? On a theoretical level, we have some plausible candidates, including communication, perspective taking, attributional mechanisms, and so on. All of these social-psychological processes have been studied in populations of children as well as adults. But there have been few developmental studies of these processes, by which I mean studies that focus upon their role in the phenomenon of progressive cognitive change. In such studies, change must be an independent condition of the investigation, assumed in the experimental design. The dependent variables must be the processes of social cognition that are hypothesized to enable the child to be socially influenced in a progressive manner. In this way the developmental significance of social-cognitive processes may be directly determined. At the present we must look to the future for empirical studies of this sort, although I believe that some paradigms presented in this book may make a contribution in this direction. More about this issue, therefore, shortly.

4. On Question 4, concerning relations between children's social cognition and their real-life social conduct, we are not much further along than when Shantz (1975) wrote: "One might well expect that there would be a good deal of information relating the child's understanding of other people to his actual social behavior, but there is not" (p. 303). A few more studies have been done, particularly in the moral-judgment area. In general, both consistencies and inconsistencies between children's understanding and their conduct have been reported, depending upon the measures used and the aspect of social interaction studied. Some progress has been made constructing models relating understanding to conduct (Berndt, in press; Gerson & Damon, 1978). We now have some systematic bases for making predictions concerning when to expect consistency and when not to expect it; and, in the latter case, what kinds of inconsistencies to expect. But empirical tests of such predictions are laborious and time-consuming, so that once again many of our assumptions and hypotheses have not yet been shaped into concrete forms. Here is an area where empiricism of all types is welcome: We simply need more data linking children's reasoning to their conduct in a wide variety of social settings dealing with a diversity of social problems.

5. Question 5, concerning the special relations between social cognition and affect, is the easiest to review because almost no one, to my knowledge, has come to terms with it. Yet it may be the key to some central features of social cognition. In particular, as I noted above, we should be curious about the nature of social reasoning on affectively charged issues like self, morality, sexuality, hostility, and so on. Intuitively, it is difficult to accept the assertion that affect plays no role distinguishable from cognition when such issues are considered. Yet the affect relation has been practically out of bounds as a research topic in developmental psychology.

Now that I have laid out my view of where we stand in the study of children's social cognition, I shall be able to comment on the contributions presented in this volume. My comments will follow the organization of the previous discussion, considering each of the five questions in turn.

1. Although several chapters in this volume discuss age differences in children's social cognition, there are few attempts to uncover or describe new ones. Consequently, there is not much to be learned from this volume as to how, for example, 10-year-olds are different from 4-year-olds in their understanding of the social world. There are some exceptions to this statement, but they will be more appropriately reviewed in the context of other questions.

In some research presented in this volume, there is a deliberate obscuring of social-cognitive age differences. Generally this "leveling" has been done intentionally, out of the belief that there is more in common between children at different ages than has been previously asserted by developmentalists. The clearest case of leveling is the presentation by Pool, Shweder, and Much, who argue that young children are neither global nor confused in their moral thinking. These authors describe some sophisticated distinctions between social rules that children commonly make in their everyday behavior, in contrast to the theories of Piaget and Kohlberg. In a similar vein, Costanzo and Dix challenge the Piagetian notion that young children have trouble understanding moral intentionality. Through a series of systematic studies, Costanzo and Dix demonstrate that young children do appreciate considerations of intention, volition, and subjectivity if these notions are presented to them without distracting social-contextual issues (like the presence of adult social regulation). Berndt has shown that children's notions of friendship-related acts do not develop according to a three-step sequence similar to Kohlberg's moral-stage progression (from a consequence orientation to a social-norm orientation to a personal-norm orientation).

But even developmental psychologists interested in age differences will find some of this work helpful in separating the wheat from the chaff. Certainly not everything about children's thinking changes with age: The study of cognitive development must be as much a search for constancies as it is a search for the dynamics of progress. Indeed, I am personally delighted that work reported in this book has cast doubt on certain structural-developmental notions that have long been my favorite candidates for junking: the notion, for example, that cognition proceeds from the concrete to the abstract (Higgins and Parsons), the "myth of the hetronomous child" (Pool, Shweder, and Much), the notion of total cognitive deficits like egocentricism (Costanzo and Dix; Hartup, Brady, and Newcomb). Such notions impeded progress toward developmental models that accurately convey the ways in which children's social conceptions change and improve with age. These notions lead to predictions that are easily disconfirmed and are in any case too general to tell us much about how children operate within specific social contexts.

But work that dismisses certain types of once-suspected age differences can contribute to a developmental model only if it is placed within a context of age changes that continue to be confirmed. Otherwise, one ends up with the implausible notion that 4-year-olds think and act like 10-year-olds. Here much of the present volume falls short, mainly because little concern has been paid to defining areas of social knowledge that might yield stable, consistent, and predictable differences between children of different ages.

It is not that age differences are entirely missing from the research presented here. Some are reported, and these could be potentially informative to a developmental model of social cognition. But, as we shall see, too often the age differences reported here are difficult to interpret because we do not know enough about the social phenomena to which they apply. In fact, often we do not even know whether these occasional age differences are specific to social or to general cognitive processes. This brings us to the issue of developmental description, which is embedded in Question 2 and in terms of which I shall discuss the few age changes that are reported in this volume.

2. Ruble's research has uncovered an intriguing instance of social-cognitive change in children between the ages of 4 and 10. It seems that the younger children in this age range do not readily make use of comparisons between themselves and others in their self-evaluations, whereas older children do. Ruble demonstrates the robustness of this age difference with several kinds of behavioral data, including evidence that only older children (fourth-graders) take social-comparison information as an index of competence sufficient to maintain their intrinsic interest in a task. This is a compelling demonstration not only that age differences in children's social-comparison processes exist but also that these differences affect children's real-life social interactions.

To what should we attribute such differences in the first place? In a careful analysis, Ruble rules out general cognitive capacities, motivation, and strategy styles. Put simply, even preschool children have the ability and the will to make comparisons between people in certain situations. But they do not construct self-evaluations out of such comparisons. Why not? Here Ruble tries out some answers that provide only a shaky basis for an adequate developmental description. The notion of "surface to depth" no doubt will go the way of egocentrism, concreteness, and all similarly global descriptions of children's inabilities once this notion is closely analyzed. Surely we would have no trouble finding counterexamples of young children considering internal states, wishes, likes, and dislikes of others under certain conditions. In any case, the point is not that young children never think in depth about physical and social phenomena but that they do not make comparative inferences about the self.

As descriptors of the age change that Ruble has documented, the notions of stability and self-reflection are somewhat more valuable, because they begin to capture the specific kinds of understanding that children must develop in order to make self-evaluations on the basis of social comparisons. Certainly the notion of continuity of personal identity as well as the notion of distinctness between self and other must play some part in the development of the process that Ruble wishes to explain. But these are only beginnings toward a definition of the particular social-conceptual problems that children encounter in the course of Ruble's tasks. Such a definition can be accomplished only through a framework that specifies, orders, and integrates the varous categories of social knowledge that children must master in the course of development. Such a framework would no doubt reveal that Ruble's tasks tap into a very central category of social knowledge indeed: the concept of self. The problem for the developmentalist then becomes analyzing the changing basis on which children construct their self-understanding at different periods in their lives.

Cast in such a light, Ruble's findings would take on an added dimension. They might indicate, for example, that children in the preschool years understand themselves mainly with reference to activities that they are capable of performing and that only later do they select those activities at which they are relatively talented as criteria for self-definition. In fact, these findings are in line with the scarce existing developmental data on preschoolers' self-understanding (Keller, Ford & Meachum, 1978), although Ruble's research goes beyond this earlier study in many regards. Much more needs to be known about the development of children's self-understanding. The extent of our ignorance in this area is legion, despite the many attempts to measure children's self-esteem (Brim, 1976). For now, my point is twofold: (1) If an age change is not simply a reflection of a "background factor" (to use Ruble's phrase), it must be described in terms that specifically indicate the pattern of behavior or conception that is changing, and (2) if the significance of the change for the child's social-cognitive development is to be understood, it must be systematically interpreted with reference to fundamental categories of social knowledge.

There are, of course, a number of possible ways to categorize domains of social knowledge. My own approach, similar to that of Hinde (1980) and Youniss (1980), is to begin with categories of interpersonal relations (friendship, authority) and of social regulations that maintain these relations (justice, rules, conventions) as the basis social-integrating categories of knowledge and with categories of personal identity (self, self-interest) and of individuating transactions that establish this identity (social selection, hostility) as the basic social-differentiating categories of knowledge. Turiel (1978) has another approach, based on divisions between moral, social-conventional, and psychological "domains"; Shantz (1975) has yet another. This is neither the place to explicate these approaches nor to argue their merits. Suffice it to say that the differences between them are minor in comparison to approaches that begin without any kind of categorical overview.

As a thematic comment on the selections in this volume, I find a general failure to approach the study of children's social cognition with a clearly defined set of social-cognitive distinctions that could give some perspective to the research and its findings. I cannot imagine, for example, why Berndt would take children's *friendship* development as a test of a sequence derived from Kohlberg's *moral-judgment* model. Kohlberg's stages are already overextended enough (Damon, 1977) without bringing them out of the morality arena. Many concerns of friendship have nothing to do with either justice, obligation, or moral responsibility. Berndt himself (in press) has found that children speak of friendship in terms of intimacy, common interest, companionship, support, affection, fun, and so on. But for the present purposes he does not distinguish any of these from moral concerns. As far as I can tell, the study that he reports does not even distinguish prescriptive intentions (how one *should* act) from descriptive ones (how one *would* act). How can findings generated from a methodology that fails to make even the most rudimentary distinctions between types of social knowledge tell us anything interpretable about social-cognitive development?

I have similar conceptual difficulties with other studies reported here as well. Emmerich and Goldman use a "general index of cognitive functioning" as a test of whether interpersonal values are acquired "directly" through social experience or "mediated" through cognitive processes. If these values are really interpersonal in nature, we should need an index of *social*-cognitive functioning to assess their place in the developmental picture. In addition, although the authors propose to make certain distinctions between the various values that one "holds" (the authors' term), their treatment still conflates a fairly diverse set of social, personal, and moral values. The notion of "social norms," for example, has very little uniformity in a value sense if one examines it closely. Norms vary drastically from social group to social group: Monks, office workers, bookies, tennis players, and terrorists all have norms peculiar to their own collective activities. Are we to treat the values manifest in these norms as functionally equivalent with regard to either developmental processes or the guidance of behavior?

Grusec's chapter shows a similar conflating of functionally dissimilar social concepts. She writes of socialization as the suppressing of "antisocial" or "unwanted" behavior. But any kind of behavior is antisocial with respect to *some* social group, unwanted by *somebody*. In this and other accounts of socialization we need principles that distinguish moral from immoral behavior on grounds beyond social acceptability, because social acceptability still does not resolve the issue of to whom the behavior should be acceptable. Hoffman makes this same point in rejecting the use of compliance as a moral index: "Compliance is a questionable moral index to begin with, in view of Milgrim's finding that it may at times lead to immoral action."

However, in fairness to the contributions, the charting of developmental trends in social knowledge is not an important goal for any of the present authors. Consequently, it is not surprising that this collection does not present substantially new ways of describing age differences in children's social cognition. In fact one group of authors (Hartup, Brady, and Newcomb) report an age difference that they do not even treat as particularly interesting in itself. Rather, these authors consider their age-difference findings to be a handle on the cognitive processes that guide children's action in real-life social situations. We shall therefore return to this research under Question 4. For now, we can only note that substantial new contributions to our present knowledge of social-cognitive age trends must await research that is more systematically grounded in basic categorical distinctions than is the research in the present volume.

Beginning with Question 3, I believe that this volume does present some "new directions" that promise to further our understanding of children's social-cognitive development and social behavior. Many of these contributions speak for themselves, so that my comments will focus more on potential problems that I foresee than on the evident strength of some of these new approaches.

3. Most previous developmental accounts of children's social cognition have been primarily descriptive. Unlike these previous accounts, several chapters in the present volume explicitly analyze processes of social-cognitive change. There is attention both to the antecedents and to the mechanisms of change. Most welcome of all, there is in this collection widespread consideration of the social-contextual conditions that foster the development of social knowledge.

Higgins and Parsons provide a general framework for studying the developmental influence of social context, offering along the way a provocative reinterpretation of some well-known social-cognitive phenomena. They point out that the development of children's social thinking proceeds in parallel fashion to systematic changes in children's social environments as they grow older. It is therefore absurd to portray social-cognitive development merely as an increase in intellectual capacity isolated from particular social experiences. This is a point well worth making, as most cognitive models operationalize thinking as a process of reflective reasoning occurring in a social vacuum (Damon, 1979). Higgins and Parsons present a developmental model that takes seriously the crucial interaction between social experience and cognitive growth. Their use of this model to explain the development of accurate social prediction is far more convincing than anything I have seen in the perspective-taking literature.

In their presentation, Higgins and Parsons often treat changing characteristics of social context as antecedents to social-cognitive development. This may indeed be necessary to counteract the impoverished view that social knowledge is solely a product of "general" cognitive development. But the authors also recognize that it is usually impossible to determine the direction of causality between age changes in social cognition and age changes in a child's social context. Social thinking must reflect cultural realities just as cultural expectations are kept more or less in tune with children's changing perspectives. In a general sense, social development is a process of mutual adaptation between society and the child.

Within this general state of adaptation, however, there are many variations between the practices of different cultures, subcultures, families, and so on. Through systematic study of such variation, Higgins and Parsons propose to sort out the distinct contributions of social experience and individual development in the child's construction of social knowledge. As long as Higgins and Parsons can preserve the notion that social knowledge is an interaction rather than a summation of these contributions, this will be an exciting prospect. But this means that the authors must avoid temptation to dichotomize and isolate the "effects" of social context from the "effects" of developmental change. To borrow from Kagan's (1976) metaphor, this would be like a meteorologist trying to determine the extent to which snow is produced by *either* cold temperature or high humidity. Rather, the study of interactional phenomena (such as social cognition or weather) must be directed at discovering the forms that the interaction takes under specifiable conditions. In the case of the Higgins and Parsons proposal, this translates as the following kinds of questions: Do social experience and development interact differently (a) under different social-contextual conditions, (b) as regards different types of social concepts, (c) at different periods in development? Ideally, such an investigation might lead to a specification of different social-developmental processes associated with different kinds of social-knowledge acquisitions. (As we shall see, Lepper also suggests this possibility in his chapter.) It should also lead to a determination of cognitive structures that are truly social in nature, rather than watered-down versions of general intellectual abilities.

My main reservation about the Higgins and Parsons contribution concerns the presentation of the changing social environments of children and adolescents. Their portrayal reads like an unanalyzed list of experiences that children in our society may or may not encounter. What are the critical elements of these different life periods? What are the organizing principles of the social networks in which children are engaged during these different periods? Without such an analysis, it is impossible even to determine whether the "typical" North American social context is different from that provided by other cultures with respect to the socialization of children. In this sense I would disagree with the comment made by Higgins and Parsons that "the scarcity of empirical evidence on these issues is the current domination of the Piaget–Kohlberg cognitive perspective on social development." Rather, I would guess that the scarcity of such evidence derives from weaknesses in our understanding of the social environment during childhood and adolescence. A unified and systematic account of contextual differences between the various social worlds of childhood and adolescence would in itself force us to broaden the focus of our social-cognitive studies. Some initial moves in this direction are under way (see Hartup, 1979; Youniss, 1980), but the magnitude of this endeavor should not be underestimated.

Collins's paper also discusses the interaction between social experience and social-cognitive growth, focusing on television as the social agent of interest. Collins's series of studies is an admirable example of how to capture the interplay between social information and children's changing abilities to appreciate that information. Further, Collins suggests the dynamic nature of this interplay by showing how children structure the information that they receive at the same time that certain kinds of informational presentations foster changes in children's structuring capacities. Not only does this give us a more accurate account of the "effects" of television than does the standard TV study; it also tells us something about the socialization process. I only wish that Collins had paid more attention to the particular effects of television as a unique presentational medium. Is there anything special about information conveyed by TV, as opposed to that conveyed by a person or a book? Here I am thinking of research along the lines of Saloman's (1979) study of television peculiarities, like zooming, and of Hope Kelley and Howard Gardner's (1981) comparisons between televised and read-aloud story narratives. Both researchers found reason to believe the McLuhanesque message that the nature of the medium itself largely determines its effects. I bring this issue up to once again emphasize the need for attending to specific features of social context and social knowledge as one designs studies in social cognition. I believe that Collins's research would be greatly enhanced by such an extension.

Several authors (Lepper, Costanzo and Dix, Grusec) present attributional analyses of social-cognitive development. The value of this approach is that it specifies mechanisms of social influence rather than merely asserting in a global way that social cognition owes a debt to social experience. The unifying notion in these chapters is that social influence has its strongest and most permanent effects upon children when children believe that they are an active part of the influence process.

There are certain different emphases that separate these authors. Grusec alone believes that punishment is the key mechanism of change. From her point of view, the primary value of a parent's reasoning with the child is to make the punishment less "salient" and therefore more effective. One problem with this view is the lack of a coherent definition of punishment: Grusec collapses this notion with generalized anxiety (including loss of self-esteem), implying that all forms of discomfort are functionally equivalent as socializers (keeping constant their "salience"). Aside from the implausibility of this view, it does not even account for the child-rearing data. For example, Baumrind (whom Grusec cites) has reported favorable child-rearing results of harmonious, as well as authoritative, parents (Baumrind, 1971). The common bond between the two is certainly not punishment, because harmonious parents rarely punish, but open communication channels and parental concern. In fact, back to Baldwin (1948), child-rearing studies have dismissed punishment as an effective means of socialization: The key variable is parental communication and control, not discipline (however nonsalient). In addition, unless the definition of punishment is extended beyond all bounds, it cannot explain the considerable social influence exerted by peers and other nonpunishing associates during the course of a child's social development.

Lepper's "minimal sufficiency" principle is a more satisfactory means of organizing the literature on social influence. This principle accounts for the effectiveness of subtle means of social control without restricting our view of the multiple processes that account for social-cognitive development. Within this framework it is possible to envision the following developmental scenario: (1) Psychologically "minimal" social guidance draws a child's attention to key interpersonal values or social norms and to some reasons behind these values and norms; (2) the child initially interprets these according to his own way of understanding the social world, but his behavior is altered in accordance with the direction of social influence; (3) this process of behavioral accommodation leads the child eventually to reconsider his conception of interpersonal values and social norms. Such an account captures the child's active role in constructing social knowledge and at the same time specifies the mechanisms by which the child is socially guided during this constructive process. It also is the best explanation of American child-rearing findings like those reported by Baumrind and Hoffman and corresponds to Soviet treatments of the same type of data (Luria, 1976; Elkonin, 1971). Although I may be stretching Lepper's presentation a bit in deriving such a model, I believe that his analysis of social-control processes ultimately leads us in this direction. Most important, it explains the process of social influence in a plausible and nonrestrictive manner.

Lepper also makes an important distinction between the child's acquisition of specific attitudes *versus* the child's construction of "coherent" belief systems. Lepper sees the latter as a "long-term" enterprise, suggesting that there may be differences between the way it and the former are accomplished. This leads us to a multiprocess model of social-cognitive development, certainly a reasonable direction considering the many-faceted nature of this complex phenomenon. One explicit version of a multiprocess model is offered by Costanzo and Dix in this volume. Others have been suggested by Nucci and Turiel (1978), Youniss (1980), and Flavell (1977).

4. Although much of the research in this volume focuses on children's actual behavior, only two chapters directly explore relations between children's social behavior and their social cognition. Berndt discusses this issue in the context of children's friendships, correlating children's expressed behavioral intentions toward their friends with their tendencies to help and share with one another. He finds that consistency between intentions and actions was higher for friends than for acquaintances, a finding that confirms the real-life importance of friendship during childhood. The correlations that Berndt reports, however, are no stronger than those reported in previous judgment-conduct studies (Gerson & Damon, 1978), which means that they account for very little behavioral variance. As Berndt states, the technique of summation across situations (suggested by Epstein) might strengthen such correlations somewhat, because the behavioral measure would then come closer to tapping a pattern of action rather than a discrete behavioral response. Apparently Berndt's study went only part way in this direction, and it would be informative to see the study replicated with cross-situation behavioral measures.

In two coordinated studies, Hartup, Brady, and Newcomb establish firm connections between children's social cognition and social behavior. This connection is demonstrated in their first study by age differences between children's use of reward information in a competitive/cooperative game. These age differences suggest that the younger children do not interpret the game's conditions in the same way as do the older children. In their follow-up study, the investigators manipulate their subjects' interpretations of the game through training procedures designed to increase subjects' awareness and comprehension of the game's critical features. The finding that the training did indeed affect children's cooperative and competitive behavior clearly demonstrates the guiding role of social understanding in this game situation.

The appealing feature of the Hartup–Brady–Newcomb approach is their treatment of the cognition-behavior relation as dynamic and interactive. As the authors themselves suggest, there is little to be gained from looking for static relations between intellectual ability and social "competence" (whatever these are). Children in real-life situations do not simply play out their competencies: They continually prod and probe one another, try out new behaviors, and generally remain open to social influence. They change in the course of acting, and so their actions only partially reflect their previous developmental achievements. Not many judgment-conduct studies have come to terms with this dynamic state of affairs, and the Hartup–Brady–Newcomb effort is refreshing in this regard.

Still, I wish the authors could be clearer about what aspect of social cognition "in that dimly chartered territory known as understanding or comprehension" they were studying. Once again I would repeat the belief that I expressed in Question 2: Findings regarding social-cognitive development are interpretable only when placed in a perspective of fundamental social-knowledge categories. What, for example, does competition or cooperation mean to a child? How are these a part of children's everyday social relations? How are they connected to conceptual systems like friendship or rivalry in the course of children's social-cognitive development? If we had a better sense of children's social understanding in terms of these basic issues, the social-developmental significance of the Hartup–Brady–Newcomb findings would be easier to determine.

5. In the present volume there is one attempt to consider affect as a distinct process with important relations to social cognition. It is also, to my knowledge, the only such serious attempt in the contemporary psychological literature. This is Hoffman's discussion of guilt in relation to moral values.

Hoffman's model is still in the process of formulation, and Hoffman is quite direct about his own uncertainties regarding some critical theoretical choices yet to be made. My only comment at this point is that I would like to see this kind of attempt directed at every emotionally intense aspect of social cognition.

Guilt is one of the characteristics that make morality unique. It affects one's moral understanding as well as one's moral conduct. When intensely felt, guilt gives us important reasons to follow moral objectives, particularly when they conflict with nonmoral objectives. Moral emotions may also play a part in the long-term development of moral judgment, where a person's feelings are questioned and redefined through reasoning and then tested through conduct. Though certainly not independent of moral cognition, guilt nevertheless adds its own affectively charged "information" with which moral cognition must come to terms. Although several alternative formulations of this phenomenon are possible, there can be no debate about the necessity of attending to it in any comprehensive account of moral development. It is a necessary step toward understanding the particular problems and complexities posed by moral concerns. Other social concerns present their own conceptual and emotional complexities that must be worked out in the course of development. It is the child's task in growing up, and the developmental psychologists' task in analyzing this process, to make sense out of these complexities.

Note

1 Developmental level was assessed by calculating the statistical mode (highest percentage) of a child's reasoning on the interview. Full results from this study are available in Damon, 1980, 1983.

References

Baldwin, A. L. Socialization and the parent–child relationship. *Child Development*, 1948, *19*, 127–136.

Daumrind, D. Note: Harmonious parents and their preschool children. *Developmental Psychology*, 1971, *4*, 99–102.

Berndt, T. Relations between social cognition, nonsocial cognition, and social behavior: The case of friendship. In J. H. Flavell & L. D. Ross (Eds.), *New directions in the study of social-cognitive development*. Cambridge: Cambridge University Press, in press.

Bigelow, B. Children's friendship expectations: A cognitive-developmental study. *Child Development*, 1977, *48*, 246–253.

Borke, H. Piaget's mountains revisited: Changes in the egocentric landscape. *Developmental Psychology*, 1975, *11*, 240–243.

Brainerd, C. J. The stage question in cognitive-developmental theory. *Behavioral and Brain Sciences*, 1978, *2*, 173–213.

Broughton, J. Development of concepts of self, mind, reality, and knowledge. *New Directions for Child Development*, 1978, *1*, 75–101.

Brim, O. Life-span development of the theory of oneself: Implications for child development. In H. W. Reese (Ed.), *Advances in child development and behavior* (Vol. 11). New York: Academic Press, 1976.

Connell, R. W. *The child's construction of politics*. Melbourne, Australia: Melbourne University Press, 1971.

Damon, W. *The social world of the child*. San Francisco: Jossey-Bass, 1977.

Damon, W. Why study social-cognitive development. *Human Development*, 1979, *22*, 206–211.

Damon, W. Patterns of change in children's social reasoning: A two-year longitudinal study. *Child Development*, 1980, *51*, 1010–1017.

Damon, W. The nature of social cognitive change in the developing child. In W. F. Overton (Ed.), *The relationship between social and cognitive development*. Hillsdale, N.J.: Erlbaum, 1983.

Damon, W. The developmental study of children's social cognition. In J. Flavell & L. Ross (Eds.), *New directions in the study of social-cognitive development*. Cambridge: Cambridge University Press, 1981.

Elkonin, D. B. Toward the problem of stages in the mental development of the child. *Soviet Psychology*, 1971, *10*, 225–251.

Flavell, J. H. *Cognitive development*. New Jersey: Prentice-Hall, 1977.

Flavell, J. H. *Structures, stages, and sequences in cognitive development*. Paper presented at the Minnesota Symposium on Child Psychology, University of Minnesota, Minneapolis, 1980.

Furth, H. Children's societal understanding and the process of equilibration. *New Directions for Child Development*, 1978, *1*, 101–123.

Furth, H. *The world of grown-ups*. New York: Elsevier, 1980.

Garvey, C. J., & Hogan, R. Social speech and social interaction: Egocentrism revisited. *Child Development*, 1973, *44*, 562–568.

Gerson, R., & Damon, W. Moral understanding and children's conduct. *New Directions in Child Development*, 1978, *2*, 41–60.

Hartup, W. W. The social worlds of childhood. *American Psychologist*, 1979, *34*, 944–951.

Hinde, R. *Towards understanding relationships*. New York: Academic Press, 1980.

Kagan, J. The psychology of sex differences. In F. A. Beach (Ed.), *Human sexuality in four perspectives*. Baltimore: Johns Hopkins University Press, 1976.

Keller, A., Ford, L., & Meachum, J. Dimensions of self-concept in preschool children. *Developmental Psychology*, 1978, *14*, 483–489.

Kelley, H., & Gardner, H. (Eds.) *Viewing children through television*. New Directions for Child Development, no. 13. San Francisco: Jossey-Bass, 1981.

Kohlberg, L. The development of children's orientations towards the moral order. *Vita Humana*, 1963, *6*, 11–33.

Kurtines, W., & Greif, E. The development of moral thought: Review and evaluation of Kohlberg's approach. *Psychological Bulletin*, 1974, *81*, 453–470.

Lewis, M., & Brooks-Gunn, J. *Social cognition and the development of self*. New York: Plenum, 1980.

Livesly, W. J., & Bromley, D. B. *Person perception in childhood and adolescence*. London: Wiley, 1973.

Luria, A. R. *Cognitive development: Its cultural and social foundations*. Cambridge, Mass.: Harvard University Press, 1976.

Maccoby, E. *Social development*. New York: Harcourt Brace Jovanovich, 1980.

Nucci, L. P., & Turiel, E. Social interaction and the development of social concepts in preschool children. *Child Development*, 1978, *49*, 400–407.

Piaget, J. *Play, dreams, and imitation in childhood*. New York: Norton, 1951.

Saloman, G. *Interaction of media, cognition, and learning.* San Francisco: Jossey-Bass, 1979.

Scarlett, H. H., Press, A. N., & Crockett, W. H. Children's descriptions of peers: A Wernerian developmental analysis. *Child Development.* 1971, *42,* 439–453.

Selman, R. L., & Jaquette, D. The development of interpersonal awareness. In C. B. Keasy (Ed.), *Nebraska Symposium on Motivation, 1977.* Lincoln: University of Nebraska Press, 1978.

Shantz, C. V. The development of social cognition. In E. M. Hetherington (Ed.), *Review of child development research* (Vol. 5). Chicago: University of Chicago Press, 1975.

Shantz, C. Social-cognitive development. In J. Flavell and E. Markman (Eds.), *Carmichael's manual of child psychology,* Vol. 2: *Cognitive development.* New York: Wiley, in press.

Shatz, M., & Gelman, R. The development of communication skills: Modifications in the speech of young children as a function of listener. *Monographs of the Society for Research in Child Development.* Chicago: University of Chicago Press, 1973.

Turiel, E. Social regulations and domains of social concepts. *New Directions for Child Development,* 1978, *1,* 45–75.

Youniss, J. *Parents and peers: Their role in child development.* Chicago: University of Chicago Press, 1980.

16   What would my mother say? Reactions to gleanings from developmental studies on social cognition

Tom Trabasso

[Ring, ring, ring.]
Hello.
Hi, Mom, it's Tom.
Tom, where are you?
At a conference, Mom. In Canada.
What's it about?
Children. It's about how children develop. How they develop social skills and knowledge about getting along with other people.
Why would anyone hold a conference on that? Don't parents usually know and teach their children what they should do?
Mom, it's not a matter of should; it's more a matter of *what. What* parents do in socializing their children. Here, it's a matter of what children know and what they do when it comes to caring and sharing, giving and helping, conforming and cooperating, achieving and asserting, being friendly and knowing one's limits. Psychologists are interested in describing, not proscribing, what parents do. They are interested in what children know and how this affects what they do. It is the result of the process called socialization. You see, we want to know how children learn these "prosocial" behaviors. We want to know why they act in socially appropriate ways when someone like you isn't around to remind them.
Well, Tom, I don't know if I understand the difference between describing and proscribing. How can you separate what you believe ought to be from what you study?
It's difficult to be objective, Mom. There is a kind of liberal, egalitarian view that pervades much of the early research on child development

The writing of this chapter was supported by Grant NIE-G-79-0125 by the National Institute of Education.

and socialization. There are norms to which people want their children to adhere. Notions like cooperation, achievement, sharing, all have a positive, desirable value, don't they? These values and beliefs do influence what psychologists study.

I'm sure about objectivity in your science – it seems common sense to me. Who decides what is prosocial and antisocial? Besides, don't you know about these "prosocial behaviors" already? Didn't I teach you?

Sure you did, but so did other mothers. We're concerned with how such behaviors are acquired.

What is acquired?

You ask tough questions, Mom. Most people who claim to be studying development in children are really comparing differences between children of different ages. The better way to do it, of course, would be to follow the development of the same children so you could document the changes you observe within the same child across various social situations such as the home, parents and siblings, church, and school. That is, unfortunately, seldom done. When you compare children of different ages, the ages chosen for study are sometimes very arbitrary and convenient rather than based upon some theory about social development. One problem I've had at the conference is pinpointing what develops when and in what sequence. A second problem is something called "cohort effects." Children change with age in terms of not only what they know and do socially but also as to which groups they belong. Their social world is not constant but changes with them.

Do you mean with whom they play?

Right. Not only who their friends are but to what institutions they belong such as day-care center, church or synagogue, school, Little League, or other formal or informal groups. These are important but neglected considerations.

Why don't psychologists take into account these groups?

I'm not sure. Part of the problem is that psychologists spend most of their time studying what goes on inside the head (cognition) and what children do to others (social behavior) and very little time on where children find themselves and what happens to them with the exception of the influences of their moms and, occasionally, their dads. The larger social context is by and large ignored.

What is the concern about these . . . "cohort" effects?

Mom, different groups have different values. Some groups, say those in athletics, may stress competition. Some, say in school, stress achievement. So, what social behavior and its expression we think is important and observe may depend upon what group the child is in or what behavior is chosen for study.

If that's the case, how can you make any general claims? How do you separate out the development you want to study from these shifting social groups?

Mom, you keep on asking these tough questions. It's an old problem you raise. So much of what we study seems to depend upon the content and . . . upon the context. Yet, psychologists, in order to be general, keep trying to ignore content and context. They want to study what they call "processes," and they want them to be transsituational, hence content-free or context-free, where possible.

But, Tom, that does not seem likely. If you are interested in social skills, how they are acquired, and what people know about them, aren't you going to have to describe what the skills are, of what they consist and in which contexts they manifest themselves?

Right again, Mom. Social knowledge is not just a matter of behavior. The rules or values are dependent upon context and the cohort. Some people at the conference believe that you can control social factors and separate them from the processes involved. Others, however, think they are inseparable. What rules we use to guide our behavior may be "domain-specific" – they may be highly dependent upon which group we belong to, upon where we find ourselves, and in what kind of social interaction we engage. It remains a problem and we only have a few promissory notes on this one. At least people are worried about the problem.

What about studying people in different cultures?

That's a start, Mom. But you need to define the culture (or subculture) of interest. For example, you could begin by assuming that children are in a subculture that is different from yours. Then, you can begin to look at the system of rules that holds for their subculture.

What kinds of rules?

One can distinguish between rules, using objective criteria, but you have to decide whether the distinctions you make and the class of rules are valid for a subculture. For example, you can distinguish between rules that are moral, conventional, regulatory, or prudential.

Hold on, Tom, you're losing me.

Sorry, Mom. Let's just say that in some situations a child is more likely to view a breach of a social rule as "bad" rather than "stupid." For example, it's "bad" for me to take someone's pencil without asking for it but "stupid" for me to be late for class. The first example is a moral breach; the second is a regulation breach.

But how can young children tell you that?

They can't tell you directly – that requires a kind of reflection and development of language and other consciously controlled cognitive skills. However, the tacit knowledge can be revealed by how they behave when rules are violated or breached. You can examine how they describe others who commit breaches. If they describe them differently, you can infer that their tacit understanding of the rules is there. Rule-governed behavior need not be open to introspection. Our behavior tells us that we know.

That's hard to swallow, Tom, especially in five-year-olds.

Why not, Mom? A lot of people wiser than we are believe as you do, but their interpretation relied upon the child being able to explain or to justify logically his actions with principles. Such use of language and reflection is not usually well attained until the age of eight or nine or even later. There is a difference between acting as if you know something and being able to tell someone about why you are doing it. The awareness may follow the tacit understanding, not cause it.

Where do these rules come from? How are they taught? How early do they appear? Are the bases for the rules the same across situations? How do the rules become general or are they domain-specific? How are the distinctions made for norms, obligations, or importance? Are the distinguishing features really used or is that the construction of some anthropology professor?

Slow down, Mom, I can't keep up. The approach I described is more analytic than psychological. It provides us with a framework in which we can identify the defining features of rules. If social behavior is rule-governed – and I think it is – then the value of the approach is in the establishment of a priori criteria for contrasting rules. If the system is valid, it predicts how rules will be organized psychologically. The fact that preschool children make distinctions between violations of social rules indicates that they have formed *basic rule categories*. There's more work to do. If the analysis is valid, it has lots of implications. The basic rules can be elaborated with age – extended to new social domains and contexts or qualified – but the criteria underlying them may be context-free, independent of the culture, age of child, and so on. This approach may help us solve the cohort and subculture problems we talked about a few moments ago.

Well, I'm not satisfied that you were raised by rules.

Mom, I'm just trying to make you aware of the culture and what it transmits to the child. When children are socialized, they have internalized a lot of rules. This allows them to behave consistently in social situations without external controls. When internalized, the rules guide their conduct. They can even help children to link up the causes and the consequences of what they do. They help them relate how their goals and attempts to carry them out may conflict with the goals of others. If a child is aggressive, and receives criticism or verbal disapproval, and if the parent explains why the behavior is bad, the child not only learns a rule but recognizes the negative consequences or harm to others that aggression may produce. A more complete rule system would include positive options as well. It is important for children to understand their intentions behind their actions as well as the consequences of their actions.

Which are more important?

Well, adults stress intentions more when it comes to other adults, but I'm not sure they do so when they deal with children. Negative consequences seem to carry more weight.

I'm not sure that I did that to you.

Well, Mom, you and I had several disciplinary encounters.

You mean I used punishment to control you?

Yes, at times – especially when I might have done damage or harm to myself or others.

But, I did create a positive atmosphere in our home and I did set a good example for you.

Yes, you were a good model.

And I taught you to believe in moral values, to trust people, to associate with good people, and to study hard.

Yes, you did all those things. You're an egalitarian liberal, Mom.

But, I still don't understand how these rules you acquired actually work.

Well, in a given situation, if I'm about to violate the rule, I'm likely to feel some emotion like guilt. This is correlated with inhibiting me, possibly through some kind of anticipatory, conditional response.

That's a result of the punishment in those "disciplinary encounters," right? The punishment worked, didn't it?

Not quite, Mom. Punishment alone is not sufficient. I had to have someone point out positive alternatives as well as how my intent and action would do harm. You helped me see the consequences of what I was about to do and steered me in other directions without denying my needs.

But there were times when I felt like killing you. I know during those times I probably hit you harder.

That, Mom, may have been counterproductive. The emotions aroused may have been too strong. If so, I could not have benefited from your advice. I would have been too aroused to have seen the connection you wanted me to see. I would have needed some "time out" to cool off and regain my reflective abilities. I probably would have felt that I was being controlled by you and not by me.

But, Tom, sometimes I praised you although it was hard, and at times I wanted to ignore you.

That's another problem, Mom. You can love someone too much. It's not sufficient either. You need a balance, and the threat to withdraw affection may not work, either. Again, I might have failed to internalize the rule. I might have believed that I was doing it for you and not for me. I had to learn the intrinsic value of what I did.

You seem to be placing a lot of emphasis on "me" versus "you," on someone external versus something internal. Isn't it a bit of both, and how can it be external, anyway?

It's not external. It's the attribution, Mom. It's the attribution of source and form of control. If one feels that one is under external control, the implication is that it's less effective.

When does this "control" business start?

Don't you remember? Probably in early infancy. Probably as soon as I was capable of endangering myself or others or things around me. Your earliest regulations were taking away objects that I tried to put into my mouth or to drop on the cat.

Oh yes, I remember. You always seemed intent on destruction. But how does it all come together so that it works? So that it regulates you?

As I said, if the punishment or the reward is not too severe and if it is coupled with an exhortation about the negative consequences or a positive induction about positive options, and if the child already has some notion that certain desires lead to certain ends, and if the child experiences an emotion that is not so arousing that it disrupts the child's executive control processes or attention, then a correlation might be established between aims and outcomes, and the child might learn to inhibit those behaviors that have negative outcomes. However, for the system to work, the child presumably would have to learn from the context and the outcomes of various behaviors, especially the reactions of others, that there are some general but different sets of rules. The rules, once acquired, allow the child to anticipate a possible violation or breach, experience guilt, and inhibit antisocial behavior. Voilà, control! The experience of guilt and some kind of conditioned inhibition prevent the child from carrying out the action and to think of the other person.

I can't seem to get clear how much of the control is voluntary and how much is involuntary.

The various psychologists who study it can't seem to decide either. Their approaches are a mélange of cognitive decision making and classical conditioning. I guess this is a natural result of mixing emotions and rules.

How do you know what is too much punishment and too much reward? Too much arousal? Too much emotion?

You don't, really. It is largely a matter of judgment, intuition, the child, the parent, and something very mysteriously called the child's "definition of self" as well as how much the child values the forbidden activity.

Well, then, how does the mild punishment and small reward work? Does it matter if you are trying to teach someone a new rule or you want to evoke an old one?

An exhortation does both. It appeals to traits that are valued and it reinstates the rule. Suppose we store, in what is known as long-term memory, the rule plus an underlying concept of the prosocial behavior, its possible outcomes, and some knowledge about emotional reactions. An exhortation such as "Tommy, be a nice boy and help me with the dishes" is a kind of retrieval cue that activates the rule and appropriate social behavior. Social situations are conditions that satisfy certain states for rule application. When these conditions, plus the verbal statement, occur, it "fires" off an action. Rules, then, are conditional states and actions. When there is more than one rule, one can get a whole value system, called a production system. So, when we internalize social rules, we internalize productions similar in form to those used in processes of thinking and problem solving. The view that cognitive development is rule-governed has gained more credence lately, so why shouldn't we begin to view social cognition and social development as the development of rule-governed behavior. The rules may be tacit or accessible via reflection. The task, then, is for psychologists to find ways to describe and verify the acquisition and operations of the rules.

That sounds like a return to an older way of viewing the child.

In part it is because the condition–action rule is like a stimulus–response. However we now have better ways to represent rules formally and to stimulate their operations such as in computer models.

You said something earlier about how I taught you to make connections between intended action and outcomes. Is that a kind of inference?

Yes. Events like one's goals, plans, actions, and consequences follow a time course that correspond fairly well to simple, everyday episodes. These are readily acquired and get run off over and over again in specific contexts.

That sounds like a TV script.
It is, sort of, and you can find these episodic structures in stories, myths, fables, and morals too.
How is it done?
How is what done?
How do you make inferences of the kind you describe?
Well, you carry around with you a naive theory about others' and your intentions. You know about scripts or plans for carrying out what you desire. You know how these plans can lead to satisfaction of your goals or to resolution of conflicts. Some of your scripts, however, are too stereotyped and rigid, like the knowledge you have when you eat in a restaurant. The general knowledge you have about goals, plans, actions, and outcomes enables you to be more flexible in solving personal or social problems. I can interpret more accurately why someone acts the way he does if I know what his goals are, what his plans are, and what his operational theme is. This is more informative and flexible than being able to predict stereotyped behavior such as eating in a restaurant or taking a bus to New York City or finding a book in a library. Scripts are procedural in nature and omit *why* we do the things we do. A script helps you organize and remember something but it does not help you understand it. You need a more general system for understanding the behavior of others.
Tom, you seem to be leaving out the fact that you learn from others as well as from yourself.
You're right. Rules must operate for others in relation to yourself, especially where reciprocity is concerned.
What?
You know, the Golden Rule, Mom: Do unto others as you would have them do unto you.
Oh. That.
Yes. Peer interaction must have strong effects on children.
You always kept good company as a child and teenager. I made sure of that. But sometimes I wondered whether or not you were too self-conscious.
Yes. I did compare myself to others.
Did they set an example for you?
Probably, but apparently I was not aware of it until I was seven or eight.
Why so late? Shouldn't this occur earlier?
Good question. Some believe that I lacked the requisite cognitive skills. Another possibility, which I favor, is that the subculture in which I found myself, namely, the school, as well as your reaction to what

happened, did not start stressing social comparison until the third grade. I remember that I first became aware of intelligence tests and achievement tests when I was told that I was doing better than my grade level. Before then I guess I never thought about such relative comparisons. I was too busy just trying to learn to do what I was being taught to do. I tried to make direct comparisons, I must have found it hard to do, not having any clear information, and making comparisons could have interfered with leaving. I just tried to learn. If I tried to compare, I forgot what I was doing and made mistakes.

What about athletics?

I guess one could make comparisons there earlier and more easily because the criteria for evaluation are more open and direct. But on academic things, it was later. When teachers are concerned with basic skills, comparisons are less important.

When do you think you first had an idea as to where you stood in your class?

I don't know. I knew that I could do a lot of things well. At least I was told so at home and at school. Having an older sister helped. She taught me what she was learning in school before I went to school. I just don't remember being compared to anybody at home except on how tall I was.

We were a democratic family.

Yeah, but some were more equal than others and who was more equal depended upon size. Somewhere along the line I must have been given feedback on how well I was doing, because how well one does is relatively rather ambiguous in academic situations. I do remember the red, blue, and gold stars though. I think that psychologists who are interested in these matters should do some observational studies, in the home or classroom, and look for those instances that entail social comparison. The current work, although diagnostic, doesn't tell us much about the etiology and causes of this behavior. If social comparison becomes internalized, when was it externalized?

Do you think that TV had any effect on you?

I really didn't understand it very well until I was about eight years old.

But you used to tell us the whole plots of what you saw when you were five years old.

Those were probably scriptlike and highly predictable events. I don't think that I always saw the meaningful connections between the things I remembered. There is a question as to how deeply one processes TV narratives. Perhaps I didn't really understand the higher-order goals or more general intentions of the characters.

These are often subtle or occur at the end of the story or are separated from the actions by a lot of irrelevant filler. I may have lacked the requisite social knowledge or maybe I understood it but wasn't asked the right questions.

Television is a noisy medium for morality, isn't it?

I would agree. Studies on TV comprehension lead one to underestimate how much children can infer about motives and internal states. If one took away irrelevant filler, made the plots more explicit or well formed, clarified actions and showed them in the normal, temporal order, children would find it less demanding to work out why people do what they do. The lack of well-formed stories and the overinclusion of noncentral, noncausal filler events overload working memory and prevent the establishment of the hypothetical plans of the characters. Younger children may adhere to the more stereotyped plots because they find it too difficult to overcome the information-processing demands of the show.

Shouldn't they find that scripts help them?

Yes, they should, because scripts enable event prediction and storage into well-organized frames or slots. However, there is some question as to whether younger children, say five- or six-year-olds, can use scripts to predict events or to recognize deviations. For eight-year-olds, this should be possible. It is possible for them to do so in verbal narratives, but on TV, with the noisy input, such ability may not manifest itself. When our general, information-processing capacity is overloaded, we don't have the internal resources to allocate to prediction, verification, and other, more critical analysis. You have to recognize that children have fewer resources or less capacity in general. It is not a matter, necessarily, of one ability. It may be more a matter of the whole system being interfered with.

Well, you didn't turn out so bad.

No, and I didn't turn out to be a goody-two-shoes, either.

Right. If you had, I don't think I would have liked you as much.

But, Mom, you must have wanted me to be my own person.

Certainly. But only if you loved (and accepted) me.

You're right, Mom. I didn't want to lose your love but I needed to be on my own.

I'm not that naive. I just expected you to be moderate in all things.

OK, Mom. I'm still growing, still trying to get my act together, still trying to find out what I am, where I find myself, and how I can meet my obligations. The values keep changing too and I find myself entering into new groups and new relationships. It all requires a lot of new learning and different sets of values. I don't think that the values we learned during childhood generalize to the various adult domains in which we find ourselves as our needs shift with age and aging. The life-span people have a lot to say here. Mom, I'm sorry but I'm going to have to get off the phone soon. Some friends and acquaintances are waiting for dinner.

Are you taking them all out?

Heavens no, Mom. I might exercise a potluck principle, buy a bottle of wine for all to share, friend and acquaintance alike, and hope that later others, in turn, will buy for me.

You're a good boy, Tom.

Mom, it pays to cooperate. Others expect me to do so and I, in turn, expect them to do so. It sounds like the Golden Rule again but I have noticed that with friends I can relax and do more of what I want to do. I know the limits better and can be more of myself. I can play around, argue, compete, and even be cautiously aggressive, and my friends don't seem to mind. With strangers, the limits are less clear and I don't know what they expect or accept. So, I'm careful.

That's wise. Don't drink too much. You might start arguments, become too critical or evaluative or threatening and uncooperative.

Don't worry. There are lots of incentives to be cooperative. It depends upon when another professor gets competitive with me. If I take issue or argue and don't personalize, they may not become competitive in turn. If they don't, I usually find myself more likely to feel a sense of trust and to begin to be more polite, to pose questions in a way so as not to offend or expose weaknesses. If I start out being polite, I can stifle competitive aggression by turning the other cheek.

But I can remember that when you were younger you weren't such a pussycat. You had tendencies to be competitive or cooperative depending upon how others treated you initially and not how you were told to be.

Mom, I've mellowed. I'm growing up. I've gained social skills.

I hope so. Your conference is more than a game.

It is. I hope we're not spinning our wheels. It is a social microcosm. We need more of these kinds of social interaction.

I hope so. Social interaction. Hmm. That is what it is all about. Enjoy your conference.

Goodnight, Mom, and thanks.

Index

Abelson, R., 86, 127, 281–2, 283–4
Abrahams, B., 203, 204
accomodation, 5, 23
achievement: gender and, 45–6; and
social comparison, 135, 137
adolescence, 16, 25–9, 31, 32, 40–1,
55, 359; disruption of superego in,
238; friendship in, 168–9, 176–7,
184; maturation at, 360; moral internalization in, 270; in North American society, 42–3; role taking in,
54–5; value trait development in,
219–21, 223–4, 228
adults, 16; reaction to moral transgressions, 290, 358; see also parents
affect, 5; in internalization, 241–4,
269, 361–4; memory and, 259–61;
response to discipline, 248–54; role
of, in social understanding, 372,
380, 390–1
age-related change (difference), 3, 5,
334, 358–60, 385–90; in altruism,
288–9; approaches to, 15–18; in attributions, 73–4; in comprehension,
123–5, 126, 129; in conceptions of
social relations, 86; in development
of interpersonal values, 215–16,
129–24, 228; in discipline, 245–6,
247, 251, 252, 259, 263–5; effect of,
on social behavior, 7, 8, 9; in
friendship, 159, 160–1, 166, 168,
169, 174–5, 176–7, 178, 179, 180–1,
182–3, 184; in inferences, 72–3; in
moral judgments, 343–4; qualitative, 374; in perception of social
control, 312–13; in relation between
cognition and behavior, 91–4, 104,
105; research on, 17, 371–91; in rule
understandings, 199, 202, 203–4; in
social comparison, 137, 140–1, 143–

4, 145–53, 346; in social interactions, 339, 348; and socialization
techniques, 322; and understanding
of television, 110, 111–12, 113–23
age segregation: in school, 21–2, 32,
39
aggression, 90–1, 106, 128–9; motivation and, 118–19
Ajzen, I., 93
Allen, A., 276
altruism, 178, 253, 361, 362; internalization of, 275–93, 312; shift from
self-interest to, 363–4, 366
anthropology, 17; symbolic, 198–9,
210
anxiety, 238, 361–2, 388; re punishment and abandonment, 236–7, 253,
254; see also deviation anxiety
appraisal: vocabulary of, 63, 205–10,
211, 212
Aronfreed, J., 266
Aronson, E., 297, 299, 303, 308, 350;
and G. Lindzey: *Handbook of Social Psychology*, 5
arousal, 8, 241–2, 281, 318, 361; optimal, 248–51, 268
attitude(s), 67–8, 93, 128, 345–6; attribution of, 69, 70
attitude change, 255, 349, 364–9; processes of, 294–5, 297–301, 319; variability in, 366–8
attribution(s), 4, 9, 36–8, 91, 342, 379;
development of (model), 72–9; dispositional, 16, 335; of goodness,
287–9; inferred, 72; and internalization, 361, 364–9; relation with
value, 216, 222–8; schemas of, 72–
3; situational, 16; see also self-
attribution
attribution process (theory), 68, 349–

405

attribution process (theory) (*cont.*) 50, 356–70, 388–9; of moral internalization, 241–3, 267; of social control processes, 300, 301, 305, 309, 311, 312, 317–20; socialization in, 63–81
augmentation principle, 63
authority, 337–8, 342, 347, 383; age-related differences in understanding of, 373, 374, 375, 376; conception of, 30–1
autonomy: in friendship, 176, 179, 183–4, 185–6; in moral internalization, 244, 246, 254; in value development, 216, 221, 222, 225–6, 228, 229–30, 231
avoidance-learning, 265, 290–1

Baggett, P., 128
Baldwin, A. L., 388, 389
Bandura, A., 19, 73, 111, 239, 290–1
Barenboim, C., 149
Baumrind, D., 280, 310, 316, 365, 388
Bearison, D. J., 45
behavior(s), 7, 9–10, 19, 83; deviant, 238–9, 241–2, 245; effect of comprehension on, 128–9; effect of external stimulus on, 6–7; effect of training in role taking on, 91–2; in friendship, 158, 164–79; generalization of, 73; relation with intention, 175–6; relation with social cognition, 9–10, 140, 142, 151–2, 153, 389–90; and role taking, 90; values and, 214–15, 230–2, 234
behavior change, 276, 287
behavioral traits: in value development, 216–24, 228
beliefs, 77, 93
Bem, D. J., 276
Berlin, I., 199–200
Berndt, R., 128
Berndt, T. J., 10, 86, 92–3, 161, 164, 345–6, 381, 384, 389
Bernstein, B., 45
Berscheid, E., 105
Bigelow, B. J., 163, 164
Black, J. B., 87, 127
blame, 252, 262
Blumenfeld, P., 34
Blyth, D. A., 54

Bolen, D., 74
Borgida, E., 85
Bower, G., 87, 127, 261
Brady, J. E., 10, 381, 385, 389–90
Brady-Smith, J., 90
Brehm, S., 67–9, 70
Brickman, P., 74
Brim, O. G., 20, 55
Bronfenbrenner, U., 55
Brown, A., 88
Bryant, S., 36
Burnstein, E., 85
Butkowsky, I., 95

Campbell, E. Q., 20
Carlsmith, J. M., 296, 297, 303
Carmichael's Manual of Child Psychology, 3
Case, R., 49–50
Cassel, T., 45
causal analysis, 63, 64, 74
causal inferences, 85, 88, 356; in discipline techniques, 247, 251, 252, 253, 255, 263, 264, 267; self-generated, 287
causal schemas, 269
cause, 37, 63, 68, 72–3, 78
Chandler, M. J., 91
Chapman, J. P., 75–6
Chapman, L. J., 75–6
child (children), 6, 30; active role in their own socialization, 4, 6, 340, 348–9, 379, 388, 389; as cultural product, 16; heteronomous, 210–12, 381 (*see also* mind, savage); social cognition and social interaction in, 82–109
child-rearing, 388, 389; *see also* parenting styles
choice(s), 37, 297, 314–15, 366
Chomsky, Noam, 336, 341–2
cinematic conventions, 128
Clausen, J. A., 20
cognition, 5–7, 54, 129–30; adult, 49; and altruism, 276, 281–9, 290–1; as auto-normative processing, 194–5; change in, 47–9, 54; characterization of, 3–4, 18, 335, 340, 344; concrete to abstract, 381; diversity in, 377–8; environmental variables in, 19–20; "hot," 261; interaction and

development in, 333–55; and mechanisms of social control, 342; mediating role of, 379; modifiability of, 339, 340; in moral internalization, 242–3, 244, 245, 255–9, 268, 269; and moral judgment, 30; relation with behavior, 9–10, 92–4, 104, 128; relation with friendship, 158, 165–79, 183; routinization of, 49–51; social aspects of, 340; in social domains, 333–4, 336, 342–3, 344–5, 346, 347, 349, 351; social/nonsocial, 85–6, 337–9; term, 106
Cognitive Abilities Test, Form 1, 217
cognitive criteria: in rule understanding, 199–205, 211–12
cognitive development, 3, 7–9, 82, 339; description of, 63–70, 373–91; entails internalization, 333; interpersonal conflict necessary to, 89; mechanisms of, 336, 339; and norm application, 74; and social interaction, 82–109; social life phases and, 29–40; stages of, 196–7; wholistic transformations in, 375–8
cognitive-development theory, 15–16, 18, 54, 55, 89, 345; and change in value development, 216, 228, 229, 234; conflict with socialization tradition, 333–41, 358–9; friendship conceptions in, 164; inference in, 64, 71–2; and interaction of life phases with cognitive skills, 46–7; of moral internalization, 240–1; role of experience in, 52–3; social predictions in, 38, 39
cognitive differentiation, 193–4, 195–201, 210 12, 344; intuitive vs. reflective, 205–10
cognitive dissonance model, 300, 301
cognitive maturity: value structure and, 222, 224, 225–6, 228
cognitive structures, 15, 52; created through action, 336, 337; facilitate retention of new information, 87, 88
Coie, John, 64–6
Cole, M., 55
Collingwood, R. G., 194
Collins, W. A., 121, 122, 128, 129, 347, 356–7, 387–8
communication, 44, 45, 50, 54, 379

comparison, *see* social comparison
competition, 10, 35, 43, 74, 360; with friends, 169–71, 173, 175, 177, 178, 179, 182–3, 186
compliance, 239, 241, 249–50, 253, 254, 319, 349, 365, 366–8, 385; distinct from internalization, 294, 305, 320; forced, 296–8; initial, 313, 315, 319; without awareness, 242; willing, 368–9
comprehension, 8, 94, 100, 104; effect of, on behavior, 128–9; of social portrayals on television, 110–33; *see also* social understanding
concepts, 29–32, 344; in attribution theory, 349–50; autonomous development of, 339; of friendship, 160–5; of persons, 82–5, 86; of social experiences, 348; variability in, 343
concern for others (principle), 275–6, 286, 289, 291
conditioning, 265; of empathy, 363, 364
conflict: interpersonal, 89; moral, 267; between personal needs and social obligation, 236–7, 240–1, 243, 245, 347; role, 55
conflict resolution, 221, 228
consensus principle, 63, 72, 73
conservation(s), 71, 86
content: explicit/implicit, 113, 114–18, 119, 122, 125; *see also* information
context, situational, 7–9, 93–4; and age-related change, 385–7; of discipline encounter, 262, 268; and intent/outcome change, 33–4, 35–6; and moral internalization, 242–3, 244; in moral judgment, 359–60; and prosocial behavior in friendship, 179–84; of social understanding, 94–103, 104, 106; and value internalization, 321–3
contingency management, 316–17
control, social, 44, 45, 349; escalation/de-escalation of, 313–14; 319; and internalization of social values, 294–330; locus of, 37; objectively insufficient, 298–301; parental, 54 (*see also* parenting styles); psychologically insufficient, 296–8; psychologically oversufficient, 301–5; sense of, 368–9; subtle, 314–16, 388

convention, 343–4, 383; differentiation
from moral and prudential, 193–4,
196–7, 200, 201–5, 206, 210–11,
358
Cook, T. D., 255
Cooper, J., 95–6, 300
cooperation, 10, 74, 162, 390; and
competition, 97–100, 102, 103, 106
Costanzo, Phillip R., 8, 33, 64–6, 67–
9, 70, 343, 358, 381, 388, 389
covariation analysis, 75–6, 77, 78, 85
Craik, F. I. M., 258
Crook, C. K., 362
culture, 339, 386; and age-graded
change, 359–61; as cognitive system,
193–213; defined, 194; and social
control techniques, 321–3; symbolic,
210; variability in, 17, 18, 40–6, 53–4
custom, 198–9, 210
Cutrona, C. E., 90–1, 93

Damon, W., 11, 15, 30, 31, 48, 84,
203, 204, 357, 369
D'Andrade, R., 86
Darley, S. A., 300
Davis, K. E., 65
demographic variability, 17, 18, 40–6,
85–6
Deutsch, F., 90
developmental change, *see* age-related
change
developmental psychology, 4–7, 17,
82, 333–4; *see also* cognitive-
development theory
deviation anxiety, 238, 250, 265, 266–
7, 280, 361
Dienstbier, R. A., 74, 241–2, 311–12
discipline, 8–9, 19, 307, 342, 347, 350–
1, 361–3; cognitive response to,
246–54; love-withdrawal, 237, 247,
248–50, 253, 254, 255, 265, 266,
268, 269, 309–11, 350, 363; model
for, 265–7; minimal sufficiency principle in, 309–12; moral internalization through, 236, 241–2, 244–8,
248–67, 269, 322; power-assertive,
246–7, 248–50, 253, 254, 255, 260,
265, 266, 268, 269, 280, 309–11,
317–18, 358, 363; *see also*
induction(s)
discounting principle, 64, 68–9, 70, 73

discourse processing models, 88
discrimination, 86, 88
Dix, Theodore H., 8, 343, 358, 388,
389
Dodge, K. A., 91, 104–5, 106
Dornbusch, S., 360
Duke University studies (social-cogni-
tive development), 64–70; implica-
tions of, 70–2, 74
Durkheim, Emile, 236
Dweck, C. S., 74

egocentrism, 89, 143, 150, 377, 381
Emmerich, W., 9, 384
emotional state, 361–4; *see also*
arousal
empathy, 90, 252–3, 254, 260, 265,
266, 268, 270, 361, 362; altruism
based on, 283; capacity for, 263–4;
inborn bias to, 363–4; reverse, 364
environment, social, 38, 47, 55, 88,
357, 364; change in, 36, 387; influence of, on development of social
cognition, 334, 340; and social comparison, 147, 151
equality: in friendships, 171, 172–3,
177, 178, 179, 182–3
Erikson, E. H., 270
ethnography, 210–12
example: effectiveness of, 285, 286;
see also modeling, models
excuse patterns, 210, 212
expectations, 22, 121–2; effect on reason, 75–6; sex-role, 125–6; *see also*
social antecedents
experience, social, 48, 49–50, 51, 52–
3, 54, 64, 73; apprehension of, 379;
and attribution, 73–4; changes in,
and value development, 216; defined, 339; in discipline encounters,
268; effect of, on patterns of friendship, 181; interaction with cognitive
growth, 130, 385–8; and moral internalization, 244–6; in moral transgression, 358; qualitative differences
in, 348–9, 351; relation with social
cognition, 335–6, 337–8, 339, 340,
343, 344, 347–9, 351; scripts and,
89; universality of, 84
explanations, 241, 242; *see also*
induction(s)

external pressure, 5–6, 296–8, 299–
300, 364–8
externality: of rules, 200–1, 202

families, 55, 386; harmonious, 316,
319; reciprocation in, 369
Farnill, D., 64–7, 71
Feldman, N. S., 36, 38, 48–9, 90, 146
Feshbach, N. D., 90
Feshbach, S., 90–1, 93
Festinger, L., 135, 136, 296
Fishbein, M., 93
Flavell, J., 71, 104, 378, 389
foot-in-the-door effect, 313
"forbidden toy" procedure, 297, 303–
4, 347, 350
Freud, Sigmund, 236, 237, 267, 336
Friedrich, L. K., 279
friendship(s), 10, 152, 158–89, 383,
384, 389; age-related differences in
understanding of, 373, 374, 375;
changes in, 172–9; conceptions of,
31–2; exclusiveness of, 179, 180–2,
186; research on, 158–9, 160–79,
345–6

Gardner, Howard, 387
Garvey, C., 87
Geertz, C., 194
Gellner, E., 193, 195
gender: and friendship, 159, 161, 168–
71, 177, 178, 180–1, 183; and social
cognition, 45–6; *see also* sex role(s)
gender constancy, 153–4
generalization, 73, 86, 278; of disposi-
tion to altruism, 281, 282–3, 288–9,
291
Gerard, H. B., 95
Gilligan, C., 46
Gillmore, G., 35, 36
Gilovich, T., 315
Girgus, J. S., 94
Glenn, C., 87, 88, 259
Glick, J., 84, 88–9
Gnepp, J., 105
goals, 5, 23–4; norm acquisition, 134–
5, 136, 152; parental, 43–5
Goldman, S. R., 9, 88, 384
Goodnow, J., 43, 44
Goody, J., 193
Gottman, J., 152

Grumet, 64–6, 67–70, 71
Grusec, J. E., 8, 9, 10, 49, 64–6, 279,
287, 290, 312, 342, 361–2, 365–6,
384–5, 388
guilt feelings, 237, 261; anticipatory,
260; empathy and, 252–3, 254, 265,
266, 268, 270; encoded in memory,
260–1; in moral internalization,
243, 244, 245, 246, 259, 266, 268,
390–1; self-generated, 254

Halliday, M. S., 95
Hallowell, A. I., 194
Hamilton, D., 76
Harkness, A., 41
Harris, V. A., 69
Harter, S., 145
Hartup, W. W., 10, 19, 381, 385, 389–90
Heider, F., 264
Henrig, M., 45
heredity, 336
Hess, V., 128
Higgins, E. T., 7, 36, 38, 48–9, 342,
348, 349, 358–61, 381, 385–7
Hillman, D., 311–12
Hillman, J., 311–12
Hinde, R., 383
Hobbes, Thomas, 229, 230
Hobhouse, L. T., 193, 197
Hoffman, M. L., 8, 252–3, 279, 280,
309, 310, 347, 349, 361–2, 385, 389,
390–1
Hood, L., 55
Hopi, Indians, 43
Horton, R., 193, 195–6
hostility, 383
Hsu, F. L. K., 42
hypothesis testing, 72

identification: and attitude change,
295; with parent, 237, 278; role of,
in social control, 319–20
identity, 43, 383
ideologies, 270–1, 317, 349
illusory corrections, studies of, 75–6
impulse control system, 237–8, 267;
see also control
incentives, 296–7, 299–300, 301–3,
304, 318; diffuse, 314; minimizing,
314–15; superfluous, 306–7, 309,
311; *see also* external pressure

individual differences, 22, 89, 106, 134, 361; in social knowledge and comprehension, 123–6; and understanding of television, 110, 111–12; in value development, 216

induction(s), 246, 247, 248–63, 266–7, 268–70, 309–11, 317, 351, 358; affective response to, 251–4; cognitive response to, 251; in early discipline encounters, 264–5; of positive behavior, 361–2

inferences, 10, 63, 64, 75–6, 79, 340; re another's psychological experience, 83–4; correspondent, 65, 67–9, 72–3; in implicit content, 113, 115–16; and intentionality, 358; person, 68; self-reflective, 147, 149–51, 152; in social comparison, 138, 140, 142–3, 147–51; transitive, 144; *see also* causal inferences; information processing

information, 5, 29, 32–8, 50–1, 73, 86, 351 n2, 387; abstract/concrete, 85; amount kind of, 95; retrieval of, 267 social comparison, 134–5, 147, 150–1; stored in memory, 256; use of, 90–1, 93, 94, 96, 97—103, 104, 105, 136, 137–41; in verbal exhortations, 286; *see also* context, situational

information processing, 50, 63, 75, 87–8, 89, 334; biases in, 29, 32–8; capacity for, 143–4; deficit in, 100–1; of induction information, 260, 265, 266, 267, 268–9; inference in 72–3; levels of, 258; and moral internalization, 236, 248–67; structures in, 127; use in social interaction, 104, 105–6; *see also* social cues

information structures: hierarchical, 127

informational analysis, formal, 72–3, 74–5, 77–8

initiation, severity of, 299, 308, 350

inoculation, 365

intelligence, 336, 337; relation with social-cognitive abilities, 47, 85–6

intent, intention(s), 10, 84, 104–5, 358, 384; and aggressive behavior, 91; in friendship, 389; inferred, 95; in moral judgments, 150; and outcome, 33–6, 49, 51–2, 53, 64–8, 70, 71; predicting, 92–4; in prosocial

behavior toward friends, 166, 168–9, 171–6, 177, 178

interaction, social, 82–109, 333; and attribution, 74, 75, 78; competent, 104; in description of change in understanding, 378–9; differs according to social domains, 339; and moral development, 241; playful, cooperative, 362–3; reciprocal, 318–19, 334, 336, 340, 341, 348, 351, 359, 368–9; and social understanding in context, 94–103, 104, 106; *see also* friendship(s)

internalization, 9, 10, 333, 342, 347, 361–9; affective and cognitive processes in, 236–74; of altruism, 275, 277–9, 291; as criterion of socialization, 320–3; defined, 275–6, 294; distinct from compliance, 295–305; as mechanism of acquisition of social knowledge, 339, 348; minimal sufficiency principle and, 309–10; model for, 265–7; as process of social control, 295; research on, 246–8; of social values, 294–330; specific vs. general concepts of, 317–18, 321–2; theories of, 336–43

interpretation(s), 8, 64, 74; awareness of potential for, 258

Ironsmith, M., 316

Jardin, A., 45

Jensen, R., 74

Jersild, A. T., 20

Jones, E. E., 65, 67–8, 69

Josephson, J., 346

judgments: concrete to abstract, 147–8; egocentric/nonegocentric, 38; errors in, 85; re persons and events, 84–5; prior, 4; *see also* moral judgments; social judgments

justice, 197, 200, 383; reasoning re, 376

justification: objectively insufficient, 298–301, 305, 308, 364, 365; psychologically insufficient, 296–8, 305, 314; psychologically oversufficient, 301–5, 308, 311, 364

juvenile state, 24–5, 30, 31, 32–3, 39–40, 55

Kagan, J., 386

Kagan, S., 178

Kahneman, D., 85
Kant, I., 195
Karlovac, M., 36
Kau Sai people (Hong Kong), 42
Keasey, L. B., 47
Kelley, H. H., 68, 73, 78, 314, 387
Kelman, H. C., 295, 319
Kessen, W., 17
King, R. A., 280
Klayman, J., 105
knowledge, 83, 336, 341; increase in, 48–9, 50; intuitive, 205–10; mechanisms for acquiring, 342–3; partitioning of, 195–6; physical, as analog for social, 83–6; prerequisite to social comparison, 142, 143, 153; prior, 75–6, 85, 88, 126–8, 356; reflective, 205–10, 211–12; social, 83, 383–4; of social interaction, 86–9; value and behavioral development, 214–15; *see also* cognition; script(s)
Kohlberg, L., 15, 44, 164, 267; reaction against theories of, 357, 358, 381; stages of moral development, 30, 46, 196, 197, 199, 205, 240, 270, 338, 345, 359–60, 384
Kuczynski, L., 290
Kurdek, L. A., 90

labeling, 63, 74, 288, 311–12, 314
Langer, E., 75
language, 255, 269, 282
learning: across domains, 333–4, 336, 342–3, 344–5, 346, 347, 349, 351; theory of, 341–2; *see also* observational learning; social-learning theory
Lehnhoff,, J., 311–12
Lepper, M. R., 8–9, 10, 129, 130, 287, 308, 315, 349, 350, 361, 364–8, 386, 388–9
Lévi-Strauss, C., 193
Levinson, D. J., 55
Lévy-Bruhl, L., 193
Lewin, Kurt, 19, 295
life phases, 18–29, 53–4; cultural and demographic variability in, 40–6; and social-cognitive development, 29–40, 46–56; and social predictions, 38–9, 43; *see also* subcultures, age
Lindzey, G., and E. Aronson: *Handbook of Social Psychology*, 5

Lockhart, K., 203, 204
Lockhart, R. R., 258

McClintock, C. G., 43
Maccoby, E. E., 11, 47, 319
McDermott, R., 55
McDonald, F. J., 73
Madsen, M. C., 178
Maehr, M. L., 35, 36
Mahoney, M. J., 314
Malinowski, B., 197–8, 199, 210, 347; *Crime and Custom in Savage Society*, 198
Markman, E., 100, 105
maturation, 40–1, 54, 360
Mead, M., 42–3
memory, 4, 87–8, 243; and moral internalization, 254–63, 265–7, 268; semantic/episodic, 255–9, 262, 263, 268–9, 283
message, 255
Mexican-Americans, 43
Milgram, S., 239, 347
Miller, R., 74
Mills, J., 299, 308, 350
mind, savage, 193–4, 195–6, 197, 199, 210–12
minimal sufficiency principle, 305–20, 349, 388–9
Mischel, H., 73
Mischel, W., 73
modeling, models, 19, 290–1, 315, 318, 357; of altruism, 276–9, 362; effectiveness of, 284, 285; of moral/deviant behavior, 238–9; on television, 110, 113, 126; *see also* observational learning
modernity, individual, 44
Moore, S., 74
moral breach(es), 202; appraisal of, 205–10
moral code, 19, 22
moral development, 47; stages of, 30, 196–7, 240; theory of, 290–1; *see also* Kohlberg, L.; Piaget, Jean
moral encounter: affective response evoked in, 260–1; conflict in, 245–6, 268; *see also* temptation situation
moral judgments, 29–30, 50, 197, 271; development of, 64–9, 72; in friendship behavior, 345–6; intentionality

moral judgments (*cont.*)
in, 150; peer interaction and, 50–1,
54; situation factors in, 359–60; and
social class, 44; stages in, 337–8 (*see
also* Kohlberg, L.; Piaget, Jean)
moral rules, 357–8, 361; differentiation of, from conventional, prudential, 193–4, 196–7, 200, 201–5, 206,
210–11
morality, 342, 343–4; definitional ambiguity, 347–8; as social domain, 345
motivation, 93, 111, 300, 361–3; and
aggression, 118–19; developmentally
acquired, 77; in internalization of altruism, 279–81, 291; in moral internalization, 241–2, 243–4, 249, 253–
4, 255, 257, 259, 260, 266–7, 268–70;
to self-evaluation, 135, 136, 142,
144–5; sense of control and, 368–9
Mowrer, O. H., 266
Much, N. C., 8, 202, 339, 343, 344,
357–8, 381

narrative, *see* stories
Neisser, U., 127
Nelson, K., 87, 127, 289
Nelson, K. E., 289
Newcomb, A. F., 10, 381, 385, 389–90
Nicholas, D., 114
Nicholls, J. C., 145
Nisbett, R., 85
Noerenberg, H., 170
noncompliance, 313–14
norm acquisition goals, 134–5, 152
norms: adult, 33; age difference in,
66–7, 68, 69–72; application of,
73–6, 77–8; cultural, 34–5, 239–40;
moral, 194–5, 243–8, 254–63, 266,
268, 347; personal, 345; social, 233–
4, 236, 345, 347, 384
Nucci, L. P., 203, 290, 389

obligation, 200–5, 211, 236–7, 240–1,
245, 347; guilt as, 253; in moral internalization, 243, 244, 268; and
value, 215, 216, 228, 232–3, 234
observational learning, 111, 269–70,
290; role of, in socialization, 356–7
Olds, J., 20
O'Leary, K. D., 316
Omanson, R., 114

Osherson, D., 203, 204
outcomes, consequences: anticipated,
93–4; past, 38–9, 43; relative standing of, 144; response, 279–81

parent-child interaction, 318–19, 368–9
parental goals, 43–5
parental image, 262, 263, 266
parenting styles, 237, 280, 310–11,
318, 363, 365, 388; and personality
development, 5–6, 41
parents: attitudes toward stability of
performance, 39, 40, 43–4; lower-
class, 44–5; reactions to moral transgressions, 290, 358; use of verbal rationales, 40 (*see also* induction[s])
Parkhurst, J. A., 152
Parsons, J. E., 7, 33, 34, 35, 39, 342,
348, 349, 358–61, 381, 385–7
Parsons, T., 20
peer group(s), 10, 19, 20–1, 47, 51,
70, 182, 337, 338, 388; behavioral
competence with, 89–90; in life
phases, 21–9, 30–1, 37–8; and moral internalization, 269
perception, 104, 105–6; development
of, 63–4, 70; and interaction, 95–6;
of persons and behavior, 4, 32–3,
36, 43, 76–7, 79, 82–5, 86
personality, 334
perspective taking, 379; in friendship
conceptions, 162–3
Peter, N. V., 35
Piaget, Jean, 6, 15, 22, 46, 49, 71, 89,
159, 164, 210, 269, 344, 369; acquisition of physical knowledge, 83, 84;
causal schemas, 264; cognitive development, 336–7; intent/outcome
moral-judgment paradigm, 33, 35;
logical realism, 150; moral development, 64–6, 67, 68, 196–7, 199, 205,
241, 337–8, 348; reaction against
theories of, 357, 358, 381; scheme
(notion), 282
Pool, D. L., 8, 339, 343, 344, 357–8,
381
preadolescent and early adolescent
stage, 25–30, 39, 55
predictions, 29, 38–40, 43, 48–9, 92–4,
386; error in, 85
preference, 68, 69

preschool to juvenile stage, 20–4, 30, 31, 48, 51, 52, 55
prescriptivity, 199–200, 201–5, 211
problem-solving operations, 89
psychoanalytic theory of moral internalization, 236–8
psychological knowledge domain, 345
psychological processes: stable concepts of, 346–7
punishment, 237, 242, 265, 290–1, 342, 350; and altruism, 276–7, 279–81, 290; anxiety re, 236–7, 250, 253, 254 (*see also* deviation anxiety); effect of, 239; as motivation, 365–6, 388; reward vs., 318; by teacher, 34–5

Radke-Yarrow, M., 90, 280
reactance, 285
reasoning, 372, 376; and attributions, 72, 74–5; conventional, 210; in discipline, 350–1 (*see also* induction[s]); across domains, 343; formal analytic, 72–3, 74–5, 77–8; inferential, 95 (*see also* inferences); interpretational, 63, 64; moral, 43, 46, 210; in punishment, 280–1, 290; in social/nonsocial domain, 338, 339
Reber, A., 266
reciprocity, 159, 163, 374; *see also* interaction, social
reinforcement, 19, 276–7, 279–80, 281, 290–1, 320; attribution as, 288–9; *see also* punishment
representations: of television portrayals, 119–23, 126, 128
research: epistemological categories of, 336, 341–2, 343, 345
research needs: cognitive mediators of social behavior, 104–6; friendship, 184–6; nature and representation of social knowledge, 127; social cognition/social interaction, 83; social-cognitive development, 371–91; social-control process, 312–17; television portrayals, 129–30
response consequences, 279–81
response inhibition, 308, 318
reward(s), 279, 280, 300–3, 318
Rodgon, M. M., 90
role-taking, 15, 47, 86, 89–90; by adolescents, 54–5; correlation with social behavior, 90; training in, 91–2
Rose, T., 76
Ross, L., 85, 340
Rothenberg, B., 90
Rubin, K. H., 90
Ruble, D. N., 9, 10, 36, 37, 38, 39, 48, 49, 130, 342–3, 346–7, 382–3
rules, 23, 281, 289, 383; alterability of, 200, 201, 203–5; cultural, 199; defined, 199–200; differentiation of, 193–4, 196–7, 200, 201–5, 206, 210–11, 358; and perception, 76–7; in savage society, 197–8; understanding of 196–7, 199, 202–5, 210–12 (*see also* moral rules; social understanding)
Rushton, J. P., 90

S-O-R model of behavior, 334
Salili, F., 35, 36
Saloman, G., 387
Samburu people (Kenya), 42
Schaffer, H. R., 362
Schank, R., 86, 127, 281–2, 283–4
schemas, *see* script(s)
scheme (notion), 282
Schmidt, C. F., 105
Schneider, F. W., 90
schooling, formal, 44
Scott, P. M., 278, 279
script(s), 4, 49, 83, 86–9, 356–7; for altruism, 281–9, 290, 291; causal, 263–5; and comprehension, 121–2, 126–7; defined, 281; differentiation of, 205–10; in discipline encounters, 257; and social cognition/social behavior relationship, 87–92
Sears, R. R., 134
Sedlak, A. J., 104, 105, 128
self-attribution, 267, 268, 269, 280, 368–9; of altruism, 312; of goodness, 287; moral internalization and, 262–3
self-concept, 36, 136, 283, 383
self-control, 52; training in, 316–17
self-esteem, 383
self-evaluation, 9, 194–5, 253; use of social comparison information in, 137–41, 143, 147, 150, 151–2, 153
self-evaluation goals, 134–5, 136, 152
self-interest, 275, 383; shift from, to altruism, 363–4

self-perception, 64, 300
self-punishment, 237, 291
self-reflection, 149–51, 152, 211–12, 382
self-reinforcement, 291
self-reward, 239–40
self-socialization, 4, 6, 340, 348–9,
    379, 388, 389; social comparison
    and, 134–57
Selman, R. L., 90, 162–4, 184
sequences, 378; *see also* stage models
sequentiality, 374–5
Sesonke, A., 215
setting, *see* context, situational
sex role(s), 6–7, 22, 153–4; stereo-
    types of, 125–6
Shantz, C., 204, 357, 380, 383; "Social
    Cognition," 3
sharing, 74, 164, 166–72
Shatz, M., 49–50
Schultz, T. R., 95
Shure, M. B., 91–2
Shweder, R. A., 8, 202, 339, 343, 344,
    357–8, 363, 381
Simmons, R. G., 36
Sioux Indians, 43
situation; defined, 49; *see also* context,
    situational
Slater, P. E., 20
"sleeper effect," 255
Smith, C. L., 289
Snyder, M., 95, 96, 105
social-acceptance values, 215, 221,
    222–3, 224–8, 229–30, 231–2, 234
social antecedents, 7–9, 386; and com-
    prehension, 111–13, 119–23, 126, 130
social class, 17, 54; and inference,
    123–5; and socialization, 44–5
social comparison, 21, 43, 73, 171,
    183, 342–3, 382–3; and achieve-
    ment-related self-socialization, 134–
    57; developmental steps in, 141–51;
    prerequisites to, 143–4, 147, 153;
    research on, 135–7, 140, 147–8;
    social-cognitive factors in, 346–7;
    strategies in, 142, 145–6, 147, 153
social conduct: research re, 372, 380–
    1; *see also* behavior(s)
social cues, 118–19
social domains, 333–4, 336, 342–3,
    344–5, 346, 347, 349, 351; catego-
    ries of, 383–4

social influence: mechanisms of, 388;
    role of, in social understanding, 372,
    379
social judgments, 5, 8, 49, 51, 105, 316,
    343; age-related changes in, 15–18;
    changes in, 33–6; cognitive media-
    tors of, 4; description of, 338–40
social-learning theory, 55, 333–4, 345;
    age-related changes in, 358–9; devel-
    opment of morality in, 290–1; of
    moral internalization, 238–40, 267;
    techniques of behavior change in, 276
social life: and attributional biases,
    36–8; and social predictions, 38–9
social-life perspective, 55–6; *see also*
    life phases
social position, role, 18, 20; in life
    phases, 21–2, 23, 24, 26–7, 29
social psychology (discipline), 4–7
social responsibility, 310–11; *see also*
    obligation
Social Science Research Council, Com-
    mittee on Social and Affective Devel-
    opment During Childhood, 334, 335
social understanding, 10, 340; age dif-
    ferences in, 371–8; in context, 94–6,
    104, 106; description of, 378–9;
    studies of, 97–103; variability in,
    126, 129; *see also* cognition
socialization: affect in, 361–4; of altru-
    ism, 275, 276, 280, 283, 289, 291; of
    autonomy/social-acceptance behav-
    ior, 222–4; definitional ambiguity
    in, 384–5; degree of pressure and,
    365–8; in development of attribu-
    tion, 63–81; in/through discipline,
    8–9; ecological, etc., impact on,
    41–2; internalization as criterion of,
    320–3; minimal sufficiency principle
    and, 305–20; through modeling,
    279; of moral behavior, 239–40; of
    prosocial behavior, 10; role of expe-
    rience in, 53; role of observational
    learning in, 356–7; and social class,
    44–5; social comparison in, 134,
    153; social controls in, 294, 295; in
    social judgments, 343; taming of
    values in, 229–30; television as, 110;
    of value–behavior discrepancies,
    230–2, 234; value paradox in, 214–
    15; see also self-socialization

socialization research, 308–12
socialization theory, 5–6, 7, 95; conflict with cognitive tradition, 333–41, 358–9
socializing agents, 18, 19, 20, 134; evaluation of behaviors by, 320; impact of, 8; and life phases, 20–4, 25–6; role of, in attitude change, 365–6; 368; role of, in motivating behavior change, 363; teaching altruism, 280–1, 282, 286, 291; *see also* parents; teachers
sociocultural theory: change in value development, 216, 228, 234
Spivack, G., 91–2
Staats, A. W., 19
stability, 39, 40, 43–4, 84; of concepts of psychological processes, 346–7; perception of, 147, 148–9, 382–3
stage(s): in development of friendship conception, 162–3; as subculture, 15–62
stage models, 373–4, 377, 378; *see also* Kohlberg, L.; Piaget, Jean
Staub, E., 170
Stein, A. H., 279
Stein, N. A., 259
Stein, N. L., 87, 88
stereotypes, 73, 76, 125–6
stories, 126–8, 256–7, 259
story grammars, 88
structural-developmental theory, 333–4, 335, 336, 339, 340, 341, 345; description, 375–7; ideas of, challenged, 381
subcultures, age, 7, 74, 339, 359–61, 386; stage as, 15–62
Sullivan, H. S., 20, 32, 159, 176–7, 179, 182
superego, 237–8, 267
Swann, W. B., 95, 96

Tanke, E., 105
teachers, 20–1, 49, 269, 316; in life phases, 22, 24–5; reaction to moral transgressions, 290
television, 8, 347, 387–8; comprehension of social portrayals on, 110–33, 356–7
temporal integration, 114
temptation situation, 241–2, 243, 246,

248, 254; prior resistance to, 303–4; resistance to, 313, 368
Thompson, R., 252–3
Trabasso, T., 11, 105, 114, 144
Trope, Y., 85
Tulving, E., 203, 204, 255, 256, 257–8, 259, 283
Turiel, E., 11, 290, 357, 377, 383, 389
Turkewitz, H., 316
Turner, T. J., 87, 127
Tversky, A., 85
Tylor, E. B., 193

validity, 199, 201, 202–5, 211
Valkenaar, M. C., 311–12
value(s), 9, 44, 232, 384; development of, 214–35; internalized, 77, 231, 233; and obligation, 215, 216, 218–19, 228, 232–3, 234; social-control processes and, 294–330
value conflicts, 228–9, 232–3, 321; *see also* conflict resolution
value domain, 233–4
value orientations, 216, 219–22; structural change in, 228–9, 231
value paradox, 214, 231, 234
value system, 317, 349, 389
verbal exhortation, 283–6; *see also* induction(s); reasoning
Veroff, J., 136, 137, 144, 145
Vygotsky, L. S., 19

Walters, R. H., 19
Warren, W., 114
Waxler, C. Z., 279
Weiner, B., 35
Weiner, J., 90
Wellman, H. M., 121–2
Whiting, B. B., 198–9
Whiting, J. M. W., 198–9
Wilensky, R., 128
Wohlwill, J., 71
Wolf, J., 94
Word, C. O., 95–6

Yarrow, M. R., 278, 279
Youniss, J., 159, 163, 383, 389

Zadny, J., 95
Zahn-Waxler, C., 90, 280
Zajonc, R. B., 261
Zanna, M. P., 95–6
Zelditch, M., 20